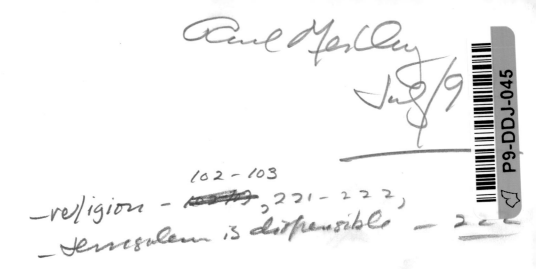

Carl Medley
Jun 9

102 - 103
—religion - ~~_____~~, 221 - 222,
—Jerusalem is dispensible — 2 2 2

Thursday's Child Has Far to Go

A ROBERT STEWART BOOK

Charles Scribner's Sons
New York

Maxwell Macmillan Canada
Toronto

Maxwell Macmillan International
New York   Oxford   Singapore   Sydney

Thursday's Child Has Far to Go

A MEMOIR OF THE JOURNEYING YEARS

Walter Laqueur

Charles Scribner's Sons   Maxwell Macmillan Canada, Inc.
Macmillan Publishing Company   1200 Eglinton Avenue East,
866 Third Avenue   Suite 200
New York, NY 10022   Don Mills, Ontario M3C 3N1

Macmillan Publishing Company is part of the Maxwell Communication Group of Companies.

Unless otherwise indicated, all photographs in the two picture sections belong to the author's collection. I would like to thank friends and relations for having helped me in my search: Mrs. F. Barkow, London; Prof. E. Beyer, Salt Lake City; Dr. J. Graham, London; Mr. S. Hermon, Jerusalem; S. Laqueur, Jerusalem; Dr. A. Lawrence, Isle of Wight; Mr. H. Lehmann, Ramat Aviv; Prof. H. Meidner, Stirling, Scotland; Y. Mikhaeli, Kibbutz Hazorea; Dr. H. Newton, San José, Costa Rica; Mr. R. Schulte, Julian, California; Mrs. H. Schultz, San Francisco; Mr. H. Ben Ya'akov, Kibbutz Sha'ar Hagolan.

Library of Congress Cataloging-in-Publication Data
Laqueur, Walter, 1921–
    Thursday's child has far to go: a memoir of the journeying years/ Walter Laqueur.
        p.   cm.
    "A Robert Stewart book."
    Includes index.
    ISBN 0-684-19421-X
    1. Laqueur, Walter, 1921–   . 2. Historians—United States— Biography. I. Title.
D15.L35A3   1992
973.9′092—dc20   92-8535

Macmillan books are available at special discounts for bulk purchases for sales promotions, premiums, fund-raising, or educational use. For details, contact:
Special Sales Director
Macmillan Publishing Company
866 Third Avenue
New York, NY 10022

10 9 8 7 6 5 4 3 2 1

Printed in the United States of America

For Rebecca, Johanna, Benjamin, and Tamar

CONTENTS

The idea to write a memoir first occurred to me when I revisited the city where I had been born and lived for seventeen years.
I once spent a lonely week in the Sahara desert, and during a
long afternoon walk, spotted on the horizon a solitary wanderer.
As he came nearer I saw that he was an acquaintance whom I
had not seen for years. I have met friends and relations, close
and distant, in some very unlikely places. But in Breslau, the city
of my birth—where I had once been surrounded by a fairly large
family and many acquaintances, where I remembered every
street and many shops within a mile from our home—there was
not a single soul known to me, and all the names of the streets
and shops, and people, had changed. The world I had known as
a boy no longer existed, and as I tried to remember the people I

had known when I was sixteen, I realized that most of them had died a violent death. Some were killed in the ruins of Stalingrad, others in Auschwitz, some in 1948 in the battles for Palestine.

I look at a photograph showing a group of a dozen youngsters, mere children, in front of a youth hostel. The date was 1936 or 1937, I was their guide and leader even though I was only a couple of years older. As I look at the faces I realize that I met only one of them in later life; I wonder what became of them and whether they had as much good luck as I had.

I can pursue the origins of my family to the early eighteenth century in both Western Europe and Russia. As so often, there are some missing links and question marks, but I do know now that the family constituted an interesting and perhaps not untypical mixture of people of rich and poor, of small-town merchants, academics, and some who had been ennobled, of rabbis and whole branches who even in the last century had given up the religion of their ancestors.

I belong to the last generation of Jews with conscious memories of growing up in Weimar Germany and under the Nazis. A great many of the generation before us, among them writers, artists, and scientists, have put their recollections on paper, but very few of my generation. The reason is obvious: We did not root so deeply in our country of origin; as we grew up we tended to look forward rather than back. Our interest in Germany faded, we used our native language infrequently, we became absorbed in the society and culture of our new homes.

It was my intention to give an account of what a child and a young man saw and experienced in a world that has disappeared. I did not want to write a requiem; it would have been untruthful if my story were predominantly one of lament and mourning or "a thousand shall fall at thy side." This was not my mood at the time nor that of my friends and contemporaries. The tragedy was only gradually unfolding and I left well before the deportation and massacres had begun.

In 1938 I went to what was then Palestine and discovered an entirely new world. I became an agricultural laborer and lived in a collective settlement, a kibbutz. Upon leaving it, I worked as a journalist, covering the political and military struggle unfolding in the Middle East and the emergence of the state of Israel. This, too, is a world now gone, the "heroic age" of the kibbutz, Jerusalem under the British Mandate, cosmopolitan Alexandria, Beirut, and Cairo, the generations of the founders. There is a famous poem by Yeats ("September 1913") with its reiterated refrain of "Romantic Ireland's dead and gone," and I feel similarly about these years in Palestine. But I was present at the creation; it was a fascinating period and an excellent training ground.

I conclude this narrative with my discovery of Western Europe and the Soviet Union in the early 1950s as a young man of provincial background with an unfinished education and as yet uncertain aspirations. The decades that followed belong to another chapter of my life; my further experiences were perhaps not unique and I have no strong urges to write about them.

In a memoir such as this, the emphasis could not possibly be on the self, on introspection, the analysis of my changing moods, my relationships with fellow human beings. If I had had the good fortune to grow up before World War I in Bloomsbury or the Faubourg St. Germain, or, say, in New York or California after World War II, I would have written a very different book. But in the world of which I have been part, calm seas and still waters were rare. My great-grandfather was born in a very small town in 1825; I have established that it counted 1,130 inhabitants at the time. He married a local girl, and as far as I know, never left his place of birth for any length of time. The railway reached Neumittelwalde only twenty years after his death in 1870; the population was then still only 1,200. His world did not extend much beyond the vineyards and the shops on both sides of the main street, which was virtually the only street. Everyone knew everyone else; there were two minor wars, but they took place far away, were short, and had no impact on daily life. This near idyllic life came to an end in Europe in 1914. My grandfather lived just to experience World War I and the violent changes following it. My father and mother perished in World War II and I survived mainly because I was lucky. Perhaps the world will move, in the years to come, to a greater peace. I have lived to watch my Israeli granddaughter donning a gas mask. Such experiences are not conducive to a preoccupation with self-analysis. For this reason, if for no other, I have written as much about the world in which I grew up as about myself.

Homecoming

On *a fine summer evening* in the early 1960s, I found myself in a bewildered state of mind, sitting on a bench in the Południe Park in the Polish city of Wrocław. The sun was about to set, some well-nourished swans were effortlessly crossing the little lake, a cuckoo was calling, and rows of pansies—a flower that is to the Poles what the shamrock is to the Irish—were in bloom. I had not lost my way, in fact had once known almost every path in this splendid park. A few hundred yards to the north was the primary school that I had attended, beyond the railway line to the south was the sports club to which I had belonged. I could even recall having once sat on this very bench and listened to what might have been the grandparent of that cuckoo. But then it had been the Südpark in the German city of Breslau. Now beyond the confines of the park almost everything seemed different, the new hotel (Novotel), the Soviet war cemetery, the streets and the houses. The city I had known had disappeared like Herculaneum and Pompeii, or, as some might prefer, like Sodom and Gomorrah. Certain landmarks were still the same, the river Oder still flowed through town, and in the center of the city quite a few streets and buildings looked exactly as I remembered them. They had either not been destroyed in the war or had been rebuilt as before. But then I had had parents, acquaintances, friends, in this city, and now I did not know a soul. The character of the city had basically changed, the new people about talked a language that I could understand only in part and with great difficulty when they talked slowly. I felt like the hero of H. G. Wells's *Time Machine*. The combination of the déjà vu with the totally unexpected was most confusing; it would have been easier to accept if the city had disappeared altogether.

I try to concentrate on the present, and yet my thoughts return to those days in May 1938. I had just graduated from school, and my future was entirely in the hands of various committees, boards, and consulates. I had much free time and came to the Südpark almost every morning; I remember reading here Céline's *Voyage au bout de la nuit*. What fascinated me in this story of cynicism and despair, I do not know; perhaps I had an inkling that another journey to the end of the night was about to begin? Or would it be wrong to attribute so prophetic an instinct to one who had not yet turned eighteen? I recall meeting an old teacher of mine one of those mornings in the Südpark. He was no Nazi and had been forced to retire before he had reached retirement age. He was deeply pessimistic about the future, and strongly advised me to clear out as soon as possible. He spoke about very difficult days ahead, about envying my ability to get away, and he ended by asking me to come back when the worst was over. He turned to go but suddenly seemed to remember something and said: "You will recall that I tried to explain to you, not always with success, the song of the Nibelungen. Do look up Hagen's story one of these days."

That was the last I saw of Dr. U., walking away from me with his ebony walking stick. There is no trace of him now, nor of the other teachers. I have looked up the story of Hagen, but I am not sure what he meant. He may have referred to Hagen's last words before he went to his last battle, that everything had happened just as he had foreseen (". . . *es ist auch so ergangen, wie ich mir hatte gedacht*"). But there is another incident in the story of the Nibelungen that has intrigued me for some time: when Hagen crosses the Danube together with King Gunther's armed escort on his way to Attila's court, a party of mermaids tells him that they are all going to perish—with the exception of the King's chaplain. To prove them wrong, Hagen pushes the priest into the torrent. But he is carried by the current to the safe shore, while Hagen and his comrades are killed in the battle they foolishly provoked.

The stranger coming to Breslau in the 1930s would receive a brochure at the central railway station telling him all he needed to know: that the city was located in the alluvium of the Oder Valley, 119.98 meters (394 feet) above sea level, that it was the biggest, the most beautiful, the most important city of East Germany, with a population of roughly 625,000. He was advised to look at the magnificent baroque buildings as well as the monumental modern structures such as the Jahrhunderthalle, with the largest cupola (and the biggest organ) in the world. He learned that there was a "very attractive social life" and, generally speaking, a very gemütlich atmosphere. If he was a philosopher, he could join either the Kant or the Schopenhauer Society; as a Mason he would find Hermann zur Beständigkeit or Settegast zur deutschen Treue very hospitable lodges, and the "Association of Christian Maidens" would take care of young women without relations in the city. Anyway, he was bound to like Breslauer Korn (a local schnapps) and Schlesisches Himmelreich, a dish that, if memory serves me right, consisted mainly of baked fruit.

The guide was well-meaning but somewhat misleading. In fact, Breslau did not differ greatly from other cities in Eastern

Central Europe. The streets in the older parts of town were rather narrow, the facades of the houses very much like one another—and not only the somber, dark-gray blocks of flats of the working-class quarters—and there were large factories and markets. In brief, it was a city of work, not of savoir-vivre. There were no aristocracy or high society as in Berlin, no royal merchants as in Hamburg, no artists' quarter as in Munich. The university was a fairly recent establishment by Central European standards, and the city had not produced any important politician with the single exception of Ferdinand Lassalle—but of him the burghers preferred not to be reminded. There were some fine actors and musicians, but they went off to Berlin as soon as they had made their names. There had been some outstanding writers and poets, but that was after the Thirty Years' War, a long time ago. People did not travel much in those days and many thought, therefore, that Breslau was simply wonderful.

Before 1914, people said, things had been different; my own recollections go back only to the late twenties. But my father came to Breslau from a little provincial town around the turn of the century, and I remember him and his friends telling me about the "good old days": the colorful parades on the Emperor's birthday, the concerts with Bülow, Nikisch, and Mahler, the *Frühschoppen* breakfasts at Hansen, Kempiński, or Brill (dinner à la carte for seventy-five pfennig, and what a dinner!), the Sunday morning walks on the promenades along the former city walls and the town moat. They seldom mentioned the other side of the picture: poverty and drunkenness in the working-class quarters; the insipid taste manifested in paint, furniture, and interior decoration; the Byzantine manners and customs of Wilhelminian Germany, led by an aristocracy that had long ago outlived its social function, and an arrogant officer corps that deemed itself far superior to all other mortals.

Yet despite ugliness, poverty, and the lack of fresh air, it must have been a very confident age. Progress was in evidence, prosperity was widespread, technical advances were made almost each year; amenities that became known in England only after

World War II, such as central heating, were already in general use. There had been no war for forty years and everybody was very optimistic, including those sinister radical revolutionaries, the Social Democrats. The first taxicabs appeared in front of the central railway station and gradually replaced the horse-drawn carriages; first-class coachmen had white, lacquered top hats, their second-class colleagues wore black hats with silver lace— there must be no mistake about a man's station in life. Everybody was very patriotic and, in 1914, went off to fight for *"Kaiser"* and *"Vaterland."*

When the war was over, the province of Posen and parts of Upper Silesia had to be ceded to Poland; Breslau lost much of its hinterland. There was a feeling of stagnation, of narrowed horizons and limited prospects, though economic progress continued on a modest scale despite inflation and the world economic crisis. Yet the former confidence had disappeared; Breslau, once an important junction, had become a terminus.

I have some memories of the city as it was around 1930: the crowds of unemployed men in the streets discussing politics, the frequent elections, and the brawls almost every Sunday in which a few people usually got killed. My own interests at the time were directed more to soccer and athletics, in which, unfortunately, my hometown never excelled; I remember the terrible thrashing a Budapest team gave our city eleven. We had half a dozen daily newspapers, and I tried to see all of them. The *Schlesische Zeitung*, archly reactionary and very proud to have published in 1813 the King's "appeal to his people" to rise against Napoleon; the democratic *Breslauer Zeitung*, which folded because there were so few liberals left apart from the Jews; and the Catholics, the Social Democrats, the Communists, and of course the Nazis, had their own papers as well.

Now the Polish journalists have a magnificent club near the town moat with first-rate abstract paintings on the walls, very good coffee, and modern furniture. But the two newspapers they produce are not very impressive. In the election of March 5, 1933, the National Socialist German Workers' Party received

5

50.2 percent of the votes in the Breslau district. What happened subsequently in the city did not differ greatly from events in other parts of Germany. I vividly remember the speeches, the demonstrations, the torchlight parades that hailed the dawn of the new era. The teachers told us, with varying degrees of conviction, what bliss it was to be alive in that dawn.

I wanted to see the house in which we lived when I was a child, but had some difficulty in finding the street. The names of the streets had, of course, been changed; but that was not the main problem. I had expected to see a house, or its ruins, or perhaps a new building, but there was nothing, not even a trace that human beings had lived and died there. There was a forlorn signpost in the middle of nowhere, marking the spot as ULICA SKWIERZYŃSKA—CROSSING ŻELAZNA. The rubble had been removed years ago, weeds were sprouting, and dandelions, a few shrubs, and a solitary tree had taken root. Some children were playing in a nearby street in which a single house was standing; they did not hurry to let me pass; cars are rarely to be seen in these parts. Half a mile or so farther on was Saint Carolus Church. In a different direction, a few hundred yards away, there were signs of life in a big, ugly red-brick building, apparently a school. For a few minutes I stared at the great sundial and the city coat of arms beneath it—of course, there were trees in front, we used to collect chestnuts there! The area would have seemed, to visitors who had not known it before, very peaceful and utterly empty. The effect it had on me was different; nothingness can make a stronger impact than destruction and ruin.

In this area, the southern part of the town, tens of thousands of people had once lived; yet the story of its destruction is very brief. During the first five years of the war Breslau was a long way from the front. It became, in fact, the air-raid shelter of the Reich at one stage, and its population grew to about a million. In January 1945, with the approach of the Soviet armies, a fanatic *Gauleiter* (area commander), Hanke, had the defeatist burgomaster hanged in public, and organized a last-ditch defense. In this Hanke was, in a way, successful; it took the Russians about three months to advance a mile and a half. As a reward, Hitler, in his will, made him supreme leader of the SS in succession to the traitor—Himmler. By that time, however, the SS had ceased to exist. Gauleiter Hanke literally vanished into thin air; he flew out of Breslau a few days before the city capitulated (it was the only major city not to surrender before the armistice). We do not know what became of that efficient *Gauleiter*. The price the city had to pay for having been turned into a fortress was appalling; the whole southern and western part was destroyed, and the center of the town was in shambles. When the surveyors came to assess the damage they said that 60 percent of the city had been destroyed, which was a lower figure than that for Warsaw and some other German cities. I do not know how destruction is measured beyond a certain point; in Breslau, at any rate— unlike Berlin, Kassel, or Nuremberg—it seemed fatal because it coincided with the expulsion of the population of the city. Fewer than 200,000 had stayed there when it became a fortress, the great majority having been evacuated before.

Then *Breslau* became *Wrocław*. In the following year all but a few thousand of the remaining Germans were expelled. Slowly, the immigration of Poles got under way. By 1947 the city again had 200,000 inhabitants; in 1949 it passed the 300,000 mark. The newcomers were people of very different social and cultural backgrounds: peasants from backward Carpathian mountain vil- lages that had been ceded to Russia; intellectuals from Lvov (its university was transfered to Wrocław); soldiers from German POW camps; reemigrants from Western Europe. Russian mili- tary administration handed the city over to the Poles, the big railway wagon factory resumed production, and the local theater staged *Pygmalion*—all this happened while the rats were still feeding on corpses in the streets that had once been a battlefront. Wrocław remained a rubble heap long after other cities had reemerged from the ashes.

The leading bookshops were on the west and north sides of the central city square, opposite the statue of a Prussian king. The statue, needless to say, has been replaced by a new one—

of Aleksander Fredro, the Polish Molière. The secondhand bookshop provides a welcome surprise; the employees are knowledgeable and helpful, the prices reasonable, and—unlike in Russia—one is permitted to approach the shelves. Many of the books are in German; I even spotted copies of the telephone directory for 1937 and 1942, and similar items of local interest. There are hundreds of books, side by side, claiming that Silesia and Breslau were "always German," and others that maintain that Wrocław and Dolny Śląsk have been "Polish from time immemorial." The Germans take the year 1241 as their starting point; the German city of Breslau was founded after the Mongol assault had been repulsed. But "No," say the Poles, "we were there much earlier!" Excavations in the city and the suburbs have proved the existence of pre-Slavonic settlements during the early Stone Age. During the Iron Age, the Lusatians lived there, and they were, for sure, the forefathers of the Slavs. The Germans violently disagree. During the excavation for the autobahn south of the city they found two big subterranean caves containing tons of amber, which they say "could only have belonged to the Wandalers" (not to be confused with the Vandals). And who were the Wandalers but the forefathers of the Germans? Nobody seems to dispute that. The Poles, however, counter this by saying that around the year 1000 Wratisława was a Polish city. At that time the Polish kings, the Piasts, called in German settlers to help colonize the country. True enough, the Germans reply, but "the Piasts became Germans by intermarriage, and anyway, who made the miserable village of A.D. 1000 what it subsequently became—one of the most important towns of medieval Europe, more important as a trading center than Frankfurt, or Berlin, of which hardly anybody had heard at the time?" I have always found these arguments somewhat tedious; how can serious people invest so much time and energy in proving and disproving half-truths? But the struggle continues unabated, each side insisting on its version of the past. The Germans insist that a great historical injustice has been done them; the Poles conclude that the German *Drang nach Osten* (eastern expansion) was always aggressive and reactionary.

The Poles felt strongly about those Pan-German ideologists who claimed that the conquest of territory and the assimilation of the Slavonic people was a "historic trend," one which indicated the "physical and intellectual vigor" of the German nation, and which had "spread civilization in a part of the world in which there existed the necessity to import all elements of culture from Germany." The quotations I have used are from Karl Marx. I know that is unfair. But the Poles, too, ought to be reminded of some of the facts of life. Like the Russians, they prefer not to rely on what Marx wrote about their country; their heroes are Boleslaus Wrymouth, Ladislaus the Short, Casimir the Restorer, and their like. These absurd exercises were provoked, it is only fair to add, by generations of *Ostforscher* (specialists in East European studies) who proclaimed that the Slavs were and always would be an inferior race.

At school we were never told that there had been any Poles in Silesia; but there was an organization called Bund Deutscher Osten (headed by a Professor Oberlander from Königsberg), which distributed maps and leaflets on the German East, with many quotations starting with Tacitus and Procopius and ending with Adolf Hitler. One of them I found again in my Wrocław bookshop. It ended with the following words: "So let us all remember the old inscription on the Reval town hall,

'He is right who fights.
He who stops fighting
Has lost all rights. . .' "

It made curious reading that morning in the Polish city of Wrocław.

I cannot recall having met a Pole when I grew up in Breslau in the twenties and thirties. True enough, there were many people with names like Stefański or Matuszewski, but this was not uncommon in Germany; the forward line of the German soccer team used to read like an excerpt from a Warsaw telephone directory. Anyway, these bearers of Polish names were completely assimilated, they were 150 percent German. There was a small Polish minority, but somehow one never met them, or more probably one did not recognize them; they had been to local schools and they spoke German without an accent. In Upper Silesia the situation was different; east of the Oder there had been a Polish majority, particularly in the villages, until 1914.

When the war ended, there were some forty thousand people in Breslau who opted for Poland. Some were slave laborers who had worked in the city, others were Polish prisoners of war, but the majority consisted of local residents. Some had never made a secret of the fact that they belonged to a national minority. Others discovered their Polish patriotism only when faced with the threat of expulsion and loss of property; because they were Catholic, had a Slavonic family name, and remembered a few words of Polish, they thought they would pass. (Many of them did pass, but the new authorities had to introduce Polish language courses for them.) The percentage of these autochthons, small in Wrocław, was substantial in Upper Silesia; the newcomers from eastern and central Poland regarded them as Germans, and often as ex-Nazis; there was tension and it continues to this day.

There is a great deal of anti-Polish literature on the shelves of those bookshops, starting with publication from the early years of the century. By their side are the Polish anti-German publications (from Roman Dmowski to the books and magazines of the Polish Western Institute in Poznań). I cannot help thinking that these historians could be more profitably employed. Breslau/Wrocław has a past that is both German and Slav. But what happened to the city in 1945 has nothing to do with medieval history, nor even with events in the nineteenth century. Don't we all by now know the causes?

All traces of German rule in Breslau have been very carefully removed. This includes statues, inscriptions, memorial tablets, road signs, and so on. Sometimes the old inscriptions have been erased but nothing put in their place, and the result is confusing, particularly in certain public conveniences. The German language is not heard or seen, except in conversations with strangers who want to help, in the secondhand bookshop just mentioned, and in cemeteries. There was a small German-language newspaper in Wrocław in the mid-1950s, but it has since disappeared. There was one remaining sign—an inscription in Ulica Włodkowica (Wallstrasse); it indicated that this had been the office of the Jewish community. (It still is, but of an infinitely smaller Polish Jewish community that had nothing to do with the German Jewry who had lived in the city.) The inscription was cut into the stone and so could not have been removed without doing damage to the building. It is a bitter irony—and yet somehow it seems appropriate—that chance should have singled out the local Jews to bear witness to the German past. There were some 20,000 Jews in Breslau, of whom half emigrated in time, the remainder being deported and killed. The assimilation of a large section of German Jewry was very far advanced (much more so than in Britain or the United States). The result of the German-Jewish symbiosis was a culture disapproved of by German nationalists. Nevertheless, it had an impact, the effects of which can be discerned to the present day.

Its influence extended far beyond Breslau, for writers and musicians who were born in the city and who became prominent, emigrated to Berlin. There were also many physicians, physicists, chemists, botanists, and biologists of Jewish origin of world distinction who had been born in Breslau or the surrounding countryside. Looking through a biographical dictionary of the world's leading scientists recently, I noticed how often the entries read "b. Breslau," or even more frequently, "b. Lissa" (or "b. Ostrovo"); villages such as these on the former German-Polish boundaries produced more leading scientists between 1860 and 1910 than any Western capital, with the possible exceptions of

London and Paris. With official careers virtually closed to them in pre-1914 Germany, many bright young German Jews were almost inevitably drawn into the then rapidly expanding sciences.

The fact that Breslau became a cultural center in the nineteenth century was to a great extent a Jewish achievement. True enough, the German-Jewish symbiosis was a hybrid, and therefore dubious, problematical; but it had outstanding achievements to its credit. Who could have foreseen that it would end as it did, with a few thousand elderly people assembled on the platforms of the central railway station one summer night in 1942? Fortunately, most of them did not know that from this journey there would be no return. My parents were among them.

As I write these lines in the late hours of the evening in my hotel room, the figure of the city's liberal rabbi comes back to my mind. He lived very near this place, on what is now Kościuszko Square. Dr. Vogelstein was one of the most widely educated men I have known, and one of the kindest; he had written a most erudite book on the history of Rome and had one of the largest private libraries in town. Sometimes I saw him in the municipal library with an apologetic smile: "I am sure that I have that book somewhere at home but I can't find it." When I went to see him last in 1938 he was a broken man. He had always been a German patriot, bitterly opposed to any Jewish nationalist aspirations; his whole world was now in ruins. These were the days of Hitler's great successes, and we talked about the uncertain future. He was a mild man, yet on that day there was something of the fire of an Old Testament prophet in him; he quoted Isaiah to me, the passage about the coming day of vengeance, and even Paul's epistle to the Romans (12:19)—I have mentioned that he was a liberal rabbi. . . . When I was already in the corridor, he added as an afterthought: "Though the mills of God grind slowly, yet they grind exceeding small; / Though with patience He stands waiting, with exactness grinds He all" (the Longfellow translation).

Gottesmühlen mahlen langsam, mahlen aber trefflich klein;
Ob aus Langmut Er sich säumet, bringt mit Schärf' Er alles ein.

Friedrich von Logau

I often read with interest the sophisticated travelogues, in magazines like *Holiday*, on the charm of the quaint little streets on the *rive gauche*, the enchanting corners of the Ile Saint-Louis, and the appeal of the Champs-Elysées on a sunny Sunday afternoon. I wish my task were as easy. For all the world loves Paris, but who is interested in Breslau, let alone Wrocław? A detailed description of the strange charm of the cemetery in Cosel, the exquisite beauty of the abattoir in Ulica Legnica and its surroundings, the splendor of the ruins at the Neumarkt, or the fascination of the desert south of Gartenstrasse would probably create the effect the Spaniards call *contraproducente* (counterproductive). I did see the sights, but the written word does not seem an adequate means of communication in this context; a film using the flashback technique would perhaps be more appropriate and more convincing.

The Monopol had been the best hotel since the turn of the century; it still is, though its name was somewhat provocative for a hotel in a Communist country. After 1945 its reputation for bad service became legendary; one day even an otherwise unflappable British ambassador is said to have shown signs of annoyance. It is much better now; a local wit maintains that a few waiters were shot *pour encourager les autres*. It would be almost perfect if only Polish economic planning had made provisions for the manufacture of sleepable-in beds.

To the right of the hotel there was, and still is, a big open square, which has changed its name and function several times during the last hundred years. In the nineteenth century the local garrison held its exercises here. Subsequently, agricultural machinery was sold, and still later Adolf Hitler used to address mass meetings from the ramp of the castle on the north side of the square. The castle was destroyed but the square is decorated

with little red-and-white flags and it is full of people; a Polish
military band plays marches; it is the anniversary of the capitula-
tion of Breslau. Beyond the square there were the enormous
courtyards and warehouses built in the eighteenth century; Breslau was then a big center for trade with the East. The houses
now look shabbier and more dilapidated, there is little trade,
and children play where carriages and trucks once unloaded
enormous bales of cotton and other large freight. It used to be a
very orderly city, the tanners had their own little street, and so
did the coppersmiths and also the prostitutes. Krullstrasse lies in
ruins, is uninhabited and cordoned off—one cannot even enter
it by car. This is the very center of town: There are old churches,
old inns, most of them in ruins now; whole streets have disappeared, but the house where we lived for some years in the
thirties still stands. I had always thought of it as dark, and in
no way distinguished. Now it looks much brighter and quite
imposing, because so many buildings in the neighborhood have
disappeared. It has become something of a national monument,
because it was designed by the architect who built the Brandenburg Gate in Berlin. Someone looks down at me from our old
flat; he must be the "specialist in nervous diseases," who, according to the doorplate downstairs, now lives there. Business
appears to be slack.

It used to take me twenty minutes to reach school; it should
have taken half the time, I realize now, but there were so many
distractions. Alas, I can't see any now. Half the buildings have
come down, and most of the shops have disappeared. There is
hardly any traffic at all in the side streets. All the life is concentrated in the main thoroughfares. The school is there all right, a
very ordinary gray building, smaller than it appeared to me in
memory. It is still a school—the Wrocław Economic High
School. Overcoming some strange fear of authority (these things,
it seems, last forever) I ventured into the building. The teacher's
lounge still gives comfort to tired lecturers, but the colored-glass
panel commemorating those fallen in World War I (*dulce et
decorum est* . . .) has been removed. The little shops nearby that

sold exercise books, toy guns, sweets, and buttermilk have disappeared; there are heaps of coal in the street, an execrable but widespread custom in Polish cities.

I only dimly remember the other things I saw on this day; there were some surprises but no major shocks, one got accustomed to the different character of the town. I went to see Wertheim's, once a big department store, and the city's most modern building (built by Erich Mendelsohn), now the Powszechny Dom Towarowy (the leading chain store). When it was established in 1930, the small businessmen made a terrible fuss; they were going to lose their customers, they said, and they threatened to support the Nazis (which, I suppose, in the end they did). The outcry was not worthwhile; after 1933 the place was aryanized; in 1945 they polonized the store and very faithfully rebuilt it. The selection and the display compare favorably with those in Moscow; there are good inexpensive cigars and a lot of well-made (and highly priced) motorcycles. In the olden days prospective customers were invited to taste the products of new baking mixes and custard powders and whatnot.

Then I went to see the hospital near the big water tower in the south. A doctor had decided one day long ago that I would be better off without tonsils; he was right, I suppose, but the timing was all wrong. Some slight complication developed. I had to stay a few days longer than planned. It was September 25, 1938; Chamberlain had just returned from Bad Godesberg to London; war seemed imminent. Never had I felt so helpless; it was like being in a mousetrap about to close. But I will tell this story later.

I went to see the cathedral that, dating back to the thirteenth century, was largely destroyed in the last war but has since been rebuilt by the Poles. There were groups of sightseers; the new Silesians are certainly eager to know their new homeland and to grow roots. There is the university on the other side of the river; nothing much has changed there. The new dean, recently elected, is himself a graduate of this university.

How curious that while trying to eradicate all traces of the

German tradition, the Poles should in some ways be so eager to continue where the Germans left off. The original function and character of many shops, public buildings, institutions, have been preserved. The place where I got my first spectacles still sells eyeglasses, and the C&A shop opposite has merely given way to the Polish "state trust," selling coats and trousers.

An elderly relation was bound to ask me what became of the Jahrhunderthalle, so I went to see it too. It was built in 1913, in commemoration of the war against Napoleon a hundred years earlier; at the time it was one of the world's seven wonders, a building of concrete and iron covering 10,000 square meters (110,000 square feet). Gerhart Hauptmann wrote a bad play for its opening; there was also an enormous orchestra and choir of a thousand. Now they call it Hala Ludowa; it houses a cinema, the biggest in Poland.

Not far off, the Oder steamers anchored on their run upriver. On sunny afternoons the ships were full, the families went to a big open-air restaurant where they spent a few hours by the river, fighting off the gnats, eating huge pieces of cake and drinking lemonade. There were small motorboats and canoes and people in all sorts of bathing costumes. The little orchestra played: *"Nun ade, du mein lieb Heimatland"* as the steamer left for the city once again. How peaceful it all seemed. One Sunday evening in 1932, on our way back, a swimmer clambered onto the ship and wiped his bottom with the black-red-and-gold flag of the Weimar Republic. There was a roar of laughter; few of the passengers thought much of the flag. The tranquillity was deceptive.

I was not eager to mention the fact that I was born in Breslau, for whenever a Pole heard about it, there was the inevitable question: "And how do you find the city now?" It was a question I would have preferred not to answer; it involved comparing two different peoples, cultures, ways of life, political regimes, and going on to pass value judgments. German Breslau was not only a bigger city than Polish Wrocław, it was more orderly and prosperous, it had a culture of its own and a certain character. But is it fair to compare the toughs from Carpathian mountain villages who now lounge about the Blücherplatz with the local intelligentsia of 1910 (or 1930) assembled in the Café Fahrig after an evening at the opera? German Breslau was not only efficiency, *Gemütlichkeit*, and culture. The head of one of the West German refugee organizations said the other day that most of his compatriots who now visit Wrocław are not really qualified to judge the present state of the city because they had not known the place in "the good old days." Maybe so, but what past does he have in mind—1910 or 1938—or perhaps 1945? Does he remember only the fair on Saint John's Eve? Or also the guillotine in the local Gestapo prison? The frenetic applause when Hitler came to watch the gymnasts in 1938? The deportation and murder of thousands of Jews? The rowdy student demonstrations (Middle Eastern style) against professors who did not display enough enthusiasm for the Nazi cause? "Temporary aberrations," some will say; German history does not begin with Hitler, nor does it end with him. True enough, but for such historic aberrations nations pay dearly.

There is a great and growing literature on the new Wrocław and I had bought in Warsaw some of the more important publications: the urban survey of 1956, the development plan for the city published in 1961, and Irene Turnau's investigation into the social composition of the new population. They all help one to understand the present state of affairs—but only up to a point. The cultural and social differences between the planners and many of the local population are simply too great. They have helped to clean up the shambles and to get the factories working again. Their children and grandchildren may make Wrocław a modern city that is more than a conglomeration of factories, shops, and schools. It must have been a dreadful place in the early fifties; even the most orthodox party members tell you that life was grim in those days. The reconstruction of the city had not yet gotten under way, but a local underworld had developed—drunks, prostitutes, criminals. There was nowhere to go in the evening, the general mood was one of gloom and despondency. After October 1956, conditions improved. The number of inhabitants, less than 200,000 in 1946, was up to about 450,000 in 1963, and is now about 600,000. (It was 625,000 in 1939, and in 1943, following the Allied air attacks against the West German cities and Berlin, it reached the one million mark temporarily.) The central city square with its baroque Bürgerhäuser has been most faithfully reconstructed, with its gables, portals, and richly decorated attics. The Gothic town hall has been repaired, and with its triangular gable towers, its turrents and sculptural ornaments, is still one of the noblest monuments of Gothic architecture in Europe. There were 30 bookshops in 1964, 27 pharmacies, 23 cinemas, 6 theaters (counting the opera), and 650 taxicabs (of which 90 percent were privately owned). Some of the shops too were still in private hands, and about 15 percent of the smaller workshops. And now (1991) almost everything is to be reprivatized—but how are they going to do it? The cinemas show films from all over the world; the graffito mark of "Zorro" on the town hall showed the progress of Western civilization. A lethargic elephant in the Zoological Garden may be one of the few survivors from the German era. Perhaps the SS omitted to kill him in the last days of the siege.

Thirty-seven percent of the population of Wrocław are engaged in industry; employment in machine industry has gone up, in textile plants it has gone down. Public transport is mainly by a noisy and not very fast streetcar service and no radical change is envisaged for the future. I am not a city planner, but I foresee certain difficulties. Few people want to live in the inner part of the city; the local intelligentsia lives in such suburbs as Biskupin, or Oporów. There are museums, milk bars, and a number of new, very big, and always overcrowded coffeehouses around Kościuszko Square; old General Friedrich von Tauentzien, one of Frederick the Great's paladins who is buried there, had to give way. There is an International Press and Book Club, where the *International Herald Tribune* is sold, sometimes with only three days' delay. (The British press seems in less demand.) There are even a few filling stations, though it takes some effort to find them. According to the city plan, the destroyed quarters in the south of the city will be rebuilt in the next few years; I saw a few surveyors at work. There are many schools; Polish Silesia is demographically a young country; there are more schoolchildren now in Wrocław than there were in Breslau.

All this does not sound too bad. It is a real achievement, considering that the Poles started from very nearly nil in 1945. In Silesia the Poles do not merely want to make their own lives more tolerable, they want to show the Germans that they are capable of building a city as well as, if not better than, the Germans. These, then, were my impressions of the city of my birth less than twenty years after the end of the war. But the optimism of 1962 was not borne out by subsequent events. Stagnation set in and even decline; the city now suffers from the same urban problems as all other Eastern European cities, and life is hard.

One recent autumn evening, during an interval at a conference near Athens, the conversation turned to "the need for roots." We were eight around the table, and it emerged that none of us lived where we were born and that only one would again be able to see the parental home if she went back to her birthplace. (This was a girl who came from a small northern Italian village that had been bypassed by the war.) The destruction of houses and the uprooting of many millions of people has been a commonplace on the continent of Europe in our time, and not only there. I envy those who survive and manage never to look back; from the point of view of mental hygiene I suppose it is the right thing to do. I was glad, nevertheless, that I had come back to my native city despite the unquiet memories. I was even more glad when the visit came to an end.

The importance that Breslau had in the nineteenth and early twentieth centuries will hardly be regained, if only for the reason that it was then part of the leading country in Central Europe; the language spoken in Breslau was the *lingua franca* of all Central, Eastern, and Southeastern Europe. All this is gone and past help; it should also be past grief. It is also, as far as I am concerned, past personal interest. I will not deny that I was excited when the train that was bringing me to Wrocław entered its suburbs, and for the benefit of my wife I gave a running commentary from the open window, interrupted only by exclamations. But when we entered the train that was about to leave the city in the early hours of the morning, I took no "last look." I went into my empty compartment and almost immediately fell asleep. An utterly confused dream is all I can remember: "Deutschland, Deutschland über Alles" played by an enormous brass orchestra, directed by a gentleman in very old-fashioned attire. It must have been my Breslau neighbor, Hoffmann von Fallersleben, who wrote the text. Yet the German anthem was soon drowned out by "*Jeszcze Polska nie zginęła*," played by a group of ladies and gentlemen looking even more anachronistic. The trumpets took up the Polish anthem: "Poland has not yet perished! . . . March, march Dombrowski!" Among the musicians one excelled, Jankiel the honest Jew, about whom I know only that he was the best performer with the dulcimer at Pan Tadeusz's marriage. Yet even this touching scene did not last long. The Poles disappeared as on a revolving stage, a calm, measured voice came on, announcing that this was a fine morning in London, and that a gentleman in Asmara had asked the BBC General Overseas Service to play "Abdullah, the Bulbul Amir." "The sons of the prophet are brave men and bold, and quite accustomed to fear, and the bravest by far in the ranks of the Shah was Abdullah Bulbul Amir. . . ." And so to this cheerful tune the East European confusion dissolved and gave way to British certainties. I reached out and turned the dial of the little radio. The train had just passed Opole (Oppeln). I had left my native city for the second and, I suppose, the last time in my life.

PART ONE

A German Childhood

Childhood

I *was born on Thursday*, May 26, 1921, the only child of not-very-young parents. My father worked in town or traveled, my mother spent most of the time with me. We had a small apartment in a southern suburb of Breslau, Schwerinstrasse 64, third floor. right entrance. In my early memories, the apartment and the house figure prominently. There was a balcony in front, and one in the back, with geraniums grown in front and tomatoes in the rear. There is a photograph taken on my fifth birthday in which I am critically mustering the presents, which include a tennis racket (my interest in sports goes back to an early date). I was dressed in a then-fashionable sailor suit, with high shoes, well over the ankles. My parents were serious people, but on this occasion they had engaged in a practical joke. I loved cherries more than anything else; my father on one occasion wrote a poem on the subject. Thus, my parents had put a few cherries on top of the tomato plants, arguing that in my honor, and in recognition of good behavior, the plants had produced cherries. I did not believe their story.

Once I began to explore our apartment I found the telephone an object of great fascination. These were the pre-direct-dial days and one got a connection by way of lifting the receiver and operating a handle, whereupon the lady at the central telephone exchange would answer and provide a connection. Of even greater fascination was the radio. We had a little crystal set, also called a detector set, with headphones. Reception was indifferent and limited to the local station. It was by means of the little radio that I came to know the hit songs of 1926 and 1927, and many of them I remember today; the late twenties were the golden age of the *Schlager* (pop tunes), even more so in Germany than in the United States. My father did not read much and probably never went to a museum, but he was a man of considerable musical culture, and my lowbrow taste and whistling "Oh, Donna Clara" and "Valencia" must have pained him, but he did not try to influence me until much later.

My parents did not have many books; I do remember a two-volume encyclopedia published in 1880 or thereabouts, from which I got my first political (and sexual) knowledge as well as much other useful information. But there was much sheet music, and occasionally father and mother would play the piano. I liked best the adaptation for piano of the classical operas and operettas and so did they. I grew up with Leporello and Count Almaviva, with Papageno and "*La donna è mobile*," even though I could not possibly understand at the time their reflection on love, jealousy, and the war of the sexes. I knew considerable stretches of *Freischütz* and *Martha* as well as the *Fledermaus* by heart well before I had ever read a serious book. I could whistle the *Si j'étais roi* overture and arias from operas by Rossini, Lortzing, and Boieldieu, not to mention *Alessandro Stradella*; the *Postillon de Longjumeau* and other opéras comiques by Adam that are seldom, if ever, performed today were among my favorites. In my father's generation such knowledge was commonplace. In the 1950s, in London, I became friendly with Robert Weltsch, the distinguished editor who had grown up in Prague before 1914, a contemporary of Kafka and Werfel. His knowledge of opera and operettas was far more profound than mine, if only because it included Wagner, whom I did not like except for the *Meister-singer*. In my generation, alas, such interest was no longer part of *Allgemeinbildung* (general education), except among professionals and experts. True, during the last two decades there seems to have been a revival of interest in classical music among the young, but by and large the one culture of 1900 has become two, three, or more cultures.

My parents were not well off. Most of my friends had more— and more elaborate toys. I was deprived, for instance, of an electrical railway, but I remember always having had a football I also got a bicycle early on. Not a new one, of course, but a sturdy NSU, which almost certainly predated World War I. It even had three gears, which aroused general curiosity, for at that time bicycles with gears had gone out of fashion—not to come back until recent years. Even though my family was not well-to-do, they had live-in help, usually countrywomen from Upper Silesia. Some stayed for a short time, others for years. I remember Anna, tiny, good-humored, simpleminded, in her fifties; she had lost two fingers in an accident. The main meal, as customary then, was lunch and there were always three courses. I was a great devotee of beefburgers, called German beefsteaks in those parts. My mother attempted to induce me to eat fish; she probably tried too hard, because I strictly refused to touch it until many decades later, when I became a fish addict. My grandson shares my predilection for beefburgers and my former aversion to fish, though his parents, who believe in progressive education, have never compelled him. Perhaps there is something in genetics after all. Evenings we had a sandwich or two; on fine summer days the table was set on the front balcony. Food was well prepared, but wine was drunk only on holidays. To clear one's plate was imperative. This had to do with the war and inflation, when food had been rationed and very scarce, but also the general Prussian ethos.

I do not remember when I first received pocket money, but it must have been very little and for this reason, if for no other, the visit of an uncle or some other relation was a welcome event. It invariably meant a present—one mark, or even two or three. I do not want to sound virtuous but from an early age I spent my pocket money on books—not, alas, Kant and Goethe, but adventure stories of the Karl May variety, immensely popular in Germany from the turn of the century to the present day. Some books allegedly written by Karl May continue to appear even now, eighty years after his death. Fifteen years ago an attempt was made to acquaint American readers with Winnetou and Old Shatterhand, the Indian chief and the eminent trapper, the main heroes of this unending series. I did my share by favorably reviewing them in the *New York Times*. The books were a total failure.

Certain events in my early childhood stand out in my memory more vividly than others. I must have been five or six when I had pneumonia and a high fever. I remember Dr. Weigert, our physician, by my bed prescribing very unpleasant cold compresses. My father seemed even more serious than usual; only later was I told that his mother had died the very same day. Then a little later, lying quietly in bed with the curtains drawn, I observed moving shadows on the ceiling—reflections of the cars and horse carts passing in the streets. These reflections have remained a mystery to me to this day. My scientific understanding was never really developed.

These were the prepenicillin days, and the diseases of infancy were taken seriously—a week or two in bed after a flu was the rule. Each winter I suffered from unending colds, and the doctors could do little but paint the throat with iodine, a most unpleasant experience, which helped not at all. At the age of five or six I had part of my tonsils removed, which hurt very badly; the old-fashioned kind of anesthesia with a suffocating mask put on one's face remained a trauma for many years. My parents told me that Amanullah, the then king of Afghanistan, underwent the same operation the very same day. But this did not comfort me at all. The doctor prescribed ice cream from the nearby Gelateria Italiana and this had a better effect.

The apartment was small; the house, on the other hand, was big, with a sizable courtyard, where carpets were cleaned with much noise and linen was dried. On the floor below lived a little girl, my friend Helga; still farther below, a strange elderly couple named Lichtenstein. He was the editor of a spiritualist or astrological journal. I had no idea what it meant. Ours was a corner house; one could enter and leave it from two streets.

Schwerinstrasse was purely residential, but there were shops around the corner in Opitzstrasse, named after a seventeenth-century pioneer of German poetry. Frequently, I went shopping there with my mother at a stationery shop full of interesting things such as colored picture sheets and fancy pencils. It was run by an elderly lady who did not like loitering little boys with no money to spend. Then there was Matuszewski's, the drugstore and perfumery, a great favorite because it had all kinds of samples to give away, such as Krügerol cough drops. I liked these very much, another curious predilection shared by my grandson Benjamin. A corner away there was the Konsumverein, the cooperative food store. I was sent there on my first purchasing missions to buy bread, which came by weight—usually three pounds or four. Nearby was a large ("Pomeranian") dairy; I still remember the notice in the window advertising their FOUR-FRUIT MARMA-LADE—10 PFENNIG ONLY. It was the cheapest they offered, but I could not get enough of this delicacy. In front of the dairy there was a taxi stand; if I remember correctly there were also horse-driven carriages, which I found more interesting. But they disappeared one by one. A taxi ride was a rare luxury, and I cannot remember more than one or two such occasions in my childhood. Usually, one went by electrical tramway, slow but reliable, which passed every five or ten minutes. There were also a few buses, but they went crosstown, not to the city center, and we used them less frequently.

I have not yet mentioned the two shops that greatly intrigued me when I was a little older—the travel agent's and the news-stand. The moment I could read, at the age of six, there was nothing that interested me more than travel prospectuses and atlases. In the beginning I went with my mother to the travel agent's, and following my instructions, she asked for timetables and leaflets for faraway, exotic countries. When she refused to ask for this literature as often as I wanted, I went alone, and the employees, more than slightly amused, gave me all their illustrated booklets about Las Palmas, Colombo, Luxor. My first essay dates back to my sixth or seventh year. It was written for my father's birthday and read as follows: "Last month I went to Bangalore and shot a tiger." There was also a drawing of a person, a rifle, and an animal sitting in a tree. How did I know about the capital of the state of Mysore, west of Madras? Whatever the source of my knowledge, I knew a great deal about cities in India, China, and Latin America—how many people lived there and even what they did for a living. My interest in geography certainly predated my interest in history. I don't think I saw a black person or an Oriental until many years later, except perhaps in the movies, but in my fantasies I had always mixed with them.

Geography meant adventure, faraway countries, the discovery of the unknown. I was six when Lindbergh's *Spirit of St. Louis* landed in Paris, and I remember reading the headlines in front of the newspaper stand. The owner took a dim view of little boys trying to bend the papers displayed in good order in front of the shop, let alone opening them and generally blocking access to the kiosk window, but I was impervious to threats. On Sunday mornings my father sent me to buy the *Berliner Tageblatt*, the leading paper at that time, mainly because it had a music supplement; I remember his excitement when I brought him Prokofiev's *Love for Three Oranges*. Again, why should I remember it?

Because I loved oranges or because the title struck me as perfectly idiotic? The winter 1928–29 was the coldest on record, some days the temperature going down to minus 30 degrees centigrade (– 22° F), and for once my parents were genuinely worried whenever I did not return from the kiosk in good time. Apparently I had discovered something of such interest in the papers that, oblivious of the cold and the snowstorm, I had to finish the story, no matter how freezing it was outside.

Lindbergh was not my only hero, another was Umberto Nobile, who, in an airship he had constructed, was the first to fly over the North Pole. But the real excitement came two years later when his expedition got stranded in the Arctic region. Lindbergh was then the symbol of the spirit of independence and of freedom, whereas Nobile was a Fascist general. Who could have known that the one would end up as an advocate for Nazi Germany and the other as a Communist deputy in the Italian parliament? But nazism and communism were far away in 1928, at least for the boy glued to the newsstand. When I became a customer a few years later, I bought the Monday morning sports paper, not the party political press.

There were a lot of small parks in our neighborhood where mothers took their children for a walk. It must have been on one of these walks that I saw my first zeppelin. I don't know which model it was, for about a hundred in all had been constructed. But it seemed (and was) enormous, effortless, majestically gliding through the blue skies, much more impressive than the small planes almost daily painting the heavens with advertisements for Persil and other washing powders.

There was also the Sauerbrunnen, a little lake with a source of mineral water, and a lot of horse-chestnut trees in all directions. We children collected the red-brown conkers and the acorns and made all kind of toys from them.

Many years later I learned from the writings of learned film critics that the street in the Weimar Republic was something threatening and hostile, best to be avoided. The street meant danger; security was at home. They must have been watching other streets; those I knew seemed a perfectly neutral playing ground. At home it often was boring; the action was in the street. The street gangs assembled there, but they were not particularly violent, rather more or less accidental gatherings; their composition would change from week to week.

Not far from us there was an open stretch of land, deserted building sites and lots. In autumn we dug up occasional potatoes and roasted them; in winter many of the abandoned building sites were filled with water, and we constructed little floats to cross them. Better yet, if the temperature got below freezing, we ventured on the ice, disregarding all warnings. We believed that if one ran over the ice fast enough, it would not break, and my personal experience bore out this utterly wrong assumption. I was strong for my age and fast, but not good at skating and skiing, probably because I did not persevere, giving up after my first failures.

There was one sinister street and it took some daring to cross it: This was Krullstrasse in the center of town, a curved thoroughfare of shabby houses, the street of the prostitutes. I had only a vague idea what a prostitute did for a living, but we were told that the ugly women walking the street would snatch our caps; since I never had a cap or hat, the danger was minimal. But even the guidebook to Breslau said that this street was not to be frequented in darkness. So this was "Sinister Street."

I cannot remember that my father ever took a holiday. Apparently business was slack, and he could not afford to abandon it. Usually, I went with my mother to the Riesengebirge (the Giant Mountains) in summer and also in winter. These were not the Himalayas, as the highest peak was a mere 5,000 feet above sea level, but to a boy the elevation seemed giant indeed. The border between Germany and Czechoslovakia ran on the very ridge of the mountains; until 1933 we usually went to the German side, but after the Nazis came to power we always stayed in Czech resorts, a few miles beyond the border. Other families traveled to more distant places, the Baltic, the North Sea, or even Switzerland and the Dalmatian coast. But again, if there was a feeling of deprivation it did not run very deeply.

There was so much of interest even in the small Silesian resorts, such as the impoverished Russian grand duke in our *hôtel garni* who always kept to himself and did not even answer questions at the table d'hôte. There was the fascination of picking blueberries and mushrooms with Mother, who, being a country girl, knew a great deal about the subject. There were sunny clearings and the silent darkness of the forest, little waterfalls and all kinds of wild animals. Sometimes we would stay in a *Baude*, a wooden country inn high in the mountains, far away from the crowds and often lacking some of the basic amenities. The train from Breslau arrived in winter in the early evening at the little station; a horse-drawn sleigh was waiting and would take us and our baggage through the snow-covered forests. It was cold, but there were heavy blankets to cover us. The horses had little bells fastened to their harnesses. These drives were one of the high points of the holiday. When I read Eichendorff and other German Romantic poets or when I listen to Schumann or Mendelssohn, driving or walking through the silent, snow-covered forest in the dark is the mental image that immediately comes to mind.

If I had the gifts of a poet, this would be the right place for a rhapsody dedicated to the forest. One of the few professions I seriously considered as a boy was that of a forester; I loved the sea but I never envisaged being a sailor. After a bad night, there is nothing to restore the spirits like breathing the air of Rock Creek Park from the balcony of my Washington, D.C., home. I spent my holidays in the forest first with my mother, later with my peers in our youth group, and later still, when I worked in a factory, I regularly toured the Silesian mountains. In our youth group new members had to pass a test of courage: They were led blindfold into the middle of a forest and then abandoned, having to find their own way back to civilization. I had many fears, but that of the forests of the night was never among them.

I revisited the forests of my youth some fifteen years after the end of the war, and they seemed unchanged. But in fact, they were diseased and today they are quite dead, killed by the fumes from the chemical works on both sides of the border. It is a tragic story and the full extent of the disaster I realized only after having read the moving account of Ota Filip, a leading Czech writer, who had been to Klein Aupa, the small village on the Czech side of the frontier where I had spent so many happy hours as a child and adolescent. The mountains were denuded, he reported, and his pictures confirmed the sad story. It was the end not only of a lovely landscape and tourism but of the village. True, they were now experimenting with mountain ash and Siberian birch trees; perhaps they would prove to be more resistant. But it will never be the same again.

At the age of twelve I went through a mildly rebellious phase and ceased to travel with my mother. Instead, I went on excursions with a group of boys my own age. But this belongs to another chapter.

I have not written about friends, and I don't think I had many. The fact that I was an only child did not help. I went to kindergarten but I remember nothing about it, except that I was told on occasion by my mother that I was aggressive and moody, and that I had difficulties getting along with other children. She was a good and kind woman but given to exaggeration; in this specific case she was no doubt right, for the years from age five to nine were difficult ones for me. I was headstrong, prickly, and occasionally had a foul temper. I recently looked at some old photographs; perhaps my imagination unduly influences photo interpretation, but if so, not by very much. At five I had been a pretty child; at eight and nine I appear awkward, introverted, defiant, obstinate. When we visited some wealthy acquaintances, I deliberately smashed a *Gartenzwerg*, a garden gnome, because, for one reason or another, I had been frustrated. Since it was a valuable gnome, there was much indignation and I received a fitting punishment. I also played a leading role in causing mayhem at birthday parties. Nor were my first years in school altogether happy ones. I was sent to a private school of considerable reputation, called Zawadzki, or von Zawadzki. I did not do badly; in fact, it was suggested to my parents that I should skip a year, so that at the age of seven I found myself in the company of boys and girls aged eight or even nine, a considerable difference at that age. My handwriting was not too good, and I had difficulties with some other subjects.

There must have been other reasons for my unhappiness. Most of the other children came from wealthy families, and some were the offspring of the aristocracy. There was some snobbishness, real or imaginary; sometimes they did not want me at their games. Thus I was, or felt, a bit of an outsider and, while I cannot recall that I ever thought of running away, these were certainly not the happiest years of my life. On not a few subsequent occasions through the years I have happened to be the youngest in a group, and I have never coped well with the ensuing problems.

The situation improved once I was out of elementary school, and looking back, I think it could well be that the price I paid for being "parachuted" into a higher form was a small one. For as a result, I graduated from school in early 1938 and was compelled to make immediate decisions about my future, which is to say, to emigrate just in time. But for the head start given to me at an early age, I might not have survived.

These, then, were some of the difficulties of childhood. But I don't think the wounds were lasting. I did have some friends at school but our ways soon parted, and with a few exceptions, I don't know what became of them. A few years ago, I received a letter from someone called Karl Heinz in Germany asking me to contribute to a symposium of one kind or another. His name was vaguely familiar, and in my reply I asked whether he had lived in Gabitzstrasse and whether in the corridor of their apartment there had been the crossed sabers of his grandfather, who, as a young lieutenant, had fought in the battle of Vionville-Mars-la-Tour in the Franco-Prussian War of 1870. This was my early patriotic period, and the cavalry charge, probably the last major one in history, had impressed me no end. I got a long letter in reply; yes, they had indeed lived at this address but there had been no sabers. A few weeks later I got yet another letter—yes, he had consulted with his sister, and my description had been correct. The selectiveness of human memory has always struck me. I could only imperfectly describe our own corridor; why should another have stuck in my mind?

There were other strange coincidences. Some fifty years later I was engaged in a long and apparently fruitless search for a man who, in the summer of 1942, had been the first to reveal to the world the information about the "terrible secret"—Hitler's decision to annihilate European Jewry. After a long time and many efforts, it was established that this unsung hero had been Eduard Schulte, the chief manager of one of East Germany's leading industrial corporations. I have described this search in a book entitled *Breaking the Silence*. By the time we discovered his identity, Schulte had been dead for years. But I established contact with his son Rupprecht and went to see him in a little town overlooking San Diego, where he now lives. It took just a few minutes to establish that we had been classmates at Zawadzki's.

I should have written more about the joys of childhood even though I have nothing particularly original to report. There was the Circus Sarasani at the Luisenplatz, enormous by the standards of those days, seating three thousand people, where elephants, lions, tigers, and horses performed all kinds of surprising feats. Even more amazing was Mr. Kassner at Liebich, the local variety theater, who made an elephant disappear from the stage. (My grandson, aged eight, recently explained the technique to me, but he has a special interest in magic that I lacked.) Out in the northern suburbs there was the six-day bicycle race (*Sechstagerennen*), which attracted many thousands of spectators. There was an inimitable atmosphere at these races; a vocal public was encouraging the competitors, of whom van Kampen, a Dutchman, was the most outstanding at the time. The orchestra was playing the "Six-Day Race Waltz," written by a distant relation named Translateur. Again, it was beyond my comprehension how people could possibly cycle at that speed for six days without a break. Knowledgeable friends explained: They were cycling in pairs, so one could always rest—and there were, of course, breaks at night. This is one kind of sport that never really flourished outside Germany and there, too, it gradually vanished in the 1930s.*

Each variety theater, from the Moulin Rouge down, had its signature tune. In the case of Liebich it was Ponchielli's "Dance of the Hours" from *La Gioconda*. When I hear the Translateur waltz I think of the cycle races; when I listen to street organs, the Neumarkt on Christmas Eve comes to mind—stalls selling Christmas trees, tinsel and other tree decorations, gingerbread, and so on.

Then there was the cinema. I have no vivid recollection of the silent films, although I must have seen Charlie Chaplin, Harold Lloyd, Jackie Coogan, and whatever the names were of the stars of those faraway days. But there was no shock of recognition when I saw these films in later years, except in the case of Pat and Patachon, two of the better known clowns of the twenties. There were in Breslau at the time as in most major cities, two kinds of cinema—impressive large halls with cinema organs named Capitol or Gloria Palace, and small and run-down places, flea pits, usually showing old films. For years I went at least once a week to watch a film—the early 1930s were the great age of the German film industry and foreign films were also frequently shown. The first film I recall seeing was *Es Zogen Drei Burschen über den Rhein* (the title of a student song); it must have been a very undistinguished movie, I have not been able to find it in any filmbook, however detailed. Next came the comedies with Siegfried Arno and Felix Bressart, which were quite funny; both stars went to Hollywood after Hitler came to power, but neither made it—though Bressart played a minor role in *Ninotchka*. Then there were the patriotic films mainly about Frederick II

---

*A Swiss friend tells me that this entertainment still exists in Zurich but is seldom reported in the media.

(the Great), not very distinguished, but very well played, usually with Werner Krauss or Otto Gebühr in the title role. Generally speaking, the German cinema had more powerful men than women actors, what with Heinrich George and Emil Jannings, whose performances seem impressive even now, many years later; the women were pretty and sometimes even vivacious, but most of them somehow lacked character and depth. Then the French movies came; I must have watched *Sous les toits de Paris* a dozen times, and for years I went to see every new French film. The German cinema by and large kept its level even after 1933; it had more freedom than the other arts, and, with some well-known exceptions, it remained unpolitical.

I was smitten by this art, for a number of years I read the film magazines (though not with quite the same enthusiasm as the sports journals), and one of my ambitions was to become a filmmaker. Strange as it may appear, Breslau had been at one time a center of the German film industry, what with companies such as Wotan and silent films such as *The Battle of the Katzbach*. By the time I grew up, these companies, alas, were bankrupt, and since I knew no one at Ufa, Tobis, or the other companies, my dreams came to nothing. It has been one of my lasting regrets in later life that I never had a chance to test my ambition. At best I have been employed as a consultant on some specialized topics. I had ideas and imagination; how often in later years watching a bad film (or a bad scene in a good film) I knew instinctively what went wrong and how it could have been put right.

BADENWEILER, AUGUST 1991. This is one of my favorite resorts, situated in the southern Black Forest, inside Germany but a few miles from the French and Swiss border, Baden-Baden on a much smaller and less pretentious scale. Tamar, that bundle of nervous energy, our youngest granddaughter, aged four, had been even more restless than usual; it is difficult to blame her, what with all the elderly people around suffering from rheumatic diseases. After dinner we took her to the park next to the hotel where the local orchestra gave its daily open-air concert.

Until a decade ago this was a sizable orchestra, but it had to pare down costs and so are down now to ten or eleven players. We arrived at the beginning of one of these unending potpourris of German hit songs of the 1920s and 1930s. The child was transfixed; she was sitting quietly listening to the tunes so different from the ones she had heard and sung in her Jerusalem kindergarten. She was surprised and perhaps a little envious that most of the adults around her seemed to know the songs and were humming the melody or even singing. The transformation was remarkable, and after a while I asked her whether she was tired and wanted to go home. No, no, she wanted to stay.

So I got immersed in my own thoughts. I had grown up with these tunes; it had been the golden age of German popular music, the songs of the handsome gigolo, of Bel Ami, the darling of all women, and of Lola, the femme fatale of suburban bars, playing her pianola, the songs of Jan Kiepura and the legendary Comedian Harmonists, the tunes from romantic comedies such as *The Congress Dances* and *The Three of the Gas Station*. Some of the songs were quite witty, such as the one telling the story of the brother who makes the noises at the talkies. But in most cases, needless to say, it was the melody and the rhythm that counted. I have acquired since a fairly comprehensive knowledge of American and British popular music and I have some grounding in French and Russian; I play these melodies at least once a week. The twenties and thirties were the golden age of popular music. I am sure the best of these tunes will last another hundred years. But I feel the Germans' were the best, and while there was a decline after 1932, some exceedingly catchy tunes made their appearance well into the Third Reich. The same is true, incidentally, with regard to Stalin's Russia; the high tide of Stalinism coincided with the creation of some of Russia's finest songs. I have no explanation for this phenomenon, nor do I know why most of these German songs never caught on in other countries. There are, as usual, a few exceptions. *"Das ist die*

Liebe der Matrosen," became *"C'est nous, les gars de la marine,"* the unofficial hymn of the French navy, and *"C'est mon gigolo"* was also quite popular for a while, not to mention "Lili Marlene." These tunes became part of my cultural interests, and I never felt the need to be defensive about it. I realized in later years that my predilection was shared by other men and women of impeccably highbrow credentials and I have never tried to analyze too hard this weakness of mine; I am not even sure it is a weakness. In the shops these records, tapes, and discs are now sold under the general heading of "nostalgia," but this is not how I feel about them. I do not love them because they remind me of a particularly happy period in world history and my own life, when our hearts were young and gay. I just like them—period.

At this stage, almost an hour later, Tamar came out of her trance and we took her back to the hotel to the tune of the song about the people who decided to stop paying rent because they couldn't afford it anymore. The year was 1932, and it must have been a topical theme, but did they get away with it?

Families of Yesteryear

The name *Laqueur is unusual* and I have become accustomed to seeing it misspelled more often than not. My father's mother was called Friedensohn; her family came from another little town in Central Silesia. Just last night I had a call from the percussionist of the Boston Symphony Orchestra, who proved to me that we are doubly related both by way of the Laqueurs and the Friedensohns. My mother was née Berliner and her mother had been born Cassirer. For all I know, I might be related to the coinventor of the telephone, to the philosopher Cassirer, or to the famous art dealer of that name; Emil Berliner emigrated to the United States in 1870, at the age of nineteen, and, in his late twenties, based in Washington, refined Alexander Bell's telephone with his invention of an effective microphone and an induction coil. Later he achieved a breakthrough in improving Edison's phonograph, replacing the cylinder with a shallow-groove, flat disc—the modern record. He went on inventing; in his middle seventies he constructed several helicopters and acted as his own test pilot.

It could not, however, be a very close relationship, and I have never investigated my descent from these lines. Nor for many years was I interested in the Laqueurs, not until my own children were growing up and began to ask questions. Since then I have invested a little time and effort and established some facts of interest—at least to myself—though some questions remain unsolved. What emerged is very briefly the following: In the early eighteenth century, in a little village called Städtel in Silesia, there lived a Jew named Eleasar Alexander, an innkeeper by profession. According to one version, the family, like most others in the neighborhood, had moved there from the east, following the ravages of the Polish-Swedish war; they might have reached Städtel via Upper Silesia. The name was Laquer; the second "u" was added only a generation later—and not by all the descendants either. Two learned genealogists have informed me that Eleasar must have come from Alsace, probably from the village of Winzenheim, which is now virtually a suburb of Colmar. I have been to Winzenheim three times and had no difficulty in finding the old Jewish cemetery, which is just off the main street of the village. Once there was heavy rain; on the other occasions it was very hot and the mosquitoes were troublesome; I had no difficulty in reading the twentieth-century tombstones, but my interest was in the earlier graves and the inscriptions on these were largely illegible. When I first came to Colmar, I got the local *grand rabbin* out of bed at a late hour, and he told me, not too politely, that there were no archives dating back to the period prior to the French Revolution. They had been destroyed or transferred to Paris. I revisited the place in 1991, but again it was a fruitless search.

Back to Eleasar in the village of Städtel. I have seen a list of the families who lived there two hundred years ago, and there were some strange circumstances. More than one third of the village was of Jewish origin, and of these, not a few had names that were clearly French sounding—such as Graveur, Translateur, and so on—names found seldom, if ever, in France. Did my ancestors come from Alsace proper? There is an explanation; the evidence is strong but not absolutely conclusive. The lands around Städtel belonged to the Grand Duke of Württemberg. According to this version, the Grand Duke, who also had land in Alsace and Lorraine (Montbéliard), moved families to East Germany to help with the management of his holdings there.

Eleasar had several grandsons; one was called Joseph (d. 1838), another David (1772–1846). About David a few facts are known: He was the local rabbi, but since the community was very poor they could pay him only a taler a week and, as was customary in those days, supplied some provisions. He was under considerable pressure from his family to look for a better-paid job or another profession. But David was an idealist and steadfastly refused to do so. According to Dr. Brilling, the historian of Silesian Jewry, he argued that the community could not possibly find a rabbi at that kind of remuneration and that therefore it was his duty to stay. He was also a chess player of renown. When the Grand Duke of Württemberg was bored, he sent a messenger to fetch the rabbi to play a game or two. Many years later someone intended to write a long article or even a book about David, but the writer died before he could carry out his project.

A few more words about Städtel. It is not easy to find even on detailed maps; the first time I discovered it was on an eighteenth-century map, surrounded by forests, close to the border between Upper and Lower Silesia. It was called Miejsce and was first mentioned in the thirteenth century; Merian, the great seventeenth-century geographer and cartographer, mentions it as Stadlin. It was totally destroyed in the Thirty Years' War and steadily lost population. In 1840 the village counted 800 inhabitants, out of which 241 were Jews. This was an untypically heavy concentration; unlike in other villages, the Jews of Städtel could be found in almost all professions: There were bakers, butchers; they made shoes and gloves and potash; bound books; traded horses and tobacco; only agriculture was closed to them, because up to their emancipation in 1812 (when they became full-fledged citizens of Prussia) they could not own land.

It was a desperately poor community; in an open letter published by the local community it was said that Städtel was indisputably the poorest community in the whole of Silesia. Even the Duke took pity and contributed wood so that the community would not freeze to death in winter. An exodus got under way; by 1856 a mere thirty families were left, and in 1925 the last Jew left Städtel.

Among those who moved out was my family, first to nearby little towns such as Carlsruhe and Neumittelwalde, later on to Breslau. My grandfather Louis was born in Neumittelwalde around 1845; his father, Wulf, was a "*distillateur*," that is to say he made schnapps in a cellar and sold it. This installation seems to have acquired a certain reputation; it still existed almost a hundred years later. Shortly before the outbreak of World War II my father wrote to me that on his sixtieth birthday a friend had given him a rare present—a bottle of spirits distilled in the very place his grandfather had established. For all I know, spirits may still be made in Międzybórz (as the place is now called), but I have no way to find out.

The Dukes of Würtemberg played a certain role in the history of my family. The little town had become their property in the seventeenth century, and about a century later the Dukes encouraged a group of vintners from southwestern Germany, under the leadership of one Johann Jakob Lutz, who subsequently became mayor of the city, to settle there. They planted vineyards, and in 1745, there was the first harvest. This, to the best of my knowledge, was the very first attempt to grow wine in East Germany and the effort lasted for more than a century and a half. It was never a great success, however, and eventually the attempt was given up. I am told that the vineyards still exist but are now largely ornamental. In any case, the Würtemberg initiative tends to explain the preoccupation on the part of my great-grandfather (and his father) with producing brandy.

From this stage on, the family tree can be documented fairly accurately. Quite a few of the next generation and the following studied medicine; one wrote a standard nineteenth-century text-book on eye diseases, another was the first to produce syntheti-cally the male hormone testosterone. There were a few historians among them; some converted to Christianity, others did not. I had a cousin once removed, named Hans, a few years older, who belonged to the (almost) "Aryan" branch of the family. He had coached me in mathematics, my weakest subject in school. Then I lost track of him; many years later I heard that he had been killed on the last day of World War II, defending fortress Breslau. Hans had never known his father, who was killed in the last month of World War I.

There is a limit to family research, in my case this limit being reached when I realized that there had been intermarriage with the Warburgs, a very well known family; their pedigree prepared in the early years of the century is so enormous it has to be seen to be believed.

One day in London a British lord of Hungarian provenance (and a distinguished economist) confided in me—his mother had been née Laqueur. I was told the same story by a former U.S. ambassador to South Africa. But the most amazing story came from another, quite unexpected direction, and since it had to do with my interests in later life I shall relate it in some detail.

When I was a boy my father told me that according to oral tradition a great-granduncle had been the personal physician of the Russian empress, he was not sure which one. It sounded most unlikely, and in any case I was not curious at the time. Fifty years later I received a letter from a professional genealogist asking for my help in the preparation of an entry on the Laqueur family for the multivolume *German National Biography*. I learned that there had been a Moritz Laqueur, born in Karlsruhe on March 4, 1787, who had studied medicine and had migrated

to the East. Moritz became Boris, Laqueur became Lakier—
there is no equivalent for ö or *queu* in Russian—and became
head of the quarantine station in Taganrog, on the Azov Sea in
South Russia. This was not a very prestigious appointment. But
Czar Alexander I happened to visit Taganrog in late autumn
1825, fell seriously ill, and Boris Lakier happened to be one of
the few European-trained physicians on the spot. His efforts
were in vain; Dr. Lakier's signature appears on the Czar's death
certificate. Soon after the good doctor was ennobled, he became
a member of the landless aristocracy, the *dvorianstvo*. He moved
to Moscow, where he died in 1851.

Boris had three sons; the third, who interested me most, was
a man of letters, Alexander Borisovich Lakier (1825–1870). He
studied law, and became a secretary of the Imperial Committee,
which prepared the emancipation of the serfs. He married the
daughter of P. A. Pletnev, rector of St. Petersburg University, a
close friend of Pushkin and many other leading literary figures
of the day. Alexander's wife died in childbirth, there having been
one son, Peter, from this marriage.

After the death of his wife, Alexander for many years found
no peace in his life. He traveled a great deal, to Western Europe,
the Holy Land, and even to America, and wrote long articles for
leading Russian journals.

Alexander's two-volume American travelogue, written in
1858, is the most interesting of his books. The University of
Chicago Press brought out an abbreviated translation a few years
ago. It was perhaps the first serious systematic Russian study of
America; he was the first traveler from Moscovy to venture west
of the Mississippi. He went to most major American cities, called
on the president of Harvard, a venerable man whom he found
by his cottage pottering about the flowers. Alexander was surprised that any U.S. citizen could call on the secretary of war in
Washington without a previous appointment. Above all, he was
impressed by the spirit of mutual aid. In New York he more than
once watched how ordinary citizens hurried to the scene of a fire
and pitched in to help the firemen. Lakier commented: "The

duty of everyone to run to a fire is incomprehensible to a Russian. In this lies the difference between American society and ours, that no one can, no one must, and no one wants to refuse labor for the common good." Alexander Borisovich was no Tocqueville; he did not engage in far-reaching conceptualization, nor was he a political prophet. But he had common sense, was a shrewd observer, and worked hard, and thus correctly discerned trends in American life that escaped the more sophisticated French count. He was struck by the fact, to give just one example, that American farmers, in contrast to Russian *muzhiks*, were well fed.

Eventually, Lakier married a wealthy lady of Greek-Venetian origin, Comneno-Varvatsi; the Comnènes, it will be recalled, had been the imperial family of Byzantium. He worked as a lawyer in Taganrog and had six children but did not publish any more books.

In the course of my investigation I received a letter from a gentleman with a Greek name, probably one of the Comnènes, rejecting with some disdain the German origins of the Russian Lakiers. He based his claim on the semiofficial handbook of the Russian aristocracy, according to which the family had come from somewhere in Central France; Alexander's grandfather had arrived in Russia as an officer during the Napoleonic wars.

If so, I had been chasing a chimera. In Brezhnev's Russia, genealogical studies by foreigners were not encouraged. I could not travel to Taganrog, and there was no access to other archives. Then quite suddenly, there was an Alexander Lakier renaissance in Moscow. He had been the first to write an authoritative history of Russian heraldry; in 1990 it was republished in 100,000 copies. The editor of the book, Dr. Soboleva, had access to all the files I had looked for in vain. There was a longish essay on Alexander. The author called him "one of the best representatives of the Russian intelligentsia in the middle of the nineteenth century." But she was silent on the subject of his antecedents. Then, in summer of 1991, there appeared another essay in the leading Russian historical journal *Voprosy Istorii*. Dr. Soboleva had been to Taganrog and had consulted the church register, which had miraculously survived both the Crimean War and World War II.

A strange story emerged. Dr. Boris (formerly Moritz) had arrived in Russia in 1816, a Prussian subject who had studied medicine (and rhetoric) at the University of Berlin. His parents had been poor people (his own words), and he had been married before. His first wife's name had been Leah, and there had been a son, named Sigismund. What had happened to her we do not know, but in any case this first marriage was not valid in Russia, and thus he was within his legal rights to call his marriage to the Baltic-Swiss lady named Schaufuss-Schaffhausen-Eck his first.

Whence the story about the Napoleonic officer and the pure French origin? I do not know the answer; perhaps it was more acceptable in Russia at that time to have a French background than a German-Jewish one. But at least on two occasions Dr. Boris provided an accurate curriculum vitae—when he enrolled at the University of Dorpat and again when he married. He did come from Silesia, specifically from Carlsruhe; he must have been David's younger brother.

Having established this much, I then found it not too difficult to find out more about his descendants. He had four children— a daughter, Akulina, who died young, and three boys: the one from the first marriage, Sigismund, who became Nikolai, Wilhelm (who became Vasili), and lastly Alexander. They and their children married into the nobility—the Chelgunovs, Tolstoys, Golovins, Khvostovs, and Jordanovs. They were in the higher echelons of the state bureaucracy. Some were judges or lawyers; one was commander of the Black Sea fleet that has been so much in the news of late. I was particularly interested in Peter Alexandrovich, whose mother had died in childbirth. He was a godchild of the Czar and died, a political émigré, in 1892 in Switzerland; he is buried in a cemetery in Clarens, near Montreux. Why did this godson of the Czar become a political émigré? There are still more than a few loose ends, and I hope I will find out one day. As I write these lines I am expecting to receive from a St. Petersburg archive the letters written by his father, Alexander, who wrote the book about America. He had also been to the Near East (as it was then called) in the 1850s; there are descriptions of Cairo and, above all, of Jerusalem.

This, in briefest outline, is the strange story of the lost branch of a family. Some may have stayed in Russia after the revolution; others emigrated to Yugoslavia, France, and even Argentina.

I did make some progress in my research concerning the duke who regularly invited Reb David to play chess. On various occasions he helped the family, and he might have been instrumental in getting Moritz, the physician, to Russia. The kings and dukes of Württemberg did not have a good reputation in the eighteenth century, but Eugen Friedrich Karl Paul Ludwig (1788–1857) was an exception. His father had been a general; the son joined the Russian army at an early age. At twenty-three, he was a general, an unusually young age even in those days. The wife of Czar Paul I was his aunt; when Eugen, aged thirteen, first visited Moscow, the czar liked him so much that he wanted to make him his successor. However, within a few months Paul I was killed, and while Eugen remained in Russian service, Alexander I (the son of Paul) took care that the career of the gifted young foreigner would not be too spectacular. Eugen fought in the Napoleonic wars; in the Battle of Borodino (1812) four horses were killed under him and in the Battle of Kulm (1813) he played a leading role in defeating Vandamme, one of Napoleon's generals. He fought against the Turks under Diebitsch, the supreme commander who had once been his tutor. He then retired to his properties in Silesia. A patron of the arts and an amateur composer, he rebuilt the Carlsruhe castle so as to have both a concert hall and a theater at his disposal.

After a long search I managed to obtain a copy of the autobiography of Eugen of Württemberg, written toward the end of his life. The personality that emerged was complicated, tortuous, in some respects not unlike that of a modern intellectual. As a child he had been an introvert—in his own words, "abnormally withdrawn"; mockingly he was called "little girl." As a young man he had been more interested in the cultural life of his time than in politics and war. He read much philosophy and psychology. True, he had talked to Napoleon on a few occasions, but he preferred conversations with Goethe, Wieland, and particularly Schiller, in whose house he was a frequent guest. He played the cello passably well, and the one opera he composed (*Die Geisterbraut*) was actually performed in Breslau. True, he had to pay for it from his own pocket, but then it was performed on twenty-six evenings and in the end there even was a profit.

The timid young man became a soldier and seems to have enjoyed it. He did not like all his superiors, and in his recollections there are too many complaints about his achievements not having been fully recognized. He was also something of a radical even though he had no sympathy for the Jacobins and the revolutionaries of 1848. But he did believe in the "moral fraternization of all mankind," that is to say, in the idea that in the final analysis all men were equal. Hence apparently the invitations to Rabbi David Laqueur to join him in a game of chess. A strange, gifted, not very happy man, brooding in his castle, which he compared to an "oasis in a sea of pine trees," preoccupied with his own imperfections and those of mankind. The castle where David Laqueur became a frequent guest was located within a circle at which eight large avenues met; seven of them led nowhere.

Enough about famous and exotic relations: The great majority of my family, as of German Jewry, as of mankind in general, were neither outstanding scientists, nor moral philosophers, nor great writers or artists, neither tycoons nor geniuses but simple God-fearing people, living in modest circumstances, unconcerned with the great philosophical or political issues of their time, trying to provide for their families. There was the usual black sheep; one uncle had to leave posthaste (for reasons never fully explained to me) for Chile around the turn of the century and he did very well there.

My parents were born in small towns in Silesia, my paternal grandfather sold spirits in a dark, old building on the central square in Schweidnitz (now Świdnica). My maternal grandfather was a miller in Krappitz (now Krapkowice), a very small town in Upper Silesia. Krappitz has a baroque castle; it began to flourish in the late nineteenth century when the railway connected it with the outside world and when shipping on the Oder was regulated. My grandfather was a good customer, shipping his flour downstream. Even when I was a little boy, many years after his death, captains of these ships used to turn up to chat with my mother, always with a present such as a chicken or a duck or even a goose.

My father was born in 1879, and since he was the younger son, he did not inherit the wineshop but was sent to work as an apprentice in a Breslau textile company. He worked for it for many years. In 1914 he was too old for frontline service, nor was his health perfect, so he was posted to Łódź in Poland to help run a local textile factory. But his service there almost came to a sudden end when a flowerpot from his windowsill detached itself and narrowly missed by inches his superior officer, who was passing the house just at that moment. My father was a paragon of rectitude, a wholly nonrebellious man, and he had only friendly feelings for his superiors. Still, it took a major effort to explain that there had been no attempted assassination.

While not withdrawn, he was very self-conscious. He was not a widely traveled man—a trip to Lucerne was the high point in his life. I have already mentioned that he was frugal in his taste and that his cultural interests were restricted mainly to music. He belonged to the generation of enthusiasts who would stand for hours on end to listen to a performance of Wagner's *Ring*— not once, but every year—and he would recall the first performance of Mahler's Eighth ("*Symphony of a Thousand*") in Breslau. Breslau was at the time one of Europe's most important musical centers from the days when Carl Maria von Weber was kapellmeister at the municipal theater to Walter Damrosch, Bruno Walter, Leo Blech, Otto Klemperer (who, like Damrosch, was born in Breslau—so, too, was Kurt Masur), and many others who had worked there before moving on to Berlin or Vienna.

My father had listened to most of the great conductors and soloists of his time and liked to compare them.

He was not resourceful enough to be a successful businessman when he became independent after the war. He produced overalls with the help of a few employees, and since he had no distributing network, he had to travel regularly to shops in the provinces. All this went tolerably well for a number of years, but then came the Great Depression, demand sharply declined, and the larger corporations were squeezing out the small independent producers.

My father was forty-two when I was born, an elderly man by the standards of those days. We never shared confidences, since we were too far apart in age: he was not a strong father figure in the classical sense. Nor do I recall that we ever embraced or kissed. I don't think it was customary at that time, in this milieu; furthermore, my father hated exhibitions of feelings. I was sorry for him as I saw him absorbed in his worries. It would have been positively indecent to rebel against a man so obviously facing great difficulties in life, and finding himself unable to cope with them. To the extent that he tried to influence me, it was toward caution, not to take unnecessary risks, not to attract attention. I was a disappointment to him in later years because he thought me reckless, irresponsible, unable to settle down, incapable of disciplining whatever talents I had. He made few allowances for the exuberance of youth and, not having been a great worldly success himself, probably suspected that I, too, would be a failure. He was horrified when he heard, early on in World War II, that I had married, not yet aged twenty. Marriage meant being tied down and added responsibilities. He had postponed this fateful decision until he was twice my age. He passionately believed in the sterling qualities of the *Bürgertum*, and I was in his eyes the incipient bohemian.

From time to time he would take me for a walk along the Stadtgraben—a canal that had once been part of the fortifications of Breslau. I have mentioned that I liked him to play the piano, sometimes together with my mother; however, in later years he was less and less in the mood to do so. I inherited his catholic taste; he was not only interested in Wagner, Brahms, and Richard Strauss but also in the great operettas such as *Die Fledermaus, The Gypsy Baron*, but above all Karl Millöcker's less well known *Bettelstudent*. He was also an aficiniado of good brass bands. This was the golden age of Paul Lincke and Willy Kollo, of Fucik, Sousa, and the other masters of marches. In Schweidnitz, where he had grown up, there had been a garrison, and as a boy he had followed the regimental band on its parades. To this day I can listen for hours on a sunny afternoon or evening to open-air concerts of this kind, which, unfortunately, have become much rarer.

Once the outbreak of the war had separated us forever, I contacted some relations and acquaintances who had known him from a different angle, and in some ways better than I did. How had they seen him? They told me that he was a most decent man, utterly reliable, a man of honor and deep moral principles, incapable of a mean thought or deed, too mild, too self-conscious, perhaps too weak.

My mother was different in almost every respect. She had grown up a country girl, one of six children, without much schooling, but she was very feminine (in the best sense), warm, spontaneous, led by her instincts. To her, there were only good and bad people and things, with no shades in between. She was good-looking even in middle age. She was nearly forty when I was born, an unusually advanced age in those days. It must have been a difficult birth, since I was a large baby. My mother could not breast-feed me, and another mother in the hospital consented to wet-nurse me. One day I found out that my "milk brother" was running a car repair service near Baltimore, not far from where I live. Mother had been married first to a man in the city of Beuthen—today Bytom—in Upper Silesia. My parents never told me this; I discovered it by chance when I was eight or nine years of age, rummaging among old letters and photographs. She was a war widow, as was her sister Clara and her cousin Elli. (It was strange for me to hear in later years that

German Jews had allegedly shirked their duty in World War I. In retrospect, a good case could be made in favor of the proposition that they should *not* have shown excessive enthusiasm, but then they did not know at the time in what way the fatherland would later convey its gratitude.) My parents were shocked about my discovery and the possible psychological consequences. But I recall no trauma; if anything, I was slightly amused by their concern.

Education in Krappitz had been limited in scope and depth, and so my mother was sent off to a girls' *pensionat*, a kind of finishing school, in Breslau, owned by a lady with the unlikely name of Holzbock. There my mother learned some French, had piano lessons, was taught the social graces and, of course, cooking. (She was an excellent cook.) About her first marriage she never spoke to me. I suspect she married my father mainly because she did not want to be lonely. Probably she came to love him later but not with the passionate, romantic love that must have burned in her in earlier years. Later in life I detected a certain unhappiness in her. Perhaps it had to do with the fact that she lacked some of the comforts she had expected; perhaps it was connected with the tense and dangerous political situation, perhaps with the menopause. She transferred all her ambitions to me. I don't know what she wanted me to be, perhaps a physician like Curt, her favorite younger brother. In any case, she wanted me to be a success, and in later years I regretted that she was not there to share whatever achievements I had accomplished. One evening, many years after her death, I was invited to dinner in Vienna by Fritz Kortner, one of the great actors and theatrical producers of his generation, and also a most difficult human being. In the course of the conversation I asked him how important critical reviews had been in his life. He thought for a moment and then said: "Very important, as long as my mother was alive." It was not perhaps the whole truth, but I felt there was much in what he said.

I had a dozen uncles and aunts and quite a few cousins, all of them older. It would be confusing to introduce all of them at this stage, especially since some will appear later in the course of my narrative. Suffice it to say that family life was close and that we met frequently. There were tensions and quarrels, sometimes deep and permanent, but these were seldom permitted to get out of hand. If a member of the family was in trouble in one way or another, it was self-evident that the others would help. I owe my survival to this family solidarity, but that, too, belongs to another chapter of my story.

The maternal part of the family met almost every Sunday afternoon for coffee and cake in the apartment of my mother's oldest brother. He had been a successful banker but at one stage decided to engage in a speculative venture. I believe it had to do with the recovery of a ship carrying gold bullion that had been sunk in World War I. The venture was not a success—not that it greatly mattered, for a few years later his business would have folded in any case.

Sometimes my maternal grandmother, whose name was Jenny, the widow of the miller, would preside. She had been persuaded to move to Breslau, where five of her six surviving children lived. She was well in her seventies at the time and if she had an aversion it was to modern fashion. Day in, day out, she wore the long crinolines that had been customary in the provinces in the 1880s. She always carried a handbag made out of little pearls called *pompadour* that also dated back a century. At the same time she was quite vain as far as her appearance was concerned. No one must know that she had artificial teeth, and, of course, everyone knew. She did not have much to say, but like Mynheer Peeperkorn in *The Magic Mountain*, she had a certain indefinable commanding presence: She did not have to talk to gain recognition. In later years she gave up her apartment and moved in with us. But she always insisted on having her meals alone in her room; she was a woman of principles very much concerned with her and our privacy.

On these Sunday afternoon reunions, the men smoked their cigars, the women talked and embroidered or knitted. I excused myself and went into the next room, in which there was a gramophone with all these wonderful Electrola, Parlophon, and Odeon records and also a fairly good library. My taste at the time was for tales of gods and heroes, especially Greek; I also read the classical German myths and legends, but they were too sinister for my taste, with too much cruelty and treason, always ending in disaster, like the story of the Nibelungen.

If the Nordic legends most of the time proceeded in darkness, Odysseus and Diomedes, and whatever the names of my heroes were, lived in a world of sunlight that was so much more appealing even though there was also a great deal of murder and thievery, of fraud and abduction. But there was also a sense of humor. My introduction to that world of magic was a book a German professor named Gustav Schwab had prepared for children early in the nineteenth century. It was a brilliant book, and successive generations in continental Europe owe to Schwab their first knowledge of this wonderful world. Schwab's work, quite different in approach from *Bulfinch's Mythology*, appeared in English with almost exactly a century's delay, with an introduction by Werner Jaeger, the greatest scholar of Greek mythology of our time. From his introduction I learned that in Plato's ideal state the children were to be told myths first; the facts would come only later.

Why Homer; why not the Bible? It was probably connected with our education; there were wonderful stories in the Bible but they were not to be read as literature. The Bible was taught in religion classes at school, seldom by inspired teachers, and most of us found it boring.

While the adults were talking and I was reading, listening to music, and dreaming, the world went on its course. Wasn't it a fearful world, full of dangers and uncertainties? It might have appeared that way to those who had grown up in the climate of stability and security of Imperial Germany, of a world that had come to an end in 1918. But I knew this world only from stories and books; the world I knew was far less peaceful and orderly; people were fighting or making revolutions somewhere most of the time. This usually happened in faraway places such as China and had no direct bearing on one's life. But the inflation had enormous psychological repercussions, and the same is true with regard to the great economic crisis of 1929. Even the possession of money no longer meant security. But as I think back it is astonishing how small the impact was at first on daily life, how the great changes on top percolated down only gradually. It was not difficult to remain oblivious of them for a long time, particularly for a child or an adolescent.

The Sunday afternoon gatherings took place in a house in the south of the city—substantial villas, spacious gardens, broad alleys lined by trees—the very names of the streets, Chestnut Avenue, Limetree Road, Maple Avenue, Oak Tree Walk, conveyed an accurate impression; after 1945 the Poles kept the names, but in translation, of course.

We used to walk home from these family reunions. It was a walk of twenty minutes perhaps, crossing Kaiser Wilhelmplatz, the large round square in the south of the city, where a half-dozen major roads converged. This had been its old name, the republic found it unsuitable and changed it to Reichspräsidenten-platz, in honor of the highest elected official in the Weimar Republic. Then the name was to change again, becoming Adolf Hitler Platz. But this did not last for a thousand years either, and what remained of the square eventually became the Square of the Polish Insurgents—in honor of the Polish irregulars who had tried to stage a coup in Upper Silesia after World War I.

In later years we lived a stone's throw from a square that had changed its name even more often. In the Middle Ages it had been Jews' Square—the only guest house for Jewish visitors from the East was there—then it became Karlsplatz. During the republic it was renamed Lassalleplatz, honoring the socialist pioneer who had been born in this very neighborhood. Under the Nazis, Lassalle became a nonperson. After the war, the Poles could not make up their minds for some time, and then settled for Square of the Heroes of the Ghetto, commemorating the Warsaw uprising in 1943. This, of course, was still years ahead.

We walked home past the water tower and the hospital. There

were few people in the streets and even fewer riders on the
bridle path. It was very peaceful; there were no clashes and mass
demonstrations, the police were in full control, and there seemed
to be no reason to think that it would ever be different.

Walking and talking, we reached yet another square—Höf-
chenplatz, where again a few streets converged. At one side was
the red-brick state insurance company, a building of fascinating
ugliness. In the middle of the square—trees, flower beds,
benches, children playing in sandboxes. It must have been a
warm, beautiful evening for even at this late hour the square,
unlike the nearby streets, was crowded.

Sometimes one should give free rein to one's fantasy. I had just
been reading in Schwab's book about Cassandra, the beautiful
daughter of Priam, king of Troy, who had the gift of prophecy
after her ears had been licked by a serpent. If I had had the gift
of prophecy that evening, I would have known that the peace
was deceptive, that in the not-too-distant future almost all the
buildings would be destroyed; that of all the people present in
the square not a single one would remain in Breslau. I would
have known that not many years later this place would be named
after Dr. Ludwik Hirszfeld, the distinguished immunologist and
serologist, the discoverer of the bacteria of paratyphoid (*Salmo-
nella hirszfeldi*). Hirszfeld was probably sitting down for dinner
with his family in Warsaw at that very hour; for him, too, the
future was not yet sealed: He would have thought it more than
somewhat fantastic that he would be arrested one day, that there
would be a miraculous rescue from the Warsaw ghetto, and that
he would have a second career as the founder of the Wrocław
University School of Medicine in 1945.

My father's family was much smaller; he had a half brother
who lived in Schweidnitz. Relations were close, and I spent many
holidays there. I have written elsewhere about my uncle Emil.
A few months ago I received a letter from a professor at Wrocław
University who has a special interest in the history of Silesia.
He had found a document concerning the Laqueur family in
Schweidnitz. A few weeks later the document arrived. It was

dated June 3, 1942; a resident of the city of Schweidnitz named Herbert Klamsdorf applied to the local finance director for permission to buy a valuable violin that had belonged to Emil Laqueur. There was a handwritten comment: "The violin cannot be found. . . ."

My uncle belonged to those German Jews of which there were not a few who firmly believed that nothing could happen to them because they were so deeply rooted in Germany. He had served in the army in World War I; furthermore, Jews had lived in Schweidnitz since 1285. One evening early in the war some strangers appeared at his door. They said that the apartment had been allocated to them and would he vacate it within the next half hour. My uncle ran to the police, suffered a heart attack at the station, and died. His wife was removed that evening and deported to one of the camps, where she was murdered. Fortunately, their only daughter had left Germany a few weeks before the outbreak of the war.

Uncle Emil had no Stradivari or Guarneri, but he had subscribed, for reasons not entirely clear to me, to all kinds of political and cultural magazines in the Weimar Republic, and he had the habit of never throwing anything away. Much of my education on Weimar culture I received from old issues of the *Weltbühne*, the *Tagebuch*, and other such journals found in the dark corners of his cavernous wine cellar. Just as I associate, for obvious reasons, the smell of Gauloises with Paris, the smell of schnapps reminds me of reading about the first German Republic.

A great deal more could, and perhaps should, be written about Schweidnitz and its neighborhood, such as Hohenfriedeberg, where Frederick II fought one of his most successful battles. What do I remember of Schweidnitz? Above all, the church with the tallest spire (more than a hundred meters—330 feet—high) in Silesia, and the market square in the center of town. I recall the promenades around the city, where once the city walls had been. I remember factories that did not, however, dominate the character of the town. Schweidnitz had once been as important as Breslau (whose main street was, and is, the Schweidnitzer Strasse—Ulica Świdnica) but was totally destroyed in the Thirty Years' War and began to recover only in the second half of the last century, when the railway reached it. It was a city with a military tradition, a city in which the middle class dominated, with few very rich people, but also with no slums. All that has remained for me is the letter concerning the violin that could not be found—a motive for a novelist rather than a matter-of-fact account of this vanished world.

The Jewish community of Schweidnitz had numbered more than a hundred members in my father's day. When I spent my holidays there it had already shrunk to half; by the time my aunt was deported there were perhaps a dozen left. Yet one of them named Blumenfeld survived. It is one of those stories that has never been told and I know only the barest details. Somehow, he had escaped from a camp; a woman hid him in her cellar for two years, until the day the Russians arrived. How Agnes Faron, Kupferschmiedestrasse 20, managed to do this and to keep the secret from the neighbors—from *all* the neighbors—I do not know. To hide someone in Spain after the civil war was child's play compared with Nazi Germany, a country of strict and most effective controls. Yet it did happen and should not be forgotten.

THREE

School Under Hitler

I *was not yet quite nine years old* when I entered secondary school, *Gymnasium.* The German educational system was, and largely still is, different from the British and American, and a detailed description would be of interest only to the expert who probably knows about it in any case. School began at 8:00 A.M. and ended at 1:00 P.M. six days a week. The holidays were six weeks in the summer and shorter periods in winter, at Easter, and in the fall. Since it took me about half an hour to reach school and since I wanted to be there in good time, it meant getting up early. I think I was never late for school; my punctuality, inherited from my father, was slightly obsessive. Only graduates from a gymnasium could study at a university; there were perhaps six such schools in Breslau, and ours was a "humanist" gymnasium, with Latin right from the start, and the teaching of Greek beginning in the fourth form. Ours, the Johannaeum, had a liberal reputation, and comparatively many Jewish boys attended it. In later years the Johannaeum was merged with another gymnasium, the Zwinger. From the point of view of academic quality there was not much to choose from among the various schools. Ours had produced three Nobel Prize winners at one time or another, but we were not overawed, and in any case, the best known of them, the writer Gerhart Hauptmann, had been asked to leave at the age of eleven because his work was so much below par; the school could not pride itself on having done a great job.

The school was situated in a little undistinguished street named Paradise Street, (now named after Stanisław Worcell, a nineteenth-century Polish émigré and acquaintance of Marx); opposite was the mandatory stationery shop, next door a small food store specializing in cheap confectionery. The classrooms were adequate; the courtyard was too small—dusty in summer, wet and muddy in winter. One large room near the entrance was the teacher's common room; there was also a little first-aid station, and the director had an impressive office. To be sent up to Dr. Gabriel was considered an extreme measure of punishment, and even the most brazen faced it only with trepidation. I made the pilgrimage once or twice, but nothing traumatic happened on these occasions. He was a gentle man, despite a somewhat forbidding appearance. A democrat, he was removed after 1933 and committed suicide.

School played a central part in my life for at least a number of years, as it did for consecutive generations of boys and girls. School was not merely the time spent there; homework was quite extensive, and in any case, most of one's friends and acquaintances were drawn from among one's classmates. True, school life did not have the self-absorbing role it had for a youngster in a British public school. One was at least aware that an outside world existed. But it took a number of years until other interests asserted themselves.

My record at school was uneven. In the early years I got some prizes for my performance, but later on—at twelve, when puberty set in—it greatly deteriorated. I was still good in subjects that interested me, such as literature, history, and geography as well as physical education. I had no inclinations for science and drawing. In a gymnasium of nonhumanist bent I would have been in deep trouble; at the Johannaeum I managed to muddle through without much effort. Discipline was not too harsh. I was never really stretched, which, in retrospect, is a matter of regret.

We had some very good teachers; their place should have been in a university rather than teaching unruly and unwilling boys. But there were only a few universities at the time and even fewer chairs, and so these teachers had opted for the security of a less rewarding job. There was A.C., as everyone called him, a Jewish bachelor, bald, sarcastic, and yet liked by most of the pupils. When I met him many years later, he was living in a village in Israel, teaching kibbutz teachers philosophy, which must have been a relief after years of trying to impart the spirit of Greek and Roman culture to much less motivated ten-year-olds.

There was also Jüttner, an unworldly scientist of truly encyclopedic knowledge, but alas, without the ability to communicate it. He looked the typical confused professor and there were countless anecdotes about him. I remember but one. In the middle of a physics lesson someone knocked on the door from outside and the nearest pupil hastened to open it. He came back and reported: "Herr Professor, Einstein is outside. . . ." Jüttner hurriedly went to see for himself and there was indeed—Einstein—that is to say, one stone (*ein Stein*) on the floor.

I read much in later years about the figure of the teacher tyrant, the sadist who played such a great role in the works of Heinrich Mann and other contemporary novelists, driving pupils to suicide. They may have existed, but well before my time. Those I came to know had their weaknesses, but there was not a particular tyrannical streak in them. Many of them had been through the war; this was also a generation that had been formed by the youth movement, the Wandervögel, of which I shall write later on. No converts to progressive education, they did not believe in blind submission either.

The pupils were, I believe, almost equally tolerant; we were harder on the very young teachers, those with the stronger nerves and less experience. One of the older teachers sometimes came half drunk to school. But we also knew that he had serious domestic trouble, and no one would take advantage of him.

The advent of Nazism did, of course, cause problems at school; up to the day Hitler was appointed chancellor, the wearing of uniforms was strictly forbidden, but the following day a swastika flag was hoisted over the very entrance. The Jewish teachers, of whom there were not many, had to leave, the half-Jewish and those with non-Jewish spouses being allowed to stay on for a few years more. Most of the teachers had gravitated to the center and the moderate right politically. In 1933 many, perhaps most, joined the party, not out of deep conviction but out of opportunism, to keep their jobs and not damage their chances for professional advancement. Only one had been a Nazi, with an early membership number, and a true believer at that. He was Kaergel, my German teacher, and for all his crazy beliefs, a fair man. The lessons frequently turned into a dialogue between him and me; I had done a good deal of reading, and specialized in the right-wing writers. He gave me high marks, except at graduation in 1938, when this was practically impossible and when, in any case, marks did not matter any longer.

German and biology apart, tuition changed but little. The history books had always been patriotic and they now became a little more so, but the difference was insignificant; contemporary history was not taught in any case. There was no nonsense about "German physics," and the biology teacher who had to instruct us in *Rassenkunde* (racial theory) did it in such a way as to make it clear that he did not think the topic of much interest or relevance. The old and learned rabbi continued to visit the Jewish boys once a week to give religious instruction.

Some of the older teachers had begun their careers in the early years of the century. One of them was Czeczetka, who taught us gardening; under his guidance I got a third prize for growing dahlias. The sociologist Norbert Elias, to whom fame came late in life, mentioned to me that well before World War I he had studied with Czeczetka in the very same school; there was a great deal of continuity. In retrospect, I admire the enthusiasm of these old teachers; by and large teaching is a profession for young people, but there are born educators and I have the greatest of respect for them.

The position of the Jewish pupils was ambiguous. According to the new order, the teacher had to salute the class by raising his arm and the students had to respond with "Heil Hitler." This obviously did not apply to the Jews. On occasion the class would be ordered to participate in a mass demonstration—say, against the League of Nations, which had condemned Germany, or on the occasion of a visit to the city by Hitler. We learned by trial and error that our presence on these occasions was not mandatory, and the feeling of deprivation was not great.

Relations with the other pupils were correct; I do not recall an open anti-Semitic incident. Gradually, more and more of the students appeared on certain days in Hitler Youth uniform; later on, one or two were in the SS, some even in positions of command. They went out of their way to be polite, as if to make it clear that all this was of no consequence; they joked about their uniform and their service. And it is certainly true that I encountered little, if any, fanaticism. I am sure that elsewhere the situation might have been different; I can only report what I recall. It is also true that the situation deteriorated after 1936. That year a class excursion was to take place. When the "Aryan" students heard their "non-Aryan" classmates were to be excluded, they decided to boycott it. Two years later this would have been unthinkable, and I do not recall that after graduation anyone expressed interest in my plans, let alone wished me well.

In later years our class became smaller and smaller despite the fact that our school had been merged with another. Schoolwork also became less and less important, partly because of other interests but mainly because of the justified feeling that it was

leading nowhere in particular. By 1936 I knew that after graduation I would not be able to study or enter a profession in Germany; my future was no longer in this country. And so I did the
very minimum needed at school. My German classmates were
not highly motivated either, because they had to join the Labor
Service and later the army—three years of restriction, of not very
interesting work, and of indifferent food and accommodations.

Am I drawing a picture that is too rosy with regard to our
coexistence after 1933? A friend sent me the other day a privately
printed book, published on the occasion of the centenary of our
school in 1936 or 1937. According to one of the contributors, a
teacher named Dr. Dohn, whom I do not remember, the general
situation of the school was worse than that of any other in Germany because of the high percentage of "non-Aryans." The
teachers found it almost impossible to function and the patience
of the "Aryan" pupils was taxed almost beyond stretching point.
From this book I learned that the Hitler Youth sent delegations
not only to the head of the school but to the supreme Nazi
leader in Silesia, asking for immediate action and apparently
threatening to do it themselves if their demands were not met.
The author clearly sympathized; how could there be a true "class
community" in the presence of so many elements alien to German character and mentality? But the director—and, more im-
portantly, the *Gauleiter*—told the Hitler Youth that 90 percent
of the non-Aryans were sons of war veterans, that there was a
decree by the minister of education protecting them, and that
under the circumstances nothing could be done for the time
being. Our chronicler relates that after 1935 the waves of indignation ebbed somewhat, owing to the admirable self-restraint of
the Hitler Youth, and in any case, the number of "non-Aryans"
had steadily declined.

Of these ongoings, I confess, I did not know at the time. But
I suspect that if these emotions had truly been deep-seated, we
would have felt it. Of course, there must have been some fanatics
(and also some careerists) who protested to all kind of authorities,

but violent, spontaneous feelings I did not detect, and I still doubt whether they existed among either teachers or students.

What became of my classmates and the other friends of my boyhood? They were nineteen on the average when war broke out, having joined the army a year before—the draft had been introduced in 1936. The lucky ones survived seven years in the army; others returned from the prison camps only in 1948 or 1950, or not at all. About a third, perhaps more, were killed in the war; of the survivors quite a few were wounded, some severely. Over the years I have heard from quite a few of them; some of my books were published in German translation and this provided a lead to contact me. While touring Germany for one purpose or another, I visited several of my contemporaries. There was a striking uniformity to their fate: They truly felt victims of the war, having lost the best years of their lives, as well as their homes in East Germany and, in quite a few cases, their families.

After the war they found themselves in villages or little towns in western or southern Germany, for the big cities were destroyed and there was no room for newcomers. Nearly thirty, they had to learn a profession quickly; a few studied medicine, more became teachers or engineers. By the time the economic miracle got under way, they had families, and the transition to the big cities became difficult. Not a few were stuck in small, out-of-the-way places, with little prospect of promotion. Quite often I had the feeling that they were not very happy in their professions and at forty they looked forward to reaching retirement. Roman was an exception; he joined the Office for the Protection of the Constitution and specialized in investigating sects of the extreme right and left. Like most of the others, he is now retired. With him and others, I often encountered envy of the interesting life that they thought I was leading. When I tried to comfort them with reflections about the great advantages of small-town life in a face-to-face community (to use the sociological term) it always sounded trite and false, though it was meant sincerely. I met one classmate in Kassel, another in Kiel, a third near Frankfurt, yet another in East Berlin. They have children and grandchildren and lead comfortable lives in retirement. But I sense a feeling of regret, of missed opportunities, of sadness in this generation.

What became of my Jewish friends and classmates? Some waited too long or had no opportunity to emigrate and as a result were caught in a trap; they perished in Auschwitz or some such place. Most of the survivors have long and complicated stories to tell that, alas, will be forgotten with their deaths. In a few cases the transition was smooth. Peter had an uncle in the United States, and he was among the few lucky ones to get an "affidavit," as stage one of an entry permit was then called, and reached America safely. When war broke out, Peter enlisted in the U.S. Army, or was drafted; he saw service in Europe and then, under the GI Bill of Rights, went to college and university. He became a lawyer; others went into medicine or business. Klaus left Germany early on and graduated from a hotel school in Switzerland. His career was rapid—in the fifties and sixties he was one of Britain's main caterers. This was the era when many African and Asian countries gained their independence and there were few such festivities in which he was not involved. Klaus's last position was that of chief of catering of the P&O shipping line, but he died quite young.

Another Peter had a Jewish father but a non-Jewish Italian mother. He went back to Breslau in the uniform of an Italian officer in the middle of the war, not unaware of Germany's "terrible secret," a ghostly journey into the shadow of death.

Still others had a harder time; they arrived in Britain during the last months of peace and were shoved off to some remote place without an opportunity either to learn or to enter a profession or acquire a craft. One worked for much of his life in a shoe factory in the North of England; another became gardener in charge of the local churchyard. As far as I could ascertain, they were as happy (or unhappy) as those who lived in a Manhattan duplex or an expensive California villa. Others went to a kibbutz and, unlike me, stayed on. They do not have to worry about

income tax declarations, about losing their jobs, or about loneli-
ness as they become older.

Then there were those who survived but had a bad war: Richard became a German prisoner of war in France; the same fate
befell Hans in Greece. Unlike other prisoners of war, they did
not know whether they would live to see the day of liberation.
One of the most amazing stories was that of a boy whom I shall
call David. He came from a village near Breslau and was among
the unlucky ones who did not leave in time. When war broke
out he had no job, no special training, and there was every reason
to assume that his life span was to be counted in months rather
than years. In due course, he was deported like all the other Jews
and found himself in Auschwitz in late 1942. He was in danger
daily of being selected for the gas chambers, but by sheer luck
he was overlooked; the fact that he was small in stature might
have helped. When the camps were evacuated in January 1945,
he was just barely alive. After the war he worked for a while
for the American occupation authorities. Then he discovered a
remote relation somewhere in New England, left for the United
States, and went back to school while earning his living. David
ended up some twenty-five years later as president of a multibil-
lion-dollar high-technology company. He retired a year or two
ago, to be appointed deputy head of a major government agency
in Washington. Only in America . . .

At least two survived by hiding their identity; Jürgen, a distant
cousin of mine, aged fifteen, worked as a stable boy for the
Wehrmacht in France. As they were about to find out his true
identity, he walked over the mountains into Spain, and a few
months later appeared at my doorstep in Jerusalem. Another
schoolmate headed a small orchestra and choir, entertaining the
troops on the Eastern Front. The former is now retired in Sweden; the other has a little orchestra in Berlin.

Then there were the truly tragic stories. Kurt was a native of
southwestern Germany. I came to know him well only in 1938,
but we quickly became friends. He was two years older and a
half-Jew according to the Nuremberg laws; as a result he had

certain special privileges. He was in charge of children's transports out of Germany. I remember walking with him to the main road traversing the Jordan Valley on an indescribably hot day in early August of 1939. He was to catch the bus to Haifa—and then back to Trieste and Germany. I tried to dissuade him up to the last moment: "Do not go back; there will be a war." He did not dispute my assessment of the world situation but he had made up his mind; his duty was in Germany as long as hundreds, perhaps thousands, of children could be saved. Miraculously, he survived the war. He was among those who established the "underground railway" leading from Holland to Spain, by means of which hundreds of young men and women were saved. Like a ship's captain he decided that he would be the last to leave Amsterdam. Again, he left it a little too late; he was arrested by the Gestapo in June 1944, but by that time the Allied invasion of France was in full swing, and the prison in which he was kept was bombed. He used the opportunity to escape—only to be run over by a car in Paris a month after the armistice.

Then there was my friend Franz, a gifted painter and a talented long-distance runner. When we were fifteen, we went to watch an athletics competition. There was a thousand-meter race for our age group, and while he had never run in a competition before, he was sure he could do it in less than three minutes. We bet; he won in 2.58 minutes, running almost effortlessly on the grass without shoes. For almost ten years I did not hear from him, and I thought that he had perished like so many others. One day—it must have been in 1949—he turned up in our apartment in Jerusalem, hardly changed, as lively, as optimistic, as ever. We talked for a few hours. After an interlude in the Foreign Legion, he had spent the war years in China. Now he was looking forward to finding a permanent home. He married a girl in Kinneret, in the Jordan Valley, and at long last settled down. He worked as a surveyor. One day he inadvertently crossed the Syrian border, was shot, and died immediately.

It is preposterous to generalize about a generation. How many did I know reasonably well of my generation? A few dozen perhaps. Some were clever, others stupid, there were (and are) some sterling characters and some dubious ones. Yet as I reflect about those who survived by effort or good luck, or both, certain common features emerge: We were not particularly well prepared for the struggle for survival; in fact, we were hardly prepared at all. We were uprooted and transplanted into a totally different world. Figuratively speaking, we could not swim, but soon it became a question of swimming or sinking. In these hours of perils, a hidden strength appeared, of which we had not been aware. We were lucky that we were young and relatively adaptable; those fifteen or twenty years older faced much greater difficulties. Sometimes I tend to compare my generation, or what I know of it, with our contemporaries in other countries or with the generation after us. I envy them for a more or less normal and relaxed adolescence. They were not on their own early on in life, their homes had not been destroyed, there was always someone to assist them. But I shall not deny that there is also an occasional feeling of superiority, for they were never really tested. It is, of course, quite unfair, because we did not volunteer for our trials, and, for all one knows, those who were not tried might have acquitted themselves as well as we did, or perhaps better.

I could fill this book with the stories before, during, and after the war of some of my contemporaries, many of them more eventful than mine. But this is my story, not theirs, and while I shall make occasional reference to what happened to those who were at one time close to me, I shall have to pick up the thread of my own story.

I have briefly mentioned that in 1932, when I was eleven, my parents moved to the center of town, and I was to spend the years until my departure from Germany in this home. The purpose of the move was to save money, to have my father's business, such as it was, and our home under one roof, and also to give shelter to Grandmother. When I close my eyes I again see the street in front of me. It was less than a couple of hundred yards long, the houses were massive and distinguished in the classic style with elaborate pediments, gabled roofs, and Ionic columns. Some had been built by Langhans, one of the leading German architects of the eighteenth century. It was a business street—the main office of the savings and loan bank was located there, as well as one or two private banks, and the town's central library. There was not a single shop, and there were few residents.

Miraculously, most of the buildings in this street survived the war only partly damaged. The house next to us belonged to a well-known banking family, Wallenberg-Pachaly. Goethe had visited it more than once during his one and only visit to Breslau in 1790. Alas, he found the neighborhood "loud, dirty, and stinking," and Goethe, as usual, must have been right. At the back of the street there was in his day a little river, the Ohle, with many tanners—yards with their specific, penetrating smell. Even in my day this back lane was called Tanners Lane although the river had been redirected and the tanners had disappeared. Though the street was quite literally a stone's throw from the very center of town, called the Ring (rynek), as in many East German cities there was no traffic in the evening, but an eerie silence.

The apartment was large, some eight rooms. I could cycle from the entrance to the far end, where my parents' bedroom faced onto another street. The rooms were huge, with high ceilings; there were double doors and double windows. These were the pre-DDT days, and like all old houses, this one was infested with all kinds of vermin; from time to time the Kammerjäger— a far more elegant term than exterminator—would appear and fumigate rooms and furniture. There was an enormous old-fashioned pale green stove in my room, but it did not work very well and once I almost died of carbon monoxide poisoning. Something was slightly forbidding about this neighborhood— all the houses were gray, and there were no trees or gardens; it was a kind of no-man's-land between the elegant main street and a much poorer district, almost a slum.

Sometimes in the evening I would accompany my father on a walk; he showed me the courtyard nearby where he had worked as a young man. The whole neighborhood seemed to consist of such old cavernous yards with names like Pokoihof, Niepoldshof, and so on. They had been used since the late Middle Ages. The goods shipped from Russia to the West and vice versa had been stored here; the carriages had stopped here. Auctions had taken place. Some of these courts figured prominently in German historical novels such as the most famous *Soll und Haben* (*Debit and Credit*) by Gustav Freytag. The merchants had done well and they had been lovers of the arts. I recall terra-cotta figures all over the place showing market women, weavers, churches, even a synagogue.

The building I came to know best was the public library, which was just a few steps away. It had been founded by a sixteenth-century humanist named Rehdiger who had bequeathed a few thousand manuscripts. This was the first of my "universities," to borrow Maxim Gorky's term. To the extent that I ever got a general education, I received it here, reading indiscriminately whatever seemed of interest. Since I could only take six books out at a time, I appeared there almost daily and became one of their best customers. The main difficulty was that much of the literature I wanted was marked either BS (which meant something like *Bibliotheca Secreta*) or had a yellow spot, which meant that it was either anti-Nazi or that the author was a Jew or an enemy of the state. Fortunately, quite a few books had slipped through the net of censorship. I remember a book, quite well known at the time, by a Communist writer named Otto Heller entitled *The Destruction of Jewry*, which was a critique of Judaism and Zionism and a paean to Birobidzhan, the recently established Soviet Jewish autonomous region in the Far East. The title seemed in accord with the Zeitgeist, and so the book had passed. The librarians gradually became quite suspicious of my choices even though each time, to minimize the risk, I used to order one or two books with a pronounced Nazi tendency. These little stratagems probably misled no one, but the librarians had to stick to their rules, and since the books I wanted were not banned, they could not refuse them to me. So I worked my way through world history and German literature and art history and a little sociology as well as sexology and some economics. When there was nothing else to read, I took a volume or two of the *Enciclopedia Italiana*, which was the best of its kind at the time, astonishingly liberal, though it had been produced under Mussolini's censorship.

I had no one to guide my steps, and as a result I read a great deal of nonsense as well as books that were unnecessary. But these intellectual odysseys also had some advantages; there was the joy of discovery precisely because I had found a book of great interest that no one had recommended, and my critical sense did develop. I remember the day I took a novel home that had somehow slipped through the censor's net in view of its innocent title. It was Ignazio Silone's *Fontamara*, perhaps the most powerful truly anti-Fascist novel ever written. I read it in one sitting.

There was an element of impatience in my reading; there were so many books and so little time; *vita brevis est, ars longa*, as they taught us in Latin lessons. ("The lyf so short, the craft so long to lerne," in Chaucer's translation.) It was one of a few dozen sayings that deeply impressed me; I learned only much later that the saying went back to Hippocrates' *Aphorisms*. (As coincidence has it, my future father-in-law, an authority on Hippocrates, had written an excellent essay on it.) It also meant that too often I would read books about books—histories of philosophy and literature, historiography rather than the sources. But perhaps it was all to the good, for there was, in fact, little time, and the sources might have defied me in the absence of intellectual guidance. The assignment at hand was to get a general overview. And so my knowledge increased but also my confusion; I shall have more to say about the subject. Dr. Johnson once observed that he knew as many facts at eighteen as in middle age, and I think this is also true in my case.

The making of a young intellectual, all brain and no body? Not quite, for such was the enthusiasm of youth and its almost inexhaustible energy that my reading, extensive as it was, constituted only part of my preoccupations. There were sports and the youth movement, there were friendships and first love.

I find it difficult to write about these pursuits—there is emotional resistance, and I lack the candor of the great confessionalists, not to mention their depth of thought and power of expression. The subjects I now have to confront are inchoate, difficult to describe, and they may, in retrospect, appear of no great consequence, infantile preoccupations. Why even mention athletic competitions, hiking expeditions, and summer camps? But they were important at the time.

Why is it so difficult to write about sports? I don't know more than three or four good novels on the subject (including books by George Bernard Shaw, Ring Lardner, and the Austrian-Jewish writer Friedrich Torberg). And yet, there is almost as much comedy and tragedy in sport, not to mention ambition and intrigue, as in *Hamlet* or *Othello*. To this day in the summer months I turn first to the sports pages of the newspapers; as a friend of mine correctly noted, this is the only part of the paper dealing with human achievement rather than human failure. This is, of course, an exaggeration but not by much.

Like almost all the boys of my age I was fascinated by ball games, and the now long-forgotten giants of soccer were my heroes: Richard Hofmann and Hanne Sobeck, who could score goals from a distance of twenty-five or thirty meters, and the stalwart goalie Heiner Stuhlfauth. I know that a number of well-known contemporaries of mine shared these lowbrow interests well into middle age. A former U.S. secretary of state still subscribes to *Der Kicker*, which for decades has been the leading soccer journal. I have to confess publicly that on several occasions I borrowed his copy without his knowledge. I suspect that a distinguished colleague of mine, an authority on the Enlightenment and the history of psychoanalysis, would not have been able to resist the temptation either. As a young boy I went to watch the local clubs confronting Everton (Liverpool) and Ujpest (Budapest), and other famous champions. When England defeated Austria 4 to 3, the match of the titans in the early 1930s, I was glued to the radio.

At fourteen I was tall and strong for my age and went for boxing lessons. There was a legendary old man, a Jew (his name was Lachman, I believe), the best trainer in town. He had a pawnshop in a tough neighborhood, and according to legend, he had once knocked out three armed robbers. He was so experienced that, contrary to strict instructions, the leading non-Jewish boxers in Breslau came to train with him under cover of darkness. He used me as a sparring partner against Miner II, who went on to win an Olympic medal in 1936. I once knocked him down, not because I was hitting that hard but because his footwork was faulty and I took him off guard. This was my moment of glory; it could have cost me dearly. But Miner II was a gentleman, and I did not have to pay for my momentary achievement.

I never became an accomplished boxer; I took part in only one three-round demonstration fight and I have forgotten whether I won or lost on points. But it helped at school when we had boxing lessons in the upper forms; I got the reputation of someone who could not only hit but had coordination and experience. Many years later, meeting classmates as infirm as myself, I was surprised when they confided to me that my pugilistic prowess had impressed them more than any other qualities I might have possessed at the time.

Boxing gave me some self-confidence. Not that this was a period of all-pervasive fear, as I heard and read in later years from others who lived through the same period. But I may have felt instinctively that the day would not be far hence when I might need every little ounce of self-confidence.

At one time or another I tried many sports. I performed reasonably well but showed no particular aptitude in ball games. I took part in swimming competitions and cycle races, but again, my results were just average. In later years in Palestine I had a great deal to do with horses, but I never had a good horse and, in any case, by that time lacked ambition. I was almost hopeless in gymnastics, which was obligatory in school. My heart was in athletics and, given the right conditions, I might have done reasonably well eventually in the decathlon. But the conditions were not right—there were two Jewish sports clubs in town, one Zionist, called Bar Kochba, the other the youth section of World War I veterans. The level was not at all bad; Bar Kochba had been German champion in the 100-meter relays before 1933, and the Austrian and Czech Jewish clubs almost monopolized swimming and water polo in these countries.

We had some good trainers, but the sports grounds were incredibly bad. There were no modern racetracks or jumping facilities; not even a cinder track, but simply a football field, not very well kept either. My breakthrough came in the summer of 1936 when, aged fifteen, I came first at a regional competition in the sprint, the broad jump, and putting the shot. Many years later, when doing some historical research, I had to go over newspapers dated 1936. I found to my surprise (and gratification) that three or four of them had taken note of the achievement of the "promising fifteen-year-old," as they called me.

These achievements are not impressive, to put it mildly, by today's standards; nowadays some girls of this age group do better. But given the conditions and the virtual lack of training, there is no reason to feel ashamed. I was encouraged to persevere, but my athletic career lasted only two summers. I was taken to other cities to compete, but outside my home ground never did well; driving in a bus throughout the night was not conducive to great achievements, and I also was too nervous away from home. On one occasion while high jumping, which I disliked in any case, I injured my knee slightly, which was a warning sign. And so I gave up competitive athletics before my career had really begun. Still, I kept an interest in the field and occasionally watch competitions to this day. I have a school certificate that says there is reason to believe I have sufficient talent and motivation to train as a sports teacher, a recommendation I am glad I did not take up.

My enthusiasm had its limits; unlike one of my early publishers, Fred Praeger, an erstwhile Austrian sprint champion, I never thought of competing in later life. True, I loved throwing the javelin; it always struck me as one of the most elegant disciplines, in which technique counts as much as, or more than, brute power. When I emigrated, I took a javelin with me, and ten years later, living in an Arab village and subsequently in Jerusalem, I took my javelin out from time to time, trying to check whether I still mastered the technique. It was not a good idea, for the hills of Judaea were far too stony for the purpose. My activities attracted a certain measure of surprise and amusement; none of the Arab villagers and few of the Jews had ever seen a javelin. To this day younger acquaintances and friends from Jerusalem tell me—decades after the event—that they watched me and thought me more than slightly eccentric. I do not know what became of the javelin in the end; for all I know, it is still in some storage room. For competitions it is no longer suitable because both the shape and the weight of javelins have changed over the years. I understand it will change again next year.

FOUR

Children at Play

One *day in the spring of 1933*, a boy whom I vaguely knew from
school stopped me in the street and asked whether I would join
him and a dozen friends next Sunday on a walking tour. How
long would it take and how did he know that I would be welcome? He dismissed the questions as of no consequence. And so
I found myself early one Sunday morning at the terminal station
of one of the urban tram lines. The others were in a uniform of
sorts, with white shirts, short blue trousers, and a blue handker-
chief, also a blue anorak of a special cut, and military shoulder
bags made out of canvas. Some of the boys I knew from school,
others I was meeting for the first time. The group leader was
named Tom, a tall nineteen-year-old who had a natural air of
authority. We waited for a few latecomers, and then we started

a brisk walk that took us through villages, fields, and forests. One had brought a guitar, and when we rested, there would be a singsong. At noon the sandwiches that had been brought were collected and then redistributed. We must have walked a good twenty miles, and I returned home in the early evening, sweaty, dusty, and very happy.

Thus, I joined the group, which met at least once a week in the home of one of its members. There was a permanent meeting place, a deserted shack somewhere in a garden in the suburbs. The group leader would talk for a few minutes on a topic of his choice; then there would be a discussion, or individual group members would talk about their activities or problems they had to confront. Then someone would read a poem or two, the group leader would recommend some books to read, and finally there would be more songs and perhaps a game. Time passed quickly, and after two hours we would disperse.

I should have added that each member of the group had a nickname, some being abbreviations, or initials, or names taken from books such as Kipling's *Jungle Book*; the origin of others was unclear. On top of the weekly meetings and the Sunday walks, there were the camps and marches, usually during the summer and winter holidays. This was the climax of our activities. Someone had rented a barn or a camping site in the mountains near the Czech border, or on the shores of the Baltic. There we would spend two or three weeks, far away from the big cities, frequently joining another group or groups. Sometimes there would be a hundred youngsters in a camp of this kind, on a few occasions even more.

Such a matter-of-fact account of how time was spent walking, talking, singing, and simply sitting around a camp fire cannot possibly convey an impression of what it meant for a boy or a girl of that age. It does not describe the quality of life and friendship, or sunrise and the smell of the forest. We were in a realm of our own, far away from the pressures and interference of a potentially hostile world. Escapism, then? Yes, but much needed at any time, and of particular benefit at that time and place.

It is difficult to write about a romantic experience using prosaic language. The very term "youth movement" does not make sense in English—there is, or has been, a working-class movement, a back-to-nature movement, but a youth movement? Professional educationalists—specialists in Central European political and cultural history—will know what I mean but few others.

Comparisons with the Boy Scouts are in many ways misleading, because the youth movements were much more ambitious in their aims. They wanted something akin to a cultural revolution, not more and not less. It is so difficult to write about it, because the main feature of the youth movements was not their philosophy, the intellectual content of their written programs, but the shared experience. Thus, the statement that a group of sixteen- or seventeen-year-old boys was walking in the forests and singing songs, while absolutely correct, is not very meaningful: Why did they walk, rather than drive? Why did they sing?

To explain in briefest outline: The early history of the Wandervögel (as the youth movement was called in its early phase) started in a Berlin suburb in the 1890s with a group of high school students who went hiking through the German countryside unaccompanied by adults. But hiking and the rediscovery of nature were not the main purpose of a movement that spread quickly through Germany, Austria, and to a certain extent, also Eastern Europe. Soon the churches and the political parties established their own youth movements. They went on such excursions to escape the control of teachers and parents, to experience togetherness, the new *Lebensgefühl*, yet another of these untranslatable terms. It was a kind of neo-Romantic reaction against anemic and arid intellectualism; it reflected a fresh awakening to life, spontaneity, human warmth.

For the great majority of the members of the Wandervögel the Great War spelled the end of innocence. True, after 1918 the movement was still growing. Part of the movement sympathized with the extreme left, more tended toward the right, and

the majority was in favor of opting out of this sinful world altogether. Both Left and Right were hostile to soul-destroying capitalism, materialism, the alienation of man. Everyone agreed that
the old world was beyond redemption, and that nothing less than
total revolution would put things right. On the fringes of the
movement all kinds of eccentric theories and activities were discussed and sometime practiced—ecstatic dances, Asian mysticism, flower power. The first urban and agricultural communes
were established. All the basic ingredients of the youth culture
of the 1960s and '70s existed half a century earlier. Yet in the
final analysis, the youth movement was not political in character
and should not be judged by political standards. They inculcated
in their members sterling qualities such as sincerity, idealism,
frugality, discipline, and the spirit of sacrifice for a common
good. They lacked a historical sense and political common sense.
In the final analysis, everything stemmed from a great and deeply
moving longing. There was a great deal of cosmic despair, some
positively relishing it. I remember how at the age of sixteen I
discovered Louis-Ferdinand Céline and tried to make my father
read his *Journey to the End of Night*. He argued that life was sad
and ugly enough; why read about it? At the time I had no sympathy with such philistine arguments; over the years I have become
far more understanding.

But how deep did the revolutionism and the despair go? Many
years later, when I had become the historian and interpreter of
the youth movement, I came across a very revealing account. In
1919, shortly after the end of the war, leading members of the
youth movements met in Jena and discussed the revaluation of
all values, world revolution, Taoism, as well as Nietzsche, and
modern art, and above all the eternal question: What should we
do? Having agreed that Western bourgeois culture was dying
and should be destroyed, all the participants retired to the leading pastry shop in town to devour enormous quantities of ice
cream, coffee, and fruit cake with whipped cream. And why not?

There were dozens and dozens of *Bünde*, as these youth groups
were called in the 1920s, some countrywide, some on a regional

basis. There were frequent splits and mergers. While some were politically deeply committed, most were basically unpolitical but for a vague patriotism and the feeling of duty to serve one's people. Its views, never very consistent, were rapidly changing. One of its model figures, whose nickname was Tusk, was an unorthodox Nazi at twenty, an unorthodox Communist at twenty-five, and ultimately had to flee to England. There were Catholic, Protestant, and Jewish youth movements. These, in turn, were again subdivided. In our town, for instance, there were half a dozen Jewish youth groups, left-wing Zionists and right-wing Zionists, religious and a-religious and wholly neutral.

There were elitist Bünde and others more democratic in structure. At least one decided to opt out from the bourgeois world altogether. They thought it pointless to study or learn a profession but preferred a hippielike existence, establishing the realm of youth on earth, traveling all year round to the far corners of the globe from Lapland to Patagonia.

After the Nazis had come to power, in the summer of 1933, all the independent groups were dissolved by decree and their members were made to join the Hitler Youth. But some groups continued to exist illegally, often inside the Hitler Youth, and it took the Nazis some four or five years to suppress them altogether.

The Jewish groups were tolerated for the time being, subject to stringent restrictions: They were not permitted to wear uniforms of any kind; all activities had to be announced to the Gestapo beforehand; there were to be no appearances in public of groups of five persons or more. Once I was detained by the Gestapo out in the country on a cycling tour. There were seven or eight of us, and since I admitted being the person in charge, I had to appear in a certain office at police headquarters the next day. But the official dealing with my case, evidently a policeman of the old school, did not consider my transgression a crime against the state. Thus, I was merely given a warning with threats of unspecified consequences.

We continued our excursions a little more cautiously. At fifteen I had my own group, consisting of boys two or three years younger than myself. I do not remember what I told them but I vividly recall some of our trips, especially those to the Giant Mountains and into Czechoslovakia. We usually took the milk-and-mail train first thing on Monday morning, crowded with officers and soldiers returning from Breslau to their garrisons. There were a few ski enthusiasts. From the station at the foot of the mountains we took a bus or walked for a few hours until, in the early afternoon, we reached the customs shed at the border crossing.

This wooded part of the Sudeten was very attractive; there were spas for every taste, complaint, and almost every purse. They were free of dust (so it was claimed), had chalybeate springs and inns (*Bierstuben*) in the fake old-German style; the food was in the Austrian tradition and uniformly excellent. We usually stayed the night in one of the blockhouses on the ridge of the mountains, which were much cheaper. Originally, these had been stables with roofs of shingles; later they were turned into mountain rest houses. Or we stayed in a peasant's barn high up in the mountains. Their soil was poor, and there was employment only for a few in the glassworks—the lumber and spinning mills could not compete with the factories in the cities of the plains. So we paid a few kronen and were welcomed.

We went up to the ridge of the mountains to watch sunrise or sunset and to feed the trout in the little ponds. It was a most peaceful neighborhood, yet only two years later a world war almost broke out over our beloved village called Ober Kleinaupa and a hundred similar places in the vicinity. Mr. Chamberlain, the man of peace and good sense, saved the day: Wasn't it absurd that England should fight "because of a quarrel in a far-away country between people of whom we know nothing"? Chamberlain's good sense saved the peace—for eleven months.

For us, after many visits, it was almost a home away from home. The local population was predominantly German. Up to 1933 they had coexisted with the Czechs more or less peacefully;

after the Nazis came to power, the pull from Berlin became stronger. The militants among the Sudeten Germans resented being a minority among this "dwarf nation of domestic servants, village musicians, and concierges"—as some of them defined the Czechs. They wanted to join the Reich. By 1937 tension had risen, and one was well advised to evade political discussions.

The nearest large city, at the foot of the mountains, was Trautenau. On one occasion we had an appointment there with a former member of our Bund, a young engineer, a few years older than most of us. He had worked for a year in the Soviet Union, about which he told us horror stories that we only half believed.

That evening I fell ill, and we returned to the mountain village instead of proceeding to Prague. For a few days I was running a high temperature. It was a great pity, but we had to be back by the end of the week. I have mentioned elsewhere the subsequent sad story of this beautiful region: The forest died; the mountain villages were largely deserted, another paradise lost.

If the Sudeten gradually became too tense for comfort, I was struck by the peace and calm of Scandinavia in 1937. It opened to me a world such as I had never known. Aged sixteen, I was in charge of the group; Tom's apartment had been searched and a revolver had been found. He happened to be abroad that day and wisely decided not to return. I drew up a most elaborate plan: We were to cross the border in groups of two, so as not to attract attention, and to meet on a certain day in a Copenhagen youth hostel. For myself, I chose the most elaborate route: I went by rail to Stettin, the Baltic port, and then overnight by steamer to the Danish capital. I was the only passenger on board. According to the prevailing regulations, each of us was permitted to take out of Germany ten marks,* and how long would that last? But I was confident that we would somehow manage, and manage we did. There were free luncheons at the Salvation

* About $2.50, or one pound sterling.

Army and the Jewish refugee committee. At the Tuborg and Carlsberg breweries there were wonderful snacks at the end of the guided tour.

I have the fondest memories of Copenhagen in the sunshine. Kongens Have (the King's garden), the canals, and the fine sand at the beaches of Klampenborg and Charlottenlund on the Oresund. Many years later I found a report I had written at journey's end. From this I gather that the famous Tivoli Gardens (the children's paradise) did not particularly impress me. I compared it with the *Johannesfest*, the great fair in Breslau, and I liked neither. Then we explored Zealand, I went to Roskilde to see one of the oldest and grandest cathedrals in Northern Europe and then on to the Belt, mainly because it appeared in the well-known German lied *"Von der Maas bis an die Memel, von der Etsch bis an den Belt."* But this was disappointing, I stayed for five minutes and hitchhiked back. On to romantic Elsinore (Helsingør), Hamlet's town, with its many little picturesque houses. We met all kinds of interesting young people from various European countries, including a Jewish group from Danzig. In the evening in the youth hostel or the local YMCA we sat together and sang our songs. It struck me that many Scandinavians spoke two or three languages; it made me painfully aware of my own shortcomings in this respect. About the Danish, I wrote that they were exceedingly nice and decent people but their life seemed to me aimless and without purpose. There is no limit to the arrogance and narrow-mindedness of a sixteen-year-old. I also noted that during our whole stay we had not seen a single soldier, whereas Germany at the time was thronging with them. It was an astute observation; on April 9 of 1940 Denmark was occupied in a few hours.

The next day we crossed by ferry to Helsingborg, but the Swedish police, having established that we had little money, and wrongly assuming that we wanted to stay in Sweden, sent us back by the next ferry. Thirty years later, I visited Sweden as a guest of some state institution. I listened to more than a few speeches about Sweden's many humanitarian initiatives, past and present. Then they asked me: "Have you been to our country before?" I tactlessly told my story about my abortive visit in 1937; there was a little embarrassment.

We returned safely to Breslau and for weeks we had many stories to tell. In the meantime our Bund had dissolved itself, some key members of the group having left the country; I joined another, which was vaguely Zionist in orientation. I liked their members very much even though I was not in full sympathy at the time with their beliefs. Their great guru was Martin Buber, the religious philosopher. I found him often unintelligible, not very helpful as a guide for the perplexed; this was yet another manifestation of the intolerance of youth. True, to this day I cannot get enthusiastic about Buber's rediscovery of Hasidism, nor do I like his translation of the Bible into German. But he was, of course, a highly educated man and wrote, among other things, an excellent book about utopian socialism. High culture played an important role among my new friends—classical music, avant-garde literature, and Renaissance art. At the same time they were preparing to go to Palestine as agricultural laborers. It was all very admirable, but how would they combine these different worlds?

Then I drifted away. Much of the cultural ambitions struck me as too rapturous and highfalutin, even faintly ridiculous. But in retrospect I would not have missed the youth movement at any price. At a difficult time in my life it was an anchor, an island of peace in a world that became more and more hostile; it developed qualities of discipline, responsibility, and leadership.

Some of the friendships I made I cherish to this day. Tom went on to South Africa. One day in the middle of the war a jeep drew up at the entrance to the wooden shack in the kibbutz in which I lived at the time. He had crossed the Sinai Desert, and seldom was a visitor more welcome. After his return to South Africa, he engaged in left-wing politics and spent some months in prison. Later, he settled in Britain, where he became a distinguished professor of botany. It is astonishing how many of these youngsters, without even a secondary education, became academics. Ernst became a psychology professor. Gunter specialized in the history of political thought. Max became a much-respected professor of pathology in New York; his brother taught philosophy in New Orleans. I am not sure whether, but for the advent of Nazism, they would have chosen an academic career. Werner was almost the only one among us who at fourteen became a builder's apprentice; when he arrived in Palestine in 1938 he was the only person in the country who could build a bread oven. I watched him work with awe and admiration. Several years later, as baking bread became industrialized, he became owner and chief executive officer of a rubber factory that supplied parachutes and rubber dinghies. Hans stayed in a kibbutz and became head of a plastics factory. Another friend worked until recently as a mining engineer in Latin America; a third is an organist in Salzburg. One went to West Africa and became an honorary tribal chief; another was last heard of as a Buddhist monk in Sri Lanka. The list is, in fact, much longer. I have not mentioned Renate and Anita, who survived Auschwitz because one of them was a member of the famous orchestra there.

And then there were those many who did not make it. As I write these lines, I have a group picture in front of me to refresh my memory. It was taken in 1936 and shows a dozen boys, most of them smiling, in front of a youth hostel. I recognize all the faces, even though I have forgotten some of their names. Six left Germany in time, three perished, the fate of another three is unknown to me. "I came to the place of my birth and cried: 'The friends of my youth, where are they?' An echo answered: 'Where are they?'"

FIVE

1937: "Oh, a Nasty Song"

It is, *of course, utterly ridiculous* when a mere boy becomes interested in politics. He does not understand the issues involved, and in any case, he cannot actively participate in the debates and struggles of the grown-ups. All he sees is the commotion, the excitement, people marching, shouting slogans, singing violent songs, people with sorrowful faces, people listening as in a trance to a spellbinder. But even the boy senses that the atmosphere is highly charged, and if he does not understand what the adults are quarreling about, he watches the theatrical elements. His outlook on politics is in some ways aesthetic; he is attracted by the better-looking uniforms and sometimes by the bigger columns, arguing that so many people cannot be wrong. The drama of adult politics invades the realm of youth.

If previously the children were playing "trappers" and "Indians" or "detectives" and "robbers," it was now "Sozis" against "Nazis." True, there was as yet not much violence, but clear fronts emerged. My parents and all parents in our crowd watched the political awakening of their offspring with grave misgivings. The German *Bürgertum* and a priori the German-Jewish middle class were deeply apolitical. There is the famous scene in *Faust*, in the pub called Auerbach's cellar, when one of those present exclaims: "Oh, a nasty song, a political song." He was merely repeating a proverb widely quoted at the time, and it was for generations the credo of the middle class.

My father used to say that politics spoils the character. As he saw it, politics was nothing but corruption or, at best, naked self-interest. There was no honor in politics; all political parties were lying, some more, some less. As Roosevelt's secretary once said— one could not adopt politics as a profession and remain honest. The phrase had first been used by a Berlin bookseller in the 1880s when launching a "nonpolitical newspaper"—which was, in fact, conservative. The belief was by no means restricted to middle-class philistines; the year I was born, Max Weber had announced ex cathedra that entering active politics was like giving a little finger to the devil. Everyone knew that the devil had no interest in little fingers. To engage in politics was considered morally disgraceful, financially unrewarding, and doubly irresponsible for a Jew: His inevitable mistakes would be blamed on the whole community. Politics was a dangerous luxury in which only born demagogues or very wealthy, independent people who were already in the limelight could afford to participate, Walther Rathenau perhaps. And poor Rathenau was shot by political enemies.

A strong case can be made for these attitudes. I have watched politics professionally for the better part of my life, yet as far as I can think back I had other interests. I have come to like Washington, where I now live, but I still suffer from the relentless preoccupation with politics in this city, in particular politics in the narrowest sense. There is a great deal to be said in favor of

the much-maligned ivory tower and of Voltaire's advice to culti-
vate one's own garden. But how could one possibly escape politics in 1932 and 1933? We were born at the wrong time; in the
1930s politics was fate, whether one was aware of it or not.

One of my first political memories is of listening, one night in
November 1930, to the results of the general elections, with
the Nazis suddenly emerging as the second-strongest party in
Germany. Even before that there were indications of an ominous
change, and one did not need to read the newspapers to be aware
of it. There was suddenly much more commotion in the streets,
not on our quiet street, but certainly in the center of town. Shabbily clad people were wandering aimlessly around or lining up
in front of labor exchanges, at street corners, near party offices
and newspapers. There were few of them at first, more and more
as the months passed by. There were more and more beggars
and able-bodied men acting as sandwichmen or selling matches.
The discussion groups at the street corners got more agitated
and violent. The streets were littered with leaflets; newspapers
were distributed free of charge; every Sunday there were
marches and parades organized by the Left and the Right. The
Center was nowhere in appearance; it had melted away. People
were injured at these parades and even killed. There were major
street battles; the police were in a state of high preparedness
virtually all the time.

I cannot truthfully say that all this caused great fear. On the
contrary, it added excitement to life. We watched the parades
and spontaneous discussion groups. I went to newspaper offices
and asked for free copies, just as in former years I had collected
the prospectuses of the travel agencies. Even the fistfights were
fascinating: Why should grown-up people beat each other up
without being paid for it, like Max Schmeling or Joe Louis,
Primo Carnera or Jack Sharkey? Gradually, it dawned on me
that a major struggle was going on, even though the motives
were by no means clear.

By 1932, at the age of eleven, I knew that the Nazis were bad.
They were also the noisiest, and their faces exuded hate. The

aims of the Center party were also easy to understand; the Catholics voted for it. It was less easy to make sense of what the left and the democrats stood for. Even a child was aware that a big slump had come, that factories had closed down, and that there were millions of unemployed. There was no other topic of conversation; everyone complained that business was bad and deteriorating. Almost everyone had less money at his disposal; all kinds of little luxuries ceased. My piano lessons stopped at the time, and getting a new bicycle was out of the question even though the old one broke down once a month.

In 1932 the Nazis became the strongest party. There were two general elections that year; it seemed strange that some thirty parties should contest the elections, including several that were clearly of the lunatic fringe. We tore down placards from the walls, especially those that did not appeal to us. The name Hitler was in everyone's mouth—a funny little man, with a mustache, vulgar, speaking (or, rather, shouting) German with an unfamiliar accent that some tried to imitate. I saw him much as today's young generation sees him, shorn of the demonic qualities, a bit of a clown. More and more people were saying "things cannot go on like this." My parents and everyone we knew, including the Social Democrats, were voting for the archconservative Hindenburg, the great war leader, the victor of Tannenberg, with the sole aim of keeping Hitler out.

But it did not help, for in January 1933 Hitler did come to power, not as the result of a spontaneous national revolution, but following some horse-trading between his own entourage and the right-wing cabal around Hindenburg. The immediate consequences were less than dramatic. People were, of course, apprehensive, but so many governments had come and gone; perhaps this one would also not last long. In Berlin there was a big torchlight parade that even today is shown on television whenever a film about Nazism is screened. The Reichstag went up in flames, and books disliked by the Nazis were burned.

But I don't recall a torchlight parade in our town, though there must have been one. No buildings were burned, and the undesirable books were quietly removed. True, a few months later there was a day when Jewish shops were boycotted. There were some violent scenes, many people lost their jobs, and some were arrested and taken to a concentration camp, a few miles south of the city. A prominent lawyer named Eckstein, who had been a leader of a small left-wing group, was killed.

But this was the exception. The boycott, after all, lasted only for a day, and for everyone who was arrested, there were a thousand who continued to enjoy freedom, such as it was. The writing of the history of the Nazi era has concentrated on what happened at the top of the regime, and to a large extent, rightly so. But even though the political parties were dissolved and the media censored (or became self-censoring), life for the great majority continued as usual; even the Gestapo was not installed from one day to the next and in the meantime the same police-men continued to do their jobs. The main difference was that some of the bureaucrats appeared at work in uniform and wel-comed their colleagues with "Heil Hitler" instead of "Good morning." I was not particularly worried by uncertainties such as whether I would be able to attend school. In the end I went to school up to graduation day, eighteen months before the war.

Gibbon once said that his service as captain of the Hampshire grenadiers had not been useless to the historian of the Roman empire; attending school from 1933 to 1938 was of use to the future student of the Third Reich and totalitarianism. Being in a school under the Nazis involved a certain amount of conform-ing, but on the whole pressures were not as extreme as commonly believed. These were, after all, the first years of the new regime; it did not yet quite know how to approach its goals on the domes-tic front.

To what extent was I influenced by the general political and intellectual climate? According to the new doctrine, I was a member of an inferior race. This, if nothing else, ruled out any sympathies for the new order. Nor do I recall any feeling of inferiority. The Nazis, after all, never claimed that they hated the Jews because they were so stupid. The grotesque cartoons of

Jewish faces adorning the front pages of *Der Stürmer*, the leading anti-Semitic weekly displayed in showcases on every street corner, did not remind me of any people I knew. On the other hand it could not possibly be argued that the faces of Hitler, Goebbels, Streicher, and the other new leaders exuded harmony, let alone manly beauty. At best these were undistinguished types. However, I should stress again that race doctrine seemed something abstract. One read about it in the papers, but I don't remember people talking about it. Propaganda was not yet all-pervasive.

And yet Nazism, or, rather, the broader intellectual fashion of which Nazism was a part, did have an indirect impact. By 1933 it seemed as if parliamentary democracy did not work; the idea of the strongman, the *führer*, was spreading throughout Europe, and it did not leave anyone unaffected. I read Ortega y Gasset at an early age, and from his writings, as well as from those of others, it emerged that we were in a deep crisis, from which only an elite, or more likely a charismatic leader, could extract us. Not a Hitler, of course, or a Mussolini, but some enlightened dictator. Perhaps we misread our mentors. Ortega, after all, was no fascist, but there is no denying that Western-style liberalism was out of fashion.

Up to a much later age I never saw a real democracy at work. The late Weimar Republic had been a democracy without democrats and therefore could not function. And was it not true that the Nazis, however brutally, did restore order, that they got the unemployed off the streets, that a new spirit of pride and (relative) optimism returned? One should not exaggerate either pride or optimism, but the despair of 1930 to 1932 certainly vanished, and whoever ignored this mood could not possibly understand why Nazism was genuinely popular in the early years. True, Moscow radio, which one listened to secretly, afraid of the neighbors, told us that Hitler meant war. But this message had no impact.

The horrors of World War I we knew only from books; the trenches of Verdun seemed as far away as Napoleon. In fact, I recall a certain fascination with books on World War I, most of which appeared with a delay of ten or fifteen years. With all its horrors, the war had brought out the best in many of the soldiers—courage, friendship, sacrifice. I also read and admired pacifists such as Rolland and Barbusse and Remarque, which points to a certain form of schizophrenia that was quite typical for the circles in which I moved. Thus, we were equally impressed by the bitter satirists of the later Weimar period, such as Brecht and Tucholsky, and knew much of their writings by heart, but also by some powerful writers in the other camp even though their names, with the exception of Jünger, are now forgotten. Among the songs of the youth movement there were some glorifying the Whites in the Russian civil war and there were others praising the Reds. One admired attitudes such as courage and selflessness rather than the cause these attitudes served—a dangerous approach, to be sure.

On some occasions this schizophrenia took an extreme form. I remember a classmate, whom I shall call Rosenberg. According to the Nuremberg laws, he was a half-Jew. He was not permitted to study and after 1939 he had to do forced labor. He did not have a good war at all. I did not know whether he had survived, until one day in the 1960s I read in a leading German neo-Nazi weekly a long vituperative article attacking the Anglo-Saxon plutocrats, arguing that everything had been better under Adolf Hitler. The article was signed Johannes Rosenberg. I sent him a short message through the editorial office, trying to establish his identity. In reply I received a letter of twenty-seven pages in which my former classmate (for such he was) developed his argument in greater detail and even more perversely. What had happened to him was of no consequence; the Nazi cause had been just, but for some minor blemishes. The Allies were to blame for the outbreak of the war and the sad fate of the German people. There was clearly no point in continuing this correspondence. He has since written a book of some 500 pages proving this allegation beyond any shadow of doubt.

There was no danger that Nazism's victims would accept its doctrine, nor did the Nazis have any such intention. The impact of communism was infinitely greater. Sometime after the war, in the course of a security clearance, I was asked point-blank: "Why were you not a Communist? After all, the Communists were against Hitler, and Hitler persecuted the Jews—would it have not been natural?" It was putting crudely a complex situation. But there is no denying that not a few of us (and even more of those ten or fifteen years older than I) were attracted by some of the features of communism—more admittedly by its anti-Fascist militancy than by its sectarianism. The fascination with communism has been endlessly discussed, but my concern in this context is with the 1930s, not the earlier revolutionary and romantic period. However, even under Stalin, up to the Nazi-Soviet pact of 1939, thousand of Communists were sent to the concentration camps; some were executed. True, they were by no means the only fighters against Nazism, but they seemed to be the most active and received the most publicity. They were better prepared for illegal work than the "bourgeois" parties and even the Social Democrats. Even before Hitler they had maintained an underground organization, and thus, for at least two or three years after 1933, they managed to be more active than the other parties. By the end of 1936 the last illegal cells had been infiltrated by the Gestapo and were smashed. I knew some of the youngsters who were helping the Communists and other far-left-wing groups as couriers and in a similar capacity, such as distributing illegal literature or painting anti-Nazi slogans on the walls. These actions should not be belittled, for draconic punishment was meted out to those caught. I know of one girl my age who was arrested, spent the next five years in prison and died in Auschwitz, merely for having helped to transport a few hundred illegal pamphlets from Prague over the mountains into Germany. I knew of other, similar cases.

These pamphlets were ingeniously produced. They would look like Nazi booklets or a "how to do it" brochure or a children's book, but from page 5, or 7, the most recent speech of Comrade Stalin would be printed, or the resolutions of the last Central Committee meeting of the Communist party of Germany. A great deal of imagination and daring went into producing and smuggling these leaflets into Germany. But the impact of the contents was in inverse ratio to the risk involved. For Stalin's speeches and the party resolutions were written in what was later called "Party Chinese." These leaflets were quite irrelevant as far as the situation inside Germany was concerned. Uncommitted readers would not understand them and Communists who had not crossed over to the Nazi camp (of which there were not a few) could always get their inspiration from the German services of Radio Moscow, which was heard loud and clear every evening. Such illegal work was dangerous, romantic, admirable, and also utterly futile. To this day I feel a pain when I think of those who lost their lives trying to smuggle this ineffectual rubbish into Germany.

My Marxist education began with the *Communist Manifesto*, from which I proceeded to the *Eighteenth of Brumaire*. I even tried to read the early writings of Marx and Engels, and eventually went on to the *MEGA (Marx-Engels Gesamt Ausgabe)*—the (incomplete) collected works. I read much of Lenin and most of the Soviet novels that had appeared in German prior to 1933. I even tried to study the various unorthodox Communists such as Rosa Luxemburg and Paul Levi, Karl Korsch and Pannekoek— many years before they were discovered by a later generation in American universities. I was more impressed by the consistency and radicalism of these thinkers than by their political logic. Historical materialism seemed at first quite plausible, but the events in Germany had shown that political, not economic, power was decisive. To explain Nazism with reference to monopoly capitalism and the class struggle, as the illegal brochures did, did not make sense. No one living in Germany this side of a lunatic asylum could argue in 1937 that Krupp rather than Hitler was running the country. I was attracted by the idealism of the heroes in the Soviet novels, the genuine desire to build a new and better world. True, there were some blemishes such as the Stalin cult. But the cult was then only beginning, and sotto voce we were told that one should not measure a backward country such as Russia, where even illiteracy had not yet been conquered, by Central and West European standards.

Yet in the end there remained some nagging doubts. From all one heard, the Soviet regime had some disturbing similarities with Nazi rule—the one-party system, propaganda, the omnipresent political police. These doubts became stronger with the Moscow trials, and the Nazi-Soviet Pact was for many the point of no return. But up to that date it was widely believed that the Soviet Union was the strongest counterforce to Nazism and that it was wrong to openly criticize Stalin, for this was playing into the Nazis' hands. Thus, the question asked by the security officer, though extremely crude, was not entirely misplaced. If Stalin was not a role model, he seemed at least an ally.

What became of my friends of the far Left? I hesitate to use the term "Communist," because some of them sympathized with Trotskyism, others with the KPO (a right-wing "deviation"), yet others were identified with one of the groups somewhere between the Social Democrats and the Communists. Those who belonged to the generation before us had either emigrated or were in prison or concentration camps. As for my own contemporaries, they survived simply because they were merely sympathizers, keeping on the outer fringe of the underground. Most of them drifted away during the emigration; two returned to East Germany after the war. I don't think they were happy there; they died long before the collapse of the DDR.

There was the tragic case of Werner Jany. He had gone to Holland, but was caught in the net after the Nazi occupation and perished in Mauthausen. Robert N. was a few years older; he had been arrested in 1935, but released shortly before the war. He wrote a book after his retirement in the 1970s, in which he demonstrated in the most uncompromising manner that, economically, communism had been a total disaster, not only in the Soviet Union but everywhere else. I thought his thesis slightly exaggerated; so did the publishers. He tried some seventy of them, but they all turned him down. His timing was bad; fifteen years later his manuscript would have become a bestseller. So many lives, so many stories, each merits to be told in far greater detail. According to the famous elegy of a Roman poet, the seaman's story is of tempest, the plowman's of his team of bulls, the soldier tells of his wounds. My contemporaries had more than one story to tell, of tempests and wounds, of ideological conviction and confusion, of danger and fear, of hopes and disillusionment. Provided, of course, they lived to tell their stories.

THERE WAS TALK of war as far back as I can remember. But even for a passionate geographer like me the civil war in China was too remote and too complicated to follow, what with the changing fortunes of the various warlords. Nor did the Japanese invasion, which began in 1931, register. No one I knew had ever been to the Far East; what happened there did not impinge in any way on our life.

Ethiopia was different, and our sympathies were from the beginning with Haile Selassie and his brave but badly equipped warriors. The Italian campaign did not go well in the beginning, and the Nazi press at first reported the Italian setbacks with some glee. But later on Italian military power prevailed, and since Britain and France did not take any action against the Fascist aggressors, there were growing doubts as to whether they would ever be stopped.

The outbreak of the Spanish Civil War in July 1936 coincided with the Berlin Olympic Games. The coup by the right-wing army officers on July 17 was not a full success, but within the subsequent weeks the two camps organized and went to war. For all my interest in the athletic competitions in Berlin, the burning passions generated by Spain were even stronger. Places of which no one had ever heard, such as Teruel and Albacete, suddenly figured in the headlines; had I been a religious believer, I would have prayed three times daily for the Republicans. By late 1937 it was clear that Franco would prevail, even though the agony was to last for more than a year. Wherever one looked, the cause of freedom was suffering an unending chain of defeats; it was all very depressing.

The invasion of Austria in March 1938 did not come as a great surprise. I had just graduated from school and started work in a factory. Somehow the great jubilations in Vienna and elsewhere did not percolate down to the little town where I then lived. There were flags on all buildings, but this happened in any case about once a month. The Sudeten crisis in the autumn of that year was an event of far greater impact, largely, no doubt, because the outbreak of a world war seemed quite likely. This international crisis coincided with a personal crisis about which I shall write later on. A few weeks later I left Germany.

I have mentioned that my family and virtually all of our acquaintances were deeply uninterested in politics; an uncle once removed was a Social Democratic deputy in the regional parliament, but this was a rare exception. In school we heard the official Nazi version of things, but indoctrination was neither systematic nor obtrusive. The youth movement was not primarily politically minded, and I do not recall bitter political debates or quarrels among my contemporaries. And yet politics was all pervasive.

From where did we derive our information? It was, by and large, a process of self-education. I have mentioned my unguided reading, but this concerned books rather than current events. Up to the outbreak of the war, Nazi censorship was surprisingly liberal, at least in comparison with other totalitarian regimes. A city such as Breslau, with little more than half a million inhabitants, had five or six daily newspapers, some of which appeared twice, or even three times, daily. Their level of sophistication was relatively high; this was true with regard to domestic as well as foreign coverage, the cultural supplement, the economic and the sports sections. When the Nazis came to power, the Communist and the Social Democratic papers were closed, and the liberal *Breslauer Zeitung* did not survive long either.

But an attentive and critical reader of the conservative *Schle-sische Zeitung*, published a block or two from where we lived, could still learn a great deal about world and German affairs. Much of the foreign press, too, was available. The left-wing papers were banned, with a few notable exceptions, such as the organ of the Finnish Social Democrats; the assumption was, of course, that no one could read Finnish anyway. The Austrian, Swiss, and Czech papers in German passed sporadically; the British and French papers more frequently. I read some French and had picked up some Danish, and during critical periods, bought the liberal *Politiken*, which, together with other foreign papers, was displayed at the newsstands on the Ring. The father of a friend of mine had a subscription to the London *Economist* and passed it on to me from time to time. American newspapers were not available in our town.

Many listened to foreign radio stations. The Czechs broadcast in German and so did the Swiss and the Russians; Strassburg was too far and we could not receive it, but the Swiss newscasts were very brief and cautious, and the Russians, as I recall, were mainly preoccupied with the production of tractors and record harvests. The Czech bulletins were also very short. Only during the war, well after my departure, did foreign broadcasts acquire some importance as far as the German domestic scene was concerned.

From an early age I was an avid newspaper reader and radio listener. In later life, once I could afford it, I regularly read a dozen papers in several languages; to this day, whenever I come to a strange city, I tend to buy the local papers and periodicals. I have no doubt wasted both money and much time this way, but I developed a technique of reading newspapers very quickly, and as a result, the damage was perhaps not too great. Wasting time—in Russia these days (1992) it may take hours and visits to various parts of Moscow to get the literature one wants. But I have always found these expeditions most rewarding; I have met interesting people and discovered publications of whose existence I did not even know. It is the fascination of doing research and should, if at all possible, not be delegated; one never knows in advance what discoveries will eventually turn up.

Whoever wanted to know, even in 1938, about events inside and outside Germany could acquire such knowledge without much difficulty. The Nazis were so confident that they had the support of the majority of the population, and that the future belonged to them, that up to the outbreak of the war they did not ban the import of most foreign newspapers, nor did they jam foreign radio stations even after that date.

THE JEWISH COMMUNITY in Breslau counted some twenty thousand members. It was the third largest in Germany, after Berlin and Frankfurt, and though the Jews were only 3 percent of the population, they played an important role in the economic and cultural life of the city. There were two major synagogues: The orthodox, called the *Storch*, was hidden away in a less fashionable part of town; the New (liberal) Synagogue was an impressive building in Moorish style, built around the turn of the century. It was located next to the police headquarters and symbolized the social standing and the self-confidence of the community in the late Wilhelminian era. Even if a Jew could not at the time be an army officer or a judge, the impressive building reflected prosperity and also a feeling of security. The big Jewish hospital in the south of the city also comes to mind and the Jewish schools that some of my contemporaries attended.

I realized early on that there were all kind of Jews—rich and poor, religious and not observant, Eastern Jews (*Ostjuden*) and highly assimilated ones, Zionists and anti-Zionists, and even Jewish anti-Semites. There were those who played bridge much of their time while others congregated in the Schopenhauer Society. The panorama of Jewish Breslau was so multifarious as to be positively bewildering. Where was my place in this community, and did I belong to it except by accident of birth? My education was not Jewish, I did not attend a Jewish school, and most of my early friends were not Jewish either. I knew little about Judaism and was not particularly interested in the subject. It would not have occurred to me to deny that I was Jewish: Some people happened to be Protestant, others Catholic, and I was one of those of Jewish origin. In the life of some people religion played a great role, but in many families it did not, and we belonged to the latter category. Culture was of greater significance than religion, and our culture was, of course, German.

I must have been aware that there were people in Germany who disliked Jews and claimed that they did not belong to the German people. But even after 1933 I remember only a few anti-Semitic attacks, physical or verbal, except once at a summer camp in 1934 on the shores of the Baltic, when a group of Hitler Youth attacked us at night. Even on that occasion the damage was insignificant, and in any case, we were too sleepy and surprised to fight back. Perhaps I have repressed some memories, but hard as I try, I cannot recall any truly traumatic, shattering incident. Was it a kind of defense mechanism, ignoring unpleasant realities, or was I thick-skinned, lacking self-esteem? I find it difficult to provide an answer even now; the psychology of a thirteen-year-old is not at all similar to that of an adult. I have checked my recollections with some contemporaries, and their memories are not very different.

WHAT DID IT MEAN to grow up in Germany as a young Jew? I was born in Germany and my ancestors had lived there as far back as one could trace them. Yet those in authority told me after 1933 that I did not belong and that I had no future there.

But the adults were saying that it was by no means clear how long the government would last, and there were proverbs to the effect that dogs who bark do not bite. In any case, I was shielded from the harsh realities of life by school, the youth movement, and my family; after all, I did not have to earn my livelihood. Only as time passed, it emerged that the government had great popular support and did not change or moderate its policy. On the contrary, if in the beginning it had shown some circumspection and concern about adverse reactions abroad, it became gradually more anti-Semitic. Only a few members of our family left at first, but most were talking about emigration. By 1937, at the latest, it became clear that the general problem was also my personal predicament; after graduating from school, I would have to leave the country.

But this was only one aspect of the dilemma, albeit from a practical point of view, the crucial one; 1933 had also brought what one would now call a crisis of identity. If I was not a German, where did I belong? I knew some who defiantly argued that they were better Germans than the Nazis, that their patriotism was deeply rooted, that they were steeped in German culture. But this attitude did not seem very convincing. Whatever one's personal beliefs, if society decided that one did not belong, it was pointless to behave like an ostrich. The Nazis would probably not last forever, but this offered little comfort concerning the problem facing us here and now.

My first memories of Jewish life are of going to synagogue with my father, but this did not happen more than twice a year. There was also a religious service for young people in the Jewish hospital that I had to attend for a while, but it was very boring indeed. I probably went more often to church than to synagogue as a child; my nurse took me quite frequently to the nearby church, Saint Carolus, which I found depressing and frightening; there was too much talk about the horrors of purgatory and hellfire. I liked neither church nor synagogue. We did not observe at home any dietary laws, nor did we celebrate Sabbath, though there was always the traditional bread (challah) on the table on Friday evening. This and fasting on the Day of Atonement was more or less the extent of compliance with tradition. My parents knew no Hebrew and very little about Jewish religion. I think the same was true with regard to my grandparents, who were born around 1850. We did celebrate both Hanukkah and Christmas; like every child, I loved to get presents, but the story of the Maccabees did not leave a greater impression than the tale about the birth of Jesus. Reluctantly, I learned some Hebrew for my bar mitzvah. After that, I ceased attending religious services. My father did go more frequently to the synagogue after 1933, when it also became a cultural and community center.

My attitude to religion was perhaps a little infantile. Initially, I had thought that religious people were morally better people than others because they observed God's commandments. When I realized that morality and religious observance were not necessarily the same, I lost interest. I greatly admired one of our rabbis, Dr. Vogelstein, a true humanist and one of the most learned men I ever knew. When once I admitted to him my lack of interest in things religious, he told me that I was *"religiös unmusikalisch"*—that I had "not the right pitch for religion," a phrase coined, I believe, by Max Weber—and that it was pointless to force a change. Either my attitude would change later in life, or it would not. Some of my nonbelieving friends were converted to strict orthodoxy in later life, and vice versa; my own attitude has changed little. As a result, I have been blamed by my own children for conveying to them little, if anything, of their heritage.

Not a few members of my family had been converted in the nineteenth century, and there were also several mixed marriages. Those who did not convert were not motivated by deep conviction or solidarity with other Jews, but because it was considered unbecoming. Probably, there was also a certain feeling of piety, not religious piety but the assumption that the ancestors would not have liked it. After 1933 the very thought of converting was considered a treacherous act; only cowards would try to escape from a beleaguered fortress.

Jewish history and culture did not greatly interest me. True, I knew at the time very little about it, but there was not much in Jewish history to derive pride or inspiration from. Up to the eighteenth century it seemed more martyrology than history, an unending chain of persecutions, and a young person's tolerance is limited in this respect. To be sure, the stories about life in the Jewish shtetl by Mendele and Shalom Aleichem had a certain exotic charm, but from a literary point of view, I preferred Dickens and Balzac. Nor did the quality of life in the East European shtetl appeal to me. There was probably some snobbism in this attitude. There was not much love lost between Eastern European Jewry and assimilated German Jews. When Weizmann first came to Germany around the turn of the century, he wrote with much contempt about the Kaiserjuden, who wanted to be greater patriots than the Germans, who had lost vitality, spontaneity, the "warm Jewish heart," and the other good Jewish qualities. There was a grain of truth in these observations. There had been no specific Jewish life in Germany ever since the walls of the ghetto had come down in the eighteenth century. How could it have been artificially preserved?

The assimilated Jews had a dim view of the Ostjuden. When my mother was really angry, she said I talked like an Ostjude— loud, gesticulating, making an exhibition of myself. The Jews from Eastern Europe talked an unlovely language and had no manners, at least as we understood it. In later years I lived among them and came to know them much better—and also the great differences among them. There must have been thousands of them in Breslau, and many more in Germany, but I met only a handful—they lived a separate life. I had a few friends among this community, but they had rebeled against their own background, and became either Communists or Zionists.

Thus, the Jewish heritage might have appeared as a burden, at best irrelevant, at worst something to be ashamed of. But this was not the case either. The question of identity should have caused me sleepless nights but it did not. There was a lack of self-consciousness that may appear quite inexplicable in retrospect. I followed with sympathy (and sometimes a little amusement) the efforts of some of my friends to find new roots, having been uprooted from their country of origin. For me, for better or for worse, this was not a matter of similar urgency; I was what I was and it did not seem a life-or-death matter to belong to a group.

I don't think I was particularly insensitive, but my emotions have always manifested themselves in my relations to individuals rather than to groups.

Was this, then, the makings of a rootless cosmopolitan? Rootless to a certain extent I was, but my background was far too provincial to aspire to anything as fancy as "cosmopolitanism." Perhaps I felt instinctively that a time would come when survival rather than the search for roots and identity would be the main issue, and when in any case a great many people would be uprooted all over Europe and beyond. The loss of my native country at the age of seventeen hurt me considerably less than the loss of those I loved. Perhaps I felt, even vaguely, that the Nazis were leading the country to ruin and that the place where I was born and had grown up would be lost in any case. If my country did not want me, I was reasonably sure that I could find my place elsewhere.

My attitude to Germany has remained markedly unemotional; I have been interested in German affairs since the war, but much of the time I've been even more interested in other countries and cultures. I was not a Zionist in the usual sense of the term when I went to Palestine in 1938. There was a bitter joke told in Jerusalem and Tel Aviv in the 1930s: New immigrants were asked, "Are you here out of conviction—or do you come from Germany?" I certainly was not there out of conviction. But I did become the historian of Zionism.

A person without a country, we know, ought to be pitied. There is a Nietzsche poem which was widely quoted at the time:

> *Bald wird es schneien*
> *weh dem der keine Heimat hat.* . . .
> (Woe to him
> Who has no native land. . . .)

There was a fear of being out in the cold. On the shore I was about to leave, there was "Heimat" and my roots. There was freedom and, maybe, security on the other shore. It is very difficult to recapture the mood of fifty years ago. Perhaps I felt a bit as if I were escaping from a building about to go up in flames. What was the point of cursing my fate if it was not in my power to suspend it?

Even if I did not believe in the Jewish religion and even though I failed to see a Jewish nation comparable to others, there was a common bond born out of traditions, arising from past and present-day persecution. All this was quite inchoate and perhaps I should not try too hard to define it. It probably would have been easier if I had been a firm, unquestioning believer in either religion or nation. In any case, I found myself in the same boat with many others, and detected common sentiments and attitudes. And this was quite sufficient for me at a time when introspection had not the highest order of priority.

I VIVIDLY RECALL some scenes from my childhood, but others have been blotted out completely. I remember to this day all the railway stations, however small and undistinguished, on the way from Breslau to Schweidnitz: Gross Mochbern, Schmolz, Kant, Mettkau, Ingramsdorf, Saarau, Königszelt. Kant was the most important station because the way led from there to the summit of the Zobten, the one real mountain near Breslau, a favorite spot for excursions. Marshal Blücher was buried there, and the fact that on the top of the mountain there had been a castle inhabited by a real robber knight provided much food for my romantic imagination. Never mind that the castle had been destroyed and the last robber seized in 1471 or thereabouts. One incident I remember vividly—I must have been nine or ten when my parents took me to the Zobten open-air theater. At that time *Wilhelm Tell* was the only play of which I had heard, and I waited with uncommon patience for the arrival of the man with bow and arrow who was to aim at the apple on his son's head. But there was no Wilhelm Tell, only various romantic intrigues frequently interrupted by songs such as

Was kann der Siegismund dafür
dass er so schön ist.
(Why blame Siegismund
for being so handsome?)

In brief, it was not *Wilhelm Tell* but the *White Horse Inn.*

If this were a historical study I would have to give up in despair; as a standard French history textbook of the last century stated: "No documents, no history . . ." But childhood and adolescence are seldom documented; and in my time it was no longer customary to keep a diary. (And how full and honest are diaries?) But sometimes the curtain can be lifted a little, be it because of sudden recollections or the discovery of some letters or a photograph.

When I was sixteen I wrote a little book for a friend who had emigrated the year before. It consisted of several short reports, quotations from novels, and poems I had read, and a few pictures cut out from books. Recently I received my book back and read it with mixed feelings. My taste in painting was conventional— Renaissance statues, Dürer, Rodin, and Masereel—exactly what was admired in our circles. At about this time I went with a few friends once a week to attend lessons with a professional art historian named Lydia, a Russian émigré who had married a local painter named Aschheim. But I gained no deeper understanding and my own paintings in later years, while in the tradition of Henri Rousseau, were not even remotely up to his level. Some of the quotations were more adventurous—Dante; and Goethe's *Iphigenie* and *Faust*; and Stefan George, but also the mystic Angelus Silesius; Garcia Calderón; and Lope de Vega— when and where had I discovered them? There was also a good deal of middlebrow poetry such as Erich Kästner's (of *Emil and the Detectives* fame), and some German working-class poets of the beginning of the century. I am not ashamed in retrospect; Kästner and the other poets were natural talents, and their best work will survive. I feel more than a little embarrassed now about my adulation of Romain Rolland, and it is no excuse that the Rolland cult was widespread at the time. I quoted from his *Michelangelo* (*Michel-Ange*): "There is no heroism but to see the world as it is and yet to love it." How trite can one get? True, he had written two major works, *Jean-Christophe* and *Colas Breugnon*, undeservedly forgotten today. He had shown much courage in 1914 when he had resolutely opposed the war from the very beginning. But there was an exalted idealism in his later work, which made him more popular in Germany than in his native France—and which strongly attracted me. This surfeit of idealism led him badly astray in his later years, made him close his eyes to Stalin's crimes even though he was perfectly aware of them. For a while I came to regard Rolland as my guru, expecting from him an answer to the ultimate questions, just as Rolland as a young man had written a thirty-page letter to Tolstoy, asking the same or similar questions. He got a reply; I did not.

There was in my writing and in the selections of texts an attempt to suppress the self and to put all the emphasis on one's duties to mankind; *Verwirklichen*, to carry out in practice, was a key word. The choice of profession depended on where one could be of greatest service to mankind. This naive surfeit of idealism bothers me even in retrospect. For the choice of profession and a country of emigration became narrower every month, and here I was, an adolescent who had never been exposed to real life, who had never done manual labor, who had never had to earn his own livelihood, engaging in flights of fancy. While writing with great disdain about the philistine, wholly absorbed in analyzing the self, and swayed by changing moods, I was, of course, doing exactly the same. The phrases about *Verwirklichung* were empty, and the mental confusion was great, Nietzsche and Marx, Zionism and anti-Zionism, and so on.

But it was probably inevitable, a sixteen-year-old does not write with the ripe wisdom of age, and perhaps I should not have read what I wrote then. The same is true with regard to a bunch of letters that I wrote, beginning in 1938, to another friend; they were almost miraculously preserved and returned to me a few years ago. It was a painful experience to be confronted with the confusion of one's own youth, with mushy phrases with a presumptousness divorced from all reality. But perhaps I have forgotten what it means to grow up, that at sixteen and seventeen serenity and modesty are not the most prominent features of character, but ferment and the desire to "storm the skies," and that one learns only by trial and error. If I compare my generation with the two or three before us, I sense that we were more ambitious, more radical, more averse to compromise than our predecessors, and this at a time when there was scarcely opportunity to compromise anymore, when the cardinal question became mere survival.

So the adolescent should perhaps not be judged too harshly; if he lacked a sense of reality, how could he have known any better? I recall some contemporaries free from the exalted dreams of youth, mainly concerned with their career at a relatively early age. They were much more sensible than I was, but even in retrospect I cannot imagine them in the role of model figures. And so I went on writing about streets leading into unknown directions, about railways to faraway countries, symbols for the journey into uncertainty that would soon begin. My choice of symbols was by no means original; in later years I found that they had been used by poets and others in Germany, in Russia, and elsewhere, long before World War I.

My embarrasment today betrays a lack of empathy for the mental make-up of the youth, strong in body but immature and confused in his thoughts. The year was 1937, there was less than a year left until I would leave home—not for a university or some such institution serving as a buffer zone between the protected parental home and "real life," but a journey to another continent, a country unfamiliar in every respect. I don't think I lacked physical courage in those days; according to letters from my mother that reached me after my emigration, I suffered if anything from overconfidence.

When I was ten or eleven I used to go swimming almost every summer day at the Olympic stadium in the north of the city; it had been built by the father of a classmate named Konwiarz; I don't recall why it was called Olympic, because I doubt whether it was quite the prescribed size. But it was certainly one of the most modern such installations, with a real racing track, several football fields, and a good-sized swimming pool. One day I decided to move on from the one-meter diving board to three meters, and when this presented no particular difficulties I also dived from five meters. There was yet another challenge left— ten meters. Here my courage faltered, at least momentarily: Up from ten meters the sky looked very near and the people below rather small—what if I hit the water at a wrong angle? Opposite the diving tower, there was a building with a giant clock. I remember how the minutes passed, five, ten, fifteen. In the meantime a few swimmers had come up and dived, having scrutinized me critically, and even scornfully—or so it seemed to me. At the end of fifteen minutes I closed my eyes, dived, and as nothing bad happened, repeated the exploit a few times. I was very proud that day, and might have gone on to fifteen meters, but there was no such height.

Perhaps it was clear to me by the end of 1937 that soon I would face another dive, figuratively speaking, but this time with no lifesavers in calling distance. Deep down I was aware that the period of gushy enthusiasm was rapidly nearing its end. Toward the close of the little book I have mentioned earlier there are some cryptic remarks about the fanciful idealistic views of one who was still at school (that is, myself) who had not been exposed to manual labor, but who had watched life (to the extent that he understood it) from a relatively safe shelter. The thought that soon I would be alone in the world did not cause me sleepless nights to the best of my recollection. But a new mood could certainly be detected: impatience to leave, mixed with uncertainty regarding stormy passages and shores unknown.

SIX

1938: Farewell to Europe

A*t the age of seventeen,* as I later discovered with a confused sense of fear and guilt, one possesses an almost unlimited capacity for overlooking unpleasant facts. Until early 1938 the years had passed without major shocks and great excitement. I went to school, read many books, met friends, engaged in a variety of sports. Right into summer of 1938 I must have been so immersed in my own affairs that I only noticed the events around me out of the corner of my eye. It was a year of waiting, of unsuccessful attempts to train for a career, a year of cycling tours in the Taunus and the Sudeten; I fell in love at least twice, saw dozens of films, did a great deal of swimming. But then, suddenly, during the second half of the year, the pulse of history began to quicken, and I discovered that there was great trouble ahead, with me in the wrong place—that, in brief, I had waited too long. With all the reading of foreign newspapers and listening to radio broadcasts from abroad, I had somehow failed to draw the obvious conclusion—that Nazi Germany had more or less finished rearmament, that expansion was about to begin, and that war was therefore imminent.

In February of that year I went for the last time to my old school on Paradise Street for my final school examinations. Normally, the average age of graduates was eighteen or nineteen, but I was not yet seventeen. As a result of the introduction of compulsory labor as well as military service, the upper sixth form had been abolished. In retrospect, I have to be very grateful to the Nazis, for it compelled me to take at last the plunge that had been postponed too long.

About the *Abitur*, as the German higher school examinations were (and are) called, I remember little, except that it was the first time that I had to wear a tie and a dark suit. I had no dark suit and did not know how to tie a cravat. My written work was about Gottfried Keller, the great Swiss nineteenth-century writer, who is hardly known outside the German-speaking world. (His magnum opus, *Green Henry* [*Der grüne Heinrich*], appeared in English only well after World War II.) I liked his shorter pieces and some of his poems even better; the story of his life in Zurich was tranquil, yet Emil Ermatinger had written three huge volumes about him that I studied with diligence. Oral examination was perfunctory, and so at the end of the day I was in possession of the document that, once upon a time, had been of enormous significance. For me, in very changed circumstances, it opened no doors and meant very little. I also received a letter that said I intended to study textile engineering and that there was every reason to believe I was suited for such a career. They would have given me a testimonial for almost any career.

But opportunities for career training were diminishing day by day. I really wanted to study history, but this was wholly illusory. I got some encouragement one evening that winter when I went to a lecture with a friend: A professor from the Hebrew University

of Jerusalem was to talk about excavations in Samaria. I had no
particular interest in archaeology, but my friend who had heard
the speaker before was full of praise. In any case I had nothing
better to do that evening and went to listen to Professor Sukenik.
His command of German was far from perfect, but his enthusiasm was infectious. He knew how to make a dry subject interesting, and in this and other respects he seemed quite different
from the German professors I had then known.

After the lecture we accompanied him to his hotel. I dimly
remember that we talked about horses as we were walking in
the promenade in the municipal gardens. The professor seemed
astonished that we had not read Xenophon's book on the subject.
Still, he went on to inquire with genuine interest about my plans
for the future. "Study history—like my eldest—if only playing
soldier would leave him sufficient time. . . . Why don't you come
and study with us?" I explained to him that I was well below the
minimum age (which was eighteen), that we had no money, that
I had heard that there were very few openings available at the
Hebrew University. But these arguments did not greatly impress
him. He told me that there would always be difficulties in life
and that Palestinian Jews, unlike their coreligionists in Germany, were not so easily discouraged. Why didn't I apply in any
case, and would I send him a copy of my application—what was
there to lose? Indeed, I had little to lose. I took leave of Professor
Sukenik outside his hotel late that night, and next morning wrote
for application forms. It appeared that applicants had to pay
either £100 or £200, I forget the exact sum, which was to cover
the first two years of study, a sum well beyond the reach of my
parents.

My mother, unbeknownst to me, asked for the help of her
younger brother, Curt, a well-to-do physician in Saxony. This
was not easy, because Curt, a bachelor, was serving a four-
year sentence in the penitentiary in Zwickau, having been found
guilty of the defilement of the German race—that is to say,
having gone to bed with an Aryan woman. His sentence was
relatively light; the lady in question had first tried to blackmail

him, a fact strongly disliked by the judge, a man of the old school, who might also have been impressed by the fact that Curt had come back from the war a highly decorated officer. So despite the severity of the crime, my uncle enjoyed a number of privileges, including the right to correspond and to dispose of his property.

Since I am trying to proceed chronologically, I have to drop at this stage the story of my uncle who had defiled the Aryan race, and also of my application to study history; but before doing so I must mention, however briefly, the archaeology professor who had given me encouragement when I much needed it. Our paths were to cross again, almost exactly to the day ten years later, in Jerusalem at a meeting in the back room of a coffee-house named Palatin. It was my assignment to introduce to the assembled journalists the speaker, none other than Professor Elieser Sukenik (now Yadin), who was to make the first announcement concerning the most important discovery of biblical archaeology in this century—the finding of the Dead Sea Scrolls. Ironically, very little notice was taken at the time, for the war for Palestine had just broken out, and who cared about archaeology at a time like this? Yet another ten years later, while attending the International Orientalists' Congress at Moscow University, I turned up by mistake in the study group for Near Eastern archaeology. A lecture was given illustrated with slides; the hall was packed to overflowing. The speaker was talking about the papyrus scrolls found in caves at Khirbet Qumran near the Dead Sea. He said that his father had begun the work; he merely continued it. I do not know whether the speaker was a great archaeologist, but he was certainly a first-rate communicator— the audience was spellbound. About the dangers of "playing soldier" the father had not been entirely mistaken; the son had been the first chief of staff of the Israeli army before returning to academic life. I told Yigal Yadin after his lecture that day that it was partly thanks to the father that I had been able to listen to the son.

Back in 1938 Jerusalem and Moscow were light-years away. I was stuck in Breslau and had to find a way to get out. My father knew some of the textile plants in Silesia. I wrote letters of application and was accepted as a voluntary worker in the dyeing department of Mr. Fleischer's factory in Reichenbach. Why dyeing? Spinning and weaving was done almost exclusively by women. I had a vague plan to gain some practical experience in the field and later to continue my theoretical studies in Brno, in Czechoslovakia. I spent two months, possibly a little longer, in Reichenbach, which was then a city of fewer than twenty thousand inhabitants, dominated by three or four major textile plants. It was in some ways a most interesting experience, my first exposure to manual labor, the first time I spent most of my time with people from a very different milieu. I found the dyeing process (Indanthrene) quite complicated, even though the physical effort was not that great. I had sufficient energy to play football after work with several other unpaid trainees—"interns" they would now be called. The workers were intelligent and helpful, but one had to concentrate most of the time, and there was not much time to talk. I was attached to a foreman, still quite young, who initiated me in the art of dyeing. In the beginning, needless to say, everything was strange and unfamiliar; at the end of the first month I began to feel at home.

My daily routine was a little complicated. I lived with my uncle's family in Schweidnitz. My uncle, as I may have mentioned before, had a dry sense of humor and a feeling for music. In the old days he used to play chamber music with friends at least once a week. Now the other members of the quartet had been unable to come to see him for some considerable time. One of them was a lecturer, the second a tax inspector, and the third worked in the police department. In this small town everyone knew everyone else and they would certainly have asked for trouble had they continued their music-making with a Jew. As public servants with pension rights, they had to be careful. Occasionally, one of them would steal into my uncle's apartment under cover of darkness and talk to him for a few minutes.

Sometimes my uncle would ask me to accompany him on his evening walks. I did so reluctantly—it seemed a bore, and I had

better things to do. The Jewish acquaintances we met during
these walks were of little interest—nice elderly folk whose conversation was mainly about whether they had saved up enough
money to enable them to retire to an old people's home in Berlin.
They were too old to emigrate, or so they thought, and I heard
them say they envied me. I, for my part, envied my friends who
had already managed to get out of the country. This was April
1938, a month after the Nazis had entered Austria; the dangers
had certainly become more acute. Near my uncle's shop was a
steep drop, and it was said that the baker from next door had
fallen down there and died instantly. I often thought of death
and of dying in those days, but these were passing depressions
that did not go very deep. At night I was always so tired that I
fell asleep at once.

Reichenbach was not really far away, but for some reason or
other the only suitable train left at six in the morning, and so I
had to get up well before that time. The train ride I liked; unless
there were low clouds, one saw the Eule Mountains (the "Great
Owl" and the "Small Owl") from the distance, rolling meadows,
little rivers such as the Weistritz, and then suddenly a little red
church where Field Marshal Moltke was buried. Moltke was
famous for his habitual long silences. In fact, he was an astute
observer and a fine writer. I recently read his *Letters from Turkey*,
an excellent description of the Ottoman Empire in the 1830s.
The name of the church and the adjacent castle of modest proportions was Kreisau; after World War II it was to become famous as the former home of the Kreisau Circle, about which
many books and articles were written. Moltke's great-grandnephew
had entertained here the heads of the German resistance during
the war. They had been quite ineffectual, but almost all of them
had paid with their lives for their plots. Nearby was the manor
of the Richthofens, another famous military family.

The train arrived in Reichenbach shortly after seven every
morning, and since work in the factory began only at eight, I
used to spend some time in the station's waiting room, reading
the paper: TAKEOVER OF AUSTRIAN NATIONAL BANK BY THE REICH,

TERUEL RECONQUERED—these were some of the depressing head-lines. The *Berliner Illustrirte* was serializing a novelette entitled *Must Men Be Like That?* The advertising slogans I vividly remember, for instance, *"Sei sparsam Brigitte, nimm Ultra Schnitte"* (promoting the sale of dress patterns). This had been better known previously as Ullstein Schnitte, but Ullstein, one of the media moguls, had been a Jew and so the name had to be changed, however slightly. One day Ullstein's successor would become my German publisher, but this possibility, needless to say, did not occur to me in April of 1938. There were countless advertisements for hair care and also philosophical slogans mainly by Nazi leaders; I remember one: "The dead can be brought back to life if one lives with them in the spirit" (Hans Schemm).

Shortly before eight I proceeded to the factory, changed clothes, and then work began. The foreman encouraged me to study applied chemistry. I tried to follow his advice but my heart was not in it. From twelve to one there was the lunch break. I went to a nearby *Mittagstisch*, where I had to pay thirty pfennig, a risible sum even by the standards of those days; the quality of the food was not remotely as good as at home. In front there was a small children's playground and, immersed in my thoughts, I watched the toddlers for a few minutes. I felt I would never be a competent textile technologist, and, furthermore, it became clearer with every day that the storm clouds were gathering and that I would not be able to conclude my training. One evening I was invited to dinner by the owner of the factory. He was obvi-ously well-to-do and lived in an elegant though not ostentatious villa on the outskirts. He and his family were particularly nice to me, but I sensed that they were depressed. Did they feel that their days, too, were numbered and that it was a matter not of years but of months until they would lose their factory?

I also remember many wonderful hours driving and walking through the nearby forest at night. With the exception of six years I have lived all my life in cities, but the youth movement had helped to awaken my interest in, and love for, nature. Nature meant hills, rivers, and forests, and the neighborhood of Reichenbach was ideal in this respect. Though housing the largest textile mills in Eastern Germany, this area had never become a genuine industrial region; it was not more than a collection of overgrown mountain villages, some of them, admittedly, enormous. Langenbielau, eight kilometers long with nearly twenty thousand inhabitants (thirty-five thousand in 1990), was the largest village in Germany until, reluctantly, they made it a town. The next village was Peterswaldau, not much smaller. This place had become famous as the scene of the weavers' revolt in 1844, immortalized in a famous Heine poem ("Germany, we weave a threefold curse in thy winding sheets") and above all in Gerhart Hauptmann's play *The Weavers*, perhaps the most accomplished literary expression of social protest in German literature. *The Weavers* ends on an antirevolutionary note, inasmuch as the use of violence is shown to be futile. But the message still had an enormous impact, in that life in these villages was described as a "chamber of tortures," in the words of the weavers' song. The young Kaiser Wilhelm II was so annoyed that he canceled his subscription to his private box at the Berlin New Theater, where the play was first performed in 1894.

When I came to know these villages in the 1930s they were still poor, even though I doubt whether anyone was starving; Bismarck's social legislation had provided a cushion of sorts, however thin, in the case of disease, and for old age. Unemployment was gradually overcome. Still, many houses were derelict, few people owned more than one good suit, few possessed a radio, and virtually no one had a car. But this was true generally of the German countryside before World War II.

Great was my surprise when I visited German villages in the early 1960s; they had changed out of recognition, far more than the cities. Was it the fact that the villagers had suffered less than the urban settlements during the war, or was it the worldwide upsurge of agriculture, which had become much more productive during this short period? Be that as it may, the average villager of 1960 not only had a radio but also television and a car as well as all kinds of machinery he would not have even dreamed of in 1938. There were well-stocked shops in even the smallest villages, the houses looked new—and many of the farmers worked only part-time in agriculture.

To reach the mountains from Reichenbach one could use either the minirailway that went slowly and cautiously almost up to the top of the Eule, about 1,000 meters (3,280 feet) above sea level. This was undoubtedly the best way to enjoy the landscape in daytime, but my free time, weekends apart, was in the evenings. A friend of mine, a few years older, had a motorcycle and so we went on many an evening to explore the neighborhood. Our rides through forests and clearings, through abandoned villages, past little factories, a big water reservoir (the Schlesiertal), and castle ruins were a kind of escapism, but how we did enjoy it! There was no street lighting in those days; once we nearly ran into an army column on the march. Otherwise there was little traffic; we had the forests of the night all to ourselves. This is a subject on which I tend to get sentimental. It has always been my dream to live near the waterfront or in a forest; I realized one part of the dream, at least for a while, but, to my lasting regret, not the other. Many of the writings of the German Romantic poets are no longer to my taste, but their descriptions of the German forest are wonderful and touch me to this day. They have captured the magical quality and the majesty of the forest. I could have done without the German cities, but I have missed the German forest all my life—I was told by friends from Eastern Europe and Russia that they felt the same. True, for a time in my life I planted trees, at others I felled trees, but these were eucalyptuses and cypresses, and the climate was different and also the fauna—no squirrels, no deer, no fir, no pine trees, no spruce.

I am hankering after something that no longer exists—the forests have shrunk, and they have become sick. One has to go far these days to find wild flowers and even farther to pick berries and mushrooms, and some of the species of birds no longer exist. There must be woodpeckers around, but I have heard only one in many years and this was in Switzerland. What became of my friend, the owner of the motorcycle, the companion on these nightly tours? He was the grandson or grandnephew of Albert Neisser, of Schweidnitz and Breslau, one of the main figures in the heroic age of the microbe hunt, when the great discoveries were made. (Among many other things Neisser discovered the bacteria that causes gonorrhea.) Young Neisser wanted to emigrate soon to South America. I hope he made it; as in so many other cases, I lost track of him.*

On May 1, 1938, seventy-five million Germans were celebrating the holiday of National Labor, under the maypole. Formerly, this had been the day of class struggle, but now, owing to the National Socialist renaissance (we were told), unemployment had disappeared and it had turned into a day of comradeship and solidarity. There were festivities throughout the day: During the hours of the morning the German Opera in Berlin bestowed the German cultural award on Leni Riefenstahl for her *Olympia*, a filmic record of the 1936 Berlin Olympic Games. The main parade was in the Berlin *Lustgarten*—but there were nine parallel mass gatherings in the German capital alone. If we are to believe radio and newspapers, two million people took part, that is to say, every second citizen of Berlin. In a long speech Hitler announced that production had been restored not owing to theories, programs, and phrases, but as the result of organized, planned, thoughtful labor. He was interrupted by many shouts of "Heil" and an unending ovation. He concluded: "Ours is the faith, ours is the will. Whatever remains as yet to be done will be achieved if only all those who believe in our great ideals will march toward the future courageously, reliably, and resolutely. Deutschland, Sieg Heil."

Hitler had ended, but the celebrations continued. In the eve-

*P.S. 1992. A few days ago, by one of these strange coincidences, I heard that he did make it to Latin America. I even received a photo of the motorcycle. Only after a delay of seven years did he succeed in marrying his girlfriend— for while he emigrated to Peru, she had gone to the United States. A few years ago he died in upstate New York. RIP.

ning there was a torchlight parade with military bands and thousands of soldiers and SS men, with a speech by Göring and the inevitable *Grosse Zapfenstreich*—the great tattoo. The Breslau demonstration was much smaller, and in Reichenbach there were hardly any festivities at all—the usual pattern those days.

The day after, shortly after I arrived at work, I was told to see the manager, who informed me, in a matter-of-fact way, that much to his regret the *Arbeitsfront* (the German Labor Front, the official successor of the unions) had lodged a protest against my presence and demanded my removal. In the circumstances I would be well advised to gather my belongings at once and go home, which I did. A few days later I received an excellent testimonial stating that I was familiar with the Thies system of dyeing of both Indanthrene and sulfur dyes, and that I had also acquired some knowledge in the process of bleaching by means of chloride and hydrogen peroxide. I had been willing, industrious, and very (underlined) eager to learn. I was leaving the plant of my own volition to complete my apprenticeship elsewhere. As I returned to Schweidnitz, and the following day to Breslau, I did not feel too discouraged: I had realized that textile engineering was not for me, and as the political situation deteriorated my removal would have been only a question of time. My stay in the factory had been an anomaly; for a while they had overlooked me, but then the inevitable happened.

The following ten weeks I spent again with my parents. Time passed very slowly, waiting for the mailman and queuing at various offices. One day in the 1950s in London my older daughter asked me why I waited so impatiently for the mailman, when I knew full well that he called regularly as clockwork three times a day. (Those days, alas, are gone, in London and elsewhere.) I tried to explain that it was a conditioned reflex; perhaps she had learned about this at school. In 1938 the post was the link with the outside world and a gateway to the future. The finer points of the mail service were carefully studied. Airmail letters were very expensive, especially if they weighed more than five grams (one-sixth of an ounce). One had to use very thin paper, which sometimes made the writing illegible, and it tore easily. Letters destined for abroad had to be posted at a certain time—for sea mail to Palestine one depended on the D-126, which left the Central Station on a Tuesday; for airmail it was necessary to post in special boxes by eight o'clock on a Wednesday night, to make the connection to Berlin for a KLM or Imperial Airways plane. If one kept these instructions in mind, postal connections were quicker than now, fifty years later. A letter in town was delivered without fail within twenty-four hours, in Europe within two to three days, and overseas usually in four to five days. I used to wait for the postman outside our front door, or, if it was raining, by the bay window of our flat from where I could see the whole street. I knew he would turn round the corner into the Rossmarkt from the Schlosstrasse at four o'clock, or five past at the latest. If he had nothing for me, I would look enviously in my disappointment at the letters in his hand, bearing foreign stamps addressed to the bank next door or to the city library. Never before or after have letters played such an important role in our lives: While there was mail, there was hope.

What did I do that summer? I recall a crowded stadium on a fine summer day, many thousands of spectators, athletes in track suits, hot-dog and ice-cream vendors. The last occasion on which I saw the Hermann Göring Stadium (as it was then called) was during the Gymnastics and Athletics Festival of July 1938. It was packed to overflowing, and I still remember the monster demonstrations and the public appearance of Hitler, Himmler, and Goebbels.

The official propaganda machine had been preparing the ground for some time beforehand. There was much talk of the "precious blessing of physical fitness," of the big rally in Silesia, the borderland that had for centuries been living proof of the "binding strength of German blood" and of "the might of the German spirit," where Germans would link up with their brethren regardless of frontiers. There were many fringe events: At the Municipal Theater they were playing *Gregor and Heinrich*, Kolbenheyer's pan-Germanic play about the conflict between

Pope Gregory VII and Emperor Henry IV. Hans, a cousin of mine, a "half-Jew" serving in the Wehrmacht, was enthusiastic about developments he had seen at the Gandau airdrome: the new DO-17 (the "flying pencil") gliders and parachutists and aerobatics. He talked about Achgelis, Count Hagenberg, von Lochner, and others. He was particularly impressed by the daring maneuvers performed by some of the pilots. Hans had a great and fatal capacity for enthusiasm, a wanderer between two worlds who did not know, perhaps could not know, where he belonged.

I went to the stadium on a Saturday. It was the "Day of Community" (*der Tag der Gemeinschaft*). There was a full program, though things were a bit chaotic; there had been a heavy thunderstorm in the morning. I well remember the 800-meter race. The favorite, Harbig, was the last to take his place on the starting line while the others were jogging about impatiently. A trainer gave some last-minute advice to one of the runners, they got into the starting position, the starter fired his pistol, and they were off. The pace was not fast, and one could hardly expect a record time on a track sodden with rain. Harbig occupied a middle position. After the first lap, tension suddenly mounted. Some of the spectators jumped up; others shouted "Sit down!" The crowd was yelling "Harbig" as he sprinted and began to overtake the whole field on the outside. He reached the winning post with a 10-meter lead, but his time was rather slow. The year after, he was to establish a world record; a few years later, he was killed in the war.

Then came the ceremonial to honor the winners. It started with a spectacular display by the SS and music by massed bands of the Wehrmacht. Himmler and his staff had timed their arrival to coincide with the SS gymnastics. A little man with a mouselike face—was this the supreme leader of the feared élite corps? Then came units of the Wehrmacht parading in historic uniforms—a company of the ancient regiment of the Elector of Brandenburg, and a landing corps of the old Imperial Navy. Finally, there followed a sort of war game, a reconstruction of the Battle of

Eckernförde (1864). Flags and buntings fluttered, the bands played the Düppeler-Schanzen march, the blue coats smartly turned right and left, and the public was highly edified by it all.

After a brief moment, there was a burst of applause from the many Sudeten Germans present. On the speaker's platform appeared a man in a white shirt and white trousers—Konrad Henlein, the athletics master from Asch. It took several minutes for the cheering and shouts of "Heil" to subside; finally, he removed his glasses and started his speech. He was not an able orator and seemed altogether ill at ease. He said he was immensely impressed by the enormous progress made by the New Germany, that he himself had come from sports and knew how great a contribution athletes had made to the unification of all Germans. "With awe and deep emotion I stand before the mighty, living work of Adolf Hitler. That we Germans have found our way to this great inner unity is due to one man only, Adolf Hitler." Thunderous applause.

Henlein left the platform. Now Dr. Goebbels spoke, and a few sentences were sufficient to make one realize how fully "our Doktor" was accepted by the public. "Certain cultural apostles abroad claim that we in Germany have forgotten how to laugh," the little man said. Gales of laughter swept the stadium. Then turning to more serious matters, he screamed into the microphone that the enslaved people of 1918 had become a new Great Power. "We are fully conscious of our strength! And we know what we want!" Tumultuous applause. He waved it aside impatiently, and silence returned. Was it not a miracle that an unknown conscript of World War I was today in charge of the destiny of the Reich and of the whole nation? Tomorrow the Führer was to come to Breslau, whose citizens would be inspired to renewed faith and fresh hope by beholding his countenance. More than anyone else they needed this faith and hope "which you preserve for the greatness of our nationhood and the honor of our blood." Once again deafening applause. Press reports next morning were to describe the meeting as "a mighty demonstration of the unity of Germany on both sides of the frontier, which can no longer be sundered by any power in the world." I made my way home in a thoughtful mood.

Hitler arrived in Breslau, and on the following morning the festive procession wound its way through the streets of the city. I can no longer remember the Führer's speech on this occasion. In three ranks several kilometers long, ten and twelve abreast, the participants in the Sports Festival marched to the Castle Square, where a colossal rostrum had been erected opposite the opera house. Beneath a large swastika made of oak leaves, Hitler stood with his staff on a platform swathed in red draperies. Beside him were Goebbels, Himmler, and a third man whose name was not very well known at the time: Martin Bormann. I was impressed by the feat of sheer physical endurance: With outstretched hand, Hitler saluted column after column of marchers; the march-past continued for several hours, the Führer's face became more and more rigid: the effort clearly showed, but he stuck it out. The marchers swarmed through the beflagged streets of the town.

> *Es fragen nicht nach Spiel und Tand*
> *Die Männer aus Westfalenland*
> (They seek not fun and regalia
> The stalwarts of Westphalia.)

Then came a troupe of Swabian girls in regional costume: *"Wir sind schwäbische Mädels* (We are Swabian girls) ..." they chanted, as if anyone could have mistaken them. They were followed by the Austrian athletes, the first contingent to arrive since the Anschluss. Twelve abreast they marched past the Führer's platform.

> *Wir sind der Ostmark Söhne*
> *Unser Land das schöne*
> *Unser Kampf und der Sieg.*
> (Sons of the Ostmark [the Nazi name for Austria] are we.
> Ours is that beautiful country,
> Ours the struggle and victory.)

The procession went on and on, until at last came the turn of the hosts, ecstatic faces, sparkling eyes, tumultuous cheering. From my vantage point at the corner of Schweidnitz street, I heard them singing an old tune:

> *. . . wo vor einer Tür mein Mägdlein steht.*
> *Da seufzt sie still, und flüstert leise:*
> *"Mein Schlesierland, mein Heimatland."*
> (. . . where my maiden stands by a door.
> And she sighs and whispers: "My Silesia, my homeland.")

The SS, who were responsible for keeping the streets clear, had great difficulty in holding back the crowds.

> My Silesia, my homeland,
> We will meet again on the banks of the Oder.

The bands were playing the Badenweiler march, the York march, the Hohenfriedberg march. And then came the Sudeten Germans, thousands of them, all clad in white. A group of young girls ran toward the platform, lifting their hands up to Hitler. For several minutes, the "Heils" and spoken choruses continued:

> *Wir wollen heim ins Reich.*
> *Ein Volk, ein Reich, ein Führer.*
> *Wir wollen heim ins Reich.*
> (We want to come home to the Reich.
> One nation, one country, one leader.
> We want to come home to the Reich.)

Now for the first time they beheld the man whose countenance would inspire them with renewed faith and fresh hope, as Goebbels had told them the day before. The enthusiasm was boundless: "As through a floodgate, the broad stream of happiness and joy flows between the Führer's platform and the marchers" reported the *Völkische Beobachter* next day. "Here was an expression of the passionate love of all Germans for the man who is the embodiment of the youthful German people." The march suddenly came to a halt, and the whole procession was threatened with momentary confusion. Himmler left the platform and thanked the Sudeten German girls in Hitler's name, asking them to continue on their way, which they finally did. Further groups marched past and were welcomed enthusiastically, especially the *Volksdeutsche* (Germans living beyond the borders of Germany) in their white embroidered shirts, with long flowing ribbons, and carrying bouquets of flowers in their hands. And again and again the chanting: *"Wir wollen heim ins Reich."*

That evening, Hitler flew back to Berlin. When, at a late hour that night, I went to visit a friend in town, I could still hardly make my way through the crowds. Everybody was in high spirits; great events were casting their shadow before them. The Sudeten German brothers would not have to suffer much longer under the "despotism of the licentious Czech soldiery."

On this day I had seen and heard almost the whole leadership of the Third Reich—only Göring was missing. What did I make of it? It is difficult to convey an impression of Hitler and National Socialism in its heyday. Even the Riefenstahl film about the Nuremberg rallies does not provide a full picture. The mass enthusiasm was genuine and impressive. Those in attendance certainly believed in Hitler and Nazism; many faces radiated belief in the Führer. Hitler and Goebbels claimed that the new Germany had established a near-monopoly in idealism. It was not quite true, because Stalin could boast in the early thirties of a similar effect on the young. But there is no denying that the Nazis had channeled enormous energies in the direction they wanted; many would blindly follow the Führer. But where would he lead them? In the summer of 1938, the question still seemed to be open. Would it be toward peaceful labor, as he constantly claimed, or toward aggression? From the speeches at the Breslau meeting it was clear that Czechoslovakia's turn would be next. And it stood to reason even then that all the new divisions, the tanks, guns, and aircraft had not been assembled merely for show on festive occasions. If I needed a further spur to plan my future outside Germany, it was provided by this mass meeting.

During the same period that the *Volksdeutsche* were clamoring so loudly to "come home to the Reich" several hundred thousand Jews, including the writer of these lines, had no dearer wish than to leave Germany as quickly as possible. They were pariahs in the Third Reich and were living—figuratively speaking—in a ghetto that was closing in on them all the time. Many of them were no longer able to carry on with their daily work. In Breslau, for example, almost half of the Jewish community had to be supported by Jewish charities.

The measures by which the Jews were to be excluded from the life of Germany had by now been in force for over five years, but many thought that this process was still too slow. In February 1938, *Das Schwarze Korps*, the SS newspaper, had devoted an important editorial to the Jewish problem. In answer to the question "Where are the Jews to go?" it said: "We must point out that the Jews have not exactly been seized by a feverish desire to emigrate. The behavior of the Jews in Germany does not give the impression that they are sitting on ready-packed suitcases. . . . With admirable agility, they have switched over from retail to wholesale trade, from manufactured goods to raw materials, and have cleverly developed the art of camouflage. . . ." Needless to say, there was not a shred of truth in this statement; I did not know of a single case where Jews had "switched over" to wholesale trading or raw materials. But the intention was unmistakable. The Jews were still too well off. What was to be done to hasten their departure? What, indeed. The Jews were besieging various consulates' administrative offices for entry into Palestine, they thronged emigration advice bureaus and language schools, preparing themselves hectically for departure.

When I think back to 1938, I still hear some snatches of songs that have imprinted themselves on my memory. To me, they symbolize a whole era in Germany: "*Steige hoch du roter Adler* (Rise, thou red eagle)" and "*Geduld verratene Brüder* (Patience, betrayed brethren)" and of course "*Wir seh'n uns wieder am*

Oderstrand (We'll meet again on the banks of the Oder)." But when I recall the Jewish situation of that summer, certain phrases come to mind, among them this compulsive advertising jingle, which I can recite by heart to this day—probably because I had to spend several hours waiting in an office where there was nothing else to read:

> *Willst den Wohnsitz du verändern*
> *Sei's auch nach den fernsten Ländern,*
> *Ob nach Indien oder China*
> *Oder auch nach Palästina*
> *Zieh getrost zum fernsten Ort*
> *Eckstein sorgt für den Transport.*

> (If you are on the move
> Let Eckstein prove
> The farthest spot
> On earth is not
> Too hard to do.
> From Timbuctoo
> To Samarkand
> Or the Holy Land
> Eckstein's takes care
> To get you there.)

Most of my acquaintances would have cheerfully moved to the farthest spot on earth with Eckstein's, but certain difficulties stood in their way. These difficulties could be dryly formulated in scientifically precise terms; the clampdown on the international movement of capital and the crisis in world trade exerted an unfavorable influence on emigration overseas. Or, to express it more simply and brutally: There was no country in the world waiting for the German Jews (or *any* immigrants, for that matter). But the words that were on everyone's lips—and that in my memory characterize the whole period—were: *retraining, livelihood* ("create a livelihood" and "a secure livelihood"), *certificate of good conduct, Hachsharah* (Hebrew: "preparation for

Palestine"), *health certificate, police clearance, harbor charges, affidavit* (American English: a necessary document for obtaining a U.S. visa), *chamada* (Portuguese: the same for Brazil), and so on. In addition, there were the many new abbreviations, such as ICA, HIAS, HICEM, ALTREU, PALTREU, that had suddenly acquired supreme importance. All this must seem rather odd, if not funny. However, it soon turned out that the certificates, affidavits, and *chamadas* were a matter of life and death. I know a number of people who are by no means of a nervous or sensitive disposition but who, even decades later, have been seized with violent palpitations upon entering a consulate, although they have, in the meantime, become unimpeachable citizens of the United States, Israel, or Honduras. . . .

While rummaging among some old papers recently, I came across a hectographed leaflet, yellowed with age, that had been handed to me at an emigration office. The mind still boggles at these extracts:

LUXEMBOURG: Frontiers closed to all immigrants and passengers in transit.

MINISTRY OF JUSTICE, AMSTERDAM: In future all refugees will be regarded as undesirable aliens.

[Notice from the] UNITED STATES CONSULATE IN BERLIN: In view of the extraordinary high number of entry applications, the quota figures for the immediate future are exhausted.

The following are required in the FIJI ISLANDS: a Jewish pastry cook and a single watchmaker who must not be younger than 25 or older than 30.

PARAGUAY was looking for an "accomplished, self-employed sweetmeat cook."

BRITISH BECHUANALAND wanted "a qualified tanner"; CENTRAL AFRICA "an unmarried Jewish butcher (specializing in the manufacture of savory sausages)"; and SAN SALVADOR required "a single Jewish engineer for the construction of electrical machinery."

The greatest opportunities existed in MANCHUKUO, where there were vacancies for "a Jewish cabaret producer/choreographer" who had to partner the prima ballerina, together with a troupe of six to eight female ballet dancers able to do dance solos. In addition, they wanted a Jewish ladies' orchestra and a pianist able also to play the accordion.

There was a peremptory notice from MEXICO to the effect that a visa issued by a Mexican consulate did not guarantee official permission to disembark in Mexico. The Canadian delegate to the Evian Conference of Refugees stated that CANADA could not make any binding promises.

The British delegate, Lord Winterton, declared that BRITAIN was faced with heavy unemployment.

Such were the openings for German Jews in the summer of 1938. They could emigrate to the Fiji Islands if they happened to be pastry cooks aged between twenty-five and thirty, or to Manchukuo—if they belonged to the female sex, played an instrument, and were prepared to entertain the Japanese armed forces.

The scenes in these offices are the most harrowing that I can remember. No one was shouting or weeping; there was only deep, unrelieved gloom. At the same time as the Gymnastics and Athletics Festival was being held at Breslau, an internatational conference had been convened at Evian on Lake Geneva for the coordination of aid and emigration facilities for refugees. All the delegates expressed their deepest sympathy with the prospective emigrants (who, since the spring of 1938, also included the Jews of Austria). Most Jewish communities held a day of fasting and prayers in the synagogues. But the prayers remained unanswered, for no country was prepared to accept refugees without any means of support, and Nazi Germany made it impossible even for those Jews who had any property left to take their possessions with them. One land would have been prepared to welcome them: Palestine, the "Jewish National Home." But in

1936 there had been violent disturbances, and the British had severely limited immigration in order not to jeopardize relations with the Arabs.

Occasionally, a ray of hope broke through the clouds. Magic words like "Shanghai" or "Bolivia" appeared on the horizon, or rumors were heard about the Berlin representative of a Central American republic who was selling passports for money and flattery—but above all, for lots of money. The only drawback was the dismal fact that these passports were apparently valid everywhere except in the country that was supposed to have issued them. The desperate economic situation was driving more and more German Jews, with the exception of the old and sick, to emigrate. Large-scale arrests had not yet begun in the summer of 1938. But certain events were casting their shadows—the sad fate of the Viennese Jews during the weeks following the Anschluss, or the series of new rules excluding Jews from an ever-growing number of occupations. It was at that time that by official edict all Jews had to change their first name to "typical Jewish names," such as Chava (as a man's name), Kaiphas, Sirach, Gelea, Tana, and Rause. A ridiculous situation, for half of the Nazi leaders, including Goebbels, had Hebrew names. But no one was moved to laughter.

A Jewish cultural association had been founded in 1933. Admission was for Jews only, on presentation of a pass; here the unemployed Jewish actors, singers, and other musicians found a modest field of activity. My father once took me to the synagogue, where I listened to Joseph Schmidt and Alexander Kipnis singing arias by Donizetti and Puccini and from *Le Postillon de Longjumeau*. Though the acoustics were far from ideal, there was much applause. In the summer of 1938 one could attend lectures on "Jewish Emigration—Whither?"; "A Biedermeier Evening with Meyerbeer"; "The Origin and Nature of the Golem [a mystical figure of clay endowed with life that has been the subject of much speculation since medieval times]"; "Jewish Hellenism as a Cultural Problem"; "What Meaning Can Books Have for Us?" There were also topical revues such as "From Romeo to the

String Quartet,"; "Poor as a Churchmouse," and "All Aboard, Please—A Travel Revue in 21 Tableaux" with Max Ehrlich and Willy Rosen, or "Winterhilfe of the Soul" (*Winterhilfe* was an officially sponsored German relief organization).

Hotel Frohsinn at Bad Harzburg, it said in a Jewish newspaper, was still offering "all mod. convens." Football results: Hakoah I *vs.* ISK I, 17–0. Small ads in the Jewish press offered an "assured income" and "excellent prospects." A Mr. Simeon Victor, of Frobenstrasse 5, Breslau 18, promised a carefree old age by means of an annuity insurance paying high benefits: "Pension arrangements to suit every individual requirement."

A CAREFREE OLD AGE . . . If these days one crosses the bridge over the Oder River, where the university is located, one sees on the right the cathedral with its ruined towers; on the left, there is a small island in the river. As I crossed the bridge many years later I suddenly remembered the two open-air lidos called Anders and Kallenbach and I told Naomi, my wife, of the many hours I had spent on this island in that summer of 1938. "On this island?" she asked. "In this foul weather, in this horrible water?" But the weather was not always so bad, or the water so dirty, and in those days the island had looked so much bigger to me. For bathers there was a rectangular wooden raft in a tributary of the Oder River, a few lockers and cabins, and an outsize "Nivea" ball. Access to the small island was free of charge, Jews had not been allowed to use the municipal pools for years, and the older generation had no penchant for swimming. For most of the time, we were by ourselves—a few dozen boys and girls in the same age group and some younger children who were being taught to swim by the bathing superintendent at the end of a line, while others were moving cautiously along the edge in their first attempts to float unaided. If the sun was shining, we arrived early in the morning and stayed for hours; I usually brought some books, but never managed to read them. From the water itself one could only see the island—nothing of the people, the houses, or the traffic on land. It was easy to succumb to the illusion that the outside world was far, far away. But not for long; conversation inevitably returned to the same theme—emigration. Someone had a brother in a kibbutz in Palestine; someone else had discovered a relation in America who was willing to help; a boy talked of the difficulties he had to overcome if he was to be accepted at a hotel catering college abroad. Yet another, whom I had known since our days at nursery school, turned up during his holidays. He was training on a farm in Southern Germany, where a fairly large group were preparing themselves for work on a kibbutz. He told us that at first he had found agricultural work very hard, and that his knowledge of the declension of Latin verbs had been no use to him at all. But he was almost aggressive in his optimism.

I had a girlfriend named Lotte, whom I met here practically every day; frequently we decided to go cycling together. She had a tyrannical father, who had been an officer during the war and was proud of his decorations. He was a member of the Association of German-Jewish War Veterans. His constant refrain was that the German Jews simply had to stick to their posts "like good soldiers." Soon things would get better. The present measures were mainly directed against the East European Jews. He had forbidden his daughter even to think of emigrating. She rebelled and decided to run away from home, but her mother was in poor health and she did not want to leave her. I tried hard to persuade her, but to no avail. Once we went to the pictures. It was a romantic comedy about Paris at the turn of the century. Lotte whispered: "If only one could . . ."—an unattainable dream, Romeo and Juliet in the backyard. Lotte, blue-eyed, with long blond braids, could have served as the prototype of the Aryan girl. Like so many others she was deported in 1942, never to return.

Twenty-five years later I saw—in what was now called Wrocław—the Ida Kamińska Ensemble of Warsaw, in a comedy by Abraham Goldfaden in the same cinema that had been rebuilt as a theater. The performance—in the Yiddish language—was impressive, though I missed some of the finer points. Still, I could not bear to sit through the comedy to the end. The door-keeper was concerned enough to ask whether the play was so unpleasing. It would have been too difficult to explain.

I WAITED in Breslau and I waited, but nothing happened. Following the advice of a friend, I even wrote a letter to the editor of the *Manchester Guardian* and got a very kind reply, referring me to some refugee committee in London. The financial situation of my parents further deteriorated; they talked about closing the business altogether and moving to a much smaller apartment. My father became even more taciturn; my mother had fainting spells. From letters written during those weeks I gather that I frequently thought of death and dying.

But in the end the buoyancy of youth prevailed: Perhaps I ought to go as an agricultural laborer to Palestine? A few hundred certificates were made available under the "schedule," the annual distribution rate of the British Mandatory Government. But a few thousand were waiting, and since illegal immigration had not yet got under way, the candidates were gathered in agricultural training camps, mostly inside Germany, as well as some abroad. However, it became more and more difficult to find such places for training—the Nazi authorities simply refused to grant permission.

There was yet another kind of arrangement to help those willing and eager to go as laborers to Palestine; these were the so-called *Bate Halutz* (Houses of the Pioneers), something like a small urban kibbutz, which were to be found in various major cities. These were communal homes in which ten, twenty, or even more young men and women lived while doing various kinds of manual labor, more often than not as apprentices. The houses had usually been put at the disposal of the youngsters by some wealthy member of the community, the life-style was Spartan, food barely sufficient, and one had to share one's room with at least one other person. I had visited such communes in the past and had not been attracted. There was, by necessity, something provisional about this, as in a railway station. There was constant coming and going, as in the army—one met people with whom one had little in common, young men and women from all parts of the country. Still, in my predicament I could not afford to be choosy; there were, after all, advantages in being part of a collective. If the situation should deteriorate even further, we could together decide how best to face adversity. The belief in security-through-numbers was quite wrong but psychologically only too understandable.

So I found myself in late July 1938 in the city of Frankfurt, as the most recent recruit to the local *Bet Halutz*, situated at 13 Wöhlerstrasse, not far from the Palmengarten. The choice had been excellent, and I was lucky that they had taken me; it was, as these communes went, something like a Rolls-Royce, well equipped and clean, located in one of the better parts of the city. Life was still Spartan: I had to share a room with two others, and since I happened to suffer at this very time from a skin disease, I would have given a great deal for some privacy. But even though I did not know it, the room-of-one's-own phase in my life had ended for a long time to come.

The Frankfurt home housed something like a social, or to be precise, cultural, elite; they were all, or almost all, members of the *Werkleute*, the youth movement to which I had belonged. Now, half a century after its demise, articles, books, and even dissertations are being written about the German-Jewish youth movement. To discuss it in any detail would lead me too far afield, but I cannot ignore it altogether, because my stay in Frankfurt was by no means the end of my involvement with them.

Once upon a time there had been the *Kameraden* (the comrades), a group in the tradition of the *Wandervogel*, with branches all over Germany. In the early 1930s it split three ways: The largest faction, namely the *Werkleute* (the toilers—an untranslatable term, used occasionally by Rilke and Buber), were gradually converted to Zionism and life in a kibbutz. A smaller group remained German-Jewish in orientation, that is to say non- or even anti-Zionist; and a yet smaller faction became Communist.

The two latter groups had ceased to exist by 1934, but the Werkleute went from strength to strength. Some of its members left for Palestine in 1933 to establish two kibbutzim, by 1938 they had been followed by many more, and hundreds were still in Germany waiting for their turn to join them. I had found them very congenial as individuals, even though I had misgivings about their ideology. I had no feeling for Buber, found little interest in reading the Bible, and was not even persuaded by the writing of Ber Borokhov. Borokhov, a Russian-Jewish labor leader (d. 1917), had provided a synthesis of Marxism and Zionism. He argued that the class struggle was of paramount importance, but as long as the Jews had no state of their own, it was pointless for them even to dream about militant socialism. Although Borokhov's writings were closely studied at the time, I was more impressed by the thoughts of another Russian-Jewish leader, Arlosoroff, who had received his education in Germany in the same family in which the future Mrs. Goebbels was growing up. But for his murder in 1933 on the Tel Aviv beach in circumstances that have not been cleared up to this day, he might have become one of the central figures in Jewish, and later Israeli, politics.

The Frankfurt commune consisted of members of the Werkleute. Among these fine people I remained, alas, an outsider. I was the youngest, and unfortunately a difference of three or four years is of considerable importance at that age. Most of them were at the end of their apprenticeship; I had not even begun. Above all, there were no girls my age, whereas most of the others lived together as man and wife; one or two of the couples were, in fact, already married. I doubt whether I would have been very happy in the long run. There was to be no long run.

On the second or third day after my arrival I made my way to the training center in the old part of town where young people like me were trained as locksmiths, carpenters, builders, and even in the fine art of plumbing and electrical engineering. I should add here that I had never before been to western or southern Germany; Frankfurt was for me almost a foreign city, even the local dialect being difficult to understand. The Old City, located between the Zeil—one of the busiest shopping streets— and the Main, was a strange sight. I had, of course, seen old half-timbered buildings before, but never so many in one place, nor had I ever been in such a maze of narrow and dark streets. Their (unofficial) names were quite amusing—one, for instance, was called the *Lappegass* (Rags Alley), in view of the many sec- ondhand cloth dealers offering their commodities in the open air; there was also a *Fressgass* (Stuff Yourself Alley), because of the many foodstores, but this was located outside the Old City, nearer the opera. In this place, there had been the ghetto, and once upon a time the Rothschilds (as well as Goethe) had lived here. By the time I visited the Old City, attempts had been made to refurbish it for the benefit of the many tourists. Many houses were brightly painted; most of the Jews had moved away long ago, and to stress this point, the announcements in the little shops said "German shop." The Jews had lived here since the eleventh century; the Germanized Old City was to last only six years. On three days and nights in March of 1944, it burned down so thoroughly as the result of massive air attacks that it seemed pointless after the war to restore it. It was through these narrow lanes that I made my way on that July morning, with some foreboding, to engage on a new career: I had opted for carpentry, even though I lacked both dexterity and interest in the subject. Why, then, had I chosen carpentry? Probably by chance, because, not being very good with my hands, I was equally uninterested in the other disciplines.

The carpentry master to whom I reported was far too busy to give me much of his time. He led me to a bench, gave me some tools and a piece of wood, and told me something that I did not understand, partly because he spoke the Frankfurt dialect, but also because he assumed that I had at least some rudimentary experience. I knew how to use a hammer, a saw, and an ax. But the job he expected me to do called not for an ax but much more refined tools. So I did nothing; at lunch I ate the sandwich I had brought along; the afternoon I used to inspect the other parts of the building as well as the courtyard. At the end of the day, the tools were unused, and the piece of wood still intact.

This was the beginning and the end of my career as a carpenter, for when I turned up the next morning, there was a big sign in front of the building saying that, in view of the fact that there had been a dozen cases of polio in town, the school had been closed by order until further notice. Furthermore, no one under eighteen was permitted to leave Frankfurt for the time being.

I should have been sad, but such was the irresponsibility of youth that I felt exceedingly glad. For the next few days I helped wash the floors of the building in Wöhlerstrasse; later I prepared a list of the books in the communal library. But this did not take very long either, and at the end of a week I was more or less free to do what I wanted.

For almost a month I went on cycling tours, exploring Frankfurt and its neighborhood. Wiesbaden was much bigger than I had thought, not so much a resort but an elegant and wealthy town. For reasons I can no longer recall, I went to see a bad French film with Jean Gabin; perhaps it was raining and I could not sit on a bench in the park. Of Mainz I remember that the Cathedral of Saints Martin and Stefan could be seen at a great distance. The hills of the Taunus did not leave a lasting impression, perhaps because the highest elevation was only half the height of my native Schnee Koppe. But there was a fine panorama, and the whole landscape, with gardens and fruit trees, was much more harmonious than the stark views of the Giant Mountains with which I had grown up.

There was much more history and culture in Frankfurt than in Breslau, even though the city was not really older. But there was Goethe, the Lutheran Church of St. Paul (Paulskirche), where the first German parliament had been convened in 1848, and much more.

I ought to mention in passing that prewar Germany was a

much less expensive country than Britain or France; the rate for a room in the most expensive hotel in Frankfurt (or Berlin) was ten marks ($2.50); meals in the best restaurants were also considerably cheaper than in London or Paris. Rail travel was cheap; for thirty marks one could traverse the whole of Germany. But ten marks was a great deal of money, and I had to count the pfennigs. My mother sent me stamps, and I sent clothes home for washing; the postage was less than I would have paid for having it washed locally. I ought to mention this because it may explain why I seldom went to the local opera and theater, since there was an entrance fee. I was not particularly interested in natural history but the Senckenberg Museum fascinated me— above all, the antediluvian animal placed right at the entrance. From a letter written to a friend after a visit, I gather that I was also deeply impressed by an exhibit that showed an embryo in various stages of development. I learned on this occasion that arteriosclerosis was setting in at the age of sixteen or seventeen, and since I had already reached that age, my creative phase was nearing its end; what new ideas could one expect from anyone aged eighteen or beyond? I cannot establish in retrospect whether I was seriously perturbed or not.

While I was exploring the neighborhood of Frankfurt the storm clouds were rapidly gathering; one could not help being vaguely aware of the connection between politics and everyday life, one's own life. Earlier on, high politics had been something rather theoretical, which had some meaning for the professionals in Berlin, Paris, and London. True, it was an important subject such as, for instance, the study of philosophy, and I had in fact begun to study political science the year before. But since the ordinary mortal could not possibly have any influence on politics, there seemed to be little point in worrying constantly; life would go on somehow. Perhaps this crisis would pass like so many before. This somewhat nonchalant attitude toward the possible effects of politics began to change only in August 1938.

On the basis of letters and a diary, I have reconstructed a timetable of sorts for August and September 1938. August 19 was a Friday; I had taken the railway to Heidelberg, admittedly with a bad conscience because even the cheapest day return ticket was more than I could really afford. I went to see the ruins of the old castle and walked along the famous Philosophenweg, the path leading through the woods. I saw a great many students and also heard some English spoken, but the overall picture was much less colorful than I had expected. No student was seen in the uniform of his corps; there was no dueling in the street. The Nazis had dissolved the students' associations; the atmosphere was strangely subdued for a town dominated by young people and known all over the world for the atmosphere of *Altheidelberg, du Feine.* For a good hour or two I sat in an open-air coffeehouse watching the boats on the Neckar, which at this place leaves the Odenwald hills and enters the valley of the Rhine.

On the same day Hitler went to Pomerania to watch the maneuvers of the Second Army Corps, and Ewald von Kleist, a leader of the German opposition, saw Churchill in London, telling him that Hitler was preparing for war in the very near future. Churchill did not need much persuasion.

The following weekend I spent with my comrades in Frankfurt, walking in the Palmengarten with its hundreds of plants. In the evening we crossed the Main on the Eiserne Steg, a famous pedestrian bridge frequently painted by Beckmann and others (but Beckmann was then very much out of fashion). On to Sachsenhausen, originally a fishing village, where in a cheap restaurant we had the local cheese and cider (*Aeppelwei*), one of the standard entertainments of the natives of Frankfurt. The same weekend, Baldur von Schirach was in Frankfurt, was honored by the mayor, and delivered a major speech in which he claimed that Frankfurt, as everyone knew, was the city of Goethe, who had admonished German youth to attain physical fitness, to train hard so as to be able to face the challenges ahead. It is difficult to think of a topic more remote to Goethe's order of values, or indeed envisage him doing calisthenics every morning. But such was the climate of those days that the speech fitted in very well with the *Zeitgeist.*

On the following Monday I cycled with a friend to Bingen. This was the first time I saw the Rhine (except at Mainz), the romantic river of legend figuring in so many sagas, songs, and poems. This, then, was the Binger Loch—the place feared for its storms by the Rhine navigators. This was the medieval Lorch, where Hagen had dumped in the river the treasure of the Nibelungen. Rüdesheim, Assmannshausen, Bacharach, the names had a magic spell even for the nonwine-drinker. It had been a fine, sunny summer and the vintners were preparing for the harvest, seemingly an idyllic picture of peace. On the same day Hitler was in Kiel with a special guest, Admiral Miklós Horthy of Hungary, inspecting some one hundred ships, virtually the whole new German war fleet. Mrs. Horthy was asked to launch the most recent battle cruiser, *Prinz Eugen*. Horthy was a cautious leader by nature, and the idea must have occurred to him that the alliance with the impetuous man to his left was more than a little dangerous. What did the future hold in store?

Ten years is not a long time in history; where would they all be, the admiral, the Führer, and the ship ten years hence? Hitler's greatest triumphs, needless to say, were still ahead. He was utterly confident. Two weeks later, at the great Nuremberg rally, he said that he had already achieved what he wanted, the victory of the young Nazi idea, and the emergence of a strong Germany, young in heart and with an iron determination. If he was to die one day, he could do so in the firm belief that victory had already been assured. A mere ten years later Hitler was dead, Horthy almost forgotten, and Germany was in ruins.

The story of the ship is equally strange: it took almost another two years to complete work on the *Prinz Eugen*, which entered battle only in August 1940, by which time the war seemed won. The *Prinz Eugen* had a good war; it caused grave concern to the Allied convoys in the Atlantic and was never caught, except at the very end, when it passed into American hands. It took part at the Bikini nuclear test, was damaged on this occasion, and had to be scuttled in November 1946.

Admiral Horthy was the only one still to be in action at the end of ten years. He had closely cooperated with the Nazis, but when it appeared that the war was lost, he put out peace feelers to the Allies, whereupon Hitler had him abducted and arrested. By 1948 he was in a relatively comfortable exile in Estoril, Portugal, reflecting about the vicissitudes of international politics and working on his autobiography.

August 1938 came to an end, but the polio alarm had not been lifted. I had not yet been to Darmstadt and the Bergstrasse, but I knew the neighborhood of Frankfurt as well as anyone. A further stay seemed pointless. Then out of the blue a special delivery letter arrived from Berlin that changed everything: It was a very short communication to the effect that I had been accepted as a student in Jerusalem, and as such I was entitled to a certificate of immigration—subject to some details to be confirmed. Would I come as soon as feasible to the Palestine Office, Berlin, Meineckestrasse 10, with my passport and certain other papers. I was also to be examined by a doctor in Berlin.

The same evening I phoned my parents. My father gently chided me for spending so much money on a phone call and strongly urged me not to burn the bridges behind me—that is to say, not to give up the (nonexistent) job in Frankfurt. After all, there were so many uncertainties ahead. It was not sufficient to pay in the money in Berlin; it also had to be transferred to Jerusalem, and this was a complicated operation. About the complexities of transfer, based on agreements reached in 1933-34, volumes have been written; all that need be said is that by 1938 there were many people waiting in line, and if I had joined them, the procedure might have taken another year or even more. But whatever good sense I had told me not to wait; there was a shortcut—namely, to find someone in Palestine to act as guarantor, which we did in short time.

I did not formally say good-bye to my comrades in Frankfurt because nothing was as yet final. However, in my heart I felt that this time I would be luckier than during the previous two false starts. At the Frankfurt railway station, uniformed police and even SS were carrying out controls, but I looked older than seventeen and was not stopped. I was too excited to sleep that night on the train to Berlin. I thought of the weeks in Frankfurt. Would I see the city again, would my path cross again the people whom I had just come to know a little more closely? As for Frankfurt—this was in a way my last visit, for though I would come again after the war, it was an altogether different place: The old Frankfurt had disappeared as the result of the war unleashed by Hitler and Co. Some of my colleagues I never saw again, but others I met, a few in a kibbutz, others in America. One day in the 1960s I had some dealings with the chief librarian of one of England's newly founded red-brick universities; only gradually it dawned on me that once upon a time we had shared a room in the Wöhlerstrasse.

The train arrived in Berlin in the early hours of the morning, I left the luggage at the station and made my way to Meinecke-strasse, hours before the office opened. When my turn finally came, they told me to return in three days when the paper work would be done. I went to see the doctor, who told me that my body was almost athletic but my throat was infected and that he would pass me only subject to a tonsillectomy. This was a nuisance, but doctors in those preantibiotic years were great believers in something they called "focal infection." There was no way around it; I called my mother in the evening, who arranged the date with Dr. Miodowski, the throat surgeon who had taken care of me since I was a small child.

I now had several days on my hands and, though I was not in the right mood, set out to walk the streets of Berlin. I did not know the city well, even though I had been there at least half a dozen times, usually to change trains, or to participate in some seminar or sports competition. It was not difficult to find a place to stay; parents of friends and even distant acquaintances, whose offspring had already emigrated, were only too eager to offer hospitality to young people. On that occasion I stayed in a largish apartment off the Alexanderplatz, in the heart of working-class Berlin.

I remember certain meetings and conversations in Berlin that week. One was with a young lady from my hometown, making a last desperate attempt through various lawyers and other contacts to get her husband out of a concentration camp. He was a dissident Communist and his case proved to be quite hopeless. In fact, she was given to understand that she ought to leave Germany while the going was good. This she did, and toward the end of the war she remarried, assuming that her husband was dead like so many others, since she had not heard from him for years. But he did somehow survive—a tragic situation, about which I have read in novels and plays, but which I thought would never arise in real life.

Then, in the youth department of the Palestine office I met an emissary from Palestine, an acquaintance who had emigrated a few years earlier and who was now back with a Palestinian passport to act as adviser to the young people preparing to join the kibbutz. I asked him about the fighting in Palestine; German papers were full of reports about Arab insurgents taking over the country. He said that the reports were exaggerated. True, there was a real national conflict that Zionism had so far preferred to ignore, but from a military point of view the Arab gangs were no match for the British—or even the Jews. Furthermore, the Arab leaders had made a fatal mistake: They had thrown in their lot with Mussolini and Hitler. Later events bore out his prediction. September 1938 was the high tide of the uprising; subsequently it declined and petered out.

Most of the erstwhile leaders of German Jewry had emigrated by that time. Some, like Leo Baeck, remained because they thought it was their duty to stay at their post; a few, like Julius Seeligsohn, even returned from abroad for this reason and were caught when the curtain came down.

What did I learn during these few days of walking the streets of Berlin and of talking with people better informed than I was? The newspapers carried horror stories about the unspeakable atrocities committed by "Bolshevik Czech gangsters" against the peaceful Sudeten Germans. But there was not the slightest war fever, let alone enthusiasm. There was a stark contrast between

the belligerent tenor of the speeches at the Parteitag in Nuremberg, just then taking place, and the indifference of the people
one met. I recall the announcements at Nuremberg about the
national prizes for art and science, the German answer to the
Nobel Prize. The recipients were Willy Messerschmitt, Ernst
Heinkel, and Ferdinand Porsche. I had never heard of these
men; we were to hear the names very often in the years to come.

Among the Jews, there was growing concern. Almost every
week there was a new official announcement limiting Jewish
living and breathing space—another ban on working in a certain
profession, more chicanery concerning passports and property,
the order to adopt a "Jewish" name unless one had one already.
Nineteen thirty-six had been a relatively calm year, for Hitler
did not want adverse publicity in view of the Olympic Games.
But in 1937 the anti-Jewish policy became more severe, and the
year after, there was a further turning of the screw. Still, there
were no mass arrests and pogroms, except in Vienna, and Vienna
seemed far away. As a result, more Austrian Jews left the country
in five months than had left Germany in five years. But it is also
true that there were more suicides in Vienna, and not a few
who tried to leave illegally were returned. A Swiss newspaper
reported heartbreaking scenes from the Zurich railway station,
when those believing they had reached a safe haven were ordered
to go back with the next train.

Having arranged my affairs to the best of my ability, I went to
the Schlesischer Bahnhof and bought a ticket for my hometown.
I was, as so often, too early and walked up and down the busy
station. I went out to have a last look at the nearby Spree and
had some guilty feelings about not having made more of my
stay. Of all the museums on my list, I had seen only one, the
Zeughaus, specializing in military history, because I happened
to pass it one day. Farther on, on the so-called museum island,
there were the truly important museums—Kaiser Friedrich, Per-
gamon, and three others. I cannot say after all these years to
what extent my curiosity was genuine, or whether I felt that I
had to see the altars, statues, and pictures because any educated

Schwerinstrasse 64, Breslau. I was born in the house to the right; my parents lived there from 1920 to 1932. The street in front served as playground, sports ground, and meeting place for street gangs. In early 1945, during fighting for the city, not a single house was left standing in that street and for a radius of more than a mile. (COURTESY HEIMATARCHIV, HORST G.W. GLEISS [HOLM])

Tanner's Lane in Breslau, the street just behind our apartment, in an 1898 drawing.

Walter Laqueur. On my sixth birthday.

Reluctantly crossing a street with my mother and cousins, ca. 1929.

My parents. The picture was taken on the sixtieth birthday of my father, shortly before the outbreak of war.

Families of yesterday. Uncle Emil's silver wedding anniversary, 1928. My parents are in center back.

Sudpark in Breslau, the scene of many childhood memories. (COURTESY WIENER LIBRARY, LONDON)

Johannes Gymnasium, Breslau, the school I attended from 1930 to 1938. It is now an institute for adult education.
(COURTESY DR. HANS-GUIDO WEISER)

Group picture of the teachers at school. The photograph was taken in 1913, but about one third of the teachers shown here were still active when I attended school.

Rossmarkt—the Wallenberg-Pachaly Building. To the left is our home; to the right, the municipal library. (Courtesy R. Schulte)

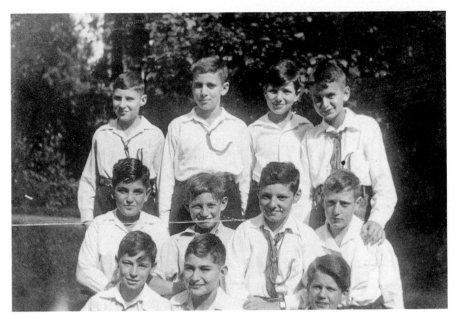

Youth movement, my group, ca. 1936.

Start of a race during an athletics competition, Breslau, 1936. My friend did not win.

At age fifteen, the athletic period.

The village in the Giant Mountains, 1936, where we often stayed in summer and winter.
(COURTESY WIENER LIBRARY, LONDON)

The same scene in 1991, with the forest dying and the village deserted.
(COURTESY OTA PHILIP, FRANKFURT)

Breslau Great Synagogue,
Moorish style, built ca. 1868.
(COURTESY WIENER LIBRARY,
LONDON)

Day of German sport, Breslau, July 1938. Hitler speaks in the presence of his ministers. (COURTESY WIENER LIBRARY, LONDON)

Breslau Central Railway Station, one of the oldest in Germany, point of departure for many excursions, including my very last one to Jerusalem in November 1938. (COURTESY WIENER LIBRARY, LONDON)

person was supposed to have seen them. But I do remember real regret and a feeling that this had been the last opportunity. My premonition happened to be correct, for during the war, museum island together with the rest of Berlin, including the Schlesischer Bahnhof, were either destroyed or severely damaged. When I went to Berlin again in 1953, the Zeughaus had been restored and reopened but had become a museum of German history in the Stalinist vein. Once again, in 1990, I went there to see an exhibition devoted to the opposition in the DDR that had brought about the downfall of the regime. The major museums were gradually restored, such as the Near Eastern Museum, but many of the fine pictures had gone forever. Under the monarchy, the Weimar Republic, and even the Nazis, entrance had been free; under the Communist regime they asked me for one mark (55 cents). The ways of Providence are inscrutable.

Time always passed quickly in a railway station, there was so much of interest to see. I belonged to the railway generation that grew up with the big locomotives—which seemed even more enormous to a child—the specific smell of steam and soot; the stationmaster in his impressive uniform, the symbol of authority; the rhythmic noise once the train was in motion. These sights, smells, and noises had been part of my childhood; I was well into my twenties when I flew in a plane for the first time. My children crossed the Atlantic before they turned ten; my grandchildren, before they could even walk. If this is progress, I don't envy them; they missed a whole age of great fascination.

I had bought a couple of newspapers for the journey; the threats against the Bolshevik rulers of Czechoslovakia and the wire-pullers in London and Paris had become even shriller. It was mid-September 1938; we were about to face a major crisis, the world at large and the young man in the third-class compartment of the Berlin–Breslau express train.

I PRESENTED MYSELF at the Jewish hospital in Hohenzollernstrasse on September 19, 1938, handed in my clothes, and was allocated a bed in the surgical ward. M., a youngish doctor who was about to marry a cousin of mine, visited me that evening and talked of wedding plans and emigration; the ward sister turned off the light at ten o'clock. A little boy talked in his sleep, an elderly man was groaning, another was telling his neighbor dirty jokes, and two were playing cards by the weak rays of a flashlight.

The operation would be ridiculously simple. M. had said it was "just a routine matter these days." It wasn't too bad. I was awake most of the time. But then there were complications; they could not stop the bleeding, and I had to stay in the hospital longer than anticipated, In the morning we were awakened early—every hospital has its own routine, but on one point all these institutions seem to agree: and that is the conviction that it is harmful to health, if not downright dangerous, to allow patients to get sufficient sleep. In the semidarkness the nurses would start walking about, talking to each other in loud voices. Temperatures were taken, and tea was handed round. M. came to see me briefly after breakfast: "You are not missing anything outside. The hospital is easily one of the healthiest places to be in at the moment. Have you heard the news?" Everybody in the ward was talking politics. Snatches of conversation drifted over to my bed: "Chamberlain will surely find a way. . . . Beneš is in a very strong position. . . . Ultimatum . . ." With a bit of an effort, I managed to find out what was going on. Since my return from Berlin, I had been preoccupied with preparations for my departure and had only glanced at the newspaper headlines. There was a crisis, this much I knew, but there had been a succession of crises since the spring almost without pause. At the beginning of September the situation had become more critical: Hitler had declared at Nuremberg that he would solve the Sudeten question "one way or another." On September 15, Chamberlain had gone to Berchtesgaden. And I was lying in bed in the surgical ward, running a temperature.

It was Jewish New Year and that very afternoon, September 22, while I was in bed feeling sorry for myself, Hitler and Chamberlain met in the Hotel Dreesen in Bad Godesberg in a last attempt by the British prime minister to prevent war. Poor Chamberlain had to realize in the course of the conversation that Hitler (accompanied by Himmler, Goebbels, and Ribbentrop) became ever more demanding and provocative. The meeting ended with Chamberlain promising to forward the German ultimatum to the Czech government.

After the war I happened to stay in the Rheinhotel Dreesen on more than one occasion, participating in various meetings. From the bedroom window one could watch the steamers on the Rhine, and whenever the fog lifted one saw the villages on the other side in great detail. The river was grayish—had it ever looked more inviting? I remember one occasion, as Raymond Aron gave one of his brilliant analyses of the world situation, when it suddenly dawned on me that the confrontation between Hitler and Chamberlain had probably taken place in the same room—where had the two delegations been seated?

My parents arrived later in the morning, looking very worried. Father said piously that I must get better as soon as possible. Mother told me the latest news about my schoolmates and friends who were already abroad, what they had written to their parents, and she mentioned the bedding she had prepared for my emigration. The half hour was painful. And what a time for an operation! Would there be war? My parents had brought me a newspaper in which I read about the "Czech-Jewish-Marxist blood terror," about a mother-to-be who had been beaten with rubber truncheons by the Czech police. The headlines ran: BLOOD LUST AND HATE PSYCHOSIS RIFE, INCREDIBLE BESTIALITIES BY CZECH BANDITS. Czech children had thrown bottles of petrol on innocent German children; old people had to run the gauntlet past rows of bayonets. A report from Annaberg said that a Sudeten German mother from Komotau had tried to flee to Germany; at the frontier she was discovered by Czech officials, who tortured her; the poor woman went out of her mind. "Prague threatens Europe with war. . . . The blood of the victims cries for vengeance. . . . Steel rods and rubber truncheons used on German workers. . . .

Moscow assassination commandos with poison gas and explosives are preparing for a bloodbath at Reichenberg. . . ." Amid
the clash of arms, the Muses were not silent. The poem of a
Sudeten writer, Wilhelm Pleyer, was featured:

> *Kein Frieden wird ihnen werden*
> *Die Gott zu Kindern uns gab,*
> *Es gibt keinen Frieden auf Erden*
> *Es gibt keinen Frieden im Grab.*
> *Nicht wollen die Hörner wir dämpfen*
> *Es schreitet die Zeit mit Gestampf.*
> *Wir kämpfen. Wir Kämpfen, wir Kämpfen*
> *Um einen besseren Kampf.*

> (No peace will ever be theirs,
> That God promised the young.
> No peace is there on earth,
> Nor is there peace in the grave.
> Let us not mute our trumpets,
> With heavy tread time marches on.
> We fight and we fight and we fight on
> To make the struggle supreme.)

There was a photo of a Sudeten German woman with the
caption: "This tormented face of a German mother expresses all
the misery of mankind." "We want war!" so the Czechs are said
to have cried. The German Embassy in Prague had lodged sharp
protests against Czech border violations at Seidenberg.

During the next few days, the mood in the hospital wards was
one of utter dejection. Everybody, it seemed, had finally realized
how things stood. Newspaper headlines and radio reports were
reflected immediately in the mood and behavior of doctors,
nurses, and patients. When Sir Horace Wilson flew to Berlin
with some new suggestions for a compromise, there was some
tangible improvement in the general atmosphere: There was
going to be a compromise, "Everything would turn out all
right. . . ." The doctors were genial; the patients no longer diffi-

cult. The man in the bed next to me said: "It is a put-up job— they have prearranged everything—and they're staging the whole show just to confuse the masses." And he continued with his never-ending game of cards. I went for little strolls in the hospital garden. The end of that September month had brought warm, sunny days, following weeks of rains and floods. The gardener was pattering about his asters and dahlias; in the morning we were awakened by songbirds. A deep calm reigned.

Then came the news that Czechoslovakia had rejected the German demands. Hitler made a speech in the Sportpalast and said that the handing over of the Sudeten region was the final German demand. Demonstrations of loyalty everywhere. *"Führer, befiehl, wir folgen!"* ("Give the order and we will follow you!") The propaganda machine was running in high gear:

This caricature of a state must come to an end. . . . Children in indescribable misery. . . . Czech women as sharpshooters. . . . In rooms requiring a great deal of lighting, the windows and skylights must be covered in such a manner that no light can be seen from the outside; this may be done with shutters or roller blinds made of wood, fabric, paper, or other materials. . . . Bohemian Woods—a living hell for the victims of Hussite murderers. . . . Announcement of the Happy Event of the Birth of a Son to Henriette von Schirach, née von Hoffmann. . . . This is the Czech: lazy, cowardly, and impertinent.

The mood in the hospital ward sank to new depths of depression. The patients suffered relapses and crises. The doctors were curt, the nurses irritable (some of them with eyes red from tears). A screen had been placed around the bed of the groaning old man, and now the card-player was lying in his bed in complete apathy, staring at the ceiling for hours.

In the bed opposite me, there was an accountant who had undergone a stomach operation. His wife and children came to visit him—the wife looked haggard, careworn, and badly dressed, the two girls, obviously twins, were spruced up in white dresses, patent leather shoes, with colored barrettes in their hair. He told me his story: He had been employed by a large Jewish firm in Upper Silesia that had dismissed him without notice over a year ago, under pressure from the "Labor Front." They had moved to Breslau, where they were living in a one-room flat at the Odertor—not one of the most salubrious parts of town. During this past year, they had gone through all his savings and were now dependent on charity. When his family had left, he said nothing for a long time but lay silently, his face turned to the wall. After supper he started to talk again. He did not know how it could go on—his wife didn't have a single pair of serviceable shoes left, and now he was sick, unable to help. Had he not thought of emigrating? That was impossible for "little men" like himself. He hadn't even enough money to travel to Berlin, let alone to faraway countries. If he were twenty years younger and unmarried, then, of course, he would try. But for people like him there was only one way out—the gas tap—that is, if the gas had not been cut off already. . . . But for the children they would have ended it all long ago.

On Saturday, a friend phoned me: "*Mensch*, the mousetrap might be sprung any moment now. I am getting out of here— on my motorbike—to Constantinople!" Did he have a visa? No, he would get through one way or another. Next day again, in the paper: "Sudeten youth caught in the pincers of Czech-Jewish blood terror. . . . The masses of persecuted Germans raise their voices in protest. . . . Rubber truncheons against weeping mothers. . . . 'All Germans are going to be liquidated,' says Czech policeman. . . . Germany's world struggle against lies. . . ."

On that morning, war seemed inevitable. Had I missed the last train? I envied my friend, who was at this moment riding his motorcycle through Czechoslovakia or Hungary. My parents arrived, tried to comfort me, pretended that in the outside world nothing had happened, discussed final preparations for my coming journey. They had bought a special pair of buttonhole scissors for an aunt in Haifa, which I was to take for her. Several minutes were spent discussing the little scissors. The nurse who brought me my supper had been crying (her fiancé was in South America; now she would never see him again). It was a long night even with sleeping tablets. The old man was louder than ever, and his groans were mixed with the radio's request program called "Nights of Old Vienna." I fell asleep to the sounds of a melody by Karl Ziehrer: "*Sei gepriesen du lauschige Nacht.*" To this day I make a point of listening to it at least once a month, and it usually acts as an antidepressant.

The next morning nothing seemed to matter. The old man had died during the night, and nobody in the ward felt like talking. Toward noon we heard the news that Chamberlain was, once again, on his way to Germany, this time to Munich. His wife had accompanied him to the door of No. 10 Downing Street. The crowd had shouted, "Good old Chamberlain, God bless you!" And the old gentleman had made a short speech: "When I was a little boy, I used to repeat, if at first you don't succeed, try, try, try again. That is what I am doing. . . . When I come back, I hope I may be able to say as Hotspur says in *Henry IV*: 'Out of this nettle, danger, we pluck this flower, safety.' . . ." The ward sister came in and attended to the little boy who had been seized with a fit of coughing. "Everything will turn out all right. . . ." There was much visiting between patients from different wards. All of a sudden, everybody was in a happy mood. There would be no war. We were not trapped, we were saved. I started to write a hopeful letter but couldn't quite manage it and put the pencil aside. On the radio, there was martial music, poetry recitals, and timely reminders: "Nations of Europe, this is the beginning of a Holy Spring. . . ." A foreign radio station reported that people in Prague were weeping in the streets. But who cared? Good old Chamberlain! All was quiet during the night of Tuesday, and on Wednesday morning I was discharged from the hospital.

I passed the Jewish hospital again some twenty-five years later. On our way back from Południe Park we had to drive past it, the main street being closed to traffic, and we took the long route along the old water tower, opposite that large building of ugly, dark-red brick. I had assumed that the hospital had been destroyed during the siege of Breslau, but I was mistaken; it was still standing, at least in part, and some public offices had been installed there. I asked my wife if she had been able to read the sign. No, I had been driving too fast. Did it still serve as a hospital? I don't know, for I did not turn back.

For the month of October 1938 I have two official documents and one long personal letter to refresh my memory. The letter said that I was recovering from surgery, that I had booked passage on a ship from Trieste on November 9, and that I felt somewhat guilty having chosen a university career rather than doing manual labor. But, I comforted myself, time was running out, and whatever I was likely to learn was not going to be in vain. Even in retrospect I find it difficult to explain this defensive reaction, for I should have known that neither by aptitude nor by interest had I much of a future as an artisan or technician. If my motivation was ideological—after all, Marx and Lenin had studied (but none of the Nazi top leaders except Goebbels). Or did I perhaps feel guilty because I was lucky to escape, whereas many others, for one reason or another, had to stay? I cannot give a satisfactory answer even now. I should have felt concern about my parents; while I was in the hospital they had moved to a much smaller apartment in a less savory part of town. Of the three rooms one went to Grandmother, and mine was to be sublet after my departure. Obviously, their financial situation had gone from bad to worse. There was nothing I could do to help, and I preferred not to think about it.

Of the two documents, one was by the mayor of Breslau, and it said that the student Walter Laqueur did not owe the city any taxes. This kind of attestation was one of several necessary for would-be emigrants. The other was a list of clothing and other personal belongings that young travelers were advised to take. From an early age I had collected guidebooks, old and new. By the age of seventeen I had a little library, with special emphasis on the Near East (as it was then called), including much advice on how to prevent (or combat) seasickness, how to obtain a letter of credit, how to buy a Mauser pistol (but to hide it from customs), and how to make use of a dragoman in Oriental markets. I also knew that the Oriental mentality was quite different from our own and that it was bad form to ask an Arab or Turk about the state of health of his wife.

All the guidebooks agreed that one should not take too much baggage, but also stated that several suits were imperative, including morning dress and tailcoat because one was bound to be invited to formal occasions. For the southern Mediterranean at least four cotton suits were needed (more could be bought locally if necessary), as well as riding breeches, a cane that could also serve as a riding crop, a lot of warm and not-so-warm underwear so as not to catch cold, two pairs of heavy boots of yellow-brown leather for walking in the mountains, one pair of patent leather shoes (to go with the tailcoat), two overcoats, at least one tropical helmet, and either a silken or camel-hair blanket.

The list for the serious traveler was well meant but quite unrealistic in my case. The much shorter one I received from Berlin did not mention Mauser, tailcoat, or tropical helmet, and my mother tried to stick to it, though some of the items we could not afford. We found somewhere an old but sturdy trunk of pre–World War I vintage that stood for a week or two in our small dining room and had to be inspected by the authorities before it was sealed and sent off. The trunk stayed with me for a number of years, and it served as a chair in the tent in which Naomi and I lived when we were first married. The cushion of eiderdown I had a little longer, and two or three books are still with me to this day.

October passed quickly, except that toward the end of that month some fifteen thousand Jewish residents of Germany, among them some friends and acquaintances, were arrested; they had Polish nationality and were dumped in the no-man's-land between Germany and Poland, for the Poles did not recognize their citizenship and did not want them either. These events would have probably entered history as a minor footnote but for the fact that the son of one of the deported families, Herszel Grynszpan, born in Hannover and at that time living in Paris, asked by his family to help them in their misery and despair, opted for a "Herostratic" act that had grave repercussions.

On November 7, my parents and I went to Breslau's central railway station. Neither they nor I had wanted anyone else to accompany us. There was a small group of youngsters departing for Trieste to catch the same boat, and we occupied one compartment. My mother wept when it came time to take leave. My father, who tried never to show his feelings, least of all in public, did not say a word. I tried to comfort my mother by saying that we would surely meet again, perhaps soon, and kissed my father, probably the only time in my life. Then the stationmaster called *"Alles einsteigen"* ("All aboard"), and the train began to move. If I now tried to reconstruct what I thought during the moments of leave-taking and the hours thereafter, it would be pure fantasy. I did not know that it was the last time I was to see my parents, nor could I imagine what was awaiting me in a faraway country. I do recall that when my parents and the station had disappeared out of view, I took out the inevitable newspaper I had bought for my trip and began to read. It was not difficult to establish what the paper reported that morning. Hitler had been in Weimar and had made another major speech attacking the warmongers. There had been ovations like never before, throughout the night. He had talked from the balcony of the town's leading hotel named Elefant, which was located in the market square where all the festivities in Goethe's or Schiller's days had taken place.

> *Lieber Führer, sieh doch ein*
> *Wir können doch nicht länger schrein.*
> (Beloved Führer, you ought to understand
> We simply can no longer shout.)

When Hitler made it known that he wanted to rest, a Hitler Youth leader ran up to him and said: "Beloved Führer! How can we sleep while you are in town!" Hitler was visibly moved and stayed a little longer.

It was at the very time while I was reading my paper, shortly after nine-thirty in the morning, that young Grynszpan went to the German embassy in Paris, 78 rue de Lille, and shot and killed one of the officials, Ernst von Rath. When we reached Munich in the late evening, there was a special edition of the local newspaper announcing the event.

But the news hardly registered; we were on the lookout for another group of young people that was to join us on the way to Trieste. There was a girl from the Rhineland, whom I liked from the moment she joined us.

In the years before World War II, the route Trieste–Jaffa (or Haifa) was by far the most common from the Continent to the Near East, and it was monopolized by the Lloyd Triestino Line. (One could fly to Tiberias twice a week by means of a hydroplane, but not from Germany, and it was very expensive indeed.) About Trieste I remember only that the railway station was near the harbor and that winter had not yet come. So the girl, whose name I have forgotten, and I walked for a few hours and then checked in at the office of the shipping company.

The days spent on the *Gerusalemme* were a delight. We had almost no idea what was happening in the outside world. As the ship sailed southward the sun came out, and passengers went on deck sunbathing. The ship's radio informed us that there had been "pogroms" in Germany; I felt a little concerned, but thought that surely it couldn't be all that bad. I did not know until almost a week later that in Germany some thirty thousand Jews had been arrested and taken to Buchenwald and to other concentration camps. But for my timely departure, there is much reason to assume that I would have been among them. By autumn 1938, Mussolini had been persuaded by Hitler to announce the promulgation of a series of anti-Semitic laws. But nothing of the new spirit was felt in Trieste, and the captain of the ship, being a thoughtful man, spared us the bad news from Rome and Berlin.

Among my fellow passengers, I met a few who were going to study at the university like myself, and others were going to a kibbutz. I went to the cinema in the evening; I have forgotten the name of the film, but Zarah Leander, whom Goebbels had chosen to be the German Garbo, or Dietrich, was singing *"Der Wind hat mir ein Lied Erzählt."*

Then we sighted Cyprus, and the boat dropped anchor at Famagusta. I tried to tell my girl the story of Othello—but she was not the literary type. Late that night we packed our things, for it would only be a few hours more. We stood on deck long before land could be seen. An old hand told us that ships used to land at Jaffa in former days, but now they were diverted to Tel Aviv because of terrorist attacks. Our ship was one of the first to berth in the new harbor. As we approached the shore, the minarets of Jaffa could be seen and finally the white buildings of Tel Aviv. A motor launch came to meet us, and a British police inspector climbed aboard. Evidently the harbor installations were not yet completed, for our ship had to drop anchor offshore, and groups of us were brought to land in small boats.

In my boat, a student from Cologne had been clutching an old battered case, and when he took out his violin, he started to play gaily, *"Bei Mir Bist Du Schön"* and then, more formally, standing up, the *"Hatikvah."* One of the Jewish port workers pushed him. "Sit down, idiot!" The boat rocked, he fell onto the seat, and his violin was soaked. It was November 14, 1938. We had come out of Europe, and the Old World was already half forgotten.

PART TWO

Young Man Adrift: Palestine in Peace and War

SEVEN

The Eve of War

I *was seventeen years and six months old* when I arrived in what was then Palestine; when I left it almost seventeen years later, it was a different country even in name. The years I lived there were not of equal interest. While the war went on in Europe calm reigned in Palestine, but I discovered a new world, a community, a way of life I had not known before. Then, from 1946 to 1949, the pulse of history quickened, Palestine was suddenly propelled to center stage in world politics, and I could watch from close quarters the establishment of the State of Israel and the war for independence. The years after 1949, important as they were for the formation of the character of the new state, were bound to be an era of anticlimax. For me, for a variety of personal reasons, they were years of stress and strain.

The first day in Palestine was one of new and unfamiliar impressions. The streets were full and loud, everyone seemingly in a hurry. Even the smells were quite unfamiliar. For someone coming from Europe it felt like summer, even though it was mid-November. The light was certainly much brighter than in the northern regions. I knew no one in the city and attached myself to a young fellow passenger who claimed to know someone who would give us dinner and possibly put us up for the night. He did both; the news about the *Kristallnacht* persecutions had made a great impact, and there was much sympathy for new immigrants. In any case, hospitality in those faraway days was greater than in later years, even vis-à-vis newcomers from Germany, who were not particularly popular in this country. There was also more trust; most owners of apartments in Tel Aviv did not bother to lock their front doors when they went out, although Tel Aviv had even then the reputation as a den of iniquity. Elsewhere confidence was even more pronounced. If the door was locked, one could be certain that the key was to be found under the doormat.

Next day I proceeded to Jerusalem, a trip that nowadays takes less than an hour, certainly at night when traffic is sparse. In November 1938 the trip was more complicated and even adventurous. One had to queue up, to begin with, in a government office for a special permit under the defense regulations that had been promulgated as a result of the riots. Having received the pass, one had the choice of taking the train, a taxi shared with four or five others, or the bus. The train was considered unsafe (and was, in fact, suspended in late 1938), the taxi too expensive. So I went by bus, and the trip took some three hours, but then I was in no hurry. The first part of the journey passed quickly, but when after Latrun the ascent began through the hills of Judaea, the bus proceeded at a snail's pace, not so much because it could not go any faster but because the road had only two lanes and there was a long row of lorries in front of us heavily loaded with sand, stone, and big barrels. Furthermore, there were military checkpoints where the bus had to halt and the passes were examined. Next to the driver was a man with a Mauser, one of the more sophisticated weapons of the day, an automatic pistol that could be used as a carbine, but was quite ineffective beyond a certain range.

Eventually, having driven past beautiful rows of pine trees and countless rocks and ravines, we entered Jerusalem at a little past noon. First we saw a few houses. Then they disappeared again as we went into a valley, and then quite suddenly we were in the Holy City. The first impression (and the second and third) was anything but uplifting. It looked and smelled like an Oriental city such as I had read about in books. I heard a horrible noise like that emanating from a rusty pump handle; it was, in fact, a donkey next to my window. I had never heard a braying donkey before. The houses were small, in ugly colors and often derelict; the streets dusty and full of merchants advertising their merchandise. Between the houses there were open spaces where rubbish had been dumped. I did not know then that the entrance to Jerusalem leads through a market called Mahane Yehuda (the camp of Juda), picturesque and cheap, but not very pleasing aesthetically. A few minutes later we reached the bus station off Jaffa Street, the main street of Jewish Jerusalem in those days.

I had only one piece of luggage; the trunk had been sent on another ship and was to arrive only a month later. I proceeded to the central immigrants' home, which was in Abyssinian Street, in the center of town. The building was modestly equipped but perfectly adequate for the purpose it served. I had to share a room with several others, and the officials told me that I could stay only for a few days because there was insufficient space and new arrivals were expected. I do not know how I communicated in those days; I knew some rudimentary Hebrew but not enough for conversation at any length. My English, Yiddish, and Arabic were nonexistent, and speaking German in public was frowned upon. I went on a walk that confirmed my first impressions: Jerusalem looked poor and dilapidated; many houses were run-down. There were very few trees and no grass, only rocks and stones. Electricity and piped water from a central supply system had come to most of Jerusalem only a few years earlier. True, I did not know then the outlying quarters, which were quite different. In any case, Jerusalem was to change in later years very much for the better, perhaps the only town I know that changed to such a degree—mainly owing to the initiative of one mayor of genius.

Walking on this first day in Jerusalem in the street of the Prophets and the Abyssinians, I saw beyond the high walls houses hidden by pine trees, cypresses, and an occasional fig tree. Still, I spied some arches and narrow passages, unusual wrought-iron balconies and gateposts, the Lion of Judah carved in stone, and some inscriptions in letters I could not figure out. (It was Amharic.) There was a strange mixture of styles, Western and Oriental, Renaissance and neoclassic. Many of the houses had been built by Conrad Schick, a Protestant missionary who had settled in Jerusalem about 1850. In later years I came to know this neighborhood well, my office was there and Shlomit, our second daughter, was born here. This was the street of foreign consulates, of the homes of leading early Zionists; Jewish Jerusalem's first leading doctors had practiced here, Feigenbaum and Ticho and Helena Kagan. These were legendary figures, but at the time I had never heard of them, just as I did not know about Ben Yehuda, who had also lived in this street; more than anyone else, he had helped to revive the Hebrew language. As one historian summarized his life's work: Before Ben Yehuda, Jews could speak Hebrew, after him they did.

But this was 1938, I was new here, and not in a sentimental mood. I also discovered that Jerusalem was a smallish city. True, it had some hundred and thirty thousand inhabitants, but one did not go to the Old City because most of its inhabitants were Arabs and it was considered dangerous. (The British had reconquered it only a few weeks earlier.) Nor did I have any business in the Jewish orthodox neighborhoods, such as Meah She'arim, the quarter of the hundred gates, or the districts where the Jews from Oriental countries lived, such as the Bukharian quarters.

My Jerusalem consisted of a few dozen blocks, and many of

its residents were soon known by sight. It differed from any city I had known hitherto in that it was divided not so much according to social and financial status but according to ethnic origin. Since its population came from all over the globe, there was a bewildering variety of styles of houses, languages, clothes, and customs. To a certain extent the city has preserved its character to this day, providing an extraordinary laboratory for students of anthropology, linguistics, and sociology.

For a week or two I lived in a very cheap hotel named Babad, a few steps from the Mahane Yehuda market. The clientele consisted of new immigrants from Europe, and the conversations were instructive, since there were people of all age groups, professions, and walks of life. Thus, I remember long talks with a Viennese psychiatrist who had experimented with scopolamine, one of the wonder drugs of the 1930s, and who explained to me that the accused in the Moscow trials had made their incredible admissions because of this drug—there was no other explanation. It was an interesting theory but, as it later emerged, not the right one. Another man had written a historical play in German that, he told me, would be performed one day by Habima, the leading Hebrew theater. I had my doubts, but his self-confidence proved to be right. It was accepted and is shown to this day.

I had no money at all; according to the then-prevailing regulations in Nazi Germany, one was permitted to take only ten marks out of the country. But I had been given by my mother a heavy gold watch chain, and after a day or two I located a watchmaker (of whom there were surprisingly many) in Jaffa Street who looked more honest to me than the others and asked him how much he would give for a few links. He established in a few seconds that the chain was indeed solid gold, took out his heavy pliers, cut off a few links, and handed me ten pounds. I was now relatively rich and decided to leave the hotel and to move in with a young man from my hometown who was also about to begin his studies at the university. He was a few years older than I. Unlike me, he was a serious student who eventually became a leading geographer and the author of standard textbooks in his field. We found a room to share in Rehavia, which I thought, and still think, the most congenial quarter in the city. It is the general neighborhood south and west of the Jewish Agency Building, which in those prestate days was the seat of the leading institutions of the Jewish community of Palestine, also called the *yishuv*. It was a bourgeois quarter, heavily German-Jewish, with a lot of trees, shrubs, and little gardens. The streets were named after leading Jewish philosophers, travelers, and other sages of the Spanish period, the medieval "golden age." I had not heard of most of them, but they all sounded impressive—Abarbanel, Bartenura, Metudela, and so on.

The name Rehavia, I am told, appears in the Bible. The quarter was founded as a garden suburb in 1921, but then nothing much happened until the Central European immigrants began to arrive. In those days one heard more German spoken in the streets than Hebrew. Aesthetically it was a far cry from the noise, the dastardly smell of hot frying oil, and the general disorder of Mahane Yehuda. The panorama of the Judaean hills was spectacular. In later years I was to spend many happy, and some troubled, hours on the shadowy streets of Rehavia, but in 1938 this seemed well beyond my imagination.

My main daily meal I had in the trade union restaurant in the center of town; it cost, I believe, three piasters (or *grush*). The Palestine pound had 100 piasters or 1,000 mil. The coins looked strange—some had a hole in the middle. The food was barely edible; the culinary standards of Jewish Palestine were lamentable in those days. True, most people were poor, but they did not know how to cook either. Even for much more money it would have been difficult to eat well. For many years one went for a good meal to an Arab, Greek, or Armenian restaurant in the Old City, especially if one could not afford Hesse's and the King David.

In part, it was a matter of ideology. For the pioneers from Eastern Europe, who were the trendsetters, food was simply not important. It was considered stupid and even asocial to spend a lot of time, effort, and money on food, just as dress was a matter of supreme indifference. Shirts and trousers of cheap khaki were the unofficial uniform of Jewish Palestine.

After I had been in Jerusalem a few days, I went up to the university on Mount Scopus on the northern outskirts of town. The idea of a Jewish university had been mooted first toward the end of the last century, and at a Zionist Congress in 1913 a resolution to this effect had been passed and a committee appointed to raise funds. But the war intervened, and work on the building began only in 1921. The university was officially opened by Arthur Balfour, the former prime minister, in 1925; three professors had actually started teaching even before that date. The drive on the bus from the center of town was interesting. It led through quarters I had not seen before, such as Sheikh Jerah, and a big military cemetery in which the British and Allied soldiers fallen in the Palestine campaign of 1917 had been buried. Number 9 bus, I came to know your route by heart, every station, all the drivers, and eventually also most of the passengers.

The university was very small, smaller, in fact, than the Hadassa Hospital, on the other side of the road. There were only about five hundred students, nor was a major further influx envisaged. I presented myself at the reception department and soon faced further disappointments. I had originally wanted to study bacteriology, having read the books by Paul de Kruif that were very popular at the time. I was told that there was no Department of Medicine (let alone bacteriology) teaching undergraduates, and only a few small research departments for graduates from abroad. Those who wanted to study medicine had to enroll at the American university in Beirut—or at some European university; the situation in this respect did not change for another ten years.

My second choice was history. But there was only one professor teaching general history, a man from my hometown named Richard Koebner. He was a great authority in his field, the author of the section on the early Middle Ages in one of the famous British multivolume histories of Europe. He was a nice man, if somewhat withdrawn and shy, and his Hebrew was worse than mine. I had no interest whatsoever in the early Middle Ages and told him that my special interest was Eastern Europe. This was more than a little presumptuous, since I did not really know what I wanted. He asked me whether I had read Kliuchevsky's four-volume standard history of Russia, and I answered, partly truthfully, that I had, whereupon he told me that he could not teach me, since this was all he knew about the subject. At this stage of the conversation it dawned on me that my future was not on Mount Scopus and that I might drop out even before having started my academic career.

I am not sure whether I attended a single class but I mixed with the students and went to meetings, which were mainly political in character. Some were sponsored by the far Left, others by the extreme Right; there were no "Centrist" students. I soon realized that the others were much more determined and purposeful than I was. They knew exactly what they wanted to study. They were all a little older than I but I do not mention this as a mitigating circumstance, for it was not just a matter of immaturity. To study for another four years seemed pointless: I had no strong inclination in any particular direction; the money would run out well before I finished my studies, however frugally I lived; and a war in the near future seemed inevitable. What, then, was the alternative? For the next three or four weeks I went to see relations, friends, and acquaintances all over the country.

Traveling was bothersome in those days; in view of the defense regulations mentioned above, one needed a permit for every journey. But one could always be certain of a bed and a meal. "Bed," to be sure, was not to be taken literally; many a night I slept in a barn in a kibbutz, or on the kitchen floor or in the bathroom of the Tel Aviv and Haifa apartments belonging to Silesian aunts. These were only aunts twice removed, but cohesion was close during these months just before and during the war; it would have been unthinkable to turn away anyone at a time like this. They would have gladly given me a real bed, only there was none; five adults were sharing a small two- or three-room apartment. These people had been accustomed to houses and spacious flats, and they were now transplanted to a country where only the superrich had more than three rooms at their disposal. But those I knew did not grumble. I knew of only one exception, the well-known writer Arnold Zweig, who lived in Haifa. His unhappiness was rooted in the lack of recognition for an erstwhile best-selling author.

I went to many kibbutzim, mostly in the Jezreel and Jordan valleys, during my first months in the country. Staying overnight there was never a problem—it simply meant finding out who of the members would be away that night; a few were always absent for one reason or another. I had to share a tent or a room in a blockhouse with someone else, man or woman, but again only a few were grumbling. I made interesting and sometimes amusing acquaintances in this way. Meals in the kibbutzim were more than frugal, the budgetary allocation for these purposes was minimal, and the girls working in the kitchen had not much experience. There was no meat or chicken, neither fish nor eggs, neither cheese nor sausage, neither butter nor margarine, but bread was plentiful, also a soup with some lonely vegetables swimming on the surface, but without much fat, and, during the season, as many oranges as one wanted. In one kibbutz they had sunflower oil in which onions were roasted—this was the gourmet supplement to a slice of bread, and people came from afar to taste it.

To reach the kibbutz was not always easy. Some were located off a main road where buses passed by, but it often meant an additional walk of a mile in heavy rain or great heat. It was safer and, of course, cheaper, to catch, in either Haifa or Tel Aviv, the kibbutz truck that carried produce to town and brought back bags of fodder, fuel, and oil as well as sundry other commodities. One had to locate the truck, which was not always easy; one had to give a hand to the driver loading it or extracting it from the mud—a frequent occurrence during the rainy season. The seat next to the driver was usually taken by a pregnant woman, and the men had to brave the elements out in the open, or under a tarpaulin, if one was lucky. But these trips had a charm of their own, and I did not consider them a hardship.

Since I eventually became a member of a kibbutz, a few more explanations may be called for. The basic character of a kibbutz and how it operates is widely known. But what is true now was not true fifty years ago; in the early, "heroic" period, life in the kibbutzim was far more primitive. When I came to Palestine, there existed some fifty to sixty such settlements; with some exceptions they had been established only a few years earlier. Their number was rapidly growing: By the end of World War II seven out of a hundred Palestinian Jews lived in these collective settlements; today the ratio is only three out of a hundred.

Virtually all members were occupied in agriculture; the basic principle for each settlement was to be self-sustaining. Almost every kibbutz used to bake its own bread and sew its own clothes. The idea of division of labor had not yet widely percolated. There were three major and several minor kibbutz movements, some more radical than others in their politics. But there were also basic differences as far as the structure of the kibbutz, its institutions, and the daily routine were concerned. Thus the "United Kibbutz" believed in fairly sizable communes of three hundred, four hundred, and even more members, whereas the other two movements were firmly convinced that a community of more than one hundred to one hundred and fifty members would be too large to conform with the original ideals of communal life. It would be no longer a big family, a "face-to-face community," in sociological terminology.

I visited settlements of all three persuasions and found the smaller, more elitarian kibbutzim more attractive; it is also true that in the smaller kibbutzim there was more talk about politics. A cousin of mine lived in Kinneret, a few hundred yards from the lake and a few miles from Tiberias. This was the heartland of the kibbutz movement, where the first settlements had been established around 1910. My cousin was married to a medical doctor, now employed as an agricultural laborer. Both complained about the negative attitude of the older members toward the newcomers, who (they thought) were spoiled, unprepared for the hardships awaiting them—the climate, hard work, and disease, such as malaria. There were the usual tensions between immigrants from Eastern and Central Europe—there were few from English-speaking countries, or second-generation Palestinians, a handful from Italy, more from France. This was a major source of conflict, and I shall have to refer to it once again.

I found some of my friends from the youth movement in the kibbutzim. They had come in groups following the initiative of Henrietta Szold, an American who had settled in Palestine many years earlier. About twenty-five youngsters aged fourteen to sixteen, of more or less the same ethnic and cultural background, were in such groups; they would work half days in agriculture and the rest of the time there would be instruction in Hebrew, Jewish history, and general knowledge. In the circumstances this was probably the best possible arrangement in theory, if not always in practice.

At first sight, the kibbutzim looked all alike—except the very recent ones. They all were a few hundred yards in circumference, protected by barbed-wire entanglements. The center was the dining room—usually a big wooden shed, eventually a building of stone—and there was the inevitable watchtower. There was animal husbandry as well as a stable for horses, mules, and donkeys. At further scrutiny one recognized the differences. Not a single kibbutz was well off at the time, and only a few could make ends meet. But the older settlements had more experience and often also better land; over the years a fair number of stone buildings had been erected, first for the children, later for adults; trees and bushes had been planted; there was a lawn around the childrens' houses. In the newer kibbutzim, many members still lived in wooden sheds or tents; many young families had to share their room (or tent) with a third person—called *Primus*. There was no time and strength to clean the place up, and the entrance to the kibbutz often looked like a garage run by mechanics who had been called away in the middle of work. It was only much later that kibbutzim began to realize that the first aesthetic impression was, after all, of some importance.

At the end of my tour I decided to join a kibbutz. The way of life attracted me, but it was probably even more important that the kibbutz offered the kind of security that I missed in the city. Seen in this light it was an escapism of sorts and the end of my academic career before it had really begun; certainly it came as a grave disappointment to my parents. But they accepted it in good grace. From a letter written by my mother in the spring of 1939: "When I went to see the dentist yesterday, I told him that my son was working with mules and donkeys. He replied: I am willing to change with him any day." I was too old for one of the youth groups, and too young to join one of the existing kibbutzim. But there was a third way, to become a member of a training group, of which there existed not a few, and more were set up as new immigrants arrived. While on the lookout for a suitable group I decided to be a guest worker in Hazorea, the kibbutz southeast of Haifa that had been established by the Werkleute in the biblical village of Yokneam three years earlier. I arrived there early in January 1939 and stayed for three months. I was to return subsequently to this kibbutz as a member, and I shall have to say more about it later on.

Today it is an exemplary settlement in many respects, and several books have been written on its history. When I first worked there, it was at the beginning of its road, much smaller in area and membership, quite poor, but also in many respects a more lively place. The generation of the founders were in their middle or late twenties; the very oldest had barely turned thirty. The camp consisted of no more than two dozen small houses, mostly wooden shacks, as well as a few tents, not to mention the "lifts," containers that had been used to ship personal belongings from Europe and that now served as living quarters. The place of a newcomer was, of course, in a tent, and since the months of winter brought both severe cold and rain, and in high wind the tent tended to collapse, there was never a dull moment. Hazorea was situated at the foothill of a chain of mountains that constitute the Carmel. From time to time Arab snipers shot at us, always at night. There was never a determined attempt to penetrate the camp and storm it, though such attempts were made elsewhere. Since the chance to hit anyone from such a distance at night was virtually nil, these "attacks" (for such they were called in the newspapers) struck me as perfectly senseless. Only once I got angry: the sniping occurred one night when I was running a high temperature, and the golden rule was to proceed to the dining hall (which was of stone) whenever an "attack" happened. That night it occurred to me that I was more likely to die as a result of getting out of bed than by being hit by a sniper's bullet. There were other such minor annoyances, such as the mud after a heavy rain; deep, gluey, all-pervasive. There were no paved paths in those days. I had never known anything like this. Luckily, I followed the advice of a friend soon after my arrival in Palestine and bought a pair of rubber Wellingtons; they were very cheap and without them one was lost. In addition, one stood a fair chance in those days of catching malaria or typhoid fever or, at the very least, paratyphoid. But I was lucky in this respect.

Hazorea did not have enough land at the time; a mere 1,400 dunam, about 350 acres. There were some fruit trees, a few cows, a chicken coop, and a sizable herd of sheep, 200 to be precise. No agricultural settlement was believed to be complete in those days without a herd of sheep. The figure of the shepherd was thought as essential as that of a tractor driver; it was the symbol of our return to nature. At the end of twenty years the sheep and shepherds had vanished; our agriculturists realized that these herds needed a lot of attention, and the income was far too low to make this branch profitable. It was part of the general revolution that took place, as a result of which agriculture has changed out of recognition. But when I first came, it still meant heavy manual labor with the same implements that had been used for many centuries.

Together with a dozen other members I was employed planting trees in the hills above Hazorea. We took a rifle or two, but no one ever bothered us. The technique could be mastered in a few minutes. I found the physical effort not too arduous, but the monotony (like that of much agricultural labor) was depressing. True, conversation went on much of the time, but after a week or two I had heard most of the anecdotes and jokes of my fellow workers. I should not complain, for I had less to contribute to the conversation than the others. The most entertaining was a young man from Baghdad, but we also had a lecturer in canonical law from the University of Sassari in Sardinia. The background of the others was similar to mine, except that one had a doctorate in philosophy, another in law.

As in Frankfurt, I was an outsider and did not make any close friends, being the youngest and more than a bit self-conscious. Still, these months taught me a bit of the spoken language and the use of the essential agricultural tools. In any case, I had never intended to stay for long, and when I heard in early March of 1939 that a new training group was about to be organized in one of the settlements in the Jordan Valley, I packed my few belongings, expressed my thanks to the secretary of Hazorea, and took the next bus to Tiberias.

How to summarize my impressions of the first months in the country? The landscape had its attractions: The winter was dreary, but the spring, with the pervasive sweet smell from the citrus groves, was wonderful. It was difficult not to feel on top of the world on a sunny spring day; alas, I did not know then how much we would suffer from the summer heat in these preair-conditioned days, especially in the Jordan Valley, which was to be my next station.

Of the cities, I liked Haifa best; its location is striking, whereas Tel Aviv always seemed to me an undistinguished and rather ugly place. In Turkish days Haifa had been a sleepy village—in my 1905 guidebook, it is barely mentioned; Tel Aviv, of course, was founded only in 1909. Theodor Herzl visited Haifa forty years before I did, and being a visionary, he wrote about the ocean liners that would one day anchor in the harbor and about thousands of imposing villas on the top of the Carmel. It did not take long for these fantasies to come true. Jerusalem, in those days, seemed exotic but dirty—and a provincial backwater.

What of the people? It was a small country but not easy to get to know, even if superficially. I was struck by the great cultural and social differences between Jews from different countries. True, even in my limited life experience I was aware of the fact that every human being was different. But I was not prepared for such a tower of Babel—groups of people looking different, behaving differently, speaking a hundred languages and dialects. Bulgaria and Romania are neighboring countries, yet Jews from Sofia and Bucharest had little if anything in common, not even their prayers, for the Romanians were Ashkenazi, whereas the Bulgarians followed the Sephardic rites. Living for a while in a Romanian kibbutz, I soon realized that those who were born in Bessarabia (Moldavia) had Russian (or Yiddish) as their native tongue, those from Bukovina had grown up in the Viennese cultural tradition, the Transylvanians were Hungarians to all intents and purposes, whereas the only "real" Romanians were the natives of "Regat" (the original "little Romania," which included such cities as Bucharest and Jassy). I had known that Jews from Iraq and Yemen were "Oriental" Jews, but socially and culturally they were light-years apart. I had known about Polish Jews, but was quite unaware of the specific character of Lithuanian Jewry, which set it apart from Galician Jews, not to mention the assimilated Jews from Warsaw and Cracow.

Would the Palestinian melting pot make one people, one nation, out of these motley groups from all over the world? It did happen faster than I, or anyone else, anticipated. Within two generations many of the seemingly deep dividing lines disappeared, with, admittedly, one major and several minor exceptions. The major exception was Moroccan Jewry, but they arrived only much later on the scene and were not part of my immediate experience.

I did mention that German Jews were not popular, and this

did not change until the first generation of them had disappeared. They had the reputation of being honest, reliable, and
hard-working, but they were also thought to be arrogant, too
rigid, lacking a sense of humor. They were said to be stiff and
formal, lacking warmth—there was, according to general belief,
very little about them that was specifically Jewish, which is to
say their mentality and manners did not correspond with the
outlook of small-town East Europeans. Their contribution to the
cultural life of the community was decisive, since most of the
leading scientists, physicians, artists, and judges had been
trained in Germany. There was public esteem for them, despite
the countless jokes about the *Jeckes*. But there was little love
lost. Six or seven of them served in later years as government
ministers, but German Jewry as such never became part of the
political establishment.

Strange as it may appear, I was from the beginning almost as
much interested in the Arabs as in the Jews. Berl Katznelson,
one of the spiritual gurus of Labor Zionism, had some bitter
words to say about the pioneers from Central Europe, who,
having just arrived, were already more preoccupied with the
rights of the Arabs than of the Jews. There was a grain of truth
in this observation, and I was certainly among those castigated.
There was an element of curiosity on our part in an exotic people,
but there was also the realization that it was absolutely crucial
to attain a modus vivendi with the other people residing in Palestine—who also happened to be the majority. Thus, a few months
after my arrival, I began to study the Arab language; I never
really mastered it, though I could eventually read a newspaper,
and after mingling with Arab villagers (and Bedouins) during
the war years and living in an Arab village for a year, I acquired
a working knowledge of Arabic. On occasion, I served as the
translator of the physician from Berlin-Alexanderplatz then residing in the kibbutz. I only hope that I have not been the cause
of any medical mishap as a result. I became friendly with some
of the leading figures in the field of Jewish-Arab cooperation

and contributed frequently to their journal (*Be'ayot*). It was an uphill struggle, and I shall report later on the setbacks and disappointments suffered by the pioneers of reconciliation between the two peoples.

When I arrived in Palestine in November 1938, the Arab insurrection had reached its climax. Virtually every day the newspapers reported the assassination of one or more Jews and Britons. The total number of victims during the year was 835 (compared with a mere 97 in 1937); it might in fact have been twice as high, because the number of reported victims among the Arab bands was usually incomplete. Considering that the whole Jewish community consisted of little more than four hundred thousand people at the time, these figures were quite high. Furthermore, in October 1938, the hold of the government outside the Jewish regions and the bigger urban centers had virtually ceased to exist. The railway to Jerusalem no longer operated; civil administration no longer functioned; police and army patrols could move about only in large groups, and eventually the Old City of Jerusalem was taken over by the insurgents. It was the height of the rebellion, and at the same time the beginning of the end.

Thus, I lived through a major civil war, yet to the best of my recollection one did not feel any special fear or excitement. It was not just the obtuseness of a newcomer; I think most reacted as I did. The brunt of the attack was borne by a few people in outlying settlements; the rest barely knew that a war was going on. It confirms an old and trite observation that unless one happens to be the victim, life goes on as usual even in a war. Furthermore, there was the news from abroad, the horrible plight of German, Austrian, and Czech Jewry, and the virtual certainty that soon there would be a world war. I read with disbelief the accounts of battles and ambushes, in foreign newspapers sent to me by parents and friends from abroad, in which I had allegedly been involved. Why all this fuss about nothing? Again, in retrospect, the lack of alarm seemed not to have been mere bravado; it was based on vague feelings that while a great deal of bloodshed might be ahead, the incidents we faced were not the first battles of that great war.

As the situation deteriorated, the British brought reinforcements from Egypt and within several weeks smashed the revolt; they systematically combed the villages and carried out mass arrests. The Arabs had made the mistake of operating in big formations, which were no match for regular soldiers. The British commander in Haifa, who made a very competent impression, was an obscure major general named Montgomery; within a few years his fame was to spread all over the world. He said in a press conference that the public should have a little patience, that within a few weeks or months the problem would be solved. He proved to be right.

By the end of 1938 the British had arrested two thousand Arab suspects (and also quite a few Jews). Of these Arabs, some were no doubt detained unjustly, but others were not, and since there was only a limited reservoir of manpower as far as the insurgents were concerned—most of them villagers, only a few came from town—the insurrection soon ran out of steam and the remaining gangs escaped to Syria. The British acted harshly: when Moffat, the acting assistant district commissioner in Jenin, was killed, the authorities blew up one hundred and fifty houses in that town; following the murder of a sergeant major in Baka al Garbia, fifty-three houses were demolished. There was an outcry in various parts of the world about these cruel actions, but they were effective. Baka simply could not afford to lose another fifty-three houses. And thus, individual acts of terror continued, but the insurgency petered out, with the heads of the bands escaping abroad.

In later years the question of political violence increasingly preoccupied me; the terrorism I witnessed in Palestine, from 1938 to 1939 and again after the war, naturally influenced my thinking. It struck me early on that the basic issues in guerrilla warfare and terrorism are quite obvious, yet there is strong resistance to accepting them. Guerrilla warfare and terrorism are the weapons of the weak, and their hope to prevail rests on the assumption that they will engage in irregular warfare, whereas the armed forces of the state will have to stick to traditional rules. This assumption may be correct with regard to democratic societies, but these, too, will be bound by their own rules only as long as the irregular enemy does not constitute a real danger. Once the foe threatens the very existence of the state, its full power will be brought against the assailant, and this sooner rather than later will spell doom for the insurgents. There have been exceptions to this rule, but little Palestine was not among them. Mao Tse-tung had once noted that what was true with regard to China did not necessarily apply to Belgium, but this dictum has been overlooked by many of his imitators.

The Arab insurrection of 1936–1938 was not a rebellion headed by saintly characters. There was much plain brigandage, and the rebels killed more Arabs than Jews and Englishmen. The figures for 1939 were 414 Arabs killed by other Arabs, 199 Jews, and 37 British. There was a tug of war between the Husseinis (the family of the Jerusalem muftis) and other leading clans such as the Nashashibis. But this insurrection was also in part a genuine movement of national liberation. Most of the Arabs felt themselves threatened by the influx of Jewish settlers, whom they considered dangerous Communists (as Jamal Husseini put it) and who, in any case, were alien elements. If it was pointed out to them that the Jews of Europe faced a catastrophe, they argued that this was not the Arabs' fault, and why should they bear the burden? Unfortunately, the Jews of Europe, their historical connection with Palestine quite apart, had nowhere else to go, whereas the Arab nation had almost limitless Lebensraum from Morocco to the Persian Gulf. It was a tragic conflict between the rights of two peoples, one fighting for its physical survival, the other for its historical rights, its land, its dignity. It never occurred to me to belittle or deny the Palestinian Arab case; had I been born a Palestinian Arab, my place would have been with them. But I was not born a Palestinian Arab, and thus found myself on the other side of an increasingly wider divide.

Individual attacks continued during the spring of 1939, in the Haifa region, in Tiberias and Jerusalem. But the spirit had gone out of the revolt; more and more Arab men could be seen wearing the tarbush rather than the kaffiyeh even though this was considered an act of national betrayal by the insurgents. More and more Arab villagers who had been terrorized before collaborated with the authorities against the unwelcome guests. The only remaining gang leader was one Abu Durra, a robber with uncertain political credentials. The adoption of the White Paper by the British government in May 1939 strictly limiting Jewish immigration and land purchase was considered by many Arabs a victory and also helped to defuse the conflict. If there were riots during this last summer of peace, they were more often than not initiated by Jews protesting against the closing of the gates of Zion. Illegal immigration became more frequent, and the security forces began to devote most of their resources to intercepting "illegal" vessels, detaining and deporting the new arrivals.

At the same time a wave of terrorism was carried out by the Irgun, the extreme nationalist organization, directed against both British and Arab; for good measure they also killed some Jews, robbed banks, and, in at least one instance, the Stern gang tried to contact the Germans after the outbreak of the war with the view of establishing a common front against British imperialism. The British authorities in Palestine retaliated by imposing curfews on the main cities, stopping traffic, and seizing miserly arms depots in outlying Jewish settlements that were quite obviously scheduled for self-defense only. There were casualties when fire was opened on ships arriving from Nazi-occupied Europe carrying illegal immigrants. The months just before the outbreak of the war were quite unhappy ones, but I did not feel the tensions so acutely simply because I did not live in town, and life in these small agricultural settlements went on pretty much as before.

This, in briefest outline, was the general political background when, in late March 1939, I presented myself in Kibbutz Sha'ar

Hagolan in the Jordan Valley, having passed Tiberias on my
way.

Sha'ar Hagolan, the gate to the Golan Heights, was then two
years old; it had been established by settlers from Czechoslovakia
and Poland in a region that was almost entirely populated by
kibbutzim. The land was fertile but the climate in summer exceedingly difficult; we were some three hundred meters (990
feet) below sea level, one of the lowest populated areas on earth.
A few minutes' walk from the dining room of Sha'ar Hagolan
one reached the river Yarmuk—rivulet would be a more correct
term—which happened to be the Syrian border. In 1938 this
border was little more than an abstraction, for there was not even
smuggling in those days; in later years the border became a
dangerous, deadly reality.

Our group gradually assembled; we were about fifteen young
men and women, almost all of German and Austrian origin,
some with more experience in agriculture than others. They put
us up in tents; work was relatively pleasant—I remember with
some nostalgia the vineyards and watering the banana plantations. True, as summer approached it became hotter and hotter
and the working day was adjusted accordingly; one went up with
the first light, and the lunch break lasted from eleven to two or
even three. Afternoons were usually more tolerable because
there was a light breeze. The nights were difficult because in this
pre-DDT age, one had to sleep under a mosquito net, which is
to say there was no air at all. Still, some very small sand flies
penetrated even these nets and they brought a very unpleasant
disease, named pappataci—a few days of very high temperature,
followed by general weakness and depression. It resembled malaria but it was not recurrent. I had a bad attack of pappataci,
and following it, I was for two weeks detailed to do guard duty
on the watchtower in the center of the settlement. Even before
that I had been sworn in as a *ghaffir*, an auxiliary policeman,
which meant that I had the right to carry a rifle at certain times
of the day or night. Furthermore, I had to work a powerful

searchlight on top of the watchtower to verify that no one was approaching the barbed wire surrounding the camp. I think I also had some Verey lights to fire in an emergency. The job was considered a sinecure, but I took it more seriously than the labor in the fields simply because of the responsibility I felt.

I well remember those nights. One by one the settlers went to bed and the lights inside the camps were put out. (We tent dwellers, needless to say, had only paraffin lamps.) In the distance one saw the lights of Tiberias and half a dozen or more searchlights from other settlements. Out in the open the temperature after midnight became pleasant, and I shall not forget the sky because never again have I seen so many stars; I wish my astronomical background had been a little stronger. While watching and listening, there was still plenty of time to think about the old world that I had left and that now was inexorably moving toward a war, and also about my past and future. Yet there was no danger of getting immersed too deeply in those dreams, for every now and then there would be the most awful noise, sometimes a solo performance by a wild dog or a jackal or even a hyena and sometimes a disharmonious choir. After midnight one of the girls doing night duty in the children's home would bring me tea and a sandwich and we would chat for a few minutes. My shift ended at dawn. It was difficult to sleep even for a few hours in the heat of the day, and my social life also suffered because I could not participate in the various activities that took place in the evening. Still, I remember with nostalgia these Jordan nights.

One day a professional photographer came to the settlement and he took a picture of me in uniform, with the rifle, and one of the kibbutz children giving a glass of water to the thirsty but smiling warrior. There was, alas, nothing spontaneous about this picture; the whole scene was carefully staged. But it looked eminently natural and spontaneous, and the picture was reproduced at the time in many countries.

On weekends and on holidays (of which there were not many in those days) one went to Lake Tiberias for a swim or for a visit to another kibbutz, such as the two Deganias, or Bet Sera, or Afikim or Ashdot Ya'akov. I always liked swimming in the Kinneret (as Lake Tiberias is known in Hebrew) even though there was not much of a beach, just a few yards of reed between the main road and the water. The kibbutzim in this general neighborhood developed well in later years. Degania was almost invaded in 1948; there is an ancient tank at its entrance. It does not look very formidable now, but since the settlers had merely rifles and Molotov cocktails to defend themselves, the danger was quite real. Sha'ar Hagolan seemed indefensible in May of 1948 and was evacuated for a day or two; when the settlers returned they found that all the houses, all their belongings, and the whole inventory had been destroyed and they had to start building the settlement from scratch.

Afikim was the only kibbutz to have a factory even in those early days; it produced plywood. Ashdot Ya'akov belongs to the many kibbutzim that split in the early 1950s for political reasons. These were acrimonious, bitter, doctrinal quarrels that made enemies out of old friends and divided families. I have a reasonably good knowledge of the recent history of Palestine and Israel, but hard as I try I can remember only vaguely what the quarrels were all about, and I am sure that the present generation of settlers knows even less. I learned at a relatively early stage in life that political views should interfere with personal relations only in extreme circumstances.

Tiberias is still a small town; then it was even smaller. It has now become a tourist center with many hotels and restaurants. There are aquatic sports for almost every taste on the lake and in water amusement parks. The hot springs of Hammat are frequented by thousands of Israelis suffering with rheumatism every winter, and Christian pilgrims take a dip in the Jordan. Only Zemah, the erstwhile railway station, no longer exists; its Arab residents left in April 1948. The annual swim across the Kinneret takes place in late spring; the finishing line is in Ein Gev, a small fishing kibbutz in my day. Now it has an auditorium that can seat five thousand during its annual musical festival.

The palms of Kinneret and Degania, smuggled out of Iraq even before my time, are still there, but the Jordan Valley is now air-conditioned, its agriculture more productive than ever, though it employs far fewer people. More now work in a variety of small factories. A good friend and Breslau classmate of mine is the chief engineer in one of them; he has to read all the professional literature and to visit exhibitions in Europe and America. All this was well beyond our imagination in those faraway days. When we shared a tent, there was not even electricity, and now I get faxes from my friend in Sha'ar Hagolan.

In the Jordan Valley, politics were far away. A visit to the city was a rare event, and newspapers arrived in the evening or only the next day. In the dining hall there was a big radio set; no individual had a radio in those days or would have been permitted to have one. Some evenings we tried to tune in to shortwave stations, mainly British, German, and Russian. I remember listening to Neville Chamberlain's Birmingham speech in which for the first time he made it clear that he had reached the painful conclusion that one could not do business with "Herr Hitler," as he was then called. But many evenings I was simply too tired to listen or the dining room got too hot despite the fans that had been installed to make it a little more tolerable.

In the meantime the British government had shelved plans to divide Palestine as suggested by two royal commissions (Peel and Woodward) in 1937 and 1938. The Peel Commission had produced an excellent, most competent, and, on the whole, fair report, which to this day is perhaps the most reliable assessment of the situation in the 1930s, a model of precision.

But the government adopted a new White Book (1939), which to all intents and purposes announced the end of the Mandate and the revocation of the Balfour Declaration. There were mass demonstrations and many arrests. A day of mourning was declared, but all this affected us only marginally in the faraway Jordan Valley. The bananas had to be watered and the cows fed. It was unreasonable to assume that a great power (for such was Britain in those days) preparing for a major conflict would be deflected from its course of action by demonstrations or even acts of terror taking place in a faraway country of no particular importance.

What had happened to my parents after my departure? They continued to write twice a week, and on occasion they sent a little parcel with newspapers and a bar of chocolate, almost hermetically sealed to survive the heat of the Jordan Valley. While they were disappointed with my agricultural career, they were glad that I was abroad. From time to time they asked whether I could not provide a document saying that they were in line for a certificate of immigration. I tried but could not help them to get visas; they did not belong to any of the few categories that still qualified, and they were too old to be considered for illegal emigration.

In their letters they could no longer write about what life was really like—the fact that their telephone had been taken away and that many other restrictions and chicanes had been imposed. They reported meetings with relations and acquaintances who were about to leave, and what some of my contemporaries had been writing to their parents from various parts of the globe. My cousin from Schweidnitz got married on the eve of her departure for Shanghai; my mother went shopping with her. My father's sixtieth birthday in July was one of the last occasions for a family get-together. He received presents—a few bottles of wine and some cigars. I had been asked for a recent photograph, which I provided. The day after, he sent me a report of the proceedings, describing his elegiacal mood, the daily walk along the promenade, thoughts about his life's balance sheet—much of his life had been concerned with balance sheets. He saw few assets; I was one of the few, and he hoped I would not disappoint him.

After war had broken out, direct communication ceased. But there was still the occasional letter sent via Holland or Switzerland. They were addressed to my Amsterdam uncle, the one who had first produced synthetically the male hormone, or to a friend from school named Alex, now in Zurich. I answered through the same channels; in this way they learned that Naomi and I were living together. We did not tell them that our formal marriage was still a year or two ahead. Nor did we describe later on the wedding ceremony—with the Haifa rabbi trying to conclude the proceedings in record time in the middle of an air raid, with rings that had been borrowed, and with building workers from a nearby site as witnesses.

Who was Naomi? Why had I never mentioned the name? I should have been perhaps a little more forthcoming. I should have told them that a girl had recently arrived from Jerusalem to join our group. I had heard many wonderful things about her before, that she would be a tremendous asset to our group. Some of my comrades had been with her earlier in Ben Shemen, the children's village. She came and, though she had no intentions of the kind, she conquered; after five minutes I ceased to regard her as an asset to the community but wanted her for myself, a typical example of bourgeois egotism prevailing over the collectivist ethos.

At eighteen one is not very communicative about one's private affairs, as I was reminded when my daughters reached that age. And in any case I could always argue that I did not want various wartime censors to read about these intimate things. So I mentioned only the bare essentials, and so did Naomi. I think we did send pictures, but I am no longer sure even about that. The parents on both sides were horrified; Naomi's father in the far-away Caucasus was mortified that I had not formally approached him. I could have explained that there were certain technical difficulties, the change in manners and customs quite apart. Wisely, I did not even try. With luck, I would have received an answer in six or eight months—an eternity, especially if one is young and in love, with a war going on.

Then Holland was occupied and Switzerland cut off from the outside world. The only way of communication was by means of Red Cross circulars with the text of the message limited to twenty-five words. I have kept these letters. They informed me that Grandmother had died, that my parents had moved to a room in Victoria Street, which they apparently shared with another relation or two. Then in June of 1942 came the last message: Soon they were to be deported to the East. The actual words used were slightly different, but the meaning was clear.

After the war, I received a letter from an uncle who lived in a "privileged mixed marriage" and thus survived the war—in Auschwitz. He had accompanied my parents on their last journey to the meeting point that had been indicated and stayed there until the police chased him away. The transport went to a camp near Lublin in southern Poland named Belžec, where they were murdered a few days after their arrival.

EIGHT

Kibbutz Life

I *stayed in Sha'ar Hagolan* during the summer and autumn of
1939, and then shortly after the outbreak of war in Europe our
group moved on to another kibbutz named Ein Shemer, located
among orange groves in a valley about midway between Tel Aviv
and Haifa, a few miles from the Mediterranean. Our status was
still that of apprentices, but after less than a year in Ein Shemer
our ways parted, Naomi and I joined Kibbutz Shamir near Haifa
as members, and when Shamir split we went to Hazorea. There
I had begun my kibbutzic career and I was to end it there in
1944. Thus, in my five years in a kibbutz, I went through the
various stages of apprenticeship, candidacy, and membership. I
soon realized that one kibbutz was not like another, that there
were basic differences between these communities, partly be-

cause of the age of the settlers, but also as a consequence of the ethnic-social origin of the members. In any case, the kibbutz of 1940 about which I am now going to write was quite different in most respects from the kibbutz of 1990. It had already moved far from the commune of the very early days (1920), even though in 1940 a mere twenty years had passed since the foundation of the earliest communes, which were something like an extended family.

About Ein Shemer I do not remember much, except, of course, that Naomi and I met there and that after a few weeks of court-ship—not quite in the tradition of the manners and customs of the bourgeois milieu from which the two of us hailed—we de-cided to move into what was then known as a family tent. But there were, alas, not enough tents, and so we had to share it with various third persons, sometimes male, sometimes female, which was not too comfortable for us, and must have been embarrassing for them. Later, in Shamir, we had a tiny room in a wooden shack, which was, in a way, progress. However, the roof was of corrugated iron; in summer the room was intolerably hot, and in winter, when it rained, the noise was more deafening than a cannonade. When it was not raining, we had to listen to the conversations, the snoring, and the other inevitable human noises from left and right, for the partition was of the thinnest plywood. On balance I preferred the monotonous noise of the rain. There was a communal washroom, and toilets, too, were a considerable distance, a nuisance in summer and a real hardship in winter because the paths were not paved.

If kibbutz food had been poor before the outbreak of the war, it deteriorated through 1939 and 1940 because of the war. Exports and imports dwindled, except from the neighboring countries, and these were not major customers for citrus fruits, the traditional export goods. There was virtually no meat, no fish, no eggs, but there were noodles, rice, and bulgur, and all kinds of vegetables and fruits. Unfortunately, those running the kitchen had no idea how to make the most of the available goods; perhaps they wanted to show that the allocation for food was insufficient. While the split along ethnic lines between the Romanian and German members of Shamir had a variety of reasons, the propensity of the Romanian cooks to prepare an inedible maize dish called *mamaliga* greatly contributed to this collective divorce. I have since eaten excellent mamaliga, just as I have become almost a devotee of borscht, but I really suffered as a result of what went under the name of mamaliga and borscht in 1940.

The communal dining room was more than primitive, the equipment even more so. Some eight people faced each other sitting at a rectangular table, of which there were a dozen. We always received the main dish first and soup thereafter; there was only one aluminum plate for each person, and the main dish had to be eaten first since, however miserable, it was rationed, whereas soup was free. Everyone got a spoon, but there were only one or two knives for each table, so one had to learn to prepare a sandwich or even to cut tomatoes or cucumbers with the help of a spoon if there was no time to wait. Needless to say, there was no dessert, except on rare occasions when something was presented as fruit soup—not-too-sweet water in which a lonely prune or erstwhile dried apricot had been placed.

Cigarettes were rationed to a few a day, and at times there were none, but tobacco could be bought cheaply from our Arab neighbors, and so I learned early on the art of rolling one's own cigarettes. I missed tobacco less than an occasional piece of chocolate or a sweet, but these were not available except perhaps for the little children. There was a semilegal way to get around it. If one worked outside the kibbutz, one was given the bus fare, and if one decided to walk instead, or hitchhike, the money thus saved could be spent on halvah, the famous Oriental sweet. On a very hot summer afternoon we would walk two miles through deep sand to the grocer in the nearby village to buy a little piece of halvah. We must have been very hungry indeed.

Perhaps it was only to the good that we were given so little sugar, for dental care was less than useless. In Hazorea we had the benefit of Dr. Hillel Schachtel, a fine old gentleman who came from my hometown, a real intellectual and a leading Zionist of the first hour. But he had evidently spent more time in politics than in dentistry, and the tools at his disposal were antediluvian. In our days of high-speed drills it is difficult even to describe the torture caused by a drill driven by a foot pedal; and pain-killing injections were not available either. At various times the kibbutz could not pay the monthly dues to the Sick Fund, and as a result, medical services were withdrawn, though never for very long.

Hygienic conditions were deplorable. Old newspapers could replace toilet paper; there were no such obvious replacements for women's sanitary napkins, and for long periods there were no condoms. If I remember correctly, there was not even enough money for postage, and we were limited to one or two airmail letters a month. There were only three or four women's overcoats that were passed around whenever one of the women had to go to town.

Clothing in those faraway days was communal; there were no "private" shirts, trousers, and often no shoes either. Every Friday afternoon one went to the communal laundry for a set of work clothes and another set for after work. They virtually never fit; furthermore, they were heavily patched and likely to disintegrate before the end of the week. Since there was no money to buy new clothing, the standing order for our seamstresses was to add patches upon patches.

I have not mentioned the furniture in our rooms. There were iron beds that unfortunately were infested with bedbugs. On alternative Sundays these had to be destroyed with the help of a blowtorch (burning on paraffin). Mattresses consisted of sacks filled with maize leaves, not the softest of material, but there was also the occasional cob, likely to cause major inconvenience during the night. There were neither tables nor chairs nor cupboards. Orange boxes were used as cupboards, and we sat on oil canisters covered with sackcloth.

The list of deprivations and hardships could be endlessly prolonged. I remember days in Ein Shemer when I could not go to work because I had no shoes. But all this did not dampen the spirit of young people, and there was no feeling of acute unhappiness. After all, there was a war on, and there were parts of Europe in which conditions were considerably worse. Shared poverty was easier to bear. At the same time, we were worse off than our Arab neighbors in Kiri, Abu Srek, or Abu Shusha. I had frequent dealings with Arab villagers; an invitation to a meal in an Arab village or in a Bedouin tent was a real event; unfortunately, there was no way I could reciprocate.

I did not really mind poverty and even subacute hunger. But I have to admit that I developed a strong dislike for various kinds of manual labor. When we were in Shamir, some miles northeast of Haifa, not far from Kfar Ata, where Palestine's leading textile plant was located at the time, almost all the men went to work outside. The kibbutz had no land and was waiting for its turn to settle, which it eventually did, somewhere in Upper Galilee. In the meantime most of us went early every morning to the industrial region in Haifa Bay. This more often than not meant work on building sites—mixing concrete and passing it by means of a bucket or a little wheelbarrow on to the builders on the scaffolding. Since the builders who came from town were paid for piecework, and we were not, there was a conflict of interest; they wanted us to work fast, and we had no incentive.

On occasion we would comply with their demand, as in the case of the Haifa refineries. After Italy had declared war, it was widely assumed that they would bomb these installations. Hence it was decided to build concrete walls between the oil reservoirs so as to prevent a fire from spreading. This was considered a very dangerous assignment at the time; we worked with one eye to the sky, since no one wanted to be engulfed in an inferno of flames. But we overestimated the ability of the Italians to inflict damage. True, they did bomb Haifa three times in July and September 1940; on the last occasion some forty Arabs were killed. Tel Aviv was bombed in September 1940, and there were more than a hundred dead. This was perhaps the greatest catastrophe that ever befell the small Jewish community; yet to this day I do not know where the bombs fell, for Tel Aviv seemed far away. Owing to censorship, no details were given in the press, and by the time I came to visit the city again, months later, the air raid was already history. How the Italians could have managed to miss the Haifa oil refineries, a landmark visible for many miles, I do not know, but after 1940 there were no more air raids.

Then I worked for a while in a big military camp named Kurdani, a much quieter place, near the sea. The British sergeant in charge, obviously a trade unionist, did not expect that we would overexert ourselves for the risible wage we received. On certain days there was no work at all because certain shipments had been delayed. We would go for a swim at the nearby beach.

Unloading ships in the Haifa harbor was heavy work but relatively well paid and more interesting. The bags we carried were exceedingly heavy, but once one had mastered the technique, it was not really dangerous or unpleasant work except if we had to carry frozen meat, because the frozen carcasses, unlike the sacks of sugar and salt, of peas and lentils, did not adjust themselves to one's back.

Lastly, and most interestingly, there was work in a factory that had just been built by a number of kibbutzim. It was called Na'aman, located near the entrance of Acre, the crusaders' town; it produced bricks and also certain ceramic products. Work in the big, hot ovens was considered unhealthy, and there were long rest periods after each shift; if one was lucky, one was sent to work on the funicular. It led to the beach on one end and inland on the other, and it carried to the factory sand and earth needed for the production of bricks. The factory, I believe, exists to this day, though its methods of production have changed radically.

There were good times and bad, but on the whole I was not too tired at the end of a long work day; we got up at five in the morning and returned home at six in the evening six days a week. But I lacked motivation and had no sympathy for the teachings of A. D. Gordon (1856–1922), which were quite influential in the kibbutzim at the time. Gordon's philosophy was, very briefly, that mankind (and the Jews more than the rest) had been swayed too much in the direction of the intellect; they had become uprooted as far as nature—the cosmos—was concerned. There was no cure for their ills but through a return to nature. Gordon preached something akin to a religion of labor, and, unlike Tolstoy, he practiced what he preached. At the age of forty-eight, quite unprepared for manual labor, he went to Palestine and worked in the orchards, vineyards, and citrus groves.

I was not impervious to the beauties of nature. I liked to watch things grow, though I never understood why my spiritual salvation should be in hard and dirty work in difficult climatic conditions. Gordon was lucky precisely because his work was in the orchards, the orange groves, and the vineyards; from this vantage point it is not difficult to admire nature's works. Something can be said even in favor of driving a tractor, though it tends to get a little monotonous after a while. But I doubt whether Gordon ever worked with a combine-harvester on a hot summer day with the enervating easterly wind, the *khamsin*, covering one's face and limbs with dirt and dust until one could not see even through one's protective glasses. I wonder whether he ever worked in maize fields a few weeks after sowing, kneeling all day pulling out the surfeit of plants. Or whether he had to dig, in stony ground, deep holes, or trenches with a pickax, or whether he was ever employed in roadwork in those premechanized days. It is not too pleasant work even now, but then it was infinitely worse and did not help to transform human life to rediscover a sense of cosmic unity and holiness.

Manual labor, as Gordon envisaged it, was the contemplative and harmonious life of a shepherd or a gardener. Agricultural work, as I came to know it, was not conducive to satisfaction and peace of mind. Much of the work seemed to me not only difficult but pointless; why not have machines to do the unpleasant work? It was my personal misfortune that I was exposed to agriculture during the last phase of traditional methods. Within the next ten years a technological revolution took place, mechanizing or even automatizing much of the work. Within one generation agriculture has changed more dramatically than during thousands of years previously. If friends and acquaintances talk these days about gardening, they mean, of course, growing roses and cutting shrubs—preferably by means of some power tools. Even work in market gardening has changed out of recognition. But for me Courbet's women kneeling in the fields rather than Watteau's shepherd in an idyllic landscape continue to symbolize agriculture.

The belief in manual labor as a redeeming factor has all but vanished in the kibbutz. Agriculture, which was the kibbutzims' obvious base, has very much declined in importance. If in 1940 it was their main, if not the only, base, industry—often high technology—now provides three quarters of their income and in some kibbutzim very little agriculture is left at all. While in 1940 everyone believed in the advantages of a mixed economy—that is to say, doing a little bit of everything—subsequently the trend has been toward a division of labor between settlements and specialization, perhaps even too much so.

My aversion to agricultural labor, such as it was in those days, triggered off a vicious circle. While my comrades opted for work in one specific branch and tried to gain as much theoretical and practical experience as possible, I remained profoundly apathetic. As a result I would be sent to wherever unqualified labor was needed, and this, in turn, would only deepen my lack of interest.

And yet, as I look back, manual labor, first for a short time in a factory, and then for a much longer period in agriculture, as well as living in poverty, was an important part of my education, even if I did not appreciate it at the time. It certainly broadened my horizon and improved my judgment. But for this experience I would probably have gone on reasoning on all kinds of important issues on a theoretical level, probably expressing all kinds of extreme views, as I did at seventeen. Much later in life I watched students and colleagues talking about decision making who never had to make a more important decision in life than where to study and what. After some of these experiences I even felt a certain sympathy for Mao Tse-tung, who at the time of the cultural revolution sent Chinese students to work in the fields for a year or two. I am sure it did not improve the level of Chinese physics, but in other respects these might not have been wasted years. What do they know who spend their whole life in an academic community or similar sheltered surroundings?

For a longish period I worked as a guard in the fields. I could ride, knew a little Arabic, and, above all, no other branch wanted to have me. At this time Hazorea, like many other kibbutzim, had some twenty or thirty pieces of land in various directions between the foothills of Mount Carmel and the Kishon River in Jezreel Valley, which was even less of a river than the Yarmuk. According to the Bible, Barak and the prophet Deborah defeated Sisera mainly because the chariots of the Canaanites got stuck in the mud of the Kishon; the prophets of Baal suffered a similar fate "on the banks of the Kishon." In my days a mouse could not have drowned in the Kishon except perhaps during a few days in winter following heavy rainfall.

Some of the lands belonging to the kibbutz were miles away from the settlement; the overall map of the valley looked like a giant piece of patchwork. It was the task of the guard to keep Arab herds out of these lands. The local villagers, on the whole, respected borders but the Bedouin (who looked down with contempt on the villagers) would behave differently, either because they were not aware of the complicated ownership or because they could not care less. Such land disputes are potentially dangerous all over the world; they could lead to major clashes and pitched battles. My job was as much one of public relations as a show of force. I was lucky, the mere presence of a mounted guard was usually a sufficient deterrent. Once a herd of Arab cows invaded our land, it was not easy to dislodge them since it was next to impossible to catch a cow. For these undernourished creatures moved exceedingly fast, and once they were stampeding they would think nothing of traversing even barbed wire.

I never had to use my revolver except once when I discovered a snake under my bed. I also carried with me a heavy wooden stick, which belonged to the guardian's traditional outfit. An earlier generation of guards had donned fancy Circassian dress, flowing robes, Arab headgear, all kinds of elaborate rifle slings. For in the nineteenth century much of this work had been in the hands of Circassians, who had migrated to Jordan and Palestine from the Caucasus. In my time such attire had gone out of fashion.

My instructor told me that my most important job was to know as many of our neighbors as possible, but since there were hundreds of them and since all looked to me pretty much alike in the beginning, this was easier said than done. My interlocutors from the neighboring villages did not volunteer any information until they came to know me much better. Nor, come to think of it, did I; I was known as "Hawaja Naboleon," since this was the name I had first given, aware of the fact that my real name was unpronounceable in Arabic, as indeed it is in most languages. (But then, most Arabs have great difficulty pronouncing the letter *p.*) However, my reputation was not equal to that of the great emperor, nor even to that of the great "historical guardians of the Jezreel Valley," such as Alexander Zeid, whose exploits have entered Palestinian, and later Israeli, folklore. Alexander Zeid was one of the founders of the watchmen's organization in Palestine well before World War I. Born in Siberia, in a little place with the unlikely name of Balagansk (which in Russian means a preposterous piece of buffoonery), he was killed at his post in 1938, a few miles from where I operated. He was also an amateur archaeologist and made some interesting discoveries. Today a statue at the entry to the Jezreel Valley marks the place where he was killed.

In those days a man's image and reputation depended largely on the quality of his horse, and mine was old and slow. While I took reasonable care of it, the only way to force it into a gallop was to return home to the settlement, when, so to speak, it suddenly changed gears. But it was blessed with an excellent sense of hearing, which made it unnecessary for me to keep a dog. We had concluded a gentleman's agreement: I would not work it hard and would feed it well and the horse would reciprocate by taking over part of my duties. I would lie down in the shade of a tree and my horse would alert me to anyone or anything approaching at a distance of hundreds of meters.

Some of my fondest memories of these years are connected with this kind of work—riding through the fields on an early spring or autumn morning with fine views from the Carmel to Mount Tabor, with the ground and the trees covered with drops of dew like sparkling pearls, with the railway line (now abandoned) traversing the valley, running more or less parallel to the river. The settlement opposite Hazorea was Kfar Yehoshua. When it was first settled in the early 1920s, the valley was a malaria-infested marsh, and since the settlers had no animals, they had to harness themselves to the plowshares. Farther to the east a few minutes' ride would take me to Nahalal, the "mother of the *moshavim*" (the cooperative settlements), where Moshe Dayan was born and is now buried. My tour of duty extended from (almost) Megiddo in the south, where according to the Book of Revelation, the last great battle between the forces of good and evil is bound to be fought, almost to Bet Shearim, with its tombs and caves, once the seat of the Sanhedrin, the Supreme Court. These two places are among the most important archaeological sites in Palestine and nowadays attract many visitors; I cannot recall a single tourist in my time.

On a quiet day I would settle in the shade of a tree and read; a watchman reading books was, of course, an abomination, and I had to smuggle my literature in the pockets of my saddle and took good care not to be surprised. In harvesttime I would, on occasion, spend the night out in the fields or up on a hill, always in the company of one or more guards from another settlement. Since we were not lying in ambush but simply wanted to show the flag, we kept a campfire burning, and my colleagues, often natives of southern Russia, would teach me the sentimental songs of their native land.

On other occasions I would be the guest of a Bedouin or an

Arab villager to whom I had been of help in one way or another. The meal would take a long time, with countless pitas consumed, much yogurt, and perhaps even a roast lamb. On a few occasions I was invited to participate in a *fantasia*, a horse race; given the age and uncertain state of health of my horse, I preferred to watch these events from the sidelines. Being a guard taught me to be careful. I don't think I ever fell asleep while on duty. But there still was much time to think, and it was during these long hours, in a landscape I had come to like, that I reached the conclusion that kibbutz life was not for me. Physically, I probably felt better then than at any time before or after. I liked riding and the campfire atmosphere, and I had become accustomed to a primitive way of life. Gradually, I was shrugging off the summer heat and the scorpion bites. But I was ambitious, and I felt that these ambitions could not be realized in a kibbutz. I wanted time to study, and I suspected that if I were to stay in our settlement I would be increasingly unhappy.

But this realization came gradually. It took me more than a year to draw these conclusions. In the meantime I was watching kibbutz life rather than actively participating in it. This is a subject that has been thoroughly studied in recent decades; some of these studies are excellent, but they usually concern certain specific issues, such as the upbringing of children. I have as yet to see an article or a book or a movie that conveys a true impression of what life was really like at that time. Perhaps social science is not the right tool for this purpose; perhaps a novel on the grand scale would be more appropriate. But novels by necessity deal with the fate of individuals, and an Israeli Balzac or Tolstoy has not yet made his appearance.

What were the main issues preoccupying my kibbutz, which had then been in existence for about seven years? Certain changes were unmistakable. The old elite, the leaders of the youth movement, were replaced by new men and women of a more practical turn of mind, doers rather than thinkers and speakers. I put the "and women" on paper with some hesitation, because women took a less active part in kibbutz life. They were but infrequently found in key positions. Was it because they were overawed by the more aggressive men? Was it because they were more drawn to the private rather than the communal sphere? It was a problem common to virtually all kibbutzim, and it was discussed for many years. No satisfactory solutions seem to have been found. Women took a leading part in education but in few other of the main spheres of kibbutz life.

It was not easy for those who had been the gurus of the youth movement back in Germany (or Poland or Romania) to adjust to the new priorities. There were certain fields of activities open to them: They could become teachers, a profession for which there would be an increasing demand. They could do political work in the trade union or the party, or clerical work in kibbutz economic enterprises. Some did very well in their new responsibilities, but by and large, power in the kibbutz passed to a new stratum of people, competent in their work, more capable to steer the community in a period of immediate concerns.

What were the issues topmost on the agenda of the kibbutz assembly—the main decision-making body in theory, if not always in practice? There was a constant tug-of-war between the radicals, who put the stress on the collective concerns and interests, and the liberals—a term not widely used at the time—who believed that the emphasis in kibbutz life was gradually bound to shift to the private sphere, the family. They were more ready to make allowances for the individual with his predilections and prejudices. They were more willing to accept the fact that while men and women were social beings, they needed, figuratively speaking, a room of their own as well as some other freedoms. They foresaw that disregarding human nature would cause growing disappointment and eventually lead to the departure of not a few of their members.

A few examples should suffice. Private property was, of course, taboo in those faraway days. If a member received a present—such as, say, a radio or a phonograph or a coffee machine—it was to be passed on to the collective. Books were an exception; a watch was in the gray zone. But then, during the war, the kibbutz members who were serving in the army came home on leave, and with their meager army pay they had bought a radio or a coffee machine or something of this kind. They were in no mood to pass it on to the kibbutz. After all, they had lived for years in difficult conditions, far away from their wives and friends; they had faced hardship and danger. Surely they were entitled to some compensation. Their case was overwhelming, but, their neighbors argued, they liked classical music (or jazz or whatever) no less and surely they, too, were entitled to have a little radio music. (Radios and phonographs were about the same size in those days—they were a piece of furniture. In retrospect, this may well have aggravated the situation.) There were stormy meetings of the general assembly, and in the end the war veterans got their way; eventually everyone got his or her radio, unless, or course, the person did not want it.

The upbringing of the children was mainly in the hands of the collective. Children were placed in the children's house immediately after birth, as soon as they came with their mothers back from the hospital. The young mothers came regularly to their children to feed them, but trained nurses and, later on, teachers took care of them. The children spent most of the daytime with their peer group and slept in the children's house. When they became a little more independent, they went during the day to visit their mothers. After work the parents regularly spent several hours with their children. For a long time it was frowned upon for parents to keep toys in their rooms. But gradually these rules became less and less stringent. At least twice a year a resolution was passed that children should not be brought into the dining hall during mealtimes, but they came anyway.

When we arrived in Hazorea in early 1942, the kibbutz had some forty or fifty children. But after the outbreak of war, the general assembly passed a resolution against having a second child, partly because of the deteriorating economic situation but also because many members felt that it was irresponsible to engage in procreation during the war. The interference of the collective in the life of the individual went very far; there were long debates whether the kibbutz could (and should) give shelter to members' parents; eventually it decided in favor.

Then there were people with special talents—such as writers, painters, musicians, photographers—whose work was not of immediate benefit to the kibbutz. They struggled for many years to be given time for what was more than a hobby. They usually succeeded, but only years later, after the economic situation had improved.

Leave, beyond the customary eight or ten days, was seldom if ever granted. There seems to have been more than a little frustration and dissatisfaction at the time, and for a number of years the kibbutz spent a great deal of money in sending some of its members to see psychoanalysts in Haifa. After the war mental health improved dramatically.

On the whole, the early war years were not very happy ones. Many members were not yet certain whether their erstwhile dreams about kibbutz life bore much resemblance to the harsh realities of Palestine; in 1943 and 1944 a record number of members left. After that the mood improved and eventually also the economic situation. The kibbutz secretary's main assignment in the early war years was to obtain short-dated loans on unfavorable terms, and frequently he did not succeed in that either.

While the general assembly was the main decision-making body, the secretary, the treasurer, and the settlement-and-labor-force coordinators were powerful figures, and there were countless committees dealing with planning, education, the admission of new members, health, culture, building, and at least a dozen other issues. I was a bad citizen and did not serve on any committee—though on one occasion, early on in my kibbutz life, I represented the community in a countrywide conference in which we initiated a new political program. But I seldom attended the general assembly and even complained to Naomi when she did, because I regarded it as a waste of time. While other members were teaching themselves the principles of the theory of agriculture, agrochemistry, veterinary science, and whatnot, I read history more or less systematically, literature, and sociology in the kibbutz library, which was excellent in choice and impressive in quantity.

Then in 1942 I broke my leg while shaving in the communal washroom. I still do not know how it happened; it may be a unique case in the annals of medicine. The floor was wet, I slipped, felt a pain, and the X ray taken in Haifa showed that the fibula had snapped. When such a misfortune befell a girl in those days she could still mend socks and trousers, but for men there was nothing to do. So while I was immobilized I decided to learn Russian with the help of Mrs. Pickman. Mrs. Pickman, born in Nikolayev, near the Black Sea, was the mother of a fellow member; I believe she had been a teacher and in any case was happy to find someone to whom she could impart the beauties of *Evgeni Onegin* and *Kapitanskaya Dochka*. I worked very hard—six, eight, even ten hours a day. Somehow I obtained a dictionary and a few newspapers. At the end of three months I could read *Pravda*, which was less an achievement than it may sound because the vocabulary of most readers of that newspaper was quite limited, so it was written in something like "Basic Russian."

My pronunciation was still horrible and has not greatly improved over the years. I never knew where to put the stress (*udarenie*)* but I had a sizable vocabulary. During the months that followed, I read a great deal of Russian literature and history. Later, things Russian had for a while to take second place to English, which I had never been taught at school. Up to the outbreak of the war, there had been a steady stream of German and French books and newspapers to Palestine, but this had ceased and whoever wanted to keep abreast of events and developments had to read English.

---

*This is a major problem for most foreign students and also for not a few native Russians. Not long ago I met a deputy foreign minister named Obukhov. When questioned, he admitted that he pronounced his name with the stress on the second syllable, but that there were also other Obukhovs who put the stress on the first or the last syllable.

Furthermore, thousands of Englishmen appeared in Palestine during the war, and a knowledge of the language was of growing practical importance. While I was still in the kibbutz, my first articles in Hebrew were published. Those in English were not— and I don't blame the editor for rejecting these limbering-up exercises. Seen in retrospect, the kibbutz was my third university, following the Breslau municipal library and the Reichenbach factory.

To what extent was it a school in interpersonal relations? Again, being among the youngest, I was more than a little self-conscious and had few, if any, close friendships. But I became accustomed to treating everyone as my equal, and later on in town had some difficulty in adjusting to the fact that there were various hierarchies even in an egalitarian society like Jewish Palestine, and that some people expected, rightly or wrongly, to be treated with the deference due their age, social standing, or achievement in life.

I have mentioned earlier on that the unquiet years in Palestine were paradoxically those before the outbreak of the war and after it had ended. But the calm was far from complete. The Stern gang continued its terrorist operations against the British well into 1942, and both Irgun and Stern renewed their attacks in 1944. The British continued to intercept illegal immigrants from Europe and carried out searches for arms caches in Jewish settlements. Several dozen participants in military training courses were arrested and given five- to ten-year sentences, among them Moshe Dayan and Yigal Alon, the two future key figures in Israeli defense; all were released after a year or two.

The danger of a German-Italian invasion seemed for a while possible and indeed likely. Four days after Italy's entrance in the war, a total blackout was ordered on June 14, 1940, from sunset to dawn. With the occupation of Yugoslavia and Greece in early 1941, enemy forces had come much nearer to the border of Palestine. In May of that year, as Syria passed into the hands of the Vichy forces and as a pro-Axis coup took place in Iraq, an invasion seemed imminent. From where we lived, there were some sixty to seventy kilometers, as the crow flies, to the Syrian border. True, Syria was recaptured within two weeks and the Iraqi mutiny was also suppressed, but then in June 1942 Rommel reached El Alamein, which was a mere one hundred kilometers from the Suez Canal.

Yet, somehow I never believed that the German forces would reach Palestine, and I do not recall nervousness, let alone even a trace of defeatism, in our settlement. If we had been privy to high-grade intelligence information, we would have known that Rommel had been gambling, that he had no reserves whatsoever, that he had overextended his lines, and that the German forces in the Caucasus had also reached the end of their tether. But we did not know this; on the contrary, the impression had been created that the German forces were invincible.

There was little we could do by way of preparing an effective defense. I was a member of the Hagana field forces, but our equipment was woefully insufficient. There were probably enough rifles but not enough munitions or hand grenades. There was no artillery except a few light mortars and machine guns. On one occasion I was given to handle a submachine gun for a few minutes; for all I know it was the only one in the whole neighborhood. A few days each month we trained in the neighborhood of the settlement—usually our strength was that of a squad, never more than a platoon. I liked being a scout, which was my usual function, moving in front of the unit, exploring the terrain; it seemed an extension of the war games we had played as children and in the youth movement. I recall several night maneuvers; once we marched over the mountains to Zikhron Ya'akov, one of the oldest Jewish colonies near the Mediterranean shores. Today this is a drive of no more than twenty minutes. But in 1942 there was no road, nor were there more than two or three small Jewish settlements on our way, and the exploit was thought to be quite daring—no one but the British army had been in this hostile neighborhood for years. Some of my contemporaries in military training went on to become colonels and even generals; my military career ended when I left the kibbutz.

In early 1943 I made up my mind to join the British army and went to Sarafend, the main military camp in Palestine and also the main recruiting center. I arrived too late in the afternoon—the recruiting sergeant had gone home for the day—and I was given a bed somewhere in a barrack. During the night I did not close an eye; never had I experienced such a combined assault of bedbugs and fleas. This provided an opportunity to rethink my decision. On one hand, there was the moral duty to do more for the war effort, on the other the near certainty that "colonial" units recruited in Palestine would at best be used as sappers in Egypt or perhaps in Persia, which made the categorical imperative appear less powerful. The next morning I left Sarafend and returned to the kibbutz without having signed up and accepted the King's shilling.

Nevertheless, I was quite obviously in a state of restlessness, and, not many months later, I found myself standing beside the road in front of the kibbutz gate, waiting for the truck to take me to town. It was quite hot. I had a good look at the neighborhood, for it was my last day in the kibbutz—the last hour, to be precise. I remember the distant water towers in the valley of Jezreel and the cypresses lining the road. A friend who was seeing me off remarked that each man had to plow his own furrow, that he could understand my decision but not approve of it, and he said a number of other things that people usually say on such occasions. He also told me that I was, to put it mildly, overoptimistic if I still assumed, as I had indicated on one occasion, that within a year or two I would be a well-known and influential political writer. I don't think I made any reply. We parted cordially, agreeing to keep in touch and promising to meet again within a couple of years. The truck arrived, late as usual, and the driver was swearing at the flock of sheep just passing by. I kissed Naomi, who was to join me in Jerusalem within a month. I threw my small case onto the roof rack, jumped onto the running board, and we drove off. I should have mentioned that, like all others leaving the kibbutz, I was entitled to an ex gratia payment of five pounds and a bed. The money was in my pocket, the bed was to follow within a week or two, once I would have an address in town.

I was not to revisit my old kibbutz for more than twenty years, but in a strange way my kibbutz past continued to haunt me. When I was invited to the United States for the first time, in the early 1950s, I went to the American consulate in London but was refused a visa. When I asked for an explanation, the consul reluctantly volunteered the information that I had been a member of a "Communistic settlement" (these were the days of Senator McCarthy) and unless I received "defector status," there would be no visa for me. But I could not receive defector's status since I had left the "Communistic settlement" many years earlier. It seemed a hopeless bureaucratic muddle, and the whole affair went to the ambassador. On that very day Walter Lippmann, widely considered the leading American journalist of the day, favorably mentioned my first book in English, whereupon the ambassador reached the conclusion that he could stick out his neck and grant me a waiver despite my doubtful political past. The whole affair was doubly ironic because in the years after my departure from the kibbutz I had become a premature anti-Stalinist and this, among other things, had been the reason for a certain estrangement with the kibbutz.

When I revisited Hazorea twenty years later, I had some difficulty finding the entrance. The settlement had greatly expanded; in my time there had been about one hundred and fifty members, and now almost a thousand lived in the settlement. I could check my bearings only by the main road that led from Haifa to Jenin. Gone were the tents and the wooden huts, gone the khaki trousers and the denim shirts, gone the horses, donkeys, and sheep. The only reminder of the old kibbutz was the tall fence around the perimeter. Not far from the entrance was an extensive parking lot, and, a little farther away, a large two-story building, evidently the dining hall, surrounded by trees and expanses of lawn. The sound of splashing and children's voices came from a large swimming pool across the way. I might have been in a country club in Westchester County. The evening meal in the dining room was excellent; there was a choice of several courses and dishes. Gone were the huge trays, the aluminum plates, and the tin cutlery. At the entrance to the dining hall I saw a cloakroom where everyone had his (or her) pigeonhole for mail. In the old days, incoming letters had been scattered indiscriminately on a table or the grand piano—a lonely reminder of the bourgeois past. But it was now equally common to have one's meal in a member's apartment, for each had a little kitchen as well as a shower and a toilet. There was a museum of Far Eastern art in the kibbutz and the House of Culture seated as many people as in a good-sized cinema in town.

I could go on for a long time dwelling on the astonishing achievements of the kibbutz—the one I knew, and the kibbutzim in general. In the 1980s they produced more than 40 percent of the country's agricultural output, and some 10 percent of the Israeli industrial exports, even though the population of the kibbutzim was only one hundred and thirty thousand in 1990. In some fields their agricultural yields are now the highest in the world, and Israeli methods of agriculture and animal husbandry are studied and emulated all over the globe.

But this would be only part of the story. Standards of living, after all, have risen in most parts of the world and there is no reason why the kibbutz should be an exception. Despite the spectacular progress, their economic situation is, in some respects, far from brilliant. The kibbutzim made the mistake of accepting too many loans in the 1970s, when money was cheap and easily available. As a result they found themselves heavily burdened at the time of an economic downturn. But neither economic success nor failure is the decisive issue. It was, of course, above all an attempt to try a new way of life, and seen in this context it is too early to draw any final conclusion.

Since I knew the kibbutz, two more generations have appeared on the scene and virtually all key positions are now in their hands. They are much more competent workers than their parents were, but their ideological motivation is much less strong. If so, why do they stay on? When I asked, I was told that they did not give much thought to this question. Some might consider this a reassuring answer but I am not so sure, and the percentage of young people leaving—often after having done their army service—is uncomfortably high, up to 50 percent and even more. What attracts so many to the city? Much as I tried to understand, I failed to do so; perhaps it is simply because they are young, and when I was their age I did behave, after all, no differently. I wanted more freedom. The question of material incentives was irrelevant; for years to come I was to live no better than in the kibbutz.

Kibbutz schools did not aim at producing Einsteins but intelligent and efficient workers, and to this extent they seem to have been a success. Perhaps contentment with one's work and pride in individual achievement, as well as the security that accrues from living in a collective, was sufficient motivation for those who stayed on. The sense of identification with the community might discourage the would-be leaver. To say that man is a creature of habit is as trite as it is apt; a person must have fairly strong reasons for deciding to make a radical change not only in his place of residence but in his whole way of life. There are, of course, many more opportunities in town, but there is also much more insecurity and there are the other drawbacks to city life, and these need not be discussed in detail.

The price of normalization has been high. I found that the young shed many of the attributes that made their parents' generation so interesting and attractive. The pioneers of the 1920s and the 1930s were an elite for various historical reasons, which no longer apply; they had the sort of chance that comes very rarely—to make a radically fresh start and to mold their lives as they chose.

With all this, the kibbutz now faces an identity crisis. It has adapted to the economic environment, developing not only industries but services for the public. One kibbutz is running a beauty parlor, another a discotheque, a third a law firm. Hazorea breeds, among other things, goldfish for export. Some kibbutzim are renting houses to nonmembers, and it is debated whether members should be paid a salary. If so, what would be the difference between a kibbutz and a garden suburb? As the pessimists see it, the kibbutz is finished, which, if true, would be a great pity, for it has been the one wholly unique contribution made by Israel to world civilization.

In the decades since I left the kibbutz I had the opportunity to watch political figures, top managers, prominent intellectuals, and, generally speaking, leaders in various walks of life in more than one country. And I still think that in the kibbutzim of the 1940s I found the highest concentration of talent I have ever met. I refer to qualities of intellect as well as of character and of leadership. Given a year or two of training, there is little many of them would not have achieved in politics, in the economy, in academic life. True, as far as politics were concerned, they were a little naive and had adopted a radical stance, which for years handicapped them. In any case there was no urgent demand for this human potential, there were too many chiefs and too few Indians in this small country, nor did they have the motivation, and probably also not always the self-confidence. By the time new opportunities for them did open in the 1950s and 1960s, they were middle-aged and no longer flexible.

Aldous Huxley, not noted for his love of utopias, once wrote that we can learn something even from the stupidest experiment in organized human coexistence. The kibbutz was not a stupid experiment; it developed under unique conditions such as prevail nowhere else at present in the modern world. Perhaps they will recur at some future date. Of all the alternative approaches to modern life it has been the most successful and the longest lasting, and it has been a privilege, as far as I am concerned, to have been present almost at the creation. The story of Lincoln Steffens is widely known—he went to Russia in 1919 and then reported back that he had seen the future and that it worked.

At a distance of more than seventy years the statement merely provokes sadness or ironical comment. Few of those who have witnessed the kibbutz in its development will make such far-reaching claims. Even inside Israel the general trend has been away from the ideals of the kibbutz—not, alas, for the better. Perhaps the kibbutz experiment will enter the annals of mankind as a mere utopian interlude of local significance only. But what would history have been but for the appearance every now and then of a group like the Argonauts of old, daring to enter uncharted waters?

Contacts with the kibbutz never entirely ceased in later years. When we lived in Jerusalem, visitors came from time to time and kept us abreast of events in what had been once our home. In later years we frequently visited Hazorea and friends in other kibbutzim. Shlomit, our younger daughter, spent a few months there in a language school headed by an old friend of ours.

The recollections of that span of our lives were to follow us for many years. Breslau was not a beautiful town, yet the years there had profoundly influenced me, for this had been home; London and Paris, which I came to know much better in later life, were far more important in every respect, but they had not been home. There are more attractive sights in the world than the foothills of the Carmel and the valley of Esdraelon (to give it its biblical name), yet the sights (and even the smells) have followed me to this day. One day in Russia in the 1960s it suddenly struck me that the street scene very much resembled Afula in 1938—except that there were no palm trees. (Afula is a little town situated in the very center of the valley.) On another occasion passing an Ingush or Cherkess *aul* in the Caucasus, closing my eyes, I imagined I was back somewhere near Kiri or Abu Shusha, the Arab village in our neighborhood. The sounds and smells (of burned dung, of roasted grain) were exceedingly similar and even the people almost looked alike—at least the men; the women's dress was quite different.

I knew my decision to leave was right, and I had no regrets

later on. Nor were there regrets about years wasted but, on the contrary, a feeling of gratitude that fate (or good luck) had made it possible for me to participate in a unique experiment. It was the kind of experiment for which no degrees are awarded but which, as I came to realize, counted more in later life than a degree.

Jerusalem

During *the last two years* of the war, Jerusalem had become a much more interesting place than before. It had been a predominantly Jewish city since the late nineteenth century, perhaps even earlier, but the old orthodox-religious community hardly ever met the newcomers and there was literally no common language. The orthodox spoke Yiddish; the Oriental Jews conversed either in Ladino or Arabic or their native dialect (Persian, Kurdish, Turkish). The new *yishuv* spoke Hebrew, with the exception of the most recent immigrants, who had not yet mastered the official language and often spoke German. The Old City was predominantly Arab, but there were sizable Greek and Armenian communities, not to mention the Jewish quarter. Monks and nuns came from just about every country; there were Copts and Ethiopians. Before the war the British community had consisted mainly of colonial civil servants and their families, of missionaries and a few archaeologists and churchmen.

All this changed during the war with the arrival of military units from half a dozen countries, of which the Poles were the second strongest contingent. Even in the kibbutz we became increasingly aware of these changes. Once I had to obtain a Swahili dictionary to converse with the soldiers stationed in a nearby military camp. Hundreds, perhaps thousands, of British civilians worked for intelligence or propaganda in Palestine; this brought a new type of resident—the intellectual. There were resistance fighters from the Balkans, a few anti-Nazi Germans, who for one reason or another had been stranded in Palestine, and also not a few spies and smugglers. There was a constant stream of visitors from Egypt, where the British High Command for the Mediterranean was located, mostly military personnel, but also some civilians.

Among the Jews, there were not a few refugees who had escaped to Palestine from Europe but had no wish to make their home there. These were mainly intellectuals, waiting for the day when the gates that had been closed with the outbreak of the war would reopen.

There was no Jerusalem society at the time, but there were a great number of societies, mostly quite small. I have mentioned some of the establishmentarians whom I came to know as customers in the bookshop. There was a small avant-garde eager to see new art books and contemporary poetry. Heinz Pollitzer worked on his Kafka biography, and there was a whole group of "progressive" (that is to say, "fellow travelers") Viennese *hommes de lettres* who were living more in the past and future than in the present. A young surrealist painter named Wolfgang Hildesheimer came together with a young Arab intellectual, Waled Khalidi, scion of a famous local family. Waled Khalidi in later years made a name for himself as one of the most eloquent spokesmen for the Arab cause in America; Hildesheimer returned to Germany and became a well-known writer. Both belonged to the salon of Kathy Antonius, the Lebanese widow of a well-to-do Christian Arab who had written an early work on the history of Arab nationalism. It was a very civilized place, with valuable *objets d'art*, good food, and fine conversation. For many senior British officials this was their introduction to Palestine.

There was a group of Communist intellectuals and they also bought books. One evening someone invited me to a lecture (in German) on Bergson; the speaker (I was told) was the greatest Marxist thinker in the Middle East, Dr. Wolfgang Ehrlich, in private life secretary of the local conservatory of music. He told us that while Bergson was technically a competent philosopher, he was wrong and Marx was right; the idealist Bergson had not been able to understand the profundity of dialectical materialism because of his bourgeois background. As the war ended, I took it for granted that Dr. Ehrlich would return to the Soviet zone of Germany, but he remained, even became a member of the Politburo of the local Communist party, with which he stayed to the bitter end. There were also Trotskyites of various nuances. One of them subsequently went to England, where, under the name of Tony Cliff, he became the guru of International Socialism, one of the more enlightened Trotskyite factions. Another, Gabriel Baer, with whom I was on friendly terms, retired from politics, became an academic, and never having been to Egypt, wrote a monumental study on Egypt's economic history.

Another frequent visitor was George Lichtheim, who became a close friend in later years. He belonged to the most exclusive and intellectually most stimulating circle called Pilegesh (Hebrew for concubine). For several years, every Saturday afternoon they met for tea and cake in George's little rooftop apartment in Radak Street, Rehavia, opposite the Italian consulate. It consisted of the orientalist H. Polotski; Hans Lewy, a classicist; Gershom Scholem the philosopher; Hans Jonas the physicist and historian of science Shmuel Samburski; and occasional visitors from Tel Aviv, Haifa, and abroad. Originally, the circle had met in Hans Lewy's apartment and had included a few women, but as one by one the members married, the circle became exclusively male in composition. All these men were polymaths—there was no surrealist nonsense, no frivolous dance music as in the Antonius salon, no vulgar Marxism. The conversations ranged from metaphysics to the analysis of the latest reports from the Russian front. Members of the group were fond of writing poems in the style of Goethe, Schiller, or Heine, in honor of a friend's birthday or some other important event. In brief, there was in this provincial town, below the surface, a cultural cosmopolitanism far more interesting than the Levantine cosmopolitanism of, say, the old Alexandria. It was equally clear that it was a transient phenomenon, which did not, however, greatly bother anyone. In a time of war and dramatic change, the next month was the long-term perspective, and few even dared to think about what would happen next year.

I once asked Gershom Scholem, the polymath and scholar of Jewish mysticism, why he had become a Zionist in his youth. He thought for a moment and then said: "I hated the restlessness and travel mania among the Jews and wanted them to settle down. And now look at them (this was about 1975)—they are traveling more than ever before. . . ." This wartime Jerusalem was, in some respects, an artificial, temporary community; many people knew, or suspected, that once the war was over they would move on, or be transferred, to other places; only the Poles did not know where they would find their new home.

The atmosphere of Jerusalem in those days has been described in several novels, including Olivia Manning's Levant trilogy; Arthur Koestler came a little later, but he knew Palestine from an earlier stay and always preferred Tel Aviv to Jerusalem. I did not find in these accounts a true portrait of the Jerusalem I knew; at best, a little segment of it. But this was inevitable because there were so many different Jerusalems and everyone spent most of the time in his or her little ghetto. On a few occasions I met friends from the kibbutzim who told me under the seal of secrecy that they were about to be parachuted into Nazi-occupied Europe. For a long time I did not hear from them; when contact was reestablished I was told that one had landed on top of a police station in Romania and had broken his leg, but survived to tell his story. Two went to Slovakia and perished, but another found his way to the Yugoslav partisans and returned. Some of their stories have become the topics of books and even movies, but others, of equal interest, have not and deserve to be recorded for posterity.

Some of these disparate Jerusalem societies met in the bookshops, and since I worked in one of these for a while it could happen that in the course of one afternoon I would see the high commissioner as a customer as well as Ben-Gurion (whose main interest was in the Loeb Classics at the time) or even Auni Bey Abdul Hadi of the Supreme Arab Council. A fair percentage of British officers, including some astonishingly young brigadier generals, were Oxford and Cambridge dons, and they came to buy books on philosophy and history. Some of these segments of transient Jerusalem society met in the concerts (on records) given in the YMCA, which always ended with "Land of Hope and Glory" and "God Save the King." Some also met in the Bet Ha'iton, a coffeehouse that, in true Viennese tradition, kept local and foreign newspapers from many countries. I should have added that in those days there was a great demand for information, but few foreign papers came, usually with three or more months of delay. Once Rommel had been defeated and the Mediterranean reopened, books from England and America began to arrive and at long last we got the wartime Penguins (price, sixpence) that we had missed for so long.

But for the many uniforms, no one in Jerusalem at the time would have guessed that a war was on; the blackout, which had never been strictly enforced, was lifted altogether in December 1943. There were relatively few motor vehicles on the road, except military ones. Much of the transport was still by horse and carriage, by camel and donkey. This changed rapidly after the end of the war. The shops were not exactly well stocked, but there was no rationing in any systematic way, and in the newly opened Palestine Restaurant one could always have a bad meal for very little money. Sweets could be freely bought, and drinks; by and large the supply situation was considerably better than in Europe. I cannot even recall the existence of a black market, even though cigarettes from NAAFI (the British military supply stores) found their way into the civilian sector. Luxuries had never been easily available in Palestine. In brief, no one greatly suffered from the war in Jerusalem. On the contrary, the economy had markedly picked up after the deprivations of the first two war years; many old and some new enterprises were now producing for the war effort.

Open conflict between Jews and Arabs had virtually disappeared; it was perfectly safe to go to the Old City. Arabs and Jews worked together more or less harmoniously in many places. There were only a few close friendships and even fewer cases of intermarriage, but a renewal of the riots seemed most unlikely at the time. Sir Harold MacMichael, the high commissioner, was the highest British official. A civil servant in the colonial tradition—his experience had been with natives of the Sudan— he had not much liking for either Jews or Arabs and made no secret of it. The Jews cordially reciprocated his dislike and the Irgun tried to kill him during the last days of his stay in 1944, after his successor had already been appointed. This successor was Field Marshal Lord Gort, a military man of legendary bravery (Victoria Cross, Military Cross with two bars). At the beginning of the war he had been picked over the heads of hundreds of more senior officers to command the British Expeditionary Force into France. In this capacity he had been responsible for the decision to withdraw his forces from Dunkirk—a correct decision in the circumstances but not exactly a brilliant victory, though it was described as such at the time. With this, his military career had virtually come to an end. He did not stay long in Jerusalem, for reasons of health, and the last high commissioner was another military man, Sir Alan Cunningham, who had led the British troops to victory in Ethiopia in 1940, but had been defeated by Rommel in the Western desert in 1941. Cunningham lived on well into the 1980s, and from his retirement in Hampshire, he must have frequently pondered whether events might have taken a different turn.

While the high commissioners merely carried out policies decided upon in Whitehall, the Jewish leaders found it psychologically easier to get along with these military men rather than with MacMichael and the colonial bureaucracy serving under him. Most of the officials found the Jews ungrateful for British protection, arrogant, always discontented, always prone to take offense, and, generally speaking, contrary, in contrast to the Arabs, who, with all their political disagreements, did at least make an effort to observe social graces and to ingratiate themselves with the administration; they must have seemed a nicer and more hospitable people.

After 1944 it became less calm in Jerusalem because Irgun declared war on the British. Attacks against officials, policemen, and soldiers followed, but they were also directed against Jewish targets such as banks. While the Irgun was more selective in the choices of its victims than later generations of terrorists, it killed and wounded, intentionally or by accident, dozens of Jews. In November 1944 Lord Moyne was assassinated in Egypt by two members of the Stern gang. I thought the cooperation between Hagana and the British authorities (between October 1944 and March 1945), to bring an end to the terror, justified. From a political point of view the wartime terror, like the Stern gang's attempts to establish contact with the Nazis in 1941, was worse than a crime, it was a fatal blunder. The Irgun "declaration of war" came at a time when the battle against Nazism was still in full swing. In fact, the Second Front had not yet been launched, and virtually all of Europe was still under Nazi rule. If the terror had had any effect, the weakening of the anti-Hitler war effort would have been an act of high treason. But the results were bound to be meager. To have any effect, terrorism needs, above all, publicity. At a time of war, when thousands are likely to be killed in any case, with strict censorship in force, who in America,

England, or anywhere else would be greatly impressed as the result of the murder of a few British policemen in a faraway country?

I found their views both repulsive and dangerous. As a victim of chauvinism I acutely felt the danger of such appeals to the dark forces that exist in every people. Their message had a powerful attraction for some, but I never doubted the long-term fatal consequences of their actions. I still tried to understand their motives. Was the flame of patriotism burning in their hearts so much more intense? I doubted it. There was machismo, boredom, and some free-floating aggression among sections of the youth—as among some of the Irish Catholics, the Basques, and other terrorist groups. The best of the young generation went to work on the land establishing new settlements, joined the army or one of the Jewish self-defense units such as the Palmach; some were parachuted behind enemy lines in Europe. The Irgun militants had to find another outlet for their energies. And there is no denying that working on a farm was far more boring than robbing a bank or shooting a policeman in the dark—the Bonnie and Clyde syndrome. Among them was a sizable element of young Oriental Jews that Hagana had never quite been able to reach. For them, I suspect, terrorism was a way of self-emancipation—just as the women of the Baader-Meinhof gang or the Italian Red Brigades had to show that they were as aggressive as their male comrades, if not more so. There was, no doubt, a variety of motives.

I remember an incident that happened as I was leaving the offices of my dentist in Ben Yehuda Street, in the very house in which Café Atara is located. On the second floor, there was a small bank, and as I went down the stairs a man waved me into the bank. Since he had a revolver and I had none, I followed his command. An Irgun robbery was in process. Although a mask partly covered the face of their leader, I recognized without difficulty the son of one of the most senior Jewish officers in the Mandatory police. One did not need to have read Freud to understand the psychological motivation of the son rebelling against the father. The bank was small, not likely to keep thousands of pounds on the premises. The whole affair was amateurish; no one came to harm, except that one or two of the robbers were caught in the street. Of course there was idealism in their ranks; of course there was courage. But I had already seen too much idealism in the service of a very bad cause in Europe to be impressed by any such fanaticism.

When I arrived in Jerusalem for the second time, about a year and a half before the end of the war, I found a city that, as initially noted, had become considerably more lively than before the war. But it was still not a very lovable city, and some of its aspects I found detestable. Many of its streets were dusty and dirty, a picture of Oriental misery and squalor. There was admittedly in those days much less talk about Jerusalem the heavenly city, the holy, the golden; this kind of rhetoric spread only after 1967. But even then an oppressive surfeit of history was in the air. It recently occurred to me that in all the years in Jerusalem I never went to see the Western (Wailing) Wall and that I cannot have spent more than a few minutes at either the Dome of the Rock, Gethsemane, or the other famous religious sites. My interest in history is reasonably well developed, but whenever I entered the Old City through either the Jaffa or Damascus gates, I encountered a world that, having lost its initial fascination, I more and more disliked: quarreling monks of every denomination, Orthodox Jews in an advanced state of trance, obsequious and overinsistent shopkeepers, beggars, peddlers, vendors of nuts and bogus antiques, shoe cleaners, guides, and sundry Oriental gentlemen offering their services at grossly inflated prices, apathetic narghile smokers, unpleasant noises and smells, idle men in pajamas playing shesh-besh (backgammon) in front of run-down hotels. True, I was no aficionado of Meah She'arim and Mahane Yehuda either, but these singularly unattractive quarters at least had no celestial pretenses.

There was no peace in the Old City, no rarefied spiritual

atmosphere, only the miasma of mankind in the raw. There is in Jewish thought the differentiation between the heavenly Jerusalem and the real one, down below; the contrast between the two was not just great, it was horrendous.

In brief, I never really liked Jerusalem while I lived and worked there; later on, my attitude became more positive even though I always felt uneasy about the growing number of religious fanatics. For some time I believed that my attitude toward the city was blasphemous, until I discovered that greater men and women had shared it without necessarily advertising it. No leading Zionist had chosen Jerusalem as his or her home, whether left-wing or right. When Herzl visited Jerusalem his impressions were exceedingly negative ("two thousand years of inhumanity, intolerance, and uncleanliness"). Ahad Ha'am, the leading thinker of cultural Zionism, found the Wailing Wall and the ultraorthodox praying there equally repulsive. Weizmann always felt ill at ease in Jerusalem, and while Ben-Gurion was the main force behind the decision to transfer the capital from Tel Aviv to Jerusalem in 1949, he never liked the city or chose to live there. Initially, most members of the government were against the move. It did not occur to Messrs. Begin and Shamir to make their home in Jerusalem before they became prime ministers. Weizmann once wrote that he would not accept the Old City even as a gift for the Jewish state, and I remember Ben-Gurion telling me, after 1967, that one ought to give up Jerusalem if peace could be bought at this price. In brief, the idea that the Jewish people could not possibly exist but for the incorporation of all of Jerusalem is a relatively recent one. I am not competent to judge how deeply this belief is rooted among the Arabs; I am told that the Koran does not mention Al Kuds (Jerusalem's Arab name) even once. But it seems unfortunately only too obvious that fundamentalist fanaticism has grown among the Arabs even more than among the Jews.

If I disliked Jerusalem, why did I settle there? I could think of more than one reason. I have singled out the negative features of the city, but these were not the only ones. Nor did I know the city that well prior to my arrival in 1944. And lastly, I had received an offer of work in Jerusalem and not elsewhere.

THE BOOKSHOP in question, called He'atid (the Future), was off Zion Square in the very center of town. It sold new books and there was a major department of secondhand books, mainly in German but also in other languages, not to mention a lending library run by a man who had once taught Latin in my hometown. Many new immigrants had brought sizable libraries from Europe, but upon arrival in the new country they found that they did not want all these books (and their children even less so) and that, in any case, they did not have sufficient space to accommodate them in their new homes. For book lovers with enough shelving space, these were wonderful years; valuable and important books could be purchased for very little money. The shop was owned by a Mr. Salingré, a polymath, once a rising star in the Berlin journalistic firmament whose German career was cut short, and Wolfgang Edinger, a very knowledgeable and polished younger man who spoke excellent English. Salingré committed suicide during the siege of Jerusalem in 1948. Edinger also died young. The bookshop survived for many years under the management of Edinger's widow, but, like so many others, it eventually disappeared. People were perhaps reading more in those pretelevision days; whatever the reason, the "people of the book" have certainly not been able to create and maintain first-rate large bookstores in their country. It is also true that books, especially in languages other than Hebrew, were simply too expensive for many people.

Salingré and Edinger offered me a very low wage; instead of trying to get a raise, I suggested that I would start work in late morning, so as to give me a few hours each day for my studies. This they accepted; there was not much business at that time of day. After leaving the kibbutz one month after me, Naomi also went to work, as a baby nurse, and, in fact, for years earned more than I did.

A bookstore can be an ideal place to acquire a good general education. It is preferable to a public library or a university because one does get paid, however little, and one comes to know the professors and leading intellectuals in their capacity as customers. He'atid was strong in the humanities and the social sciences and not bad in science and medicine. Within a relatively short time I had a nodding knowledge of the standard textbooks in the various fields; I drew the line at physics and mathematics, subjects in which my knowledge had always been well below average. Perhaps our best customers were the physicians; medicine made rapid advances in wartime and they tried to keep abreast by following recent advances in specific fields. Physicians also often had more money than others; I did not quite understand how anyone could afford to buy a three-volume work on gastroenterology that cost as much as my monthly salary. Young scientists usually came in groups. One of them would later become president of the country; at the time he was more interested in polymers.

There was at the time considerable interest in Russian books and quite a few potential readers. Russian books, furthermore, were cheaper than English, and I persuaded the owners of He'atid to open a Russian section, a decision from which I benefited more than they did. A new circle of clients arrived, among them the head of Polish military intelligence, who used to come at least once a week; he was a gentleman of considerable knowledge in things Russian and with exquisite manners. He was not a snob either, and we had long conversations on Russia, past and present. My Russian activities had attracted the attention of the CID, the political department of the police. They reached the conclusion that I must be a potentially dangerous agent of influence; the fact that Naomi regularly corresponded with her parents, who happened to live in the Caucasus, certainly did not help either. The chief censor at the time was Clarissa Graves, the sister of the poet and writer Robert Graves. Another brother, Richard, acted as Jersualem's last mayor under the Mandate.

One day a police sergeant in uniform appeared in the store

and tried to befriend me. He claimed to be a member, or at least a sympathizer, of the Socialist party of Great Britain. This was a very small group that, though very left-wing, was staunchly anti-Communist and even anti-Soviet at a time when this was not fashionable. I decided to give the man the benefit of the doubt and told him that if he was indeed interested in Palestinian socialism he should see a kibbutz. I took him to visit one and he seemed genuinely interested. But after a few weeks his interest waned. Several years later, soon after the British had gone, a friend of mine retrieved my file from CID archives, and I found my worst suspicions justified. Unaware that my job at the time consisted predominantly of selling Russian books on subjects such as hydrology and crystallography, they had truly believed that I was presiding over an important branch of the defunct Communist International. I was in good company, for virtually all their secret information was incredibly wrong. The Palestinian left-of-center parties and unions were characterized as "pro-fascist" whereas the right-wingers became liberals; I wonder whether their informers had been practical jokers who had engaged in systematic disinformation. The incident taught me a lesson: More than once in subsequent years I did historical research based in part on police files. I would never trust informers' reports unless there was further corroboration.

Since the population of Jerusalem had grown very much in wartime, and since there had been little new building, it was both difficult and expensive to find an apartment in town. Someone mentioned to me Issaviya, an Arab village on the other side of Mount Scopus, and I went to inspect the place. The houses were less than a hundred yards from Hadassah Hospital and a few minutes' walk from the Hebrew University. The panorama was magnificent, the wild Judaean hills falling down to the Dead Sea several thousand feet below. The air was fine, but even the most elementary comforts were nonexistent—no electricity, no running water, no gas, and, of course, no telephone. Water had to be fetched from a well; the scene from Genesis, where Jacob watched Rachel watering Laban's sheep, was repeated several times daily. Nothing had changed in three thousand years except perhaps that we boiled the water before drinking it. Personal hygiene was not easy, to put it mildly, in these conditions. In the beginning we had a tiny room in a house that we shared with a philosopher named Hans Jonas, who had not found a chair in the Hebrew University; since there was but limited demand for philosophers, he did not have an easy time. Later, in the United States, he became well known for his work on Gnostic religion.

Our room was so small that each evening when we put up both our beds, the rest of our highly primitive furniture was put outside in a courtyard. After a few weeks we moved into a nearby house, which we shared with a young zoologist named Janowski, a decent and helpful man who came from a place called Auschwitz on the Polish side of the Silesian border, of which very few people had heard at the time. Eventually, we moved in with an Arab family. The female members worked very hard; the wife was washing, scrubbing, and cooking all day, as well as preparing *burghul* (bulgur) from wheat. Sakia, the small daughter, took care of the few goats and hens and ran errands. Whenever she was needed, her mother would shout, in a piercing voice that could be heard on the next hill, half a mile away, "Ya Sa-ki-a." Hassan, the father, spent his time sitting in the shade with the village elders, smoking and discussing village and world politics. Mustafa, one of the sons, used to enter our room from time to time. Though we were very poor, he still found something to steal. I complained, and he was fairly frequently given a beating, whether for stealing or for having been caught, I cannot say.

Naomi and I were aged twenty-three at the time, still without children, and for a while this primitive life seemed not particularly arduous. Yet as time went by the disadvantages became only too obvious. The autobus stopped operating before ten at night, and since we had no transport of our own, we were virtually cut off from friends and acquaintances. Furthermore, as the war ended I sensed some growing tension, particularly after the ex-mufti, Haj Amin, had been permitted to return to the Middle East; bonfires were burning every evening in the village. I do not recall whether it was a case of children throwing stones or some other minor incident that made us look for another place in town.

When I revisited the village in 1991, I found it almost unchanged, except that by now electricity and telephone cables had been laid and water was pumped to the village. Most of the inhabitants were still Arabs, but in the houses nearest to Hadassah Hospital there lived some Hebrew University students who could not afford Jerusalem rents. As the preacher in Ecclesiastes said a long time ago—there is nothing new under the sun.

As the war ended, the housing problem eased somewhat and we found a room in an old building in the German colony, a suburb that extends, roughly speaking, from the railway station in a southerly direction. It had originally been established by the German Templars; it was an area of manifold styles, many trees, and a very mixed population. Many British officials made their homes there, but the Arab middle class was also strongly represented, as well as the Higher Arab Council, and there were not a few Jews. Since then the German colony has undergone further demographic change; after 1950 many Jews from Morocco and Middle Eastern countries moved in; later still, the area became fashionable among artists as well as among immigrants from the so-called Anglo-Saxon countries.

The original German colony had been called Refaim because it was believed to be the site of a battle in which, according to the Bible, David had defeated the Philistines. It had been an agricultural settlement fashioned after German villages on both sides of the Neckar, and its original character—with a village street with shade provided by high trees, with fenced-in houses with red-tile roofs—has still been preserved in parts.

During the Mandatory period this was certainly one of Jerusalem's more pleasant neighborhoods. Unfortunately, all we could afford was a small room in a fortresslike Arab (Turkish?) building; its one advantage was that the walls were so thick and the windows so small that it never got very hot in the summer. Then at long last we found a decent apartment in a nearby house just about to be finished. It was three months before our first child was born, five months before the War of Independence, and our happiness was not to last long.

On May 9, 1945, victory was celebrated in Jerusalem. The fact that the war continued in the Far East hardly registered, for our horizon, by necessity, was not the one of the White House or Number 10 Downing Street. I remember that I did not feel much joy that day; elsewhere in the capitals of Europe the crowds were dancing in the streets. I felt more like mourning and my heart was full of doubts and forebodings. Long ago I had given up hope of ever seeing my parents and the other members of my family again. But it was one thing to suspect the worst and another to have final certainty. Nor, like everyone else, had I been aware of the extent of the disaster that had befallen European Jewry. In fact, it took a while even after the end of the war to understand the magnitude of the catastrophe. There was the personal bereavement with which I found it difficult to come to terms, and that, like others, I repressed for years. But there was also the loss of hope. Until the outbreak of war there had been the feeling that we were part of a great building project—every week reinforcements arrived from Europe, individuals and groups, among them not a few friends and acquaintances all eager to cooperate in this venture. This stream had been interrupted for six years, but only now did it become clear that those we expected would never come—the reservoir of European Jewry no longer existed, the last chapter in its history had already been written.

T E N

Special Correspondent

W*hile the war had gone on* I had been drifting; it seemed futile
to make plans for an uncertain future. Now I had no more
pretexts postponing any personal decisions. But the opportunities
were exceedingly limited: An academic career was ruled out, I
had no degree and no wish to start studying in my middle twenties—nor would I have known what direction to take. I had no
aptitude for either business or a craft. I was interested in politics
but never considered making it my profession. I did know that I
wanted to write, but this was an avocation, not a way to earn
one's living. Working in a bookstore, while not demeaning, was
not satisfactory in the long run.

So I was looking out of the window of my bookstore, a little
envious of the trucking and furniture-removing business oppo-

site, owned by a Viennese gentleman named Biedermann, envious even of the Kurdish porters, squatting in front of Biedermann's office waiting for customers wanting to move their piano or wardrobes. I had made friends with one of them named Eliyahu; one day he had asked me how much I earned, and when I had told him, his comment was that with this kind of money I would not be able to raise five or six children as he did. I was envious not so much about his higher income but because there seemed a purpose to his life, whereas I seemed to have reached a dead end.

True, I had tried to perfect my English and I had written articles from time to time; a few had even been published. I knew that some people had read and liked them but I did not delude myself: No one of consequence thought of me as an up-and-coming young man or had even heard of me.

Then one morning in early spring of 1946, wholly out of the blue, a miracle happened. I received a letter from the editorial secretary of the Hebrew newspaper *Hamishmar* to the effect that they were looking for a Jerusalem correspondent, that someone had recommended me, and that, if I was interested, I should appear in Tel Aviv next morning, if possible, with some samples of my recent work.

I do not know to this day to whom I owed this good luck; of the three editors only one knew me slightly and I had no reason to believe that he particularly liked me. All I do know is that any subsequent good luck I had in my professional life can be rationally explained because of one thing somehow leading to another, but the breakthrough of 1946 was an accident wholly unexpected. I had no journalistic experience except some "think" pieces; my command of literary Hebrew was far from complete; the sample articles I took with me had been written in a hurry and were quite inane.

Nevertheless, at the end of the interview I was offered the assignment, initially for a short trial period, but since my predecessor, an American woman named Sylvia Binder, was about to return to her kibbutz, this was more or less a matter of routine.

Perhaps my enthusiasm had impressed my interviewers. I have no other explanation.

The newspaper *Hamishmar* had been founded some two years earlier by the left-wing Hashomer Hatzair movement (to which Kibbutz Hazorea belonged). Its circulation was small but it was not uninfluential. The people who edited and wrote for it were amateurs, but many were gifted amateurs, and the paper had a freshness that others perhaps lacked. It was ideologically deeply committed, but it was flexible enough to give up positions when the editors realized that they were no longer tenable. Thus, for many years they had advocated a binational state, bitterly criticizing Ben-Gurion's Biltmore program (1942) which envisaged a Jewish state after the end of the war. But when it appeared that there was little support among the Jews and none whatsoever among the Arabs for a binational state, *Hamishmar* did not persist. The paper was both pro-Soviet and pro-American, a position that became increasingly difficult to maintain as the cold war reached its climax. But it should be recalled that the conflict of the two superpowers hardly registered in Palestine at the time. Thus, the Soviet takeover in Prague (March 1948) coincided with the "war for the roads" in Palestine, and in these circumstances no one paid any attention to it. The only concern was whether the events in the Czech capital would interfere with the purchase of rifles and machine guns urgently needed for the defense of Jewish settlements.

The position offered to me was both interesting and prestigious. The Jerusalem correspondent was then chief political correspondent of the paper, for the British administration as well as the Jewish Agency and the Arab leadership were all located there. But since the circulation of Palestinian newspapers was small, the correspondent also had to report on local affairs including municipal concerns, economic problems, cultural events, accidents, crime, the law courts, and even archaeology. Ours was a highbrow paper, and, fortunately, we had no gossip column. Even so, such encyclopedic coverage gradually became a little bothersome.

The office consisted of two rooms in the building that belonged to the *Palestine Post.* We shared the second floor with two
telegraphic agencies, another Hebrew newspaper (our revisionist
antagonist *Hamashkif*), and the office of Richard Kaufmann,
one of the countries leading architects. A friendly, soigné-look-
ing, elderly German Jew, he was also a very modest man; only
gradually did I find out that large parts of what is now Israel,
from Rehavia and Talpiot to Nahalal and Afula, had been built
on the basis of his blueprints, which harmoniously combined the
principles of modern European architecture with Palestinian
specifics. He had settled in Jerusalem in 1920. I sometimes accompanied him on his way home and I learned from him much
about how Jewish Palestine had developed.

Another fascinating character was Abba Achimeir, a native of
Bobruisk in Russia. He was about fifty at the time, an erstwhile
pioneer of the Labor Zionist persuasion. Gradually, he had
moved to the extreme right, ending up writing a "Column of a
Fascist" for *Hamashkif*, admittedly in Mussolini's days before
Hitler had come to power. He had become the chief ideologist
of the terrorist groups and was in and out of prison. He was a
man deeply steeped in Russian, as well as French and German,
culture. I found him an excellent conversationalist; the great
difficulty was to steer him away from domestic affairs, for on
these topics he tended to display raving madness, calling Golda
Meir a prostitute and Ben-Gurion a murderer.

There was a great deal of talent in my little office; our assistant
accountant, Victor Shemtov, eventually became minister of
health in the Israeli government, and my Tel Aviv editor became
minister of public works. *Hamishmar* was at the time something
like a jumping-off board for gifted youngsters, not yet twenty
years of age, who worked part-time for me: Amos Eilon and
Shabtai Tevet later became writers well known beyond Israel;
Eilon was with me during the siege of Jerusalem and wrote in
record time a little book *Jerusalem Did Not Fall*, which he may
not want now to include in his collected works but which was
still a good limbering-up exercise. Tevet is perhaps best known

as the biographer of Ben-Gurion, one of the great biographies of our time. A third, Naqdimon Rogel, became a pioneer of Israeli television and created various popular programs. All three developed, in later years, a pronounced interest in history. I don't think my own inclinations had influenced them, for from 1946 to 1948 there was so much going on every day no time was left to look either back or forward. I should mention two others, no longer alive—Gavriel Stern and Arie Zimuki; the former, one of the main activists in the field of Arab-Jewish understanding, a walking encyclopedia on Arab, as well as religious, affairs. Zimuki managed to combine work as a Mandatory police sergeant with that of journalism; it is not clear to me to this day how he managed to get away with it.

Whatever success I had in the following years I owe to a large extent to this little team. I was far too inhibited to be a good reporter; unlike my colleagues and rivals I had no friends among leading figures whom I could phone in the evening to be briefed and to get the occasional scoop. My Hebrew spelling was uncertain and for this reason I greatly preferred to transmit my daily reports over the phone, much to the despair of the typists in the Tel Aviv head office, not to mention our treasurer. While others would type their stories and send them in the late afternoon by taxi, I claimed that my stories always broke in late evening so that there was no alternative to the phone. At the end of a year, and following phone bills that almost ruined the paper, my spelling improved sufficiently to enable me to make more frequent use of the taxi service.

My strength was not the exclusive interview but the think piece, and I think I anticipated events from time to time. But my editors and readers quite legitimately were more interested in current than future events, and in this sense my apprenticeship in reporting correctly, succinctly, and vividly was merely beginning. This, I must confess, did not come easily to me; it was an eventful time and every day brought two or three little sensations. There was always the temptation to transmit a story without checking its authenticity too thoroughly, but to convey it instead with no clear attribution ("According to knowledgeable circles . . ." etc.) and also with a question mark or two by way of insurance. Furthermore, there was the constant inclination to editorialize rather than to report; political passions were running higher than ever before, and it was not easy to report objectively and not suppress information that did not conform to my predilections. I don't think I always lived up to the high principles of objectivity— there were some incidents about which I do not feel proud in retrospect. Above all, I learned to write under pressure and to meet deadlines; this training helped in later years to produce a column or an editorial in a couple of hours. In academic life, I had little sympathy with students and colleagues who claimed that they needed weeks for the preparation of a paper.

It was May 1946 when I took possession of my desk in the newspaper office, just a few houses up the street from my previous place of work. It was, to be precise, only half a desk, for I shared it with my assistant. A year had passed since the end of the war in Europe, and the world was still in a state of turmoil. Empires were disintegrating and new states came into being all over Asia, Africa, and the Middle East. The future of Europe was in the balance. No great powers of political prophecy were needed to understand that the days of the British Mandate of Palestine were numbered. Britain had needed its position in the Middle East above all as a link with India; with India gone, with Egypt and Iraq having attained virtual independence, the British presence in Palestine was rapidly becoming an anachronism. The military was in favor of staying on but Britain's weakened economic situation made the retreat inevitable. What kind of future was in store for Palestine?

One of my first assignments was to cover, on April 22, 1946, the conference of Ihud, the chief protagonist of Jewish-Arab cooperation. It was a most impressive gathering. Buber was there and Dr. Jehuda L. Magnes, the president of the Hebrew University; Moshe Smilansky, a leader of the farmers; Hugo Bergmann, the distinguished Prague-born philosopher. These were the guardians of the flame of humanism, the moral conscience of the community. The speeches were logical and forceful. The resolutions favored a binational state on the basis of full equality. The speakers attacked the Biltmore program and condemned the "totalitarian and terrorist trends" spreading in the political life of the community and also in the education of the youth. And yet, as I listened to speaker after speaker with sympathy and even enthusiasm, I could not fail to notice that there were few young people in the hall and not a single Arab. In the Arab community there was no support for power sharing, no readiness to accept any of the displaced Jews in the camps in Europe. In brief, Arab-Jewish cooperation resembled the German-Jewish cultural symbiosis before 1933—it was a one-sided affair.

Six weeks later I reported the annual conference of Aliyah Hadasha, the new political party, consisting mainly of new immigrants from Central Europe. Again there were resolutions in favor of immigration and condemning Ben-Gurion's project for a Jewish state. Perhaps one should have waited for some Arab leaders to emerge who would accept the idea of political equality and power sharing or perhaps even partition. But the few that had done so, such as Fakhri Nashashibi, whom I had known slightly, had been killed. From an Arab point of view any concessions must have seemed wholly unwarranted. All over the Middle East, Arab countries were gaining independence. The previous year the Arab League had been founded. Why should the Palestinians give up a single inch? What would have happened to the Jewish minority in this case? The Mufti and Jamal Husseini made no secret: The Jews would have to return to where they had come from; only some of those who had lived in Palestine in 1917, before the Balfour Declaration, would be permitted to stay.

But the Jews, and particularly the young generation, were in no mood to heed the counsels of the Mufti. I remember many a conversation with Arabs in those last days of the Mandate. They were saying that the Jews had always been a minority and how could any fair-minded person expect the Arabs to give up their homeland or even part of it? Why should the Jews be so afraid of minority status? Was it not true that the two peoples had peacefully coexisted for centuries—under Muslim rule in Spain and elsewhere—while in Christian Europe they had been burned at the stake?

True, I said, but that had been a long time ago. In recent centuries Jews had not been that well treated in Arab countries—there had been pogroms in Baghdad and Cairo, even in cosmopolitan Alexandria. Even in faraway Tripoli in November 1945, as Libya became independent, 120 Jews had been massacred.

Once a month I went to the political department of the Jewish Agency, where they followed with a passionate intensity events in the Arab world—Eliyahu Epstein, Eliyahu Sasson and Esra Danin, Reuven Zaslani, Joshua Palmon, Uriel Heidt, Jaacob Shimoni, and others. They followed the press, and from time to time they would travel to Beirut and Damascus, to Cairo, and even to Baghdad. What could be done to engender some more goodwill on the other side? They were quite skeptical; there might be some support among the minorities in the Arab world—the Maronites and the Copts. As for the rest, the only way to neutralize the hostility was to make some judicious payments to individual Arab leaders. But since the Jewish Agency had very little money, not much could be done in this direction either.

This I found reprehensible—how could one engage in such unethical practices? I was told that I had as yet much to learn. It was ridiculous even to try to transplant European standards of political behavior to another part of the world in which baksheesh was considered a perfectly legitimate and even honorable practice. Had I ever heard of Haim Kalvarisky and his ways of making friends and influencing people? Of course I knew Kalvarisky, one of the pillars of the movement of Arab-Jewish rapprochement. Of Russian origin, he had come to Palestine well before World War I and had been prominent in buying land and supervising Jewish plantations. He had been almost the only one in this circle who had contacts with Arabs and from time to time he would even bring an Arab to meet his Jewish friends. My friends at the political department assured me that Kalvarisky's successes, such as they were, had one and only one reason. Did they have to be more specific?

I refused to believe them. Yes, passing presents from time to time was self-evident, but baksheesh as a system? Many years later, when the documents became accessible in the archives, I had to admit that I had been wrong. In 1946 I still had a lot to learn about the political culture of the Middle East.

When the war had ended in 1945, and the Labour party had come to power in Britain, this had given rise to great hopes in the Jewish community in Palestine. When in opposition, the party had passed pro-Zionist resolutions that sometimes exceeded the demands of all but the most extreme Zionists. But once in power, the party promulgated no change in policy—the Balfour Declaration was disregarded, no immigration was permitted, the displaced persons were kept in their camps in Germany. In a vote that had taken place in the camps in February 1946, under supervision of the UN refugees' organization, 97 percent had said that Palestine was their one and only destination.

Illegal refugee ships began to arrive on the shores of Palestine; first *Wingate*, then *Tel Hai*, and then on May 16, 1946, *Max Nordau*. They were intercepted, and there were clashes and victims. Bracha Fuld, a Palmach commander, was killed during "*Wingate* night" in Tel Aviv. When Jewish refugees in La Spezia, the Italian port, about to board a ship for Palestine, were arrested by the Italian authorities, because of British pressure, they went on a hunger strike—and there was an overwhelming response in Palestine. At the same time Irgun and the Sternists ("The Fighters for the Freedom of Israel") attacked individual British soldiers, and Hagana, for the first time, joined them, mining radar stations, bridges, and railway lines. When the Anglo-American Committee, which had been appointed a few months earlier, recommended that one hundred thousand immigrants should be permitted to enter the country irrespective of the political solution, the Hagana declared an armistice. But the Arab leadership rejected this out of hand and the British government ignored the recommendation. The terrorist actions continued.

THIS, IN THE BRIEFEST OUTLINE, was the state of affairs when I began my work as "our correspondent in Jerusalem." My daily routine began in the morning with the study of the daily press, to find out whether I had missed a major story. I had to read ten Jewish dailies, including the *Palestine Post*, not counting the Arabic *Falestin* and *A'Difa'a*. Then there were the press conferences, at least one a day, and sometimes two or three. Political information emanated mainly from the Jewish Agency, the government of a country that did not yet exist, and less frequently, from the Va'ad Leumi (the National Council), the representative body of the Palestinian Jewish community. However, the Va'ad Leumi was boycotted not only by the ultraorthodox and the right wing but also by the Sephardim—because their demands for electoral reform had not been heeded. It was headed by Yizchak Ben Zvi (who later became the second president of Israel) and David Remez, veteran members of the local Labour party, men of a scholarly bent, but not very effective politicians. The Jewish Agency press conferences were frequently chaired by Moshe Shertok (Sharett) and sometimes by David Ben-Gurion. They usually took place in the Jewish Agency building, except during the short period when British armed units had occupied it and arrested some of its leaders, including Shertok. Golda Meirson (Meir) had a little apartment opposite the Jewish Agency building, and we met in her kitchen during those weeks. Later still, in 1948, when the Jewish Agency building had been partly destroyed by a bomb, daily briefings took place in an office that had been rented in lower Ben Yehuda Street, near Zion Square. The meetings, usually in the late morning, proceeded like press conferences all over the world; there would be a short, or not so short, opening statement, followed by a question-and-answer period. In addition, we had to attend Jewish Agency executive meetings; journalists had access to some of these gatherings, and furthermore, heads of departments such as finance or settlement also used to call press conferences. So did the directors of the various funds such as the Keren Hayessod and the Keren Kayemet, and other organizations, important or unimportant, not to mention visiting politicians. It was physically impossible to attend all these meetings, and the journalists, quite irrespective of the political orientation of their papers, would designate an internal division of labor.

The Mandatory government kept a very active Public Information Office (PIO) in the David Brothers' Building, an undistinguished office block in a unique position at the very bottom of King George Street: from the windows of the top floors one had a wonderful view of Mount Zion and the Jaffa Gate. The PIO employed some sixty-five people, headed by Mr. Stubbs, a smallish, dapper man, immaculately dressed, always with a carnation in his buttonhole. Some said that he had no journalistic experience but had been selling dog food before the war, which was probably a calumny. He had no great sense of humor but did his job not badly; he met the international press and the Palestinian Jewish correspondents separately. I think the Arabs boycotted the PIO altogether at the time. The Jewish correspondents sorely tried him, but except on a few occasions, he was almost unflappable; he cannot have had any sympathy for their cause but tried to put the best gloss on his bosses' actions, as a good public relations officer should. The PIO provided great help to the journalists by letting them participate in military actions such as searches of settlements and the interception of refugee ships. All this would have been unthinkable before 1939, but the war had made a great difference in official attitudes toward the media. We also got special passes to enable us to walk (or drive) home during a curfew. Curfews beginning with darkness were imposed rather frequently in those days. I well remember the walks through the dark streets of Jerusalem—with not a single vehicle on the road, except some military jeeps and lorries.

Those who remember René Clair's *Paris qui dort* will have a general idea what a dead city looks and feels like, except that in the summer of 1946 there was the danger of being shot. The soldiers were trigger-happy and often inexperienced. Who could blame them after so many ambushes and attacks? From the office, I had a walk of almost half an hour to my home and I was always debating whether there was greater safety going alone or with a group. Mostly I ended up walking alone, sometimes whistling or singing a not-so-merry song, in the middle of the road. I could either walk down to the German colony past the Russian compound, past the King David Hotel and the railway station, or through Ben Yehuda and King George Street, through the heart of the Jewish sector. Quite often I was not even stopped once by a military patrol, but these walks were always an ordeal. I felt like a little boy walking through a dark forest, except that the dangers were not imaginary. Since not much happened anyway once a curfew was imposed, I made it a habit more and more often to stay home, or, if I had to be in the office late for some reason or another, I stayed with a friend who had an apartment just a few hundred yards away.

The Irgun planned to blow up the PIO at the same time as the King David Hotel (July 1946). It would not have been a great military feat, for just about anyone could enter it almost anytime. But there was a change of plans and so the PIO continued to function to the very end.

During mid-June 1946, tension rose further. In the night of the seventeenth, Palmach units mined eleven bridges that connected Israel with the neighboring countries, bringing rail traffic to Jordan and Syria and Lebanon to a standstill. It was an act of sabotage rather than of terror, but on the old *via maris*, the old coastal road in the north, it ended in a major tragedy. The Palmach unit was spotted by a British unit, which fired a flare that hit the explosives of the assault team, and all fourteen of them were killed. One of the fourteen, the son of a well-known and much-liked Zionist leader, was buried in Jerusalem. A cortège of thousands went in the procession to the Mount of Olives

Cemetery; as we passed through the Oriental quarters the women were ululating, as was the custom to express great grief and sorrow, and the rabbis were reciting psalms. I had always felt a horror of burials and left the scene as soon as I could.

Today the neighborhood of AhZiv, where the accident happened, is part of the Israeli "Golden Coast"; a kibbutz has been founded there with a well-known guest house, but there is also a branch of the Club Méditerranée, a national park, a museum, and a youth hostel. A man named Avivi even tried for a while to establish an independent Ahzivland. A black metal monument commemorates the fourteen that were killed. I had known and liked two of them; had they lived they would now tell their bored grandchildren about their exploits in antediluvian times.

The period before the establishment of the state of Israel has become the subject of many television programs based on '40s footage. They show Jewish and Arab demonstrators, British troops searching for weapons and putting up barricades, international committees arriving, and British officials making statements. On one such recent showing my daughter Sylvia spotted a young man alighting from a car, with open collar and a straw hat, dutifully following a group of dignitaries. We played the film back; it was only a fleeting moment but there could be no doubt, it was me, even though I could have sworn I never possessed, let alone wore, a straw hat. Since then I have discovered myself in several such films or pictures, always in a group, in the company of people only some of whom I can now identify.

Thinking back to those years, it sometimes seems to me that much of the time I spent getting in and out of cars, although I did not have one—few did at that time. We were constantly on the move: Thus, on August 18, 1946, the ship *Bracha Fuld* (named after the Palmach commander killed during *Wingate* night a few weeks earlier) was found empty near Caesarea, its passengers having fled during the night. The following night *Amirans*, a very small vessel, also broke through the blockade and landed 187 passengers. But most ships were caught—*Pal-*

mach with 900, *Knesset Israel* with 3,800. The routine was to take them to Atlit, a big military prison camp south of Haifa. However, when they became too many (and as an act of deterrence) the authorities announced they would be deported to camps in Cyprus. Curfew was declared in Haifa but disregarded by the population—three Jews were killed and seven wounded. Palmach tried to sabotage the ships *Empire Rival* and *Empire Heywood*, but without much success.

The PIO and the army press office let us visit the ships that were intercepted and sometimes even provided transport from Jerusalem. We had to hang around the PIO because departure would often be on a few minutes' notice. One had to develop a certain degree of indifference vis-à-vis human suffering to keep one's sanity. If one had seen one or two of the refugee ships, one had seen them all: Sanitary conditions were abominable, but the passengers survived, and I for one had no doubt that sooner or later they would find a better future in freedom—probably in Palestine. It was difficult to hate the British officers and soldiers. They obeyed orders without much enthusiasm and without unnecessary cruelty. True, on a few occasions after some of their comrades had been killed they would get a little wild. I have no doubt that soldiers from most other nations would have been more violent.

I saw a great deal of anguish and suffering during those days, but some scenes I recall more vividly than others. One of these, datelined Haifa Harbor, I described in a dispatch to my newspaper:

At three this afternoon, September 3, six hundred refugees from the *Four Freedoms* were transferred to *Empire Heywood*, which will take them to Cyprus. Those present will not forget this scene. I do not accuse the men who carried out this operation, from private to brigadier general; they merely followed orders, and they did so as decently and humanely as possible.

On board nothing was heard but shouting, loud moaning, and

tears. Half of the refugees seem to be ill, some suffering from nervous or mental diseases; they shout "water, water" and want to jump into the sea. They are restrained by fellow passengers.

In a corner I saw a mother with her daughter. The mother is weeping, the daughter tries to comfort her, but in vain. They look vaguely familiar to me, but this is probably just imagination. I talk to the daughter, and it emerges that they had come from my hometown and lived in my immediate neighborhood. The woman kisses and caresses me, sobbing all the time. She tells me about the tortures in the camp where her husband perished. After the liberation—waiting and again waiting; later still, the trip on board this ship without sufficient food and drink. She is at the end of her tether: "Who will take care of us?" "It was so horrible," she says, pointing to the tattooed Auschwitz number. She repeats it several times.

Two boys and a girl in their early teens try to explain to the brigadier that they will on no account board the other ship. Their mother is very ill and was taken to a hospital on land. The officer does not understand; the children kneel in front of him; he is clearly embarrassed. A translator is needed, and I volunteer. The brigadier hesitates for a moment. "There may be the devil to pay," he says. There is a total ban as far as the landing of refugees is concerned. But he gives orders to the authorities on land to prepare for the reception of three children—"exceptional circumstances." I murmur a few words of thanks. Seven years ago this day Britain and France declared war on Nazi Germany. The tragedy is not over yet.

I kept my composure throughout these meetings, but that evening, back in Jerusalem, I broke down, the only time I can recall during all those years. Some chord had been struck; the whole tragedy of my family, of so many friends and acquaintances, of European Jewry—which, as many others have done, I had suppressed—became alive as the result of this chance encounter. Perhaps I would have been less moved if they had not been from my hometown, or if the girl had been less attractive or their sorrow less obvious. I do not know the answer. I promised

to write them in Cyprus and I did receive an answer. I do not
know what later happened to them; in all probability they came
to Israel after the state was established and the girl of the *Four
Freedoms* is now probably a grandmother. These visits became
almost routine. I had reported a similar happening only a few
weeks earlier:

FROM OUR OWN CORRESPONDENT, HAIFA:
Together with several other correspondents I visited today some
of the ships on which 2,300 illegal immigrants are concentrated.
There are 700 on *Max Nordau*. The men, mostly young, are half
naked and unshaved. They shouted "liberty," "free immigration," as we went on board. Since the ship is so small, only part
of the passengers can be on deck at any time. Each cabin houses
100 people, the space allocated to each person is slightly less than
seven feet in length, two feet wide, and less than two feet high.
There was one little window, and the stench was intolerable; after
a few minutes I thought I would faint and went again on deck.
There were long queues for the one and only washroom and the
toilets. There was a doctor on board and he told me that the first
cases of dysentery had been reported. How long could people live
in such conditions? "I would measure it in hours rather than
days," he said. Many languages are heard, but Yiddish seems to
be the *lingua franca*. It is difficult to describe the mood of the
"illegals"; they hope that they will be permitted to go ashore in
a few hours. They complain that the Jewish community does not
know in what conditions they live and perhaps does not sufficiently care. As we leave the ship it is announced that 800 will be
permitted to land this very day. Great jubilation all around.*

The next morning brought another excursion provided by British forces. During the night some railway line had been blown
up by Irgun or Lehi. But railway lines, as even a child knew,
could be repaired in a few hours. So this was a nonstory rating

---

*I should perhaps note at this stage that while all my dispatches are given
verbatim (in translation), major cuts had to be made.

perhaps a few lines, after the unsettling encounters of the previous day.

Yet a few days later I remember walking in the sands of Rishon Lezion, somewhere near a rivulet called Sorek by the Arabs, Rubin by the Jews. Another refugee ship had landed, or was said to have landed, and by courtesy of the Second Parachute Brigade (but it could also have been the Third) I participated in the chase of those who had landed. Much as I love the seashore, I always hated walking in the dunes, which at that place extend for a mile or even two inland. It was a very hot day, every step in the roaming sands was torture, and, but for a mosque on a faraway hill, one would have lost all orientation. This was the tomb of Nabi Rubin, once a famous site visited by thousands of Arab pilgrims, but now quite desolate. I dutifully followed the captain who was in charge of public relations. The chase extended further south to the Yavneh sands up to where in later years the city of Ashdod was built.

Today the assignment would be given to a helicopter pilot who would obtain the information needed within a few minutes. But this was 1946, and the parachutists went through the motions as if it were a major military maneuver. They knew full well that if indeed an enemy was hiding under the wormwood shrubs, it would be an unarmed enemy, including women and children. They were disciplined soldiers, and although they were cursing, they cursed no one in particular. This was not the kind of raid they enjoyed. Even a general was there, either Bols (who later became chief of staff) or Cassels. After a few hours the chase was called off. If there had been any illegals in the first place, they had long ago reached Tel Aviv or, even more likely, been distributed among some of the kibbutzim.

Most of the immigrants were caught well before they reached the shores of Eretz Israel. Sometimes there would be a newspaperman among them. I recall I. F. Stone of the New York newspaper *P.M.*, an almost legendary figure at the time, hardworking, very thorough, highly opinionated, hard of hearing. We became friendly, and I shared my desk with him during the weeks (or months) he was in Palestine. In later years we drifted apart; somehow he persuaded himself that South Korea had attacked the North (and not vice versa) and that America had somehow prepared bacteriological warfare against the North Koreans and the Chinese. For many years I did not see him, but one day in the 1980s, taking a stroll along one of the branches of Rock Creek Park in Washington, near my home and his, I ran into him, and we had the first of several long talks, reminiscing about the old days. He had given up active journalism years earlier and was deep into Greek studies, which resulted in a book on Socrates. But he still thought of the years of 1946 and 1947 as one of the highlights of his professional career; he was quite angry about the editor of a magazine who had just sent him a new Ben-Gurion biography on the assumption that he would do a hatchet job on Ben-Gurion because he had been very critical of him forty years earlier. Stone said that he had been in favor of a binational state, which would have been the ideal solution. Unfortunately, it had been a noble dream. In any case, the dispute of 1946 had been a family quarrel—what impertinence by someone who seemed not to care one way or another whether Israel existed to expect him to attack someone who, with all his weaknesses, had been a great leader!

When the British government announced on August 12, 1946, that from now on illegal immigrants would be deported to Cyprus, several thousand were concentrated in Athlit and other camps, I persuaded my editors that I should proceed to Cyprus to write on the fate of the immigrants. They had some doubts—justified, as it subsequently appeared—whether my presence in Cyprus would be of any use, but gave me a free hand. Somehow I got a passport and a seat on the airplane that was commuting three or four times a week between Haifa and Nicosia. The plane could seat four or five passengers at most, and the pilot, quite obviously, had gained his experience in the war and was not accustomed to take into consideration that he was no longer alone in the aircraft. It was my first flight ever, the plane was not pressurized, and I was more than a little apprehensive. For unknown reasons we had to land in Beirut. It was a very clear day and one could see Cyprus soon after leaving the shores of Lebanon.

Nicosia was even hotter than Haifa, and since I could not afford one of the better hotels, I spent a very uncomfortable night in that city. I knew that the refugees had been brought to Famagusta, a harbor in the east of the island; next morning I took a bus from Nicosia that carried me through a landscape not unlike the hills of Judaea. We passed a dozen villages—one was Turkish, the next Greek. There were no mixed villages. From the comments of the other passengers, I gathered that there was no love lost between the two peoples. There were churches that had been originally mosques, and vice versa. In the old city of Famagusta, I even came across a Gothic mosque (Lala Mustafa Pasha). But just as no one would have imagined that peaceful Beirut, the Nice and Monte Carlo of the Middle East, would one day be a battlefield in ruins, no one envisaged that this little island would be rendered by bitter strife, and partitioned.

A trip abroad was a rare occasion, and in the few days prior to my departure I had tried to read up on Cyprus. Unfortunately, the standard book on the subject, G. F. Hill's four-volume history, had not yet been completed and as a result I knew more in the end about Richard Coeur de Lion's siege of Famagusta and about Venetian and Ottoman rule than about more recent times. One author had called Famagusta one of the most remarkable ruins; another, a city of riches and courtesans. I found neither riches nor courtesans, nor even that many ruins.

I went to the leading hotel in town on the assumption that I would find some colleagues at the bar. This happened to be the case; an Arab journalist representing one of the international telegraphic agencies welcomed me very warmly; he mistook me for a roving *New York Times* correspondent, very famous at the time but now, alas, forgotten. From my colleagues I learned that the refugees were concentrated in a place named Karaolos, north of Famagusta, but that so far there was nothing to report. I learned that a room in the hotel was out of reach given my modest budget. Without difficulty I found another, far cheaper. Unfortunately, the heat wave had become quite intolerable. To escape it, I went to an open-air cinema showing a Sonja Henie film, watching the queen of ice making her pirouettes and double axels in perhaps the greatest heat I had ever experienced this side of Nigeria. On my way back to the hotel I bought a bottle of ouzo, assuming that it would help me to fall asleep, which it did.

Next morning I hired a bicycle, and found the site of the camp without difficulty. It was situated a few miles out of Famagusta, between the main road leading north and the sea. Soldiers of the Royal Engineers were in the process of putting up barbed wire and tents. Men, women, and children were dispersed over a wide area. Some of them were bathing. I had a camera and slowly approached the camp without actually entering it; I tried to talk to some of the refugees but was sent away by a sentry who pointed to a sign: "KEEP OUT! FORBIDDEN AREA! ENTRANCE FORBIDDEN." All this proceeded without attracting any attention.

FROM OUR OWN CORRESPONDENT, FAMAGUSTA, AUGUST 27, 1946: Famagusta, 8,000 inhabitants, this is surely one of the most boring places on earth. The first person I encountered in the street was a senior British officer, the chief judge of the Jerusalem military court. After ten no one is seen in the streets; it is simply too hot. The shops remain open, but the owners sleep in their chairs—like everyone else. The town reawakens after five in the evening. Life centers on the Savoy Hotel. A little orchestra plays a potpourri of Viennese melodies. I order ice cream. The waiter tries to be helpful but says that he does not know the various flavors of ice cream in English. What color is it? It is not white . . . Give it to me anyway. . . .

I am looking for Mr. Allen, head of the Cyprus Public Relations office. Poor man, nothing ever happened in Cyprus and now this sudden influx of correspondents. "Not since Churchill's visit did we have this many journalists," he moans. I do not dare to ask when Churchill visited; it must have been a long time ago.

In another corner I meet a group of local Jews. There are some twenty-five families in nearby Larnaca—they want to be of help. They tell me that there is a sizable group of Greek Jews in the camp, families with many children; they feel isolated since no one understands their language. . . . Elsewhere I encounter the Joint Representatives.

The Karaolos camp commander visits the Savoy. I corner him: "What kind of routine have you established?" "I try to intervene as little as possible. I wish the refugees would make their own arrangements. Unfortunately, they are not willing to cooperate." (This changed after a few days.) "What is your main problem at present?" "There is no electricity; there is nothing to do in the camps after seven. I hope electricity will be installed in a few days." He is polite, not a bad sort. I talk to another British official: "I sympathize with the refugees," he says. "I know how difficult it was for the Greek refugees from the mainland during the war. And these poor people, after all they went through. . ." "But why are they forbidden to write letters?" "Quarantine, a temporary measure . . ." Inevitable. [I ended my report with an *Othello* quotation:] "Here is my journey's end"—this will not be their journey's end.

I spent the afternoon swimming and walking on the beach. I had seen Famagusta first in 1938, and the city wall had impressed me even from the distance. Now I found myself almost alone on the most beautiful sand beach I had ever seen, nor were there any other swimmers in the blue Mediterranean. The sea was actually blue in those prepollution days; more recently much of the eastern Mediterranean has become unsuitable for swimming. My eyes were not those of a developer and mass tourism organizer, but even I could not fail to realize the potential of this finest of all beaches. Ten years later the great tourist invasion began, and modern hotels were built, but the prosperity lasted only a short while; the civil war and the Turkish invasion put an end to the Famagusta boom. Cyprus's biggest harbor found itself just inside the Turkish side and it became a ghost town.

The next day I went to the Old City, mainly inhabited by Turks, the Greek "new city," and the nearby ruins of the ancient town of Salamis. Outside the harbor area there was very little traffic. The journalists were still sitting in the bar waiting for a story to break. But nothing happened except that on the third or fourth day of my stay a small item appeared in the *Cyprus Mail* according to which a Palestinian journalist had tried to infiltrate the Karaolos camp. No names were mentioned, but the item still had some sinister implications, and I decided to return on the next plane from Nicosia.

Another trip stands out that took place not long after, to the annual conference of the Interparliamentary Union in Cairo. This was an organization founded as far back as 1888. It consisted of parliamentarians from various countries who met to discuss matters of common interest—above all, the promotion of peace and democratic institutions. As far as international or national politics were concerned, it was not of the slightest importance, nor did its members take their activities too seriously. But it provided welcome holidays for backbenchers who had not as many opportunities to travel as today. Sometimes, unofficial negotiations took place that in the end led perhaps to some new initiatives. For me, it was an opportunity to meet interesting people, even though front-rank politicians seldom had the time to attend these meetings. That year the conference was perhaps of more than ordinary interest because of the participation of the East Europeans. The Russians did not appear. This was the short interval between the end of World War II and the Stalinization of Eastern Europe, and the East Europeans still had some freedom to maneuver.

I had never been to Cairo and again persuaded my editors to let me go. Visiting Egypt was easy in those days: One caught a taxi seating five or six passengers at the Jerusalem General Post Office at eight in the morning, reached Ismalia at two in the afternoon and Cairo not much later. The fare was less than a pound. My main impression of the trip was that the desert was hilly and that there wasn't much desert in the first place. Some form of vegetation could be seen all along the road, so there must have been some water after all.

Having checked into my hotel I soon spotted a fattish man, his face hidden behind a newspaper, who followed me around. I felt flattered but decided to ignore him. Next, I proceeded to the building of the Egyptian parliament to present my credentials. I had borrowed a small portable typewriter, a Hermes Baby, and this almost proved to be my undoing. The model was apparently unknown in Egypt at the time. Having seen my passport and the suspicious machine, everyone had suddenly disappeared from the entrance hall of the parliament building. Rifles were pointed at me—another Palestinian terrorist trying to blow up the parliament and perhaps even King Farouk, about to open the conference. I offered to open the typewriter but this was the last thing they wanted me to do. After a few minutes the excitement passed and a police officer ordered me to follow him to another room, where he sat down, wrote a note, and without saying a word passed it on to me. It seemed gibberish, and I told him that it was written in a language unknown to me. This surprised him no end, and he asked me to read it again. After I read it for about the tenth time, it suddenly dawned on me that it was Hebrew written in Roman alphabet letters. The police officer in question, apparently a Jew, wanted to check my bona fides.

Having passed the examination, I passed the rest of the stay more or less uneventfully. Neither Germans nor Italians had been invited. There was an influential American senator (Owen Brewster, I believe), but his speeches did not leave a lasting impression. There was a Frenchman, Marius Moutet—a Socialist, an on-and-off minister in many governments, an excellent speaker in the classical French tradition—making a virtuoso performance with his mellifluous cascades of words. At the end one did not remember what it had been all about. I found the East Europeans most interesting—Vasile Luka of Romania, for instance, a leading member of the Politburo. Cocksure, smiling, he was certain the future belonged to him and his party. Within a few years he disappeared in one of the many bloody political purges. Tsola Dragoicheva of Bulgaria was more Stalinist than Stalin; she seemed half overcome by the occasion, half contemptuous of the bourgeois parliamentarians who did not even know that their time had passed. She was luckier than Luka. Well into her nineties, she is still alive somewhere in a Sofia old-age home, having witnessed all the other Communist leaders come and go.

My idol was Károlyi, or, to give him his full name, Count Miháily Károlyi of Nagy Károlyi. He was in his seventies at the time, highly educated, a grand seigneur of the old school, who spoke all major European languages, albeit with a marked Hungarian accent. He was a radical democrat, and after the fall of the Austrian monarchy, had been prime minister of Hungary for a few months. Subsequently, he spent more than twenty years in exile, the Horthy regime not being to his taste. He had returned to Budapest not long ago and told me that he had just been appointed ambassador to France. He loved France, but somehow he had hoped that he would be able to play a more important role in the politics of his country.

I attached myself to him; he invited me for a walk along Kasr al-Nil Street and Suleiman Pasha (now Talaat Harb), Cairo's most elegant avenue at the time. I tried to sound him out: Would Hungary opt for democracy? He was not sure—"*On verra.*" He was quite outspoken and full of doubts whether for an independent-minded man like himself there was room in the new order emerging in Eastern Europe. Then, having passed countless luxury shops, cinemas, and coffeehouses, he suddenly stopped and pointed to one of the side streets, which, unlike Kasr al-Nil, was dirty, poor, in a state of advanced decay. Pointing to the obvious contrast between rich and poor, between elegance and shabbiness, he said: "Young man, mark my words, there will be major trouble in this country. . . ." I thought of this conversation a few years later when King Farouk was exiled and a new order emerged in Egypt: Midan Ismail (Ismail Square) became Midan Tahrir (Liberation Square), and many other streets changed their names. The social and economic problems of Egypt, alas, have not been solved despite all the reforms. The crucial problem was demographic: In 1946 Cairo had less than 1 million inhabitants; today it has 13 million. In 1946 Egypt had about 20 million inhabitants; today its population is equal to that of France.

Count Károlyi stayed on as ambassador for a while after the Communist takeover, but resigned at the time of the first Budapest show trial (of Rajk) and became an emigré a second time in his life. He died in Vence, a little town in the south of France, in 1955, aged eighty.

FROM OUR OWN CORRESPONDENT, CAIRO, APRIL 27, 1947:
Interview with Prof. Ludwig, an old, experienced diplomat. He was Austria's representative in the League of Nations and also chief government spokesman in the 1920s and '30s: "We have 590,000 displaced persons, 11,000 of them in camps. All the Jews want to emigrate. I wish they would work as long as they are in Austria. I was interned in Dachau with many Jews; all of us had to work. I have many friends in Palestine. And now I'll teach you how to interview someone. I happen to be professor of journalism at Vienna University." He asks me a great many questions about the situation in Palestine.

Prohaska, a leading Czech Communist: "The Palestinian problem is very complicated. The Jews should have their state, but agreement with the Arabs is a precondition. There is no anti-Semitism in Czechoslovakia."

Károlyi: "The Jewish problem is a social, not a racial, problem. I fought anti-Semitism for forty years. The fact that Horthy handed over 400,000 Jews to Hitler is one of my most bitter recollections. If the world will turn to the left, the prospects of the Jews will improve, but present trends . . ." He did not finish the sentence. "I am not a Communist but pro-Soviet. Europe needs an understanding between East and West." He criticized U.S. policy. "In any case, Hungary has no alternative. I wish we had one."

Hartwig P., a leader of the Danish Social Democrats, Danish representative in the UN: "We have much sympathy for the remnants of the Jewish people after all they suffered. There seems only one solution—partition."

On July 22, 1946, a few minutes past noon, on my way from a meeting of the Jewish Agency to the Public Information Office, I heard a dull, big bang; it was the bombing of the King David Hotel, the biggest terrorist attack so far. About three weeks earlier the authorities had occupied the Jewish Agency building and arrested the leaders. But there was no direct connection between these two events: The bombing of the King David, where the secretariat of the Mandatory government was housed, had been planned well before; it had the code name "Operation Chick." Events during that day have been described in minute detail, but they have not fully cleared up some essential questions: Had the Hagana given the Irgun the green light? There is no doubt that the Hagana supreme command had known about the plan in general terms, albeit not its extent and the likely number of victims involved. The operation had been approved by a majority of three to two. But on July 17, following an ultimatum by Chaim Weizmann, who had somehow learned about the impending operation, the Hagana command reversed its decision and demanded that the Irgun should not proceed with it. Had the Irgun given a telephonic warning to prevent loss of life? Again, the evidence is not altogether clear. Someone seems to have phoned the King David switchboard. But whether the call went through is not certain; in any case, there were a great many calls by cranks in those days and no one had seen reason to give this particular one much attention. The warning would probably have come too late for the evacuation of the building.

When I reached the PIO not long after the explosion, a curfew had not yet been imposed, and I joined the small group of journalists in front of the building. According to the first news, the whole building had collapsed, but from the distance of three hundred yards the damage looked less serious—the center of the building was standing, and so was the northern wing; only the southern wing had disappeared. At first there were incomplete figures about the loss of life because so many people were missing. Later it was announced that ninety-two had been killed, about half British, the others Jewish and Arab. It was the biggest terrorist exploit by far, even though leading British officials, such as the chief secretary of the Mandatory government, escaped. It came as a great shock precisely because the preceding weeks and months in Jerusalem had been calm. We all had good acquaintances among those killed and injured, which also included several journalists, among them Richard Mowrer.

The sequel is known: further military curfews and searches and, on the other hand, an end to the collaboration between the Hagana, Irgun, and Lehi.

FROM OUR OWN CORRESPONDENT, JERUSALEM, JULY 24, 1946:
As these lines are written, forty hours after the explosion, excavations in the ruins of the King David Hotel continue around the clock. And there is still hope that some human lives might be saved. With the collapse of these enormous slabs of concrete it seemed impossible that any living being, however small, might have survived—they must all have suffocated. Nevertheless, the experts hesitated to blow up the concrete slabs, and work continues with pickaxes, electric drills, and hammers as giant searchlights illuminate the ghastly scene. Work proceeds in conditions of extreme danger; some of the excavators acquired their skills in the London blitz. Every half hour orders are given: "Total silence. Stop work. Do not move. Do not leave your place. Do not talk." Total silence, and then suddenly the special amplifiers detect a voice underneath the rubble, and then another. During the day two persons were saved, one of them an Arab policeman. At 11:00 a voice was heard from a room on the second floor: "Who are you?" "Thompson" was the answer. He could not immediately be reached but a water hose was pushed through to the place where he was buried. Thompson informed us that in a neighboring room a man called Mantura was still alive. Elsewhere contact is established with two young women. In both cases the approach is exceedingly difficult; each stone has to be removed by hand so as to prevent any further collapse that would kill both those buried down below and those trying to save them. Work will continue for many more hours.

FROM OUR OWN CORRESPONDENT, JERUSALEM, JULY 26, 1946:
In front of the government hospital, dozens of families and friends
of the victims, Red Cross trucks, wreaths, with Arab, Jewish,
Greek, and Armenian gravediggers squatting with their backs to
the wall of the law court. Every now and then an ambulance
arrives. "Anyone alive?" "No," says the driver. British policemen
clear the road for those carrying the corpses covered by canvas to
the mortuary. Stokely and Musgrave, two senior British officials,
are buried near the Dormitio on Mount Zion. Shaw, the chief
secretary of the Mandatory government, and Fitzgerald, the chief
justice, are among those paying their last respects. More sighs,
more tears. Another ambulance arrives. "Three girls," the driver
says: Rumors quickly spread—they are alive, someone talked to
them, one of them jumped off the truck. No, they are all dead,
two Arab typists named Tuma and Buarshi, and one Jewish girl,
Lea Bacharach. Yet another ambulance—an unknown Jew, no
one had identified him; he is buried under the name Abraham
Abraham. And so the ghastly procession continues.

The King David Hotel had been my favorite among Jerusalem
hotels: Like Shepheard's in Cairo and Raffles in Singapore, it
was not so much a hotel as a landmark, an institution, the symbol
of a whole era. Opened in 1930, it originally belonged to a Swiss
consortium and to Egyptian Jews. During the 1930s and World
War II everyone who was someone, passing through Jerusalem,
stayed there. I could not, of course, afford at the time to stay
there, but countless interviews and briefings had taken place in
the lobby of the hotel.

I always found it difficult to understand why people should sit
in a bar for hours. But the bar of the King David was unique,
not with regard to the quality of its drinks but as an observation
point. During the war and even in 1946, one could see kings
passing, politicians and generals as well as the very rich, their
retinues and those who for one reason or another wanted to be
accepted as VIPs. After Haile Selassie of Ethiopia had departed,
King Zog of Albania arrived; at any time one might see the

commanders of the various British armies in the Middle East or General Georges Catroux of the Free French; Nahas Pasha and Nuri Said, the prime ministers of Egypt and Iraq; rich Muslims and rich Jews from Egypt; wealthy Christians from Beirut; the local high society; young women in and out of uniform; and ladies of a certain age, as the French say.

The terrace of the hotel is even more picturesque; it has figured in movies ranging from *Exodus* to several based on Agatha Christie's stories. Both the scenery and the interior, Assyrian-style, lend themselves as an ideal background to high life and international intrigue, with an admixture of the exotic.

In later years, once it had been rebuilt, I frequented the swimming pool of the hotel, surrounded by palm trees and cypresses. From the terrace there is an unending number of possibilities to photograph (or just to observe) the city walls across the Valley of Hinnom, and also Mount Zion.

The events that took place on that day in July 1946 are now more than half forgotten. Most of those who carried out the bombing as well as most of the survivors are no longer alive. Yet even now, after all these years, it is not easy to write dispassionately about the events, the motives behind it, and the consequences. The case for the "activists" is briefly this: Speeches and editorials alone would not have induced the British to leave Palestine. Time was of the essence: After 1947, a UN decision envisaging the establishment of a Jewish and Arab state would have been unthinkable, for with the deterioration in relations between Washington and Moscow there could have been no agreement. This is one side of the case.

But it is also true that the British would not have been able to hold on to Palestine much longer in any case, that other ways of struggle were feasible, and that partition would have ensued with or without UN sanction, even if it had come a year or two later. Did Irgun and Stern precipitate the British exodus?

The number of those killed in Palestine between August 1945 and August 1947 was 260, of them 141 British, 65 Jews and 34

Arabs. These figures are quite low if compared with other terrorist campaigns outside Europe (or with the Irish); in one single year, 1972, there were 450 fatalities in Northern Ireland but the British still did not leave Northern Ireland even though there was much more sensitivity in the 1970s with regard to loss of life than during the immediate aftermath of the war. In brief, Britain left Palestine because Palestine had lost its importance for a country that had ceased to be a superpower. On the other hand, the Irgun strategy caused tangible damage to the Jews of Palestine, some immediate, some long term. Among the immediate damage was the loss of weapons. The British authorities reacted with widespread searches. In the course of one search in Kibbutz Yagur, British army units seized some thirty arms caches, which was a sizable part of the countrywide arsenal of the Hagana. More weapons were taken in Dorot, Ruhama, and other places. When the *yishuv* (the Jewish community in Palestine) had to fight for its survival in 1948, these arms were sorely missed by the defenders and made the war of independence so costly. These tactical considerations apart, there were the long-term consequences of the terror—the belief that bombs were the solution to almost every political problem led to the Deir Yassin massacre and it contributed to a frame of mind that in later years made one of the most difficult political conflicts of our times virtually insoluble.

The great majority of the Jewish community dissociated itself from the terrorists after the King David bombing. Generally speaking, the backing of the terrorists among the Jewish community was greatly exaggerated in the media at the time. When the first elections took place after the establishment of the State of Israel, Herut, Menachem Begin's party, polled no more than 11 percent, and two years later the vote declined to a mere 6 percent. But despite its opposition to the terror, the community still did not want to collaborate with the British against the terrorists.

On occasion one got a glimpse of what went on behind the scenes of British counterterrorism. I covered the trial of Captain

Roy Farran, of the Special Air Service Regiment. Farran was accused of having abducted Alexander Rubowitz, a young member of Lehi who had been caught while distributing leaflets and was missing since—believed to have died while in the hands of his captors. It appeared that there were two small antiterrorist squads that reported not to the police but directly to Colonel Bernard Ferguson, who had been with the Chindits in the Burma campaign. The disappearance of Rubowitz was reported in the press and Farran's name was mentioned in this context. Whereupon Farran lost his nerve and fled to Syria. He subsequently returned to Palestine, and in view of the sensational circumstances of his disappearance, a trial became inevitable. Colonel Ferguson appeared, an eccentric who played much of the time with his monocle and refused to reveal to the court what Farran had told him. Since there was no corpus delicti, Farran was acquitted. Lehi later on tried to avenge their comrade, and Farran was injured by a parcel bomb. The trial demonstrated that in view of their lack of knowledge of language and people, these counterterrorists were quite ineffectual. If the British nevertheless succeeded in arresting terrorist leaders and militants, it was owing to a time-honored practice—the use of paid informers, of which there were not a few.

We knew much less about the bitter debates that went on at the time among the British Command dealing with terrorism. Cunningham, the high commissioner, argued in favor of a political solution; as he saw it, the battle against the terror was essentially a task for the police, not the army, which should be brought in only in extreme circumstances. Field Marshal Montgomery, on the other hand, now chief of staff, and General Sir Miles Dempsey, commander in chief of British forces in the Middle East, argued that the policy of appeasement had failed, that the army should be unleashed, frequent mass searches and arrests be carried out, heavy collective fines be imposed, and generally a more "robust mentality" be shown. Montgomery probably drew on his experience as commander in Haifa just before the outbreak of the war. But the situations were not remotely similar. Mass arrests were carried out, but they did not decisively affect the operations of Irgun and Stern with their relatively few militants—probably less than a thousand. In any case, the "robust" policy would have made a political solution impossible and the government in London became gradually convinced that such a solution was imperative.

In the meantime the Mandatory authorities followed a policy that constituted a compromise between a strong hand and abdication. The terrorists continued mining the roads and railways. There was one major attack in May 1947—the attempt to storm Acre prison. This was the answer to the execution two weeks earlier of Dov Gruner, an Irgun fighter. Some forty Irgun and Lehi members (and some two hundred Arabs) escaped, but eight were killed and thirteen of the attackers apprehended. There were other acts of terror during 1947, and they always attracted publicity. But by and large the terrorist campaign became of less importance.

I learned early on one of the basic lessons about terrorism: that without publicity it amounts to very little. But mere repetition of terrorist acts does not engender greater publicity; on the contrary, interest flags unless the terrorists can think of some new angle or gimmick. In any case, there were other stories to report.

FROM OUR OWN CORRESPONDENT, OCTOBER 31, 1946:
Kfar Etzion, the highest settlement in Palestine, 966 meters above sea level, lies southeast of Jerusalem, between Bethlehem and Hebron. Jewish settlers tried twice to set up their tents here; twice they failed. They had to vacate Kfar Etzion in 1936 during the riots. But they came back in 1943. Tomorrow a third settlement will be established here by a young group of pioneers of the Bne Akiba, a religious labor youth movement. They were born and grew up in Meah Shearim and other ultrareligious quarters of Jerusalem; they went to orthodox schools, and their families were bitterly opposed to the idea that their children should join a collective settlement. Yet these youngsters had their way. Last night in the Kfar Etzion dining hall we listened to the obligatory speeches,

which were, however, mercifully short. Old Rabbi Benjamin*
said: "The mountains are so high, the rocks so big—and the
pioneers so young. . . ." Then they danced the hora—and went
to sleep. This morning they went out in seven trucks to Deir Abu
Said, where their settlement will be. The soil seems to be fertile,
but an immense quantity of stones will have to be removed. The
girls started working in the fields while the young men were
setting up two blockhouses. The air is wonderfully clear. As one
looks to the west we see the Mediterranean in the distance and
in the east the hills of Transjordan. There will be difficult years
ahead for this new kibbutz in the mountains.

There were difficult years ahead. When Palestine was partitioned, the Kfar Etzion settlements found themselves outside the
Jewish state. They were cut off well before the British Mandate
ended; they had no food, their ammunition ran out, the attempt
to get a convoy through from Jerusalem failed. One hundred
and thirty-five young men and women died in the defense of
these settlements; 359 survived. They surrendered to the (Jorda-
nian) Arab Legion, which treated them as prisoners of war. They
returned after the armistice was concluded between Jordan and
Israel. In 1967, after the Six-Day War, a new settlement was
established where Kfar Etzion had once been, by, among others,
some of the sons and daughters of the settlers whom I had
accompanied in 1946.

Palestine in 1946 and 1947 was a very small country, and
within a short time I came to know the leading politicians and
public figures. It would be of no great interest to mention all of
them, for some I did not know well and the biographies of others
have been written in considerable detail. I shall therefore deal
only with some incidents that, for one reason or other, stuck in
memory, a highly selective approach, to be sure, but the only
one possible in the circumstances.

*"Rabbi Benjamin" looked like a rabbi but was not one; it was the pen
name of Hebrew writer Y. Radler-Feldman (1880–1957), one of the early
members of the League for Jewish-Arab Rapprochement.

Chaim Weizmann had been in Zionist politics for fifty years; by 1947 he was a sick, old man, half blind. Checking on his age, I find that he was just one or two years older than I am now. He certainly gave the impression of someone no longer in full possession of his faculties. He had been ousted from his position as president of the World Zionist movement. His policy—his basic orientation toward England—was in ruins, as Bevin had turned sharply against the Zionist aspirations. When he appeared as a witness before the UN Special Committee on Palestine in August 1947, he seemed so infirm that I feared he would not be able to finish his speech. In the beginning his words were barely audible. Yet within a few minutes I was spellbound; his infirmities were forgotten. Here was the authentic voice of the Jewish people—and what a voice! There was something almost demonic in his impact on people, in his combination of seemingly irrefutable logic and appeal to emotion. He was probably the most persuasive man I ever met. Some Western statesmen were most reluctant to confront him because they knew they would find it exceedingly difficult to resist him without appearing boorish. Yet all these years he had been the leader of a people without country and state, utterly powerless. He was the kind of man who when entering a room would attract everyone's attention; without his saying a word, conversation would cease. In later years I had the occasion to watch presidents, prime ministers, and national and international leaders, but I never experienced this kind of charisma—to use an overworked term. Weizmann was anything but a saint; he was fickle, a prima donna, a bit of a snob, on occasion quite wrong in his political judgment. Yet he retained his magic even in his old age. It is far easier to exude the aura of leadership if one keeps a certain distance (as de Gaulle did, for instance). Among this hypercritical and egalitarian tribe, the Jews, no such distance was permitted; it was infinitely more difficult to be accepted among them as a leader.

Only on a few occasions did I have the chance to talk to him alone. It happened the first time on King's Birthday, on a July afternoon in 1946 in the garden of Government House, Jerusalem. The Zionist leadership boycotted the party because many of their leading figures had been arrested, and most leading Arabs did not appear either. It was a small gathering—the British in one corner, the Arabs in another, the bagpipe players in the third—and since I had come early, I joined the tall, elderly man who was standing alone. Weizmann needed an audience, and for some twenty minutes I listened to a fascinating monologue, anecdotes in a mixture of Yiddish, Hebrew, and English, dire prophecies about the future, complaints that no one listened to him anymore. Then others joined us, and he turned away from me. It was a memorable occasion, not only because of Weizmann—it was also the first time that I had listened to bagpipes and that I was offered whisky-and-soda. I had far too many of the latter; it was the only time in my life that I got truly drunk. I barely remember how I reached home; someone must have taken me in his car. I felt very ill for hours. Ever since, I have consumed whisky for medicinal purposes only.

There was nothing magic about Ben-Gurion, nor did he have aristocratic pretensions. Like the other Labour party leaders his life-style was Spartan. Small of stature, he was utterly fearless, ready to make decisions, however unpopular, when others were shrinking back. He had genuine (and deep) cultural interests, but these were limited; I doubt whether he ever went to a museum or concert.

I watched him closely, but there was nothing even approaching intimacy until much later. Toward the end of his life he treated me, somewhat to my surprise, almost like an old friend. I remember a reception in London in the 1950s, when a messenger came to fetch me—Ben-Gurion knew that I was writing a history of Zionism and wanted to give me his version of the Carlsbad Congress, which had taken place more than thirty years earlier. I felt embarrassed as he talked and talked; the ambassador came and implored him to greet the chief rabbi, but Ben-Gurion waved him away—"Let him wait." After a few minutes some important members of Parliament arrived. Ben-

Gurion turned to them and said, "Tell me, is there a great difference these days between Labour and the Tories?" and without waiting for an answer, he again continued his passionate lecture on a subject that was of no particular interest to me, quite oblivious to the many hundreds who had come in his honor. In the United States, not long before his death, I interviewed him for some five or six hours on television, in a program not to be shown in his lifetime. He spoke with great animation about his early years, but refused, sometimes abruptly, to answer questions concerning the 1950s and 1960s. I asked him who had been the American Jewish leader whom he respected most. Dr. Magnes. But he had been a political foe all along, the chief protagonist of a binational state. True, but he was the only one to settle in Israel; the others just made speeches and stayed in America.

Ben-Gurion was one of the most single-minded people I ever met; this was his great strength, but in later years it often turned into obstinacy, and it became his great weakness. Unnecessary personal quarrels beclouded his last years in office.

Moshe Shertok (Sharett), for many years before and after 1948, acted as foreign minister. He lacked Weizmann's charisma and Ben-Gurion's vision and single-minded approach. But he was a gifted and thoroughly decent man, unjustly belittled by some who were antagonized by a certain pedantry, a preoccupation with seemingly unimportant details. One specific incident sticks in my mind. One day I received a call to come to his office in Tel Aviv—this must have been in the early days of the state. Having vainly tried to adjust the venetian blinds, he tried to persuade me to change my name to Yakir, since Laqueur, all other considerations apart, could not possibly be spelled correctly in Hebrew. I noted that Yakir was the name of a famous Soviet general who had perished in the Russian purges of 1937—obviously an ill omen. Sharett said that Charette had been a French general who had been defeated in most of the battles he had fought, even in the Vendée. He then continued to argue that my father, whom he had known (his memory was for once totally at fault), would have agreed with his suggestion. I procrastinated and said I needed more time. Within a week Sharett faced some domestic or foreign crisis and duly forgot. I never had the impression that he paid much attention to what I told him; I could have been his son, did not belong to his party or the political establishment. Yet when his diaries were published many years later, I found myself to my surprise mentioned more than once, albeit not on issues of great affairs of state.

Born in Kherson, Ukraine, Sharett grew up in an Arab village and served as a lieutenant in the Turkish army. He was an excellent linguist. Through ties of family or friendship he was linked to many of his contemporaries in the leadership—either they were his cousins, had married his sisters, or had been his classmates in Tel Aviv's Herzlia High School. Born in Poland, White Russia, or the Ukraine in the 1890s, they all arrived in Palestine in their teens. One of them was Elijahu Golomb, the father of Jewish self-defense in Palestine, who died far too early, aged fifty-two in 1954. Some of his functions were taken over by Shaul Meirov (Avigur), a man of few words. Born on the last day of the last year of the last century, a fact of which he was very proud. His last and major assignment was the preparation for the immigration of Jews from the Soviet Union, some thirty-five years before it became a reality.

I came to know Avigur better in later years. I tried to show him London on one occasion but never had I a more reluctant, less enthusiastic visitor. To spend time on anything but the urgent tasks at hand seemed to him frivolous. I ran into him in Warsaw and we had a long talk. He must have been high up on the Polish secret police blacklist, because after leaving him I had an unmistakable tail. Since I was driving a hired car and I did not know Warsaw well, I entered a one-way street the wrong way, which compelled my pursuers to follow me—to their evident embarrassment. For a day they seemed to have thought that someone so well versed in spycraft must be a very dangerous agent, but thereafter they left me in peace.

Above all, I remember one incident in the 1950s. I was back on a visit in Jerusalem and had contracted chickenpox, a most unpleasant disease for adults. I was running a high temperature when Shaul suddenly appeared in my room. Naomi told me later that when she had opened the door he pushed her aside murmuring that he had to see me alone. He told me that he had only a few minutes; Ben-Gurion had sent him, having heard that I had a certain knowledge of things Russian. What was my assessment of the chances of getting Jewish immigration from Russia over a long period of time? This both flattered and amused me, despite the fact that I felt miserable. Up to that date the Russian-Jewish establishment in Israel had never been particularly interested in my views: What could a young German Jew know about a country in which they had been born and educated and which they knew inside out? The fact that there had been a revolution since they left and enormous changes seemed of little importance to them.

I took a little sip of vodka, which I have often found an instant antipyretic in my particular case, did some rapid thinking, and said: "Prospects are not at all bad in the long run, but there will be great difficulties to overcome. In the short run it will make the Russians quite angry. Nor can you be sure that most Russian Jews want to come in the first place. When do masses of people leave? When the situation in a country gets desperate. In brief, the situation will have to be worse before a mass immigration will occur." This was a trite observation but subsequent events bore it out. Thus, I played a very minor role in the first deliberations aiming to strengthen relations with Russian Jewry; immigration ("reunion of families") was running at the time at the rate of a hundred a month. (As I wrote these lines in 1991 two thousand came on certain days.) A very small network was set up to intensify relations with Soviet Jews, headed by my friend and neighbor Benjamin Eliav and some others who became my friends, such as Lova Eliav (no relation to Benjamin). My assumption that there would be a deterioration in relations on the state level unfortunately became true early on. As relations improved again in the later 1980s, anti-Semitism came to the surface as one of the by-products of *glasnost*.

Of the old guard of Zionist diplomats, I knew Berl Locker slightly. Since our names are spelled similarly in Hebrew, and as we were neighbors, some of his mail ended up on my desk, and vice versa. Nahum Goldman was an independent spirit with independent means (by marriage, I believe). He was an excellent raconteur in several languages, but his political judgment was erratic and he had an unfortunate tendency to drop names, which became more pronounced with age. ("When I last saw my friend Tito, he told me to look up Charles in Paris," etc.) He had good contacts with the German government of Adenauer because he had spent his formative years in pre–World War I Germany and the Weimar Republic. I don't think that with all his charm he ever hit it off with the Americans, British, French, or Russians.

A whole pleiad of young "Anglo-Saxons" descended on Jerusalem in the immediate postwar period. Aubrey Eban, Vivian Herzog, and Michael Comay had all been majors in the British army, Walter Ettinghausen, an Oxford don, had been at Bletchley during World War II—the place where the secret German military communications were decoded. Gershon Hirsch, the youngest of this group, had been educated in Palestine, but studied in England and had been president of the Oxford Union at one time. These and some others were then young men in their late twenties or thirties. True, their experience was by necessity limited. I was taken aback, to give but one example, when one of them told me one day that in his opinion the London *New Statesman* was the most reliable magazine; entertaining, yes, under Kingsley Martin, but reliable? He was at the time the principal of the "school of diplomats," which was to give a crash course for leading cadres for foreign policy assignments in the state, and later he became the first director general of the Israeli foreign ministry.

These Young Turks knew England much better than America, let alone the Soviet Union, but they adjusted quickly to the changing balance of power. Compared to the generation of Israeli diplomats that came to the fore forty years later, they were

truly giants. I have sometimes pondered whether such comparisons are not unfair. The present generation of Israeli policymakers, diplomats, and generals are probably about as capable as
those of other countries. But in 1947 and 1948 a different type
of young man and woman was attracted by public service than
in later decades. Talented young people now opt for business or
the law, for medicine or a university career; these professions
offer greater scope for developing their talents, greater freedom,
and often also higher material rewards. In those years there was,
furthermore, an idealistic motivation that is much rarer now,
and also a greater cultural interest and curiosity.

In addition to those I have mentioned there were Ehud Avriel,
who died at a comparatively young age, and Teddy Kollek, both
Viennese by origin, both members of a kibbutz, men with inexhaustible energy and great inventiveness. These and some others
played a notable role in the prehistory of the state that is reported
in the history books. I have mentioned the "Arabists" of the
Jewish Agency, but there were also Gideon Ruffer (Rafael), who
had been a member of my old kibbutz (Hazorea); Arie Levavi,
who specialized in East European and Soviet affairs; as well as
many others.

Political leaders too tended to be young at the time; Moshe
Sneh (Kleinbaum) became head of the Hagana at thirty-two,
just one year after his escape from Poland early on during the
war. Pinchas Lubianker (Lavon) was a leading figure in the labor
movement already in his late twenties, as was Yakov Hazan. All
three were excellent speakers; the level of public speaking was
much higher then than in our present age of television. Sneh
became a Communist in later years without (his critics would
say) ever having been a socialist. Toward the end of his life
he realized that his support for Stalinism had been a grievous
mistake, that communism was not the "wave of the future." He
publicly repented like an observant Jew on the Day of Atonement. Lavon, a very gifted, highly intelligent man in many fields,
was appointed to the one post to which he was not particularly
suited, that of minister of defense; he became involved in the

most famous political scandal of the fifties in Israel. What a pity that his public career was to end in tragedy or that Hazan never played a role in the politics of Israel commensurate with his stature. Any nation would have been proud of such people, and for each of these names others could easily be substituted. Palestine from 1946 to 1948 was a country with many excellent chiefs and not enough Indians.

When I think of Jerusalem in 1946 and 1947 barbed wire plays an important part in my recollections; there seems to have been an inexhaustible supply of it. The Mandatory authorities established the first of three security zones in August 1946, following the attack on the King David Hotel. It was popularly known as Bevingrad and encompassed the Central Post Office, the Central Prison, and PBS, the radio station. As a result, considerable hardship was caused to hundreds of shop owners and tenants. In checking old dispatches, I found that I asked the Chief Inspector of Police Colonel Gray (a military man by training) whether it would not be in everyone's interest to concentrate police and army in the suburbs rather than the city's center. Colonel Gray replied with great patience that this would mean that in an emergency the security forces would reach the city center with a few minutes' delay, and that these minutes could well be decisive. He was probably right, but eventually it did not make much difference. I ended my report: "Soon we shall need a visa to enter the Old City and two identity cards to cross from one side of the street to the other" (August 15, 1946). My predictions came true within a year, and within two years even a visa was no longer sufficient to enter the Old City.

Toward the end of 1946, two more security areas were established, and I happened to become resident in one of them, the biggest, known as Number One. It comprised the German colony as well as parts of Baka and Katamon. More than half the population was Arab; most British institutions and the homes of all British officials were concentrated there. There were also a thousand Jews in the German colony, not counting Poles, Greeks, and others. There were three entrances, and only residents with a special permit could pass. We had just rented a three-room apartment that belonged to an Arab police sergeant. The day the building workers finished, we moved in. For the first time since we had left Germany, we had a decent abode, even though the furniture was rudimentary. But there was running water and electricity as well as a real kitchen and a bathroom and also a balcony with a pleasant panorama. The rent was quite reasonable—but still too high for us, so we sublet the third room to a couple of American students with whom we became friendly. They introduced us to all kinds of technological innovations such as Kleenex and various other hygienic articles of which we had not even heard.

Having acquired a decent place, we were very happy; Naomi was six months pregnant. But the joy did not last long. When we moved in, I had a long discussion with my landlord, the Arab police sergeant. "Nothing will happen here. All of us want peace," he said. And I reported a British official calling the German colony "a cosmopolitan island of peace and tolerance." Relations between the communities were excellent. But gradually tension grew, several Jewish residents were shot, Café Loy and some other Jewish shops in the main street were burned down. The local security authority permitted the Arab bus (number 4) to cross the security zone on condition that no one left or entered it. But who would check whether the ban was observed? Weapons were smuggled into the area. A young man named Husseini, a distant relation of the Mufti of Jerusalem, was made commander of the Arab forces inside the area. First he organized a protest demonstration in front of the Czech consulate inside the zone. But those who came were young intellectuals. They listened to a few speeches, passed a resolution, and went home. There was no violence.

A week later Husseini brought some young men from Hebron who were not intellectuals, and from that date on, the situation became more dangerous. It was fascinating to watch how a peaceful community turned gradually into an area of insecurity.

Unfortunately, I was involved personally. In daytime there was no real danger, but with nightfall the risk grew, and since I often came home close to midnight, I tried to obtain some means of protection. This was not easy because, outside the ranks of the police and the terrorists, small weapons were scarce. My Beretta .22 was slightly defective, as the magazine was loose, and furthermore there was the constant danger that the soldiers on guard at the entry to the security zone would look for weapons, as indeed they often did. The sentence for carrying arms at the time was between five and ten years. Naomi sewed me a belt, by means of which I could carry the weapon at a part of the body that, according to experience, few searchers would touch. It was so well hidden that it would take me about a minute to get into action, which made the pistol perfectly useless. So gradually I stopped carrying it.

During the second half of 1947, there were fewer incidents in Jerusalem than in Tel Aviv, despite the mixed character of the city. All this rapidly changed after November 29, 1947, when the UN resolution on Palestine was passed. After a few months of bliss in our new apartment, we became refugees. But the story of our escape from the security zone belongs to a subsequent chapter.

In spring 1947 World War II had been over for almost two years, but there was no feeling in Palestine that peace had really returned. This was also true with regard to Europe. In Britain the economic situation became more and more critical, which had direct repercussions on British foreign policy. In France and Italy a civil war seemed imminent, and Spain became a monarchy without a king. As I think back to 1947, the most important event was the visit of UNSCOP, the United Nations Special Commission on Palestine. Its recommendations eventually led to the UN decision of November 29, 1947, to partition, and the establishment of two separate states in Palestine, one admittedly stillborn. I took part in the open meetings of the committee in Jerusalem and all its study tours, quite literally

from Dan to Beersheba. These meetings were meant to be an intensive course on the Palestine problem for the committee members, and it certainly was one for me.

In February 1947 the British government had advised the families of its officials in Palestine to leave if their presence was not essential. Many neighbors left with regret, despite the growing insecurity. In May the British government requested the United Nations to put the Palestine problem on the agenda of the next session of the General Assembly. The burden of the Mandate had become too much, and it half wanted the international body to take over. Accordingly, a committee was appointed consisting of the representatives of Australia, Canada, Czechoslovakia, Guatemala, India, Iran, the Netherlands, Peru, Sweden, Uruguay, and Yugoslavia, "with the widest powers to ascertain and record facts and to investigate all questions and issues relevant to the problem of Palestine."

The committee met for the first time at Lake Success on May 26, which happens to be my birthday. On June 9, an advance party of twenty-nine UN officials and secretaries landed in Lydda (Lod). With many other correspondents, I went to welcome the TWA Skymaster. I talked to a young Englishman named Alexander, who looked like a rugby player (and, as it turned out, was one), and who told me there would be about one hundred technical personnel. The advance party was quite obviously surprised by the great attention their arrival had provoked; they were not accustomed to being in that much limelight. Shertok, who was on the same plane, got much less attention. He complained to me that the flight from the United States had been very long; they had to stay overnight in Cairo. A flight in those days was still a rare, adventurous, and unpredictable venture. Six days later I again went to the airport, then a small, primitive installation, even though there was already a hotel of sorts called Terminal and even a bar. Judge Sandstrom of Sweden, the chairman, arrived, together with several members of the committee. From my report I gather that he was a tall, distinguished-looking gentleman wearing a straw hat. The greetings of the Palestine government were conveyed by Sir Henry Gurney.* Someone gave Sandstrom a pita—he took a bite and said that he had not eaten this kind of bread for twenty-one years, when he had last visited the Middle East.

Then there was the inevitable press conference. More than a hundred journalists and photographers surrounded Sandstrom, who spoke very slowly and almost inaudibly. He said that it was hotter in Palestine than in Egypt, where they had spent the previous night. Mercifully, it was all over in five minutes, and a long caravan of cars set into motion in the direction of Jerusalem. I was to be part of this caravan for several weeks, but there is no need to describe in detail all its movements, the speeches and discussions that took place. (This was done years ago by members of the committee and also by outsiders.) My account will deal with some of my impressions based on my dispatches written at the time. I tried deliberately to put myself into the position of one of those judges who had been called upon to suggest a Solomonic solution to this intractable problem. Of course, I could not make myself into a tabula rasa, but I tried: How did the Palestine problem appear to a total outsider, how could it be solved?

The members of the committee and the senior staff members were housed in a strange building on Gaza Street, at the border of Rehavia, that had just been finished. It had been commissioned by the Mandatory government for its officials, but when the building was ready for occupation, it appeared that it was located in the unsafe no-man's-land between the Jewish and Arab quarters of town. I call it a strange building because it was unlike any other in the city. The twenty-odd apartments were not on top of one another, but the layout was in the form of the capital letter **H**. It was surrounded by barbed wire, and the Arab policeman at the entrance carefully checked our permits.

I became a frequent guest at this house for a number of weeks.

---

*Sir Henry subsequently went to Malaya, where he was killed by terrorists in an ambush.

By a strange accident, it became my home a year later. Long after UNSCOP had left, Shlomit, our second daughter, was born there, as was, many years later, Tamar, our youngest grand-daughter. My first book was written in this building and also two chapters of the present recollections. The building was then called Kadima House (Forward House) because it was the most exposed house seen from all directions. By now the name is almost forgotten. Only old-timers use it occasionally. Once a landmark, the building no longer stands out among other houses, and it is surrounded by high trees.

During the next few weeks, we listened to representatives of the Mandatory government giving evidence, and also to Weiz-mann, Ben-Gurion, Shertok, and Kaplan, the treasurer of the Jewish Agency. The Palestinian Arabs boycotted the committee, but several marginal groups were given the opportunity to make their views known, including Dr. Magnes and his fellow advo-cates of a binational state. The Communists appeared, too, even though their position was not enviable. It was precisely during these months that the Soviet line on Palestine changed, from unrelenting opposition to Zionism to support for a Jewish (and Arab) state. As a result, the Communists had no idea what the Soviet line was or was likely to be in the near future. The East European members of the committee also showed great caution; Yugoslavia had not yet broken with Stalin, and the Czech repre-sentative, a professional diplomat, had not yet defected from a government that was more and more dominated by the Commu-nists. Unofficially, and with all the due precautions on both sides, the chairman also met representatives of Hagana and the terrorist groups.

Some of the speeches were powerful and moving, others tiring. The question-and-answer period shed some light on what the position of the delegates (and their countries) was likely to be. The strangest questions came from the Indian representative, Sir Abdur Rahman Bahador, a distinguished judge in his homeland but quite unknown in the outside world. A prickly, aggressive man, he clearly felt the urge to assert himself. The Zionists thought this Muslim a sworn enemy, but after a few attempts to talk to him, I realized that his true motives were quite different. He belonged to a now-extinct type, the uncompromising Anglophile—British law was the best; so was British civilization. He was against partition in India; why should he favor it in Palestine? And how crazy of the Jews to oppose the blessings of British Mandatory rule in Palestine. And so he continued relentlessly with his hostile questions: "Mr. Ben-Gurion, isn't it true that the Jews fought with the Turks against the British in World War One?" He should have asked Shertok, who had been a lieutenant in the Turkish army—a liaison officer with the German military mission; Ben-Gurion, it so happened, had been a lance corporal in a British unit. Alas, Sir Abdur did not even begin to understand the intricacies of the Jewish question.

The field trips were fascinating. The caravan was always headed by Sandstrom's car, followed by the highest-ranking UN official, Victor Hoo, a non-Communist Chinese, fluent in many languages and a workaholic. Another UN official, Ralph Bunche, who was to play a greater role in 1948, was in many respects even more impressive. A black U.S. secretary of state was, of course, unthinkable at the time. But for this barrier, I am convinced he would have made a good one. The rest of the caravan went in alphabetical order, with Australia leading and Yugoslavia last, so as not to create problems of protocol. A dozen cars with journalists followed. Most of these excursions were day trips, but sometimes we stayed away overnight.

JUNE 26, 1947:
Be'ersheva, my first visit to this overgrown oasis in the desert. A small, hot, dusty, godforsaken little place. It seemed to be market day; never have I seen so many camels in one place. The police station was the only modern building in town, which seemed to have changed very little over the centuries. Be'ersheva must have been more or less the same in Turkish days, a place in the middle of the desert, which did not even appear in most guidebooks, except with reference to the Bible. To be transferred to Be'ersheva

was tantamount to demotion and disgrace for Turkish officials. An estimate of the number of inhabitants is difficult—there are perhaps a thousand or two. Most of those I saw had come to attend the market.

When I passed Beersheba again forty years later, it was a city of some one hundred and thirty thousand inhabitants, with a university priding itself for its mathematics department. I was impressed by the large number of satellite dishes—Soviet immigrants wanting to watch the television programs of their native country. In 1947 I reported to my paper:

We did 400 kilometers today, partly on very bad roads. South of Be'ersheva, Kibbutz Revivim, founded four years ago, half of the members and most of the children have not yet arrived. Hepner, spokesman for the settlers, provided information about desert agriculture. The committee members were a little incredulous until they saw the tomatoes, cucumbers, courgettes, peanuts, and even roses, carnations, and other flowers. Then the questions started: Well, you have done great work in the wilderness. But is it profitable, what about the investments needed, isn't water far too expensive to make this a viable concern? An expert replied with patience and knowledge: There is plenty of water; the problem is to channel the downpours from the wadis into reservoirs. One recent cloudburst had resulted in 200,000 cubic feet. . . . More questions, more information. Lunch in Revivim; Sir Abdur Rahman had absented himself and went for a meeting in Be'ersheva, where the local notables had refused to meet with the committee. Beyond Revivim, Ruhama and Nirám; we arrived with two hours' delay. Each morning we get a detailed timetable for the day, but the problems are many and we are always running behind schedule. More vegetables, more fruit—date palms, plums, pomegranates, peaches—for the time being, in the experimental stage, but what an experiment! Six-thirty in the evening, we should be on the way home, but yet another settlement, Hefetz Haim, founded by a religious group. Long speeches, more information also in writing. The members are tired, no more questions, they want to return to Jerusalem. The caravan was accompanied today by Messrs. David Horowitz, Aubrey Eban (Ewen), Levi Shkolnik (Eshkol).* There was no need for a police or army escort.

During the next few days the committee visited Tel Aviv and Haifa as well as other Jewish settlements. The welcome was cordial. Children presented flowers, and there were more speeches. The Arab municipalities from Ramleh to Acre, from Nablus to Hebron, decided to boycott UNSCOP; there were many individual meetings but the Jewish journalists were kept out, not only from Abraham's Tomb (near Hebron) but even from the Karaman, Dick, and Salti cigarette factory. The Arabs were, of course, perfectly entitled to keep Jews out, but, on balance, their attitude made a negative impression. Most of the committee members were desperately eager to meet leading Arabs and were bending over backward to make concessions to achieve this aim. Most of them were initially against partition. But when they realized that the hostility on the part of the Arabs went very deep indeed, they were gradually driven to the conclusion that collaboration in a single state was unlikely.

Thus, seen in retrospect, Palestinian Arab leaders made a fatal mistake well before they rejected the recommendations of UNSCOP for partition. As far as I was concerned I still had hoped that some federative solution would be possible. As I waited outside the cigarette factory, it occurred to me, not for the first time nor the last, that such hopes were in vain. I was not personally offended; my interest in cigarette factories was limited. I simply realized that, given the conflicting aims of the two peoples, partition was the only possible solution, even though it did not offer any guarantee for peaceful coexistence.

The three-day tour of Galilee was the climax of the UNSCOP

*The first-mentioned became director general of the Bank of Israel; the subsequent careers of Eban and Eshkol are well known.

activities. It began inauspiciously. The committee members were tired from too many speeches, late sessions, and excursions, even though no one wanted to show it.

FROM OUR SPECIAL CORRESPONDENT:
We left Jerusalem one hour late. Victor Hoo, as usual, turned up first. Sir Abdur Rahman did not want to come at all. First stop, Zikhron Ya'akov, south of Haifa. A reception in the municipal garden—fruits are offered and fruit juice. Short speeches: "When our grandparents came here sixty-five years ago, it seemed doubtful whether five families could make a living on this inhospitable, desolate mountain. Today we are two thousand, and many Arabs work in the vineyards and orchards." The rest of the program was a little unusual: first a visit to the local synagogue, where a psalm was read by the cantor, then an inspection of the wine cellars— Zikhron's main industry. The usual wine tasting; Professor Fabregat of Uruguay said that he had never touched alcohol in his life and, with due regrets, would not now change his habits. Dr. Hoo, on the other hand, claimed that he could drink a bottle or two without any ill effects.

We then continued through the mountains, passing my old kibbutz, Hazorea, briefly visiting a few others, drank cold milk in Mishmar Ha'emeq, and listened to explanations about life in a collective settlement. More cold drinks in Nahalal and explanations about the *moshavim* (cooperative villages).

FROM OUR OWN CORRESPONDENT:
Evening in Safed. It was not difficult to find rooms for a hundred unexpected guests in this little town, which reflects badly on the tourist season. Safed has not developed. It is a city of old people— a lot of empty houses, especially in the Jewish quarter. The younger, more enterprising native sons and daughters are leaving. Every other year another development plan is mooted, discussed, and shelved. After dinner I went out and discovered two coffeehouses and a cinema. But the cinema was shut; the only guests in the coffeehouses were British policemen, and they were about

to close. Back to the new hotel on Mount Canaan. Sandstrom and Hood, the Canadian, are playing bridge. Fabregat's voice, a room-filling bass, is heard above the din; someone had told him a joke in Spanish. During the day, from conversations with the delegations, I gained the impression that there is still support for a federative solution rather than partition. But most have not yet made up their mind.

Next day we visited several settlements in Upper Galilee. The Yugoslavs met some former partisans, the Entezam; the Persian delegate encountered Jews from Iran; the Dutch were met by fellow countrymen. The dispersal of the Jewish people had not been staged for their benefit; these were members of the settlements. There was even an Australian soldier—a non-Jew who decided to join one of the local kibbutzim, and had married a local girl.

Tiberias, the lido, a reception without speeches. We continue on a little steamer to Ein Gev. The children offer the delegates locally produced ice cream, a fantastic success. ("Do you eat ice cream every day?") It is getting late, I desperately look for a telephone to transmit my daily report. The only phone is in the secretariat, which is closed.

It has been a long day and exceedingly hot; the attraction of a swim in Lake Tiberias is irresistible. Most of the delegates join in; the secretaries, prim, proper, and seemingly unapproachable, join in the general fun. The congress dances. . . . Then a spontaneous singsong with "Volga-Volga" as the only common denominator. Was it not a little frivolous, this group of distinguished citizens from a dozen countries, commissioned to find a solution to a dangerous, historical conflict, behaving like adolescents? To a participant it seemed a natural reaction at the end of a long day.

FROM OUR OWN CORRESPONDENT:
A long drive along the northern border to Naharia and Acre. More questions and answers in Naharia, more swimming but the waves are too high. Dr. Hoo loses a Ping-Pong match against a

pretty young secretary. In Acre a short reception by Husein Ef-
fendi, the local mayor. But he strictly refuses to talk politics. One
delegate asked him about the municipal budget—no answers.
We journalists had as usual to wait outside. Later a walk through
the narrow streets of old Acre. The inhabitants showed no interest;
a few were cursing the delegates—but not very loudly. Back to
Jerusalem.

After UNSCOP finished its work in Palestine, several members
of the committee went to Amman, and there was a meeting in
Beirut to ascertain the views of the Arab governments. Some
committee members went to displaced persons' camps in Germany; others did not think this a good idea and went directly
back to Lake Success.

On the last day of August 1947, the Special Committee sub-
mitted its report and recommendations to the UN General Assembly. It was a judicious, well-informed report, but most
observers assumed that it would suffer the fate of the nineteen
reports that had preceded it over the years. I had the instinctive
feeling that, for once, this report could have an impact. As someone said at the time, "Commissions come and go, but the situation in Palestine does not remain forever—it is deteriorating
rapidly." I summarized my views in an article for an American
journal one week after the publication of the UNSCOP recommendations:

> Palestine cannot be divided without doing injustice to one side or
> another. It was UNSCOP's task to find a way out of the Palestine
> muddle, the one that would cause the least injustice and the least
> violence. Their task would have been easier if Jews and Arabs
> would agree to live in one undivided country, to establish a bina-
> tional state. Unfortunately, the majority of both peoples reject this
> solution. . . .

And I also took it for granted that there would be no peaceful
solution:

The unpleasant and unpopular truth is that the Palestine problem can be solved only by force. If there were a strong UNO, having at its disposal armed forces or an international police force, the vicious circle could be broken by carrying out the program agreed upon by a majority of nations.

What was the alternative? Permanent strife, resulting in the destruction of the country, such as happened in Lebanon in the 1980s. Ironically, Lebanese society in 1947 was the most frequently invoked example of ethnic harmony. Peaceful coexistence between two or more peoples seemed possible in either old, highly civilized countries such as Switzerland or where an iron hand imposed discipline from the center, such as, at the time, the Soviet Union or Yugoslavia. But Palestine was neither Switzerland nor the Soviet Union. Whatever the solution, I did not expect peace for a long time to come. I was glad when the United Nations voted for partition on November 29, 1947, but I was not among those dancing in the streets.

August, September, and October 1947 passed quietly in Jerusalem. The political scene largely shifted to the United Nations, to the struggle for the acceptance of the UNSCOP recommendations. I went on my usual daily rounds. More press conferences, a few more Irgun and Stern attacks, some more arrests, more sentences imposed by the military courts. On October 30, I came home late to find a note from Naomi that she had gone to the Hadassah Hospital on Mount Scopus. On November 1, Sylvia was born, a small but healthy baby. These were the last weeks of peace and, for a while, quite naturally life centered around the new arrival.

It was also a period of hard work. More and more foreign correspondents were arriving, among them excellent writers, some of the leading journalists of that generation, some of them very intelligent, experienced observers of the international scene. But about Palestine they knew little. It was a small country, but the complications were immense, and, above all, they had no feeling for the situation. Things that we, the locals, felt in our bones, seemed to them outlandish and altogether incomprehensible. They would file story after story about the terrorists on the correct assumption that terrorism always made for good copy—politically the issue was marginal, but it had all the ingredients of the detective story, and readers liked thrillers far more than boring accounts on politics. Arthur Koestler, a gifted writer, had been in Palestine before; he came in 1946 not just for a short visit, but stayed for almost a year. But he did not speak the language. He was attracted by the excitement, the dramatic elements in the situation, and had no feeling for what went on below the surface. He wrote about thieves in the night and not about more or less honest people doing their work in the light of the day.

These foreign visitors were aware of the fact that they were cut off from Palestinian realities, and, as a result, we local correspondents were in considerable demand as stringers. They wanted the facts, introductions, and sometimes also discreet guidance. I don't think I provided the world's press with many scoops, except perhaps being the first to find out that a little committee had agreed that the name of the new state would be Israel (it could have been Judaea, and there were several other proposals). I needed the money at a time the family was about to expand. On the other hand, I found it a bit ghoulish that I should be paid for the misfortunes of other people—three killed in an attack on the Etzion settlements, twenty-five injured in a bus to Mount Scopus or the Old City—for such was the news in those days. To compensate for this well-paid hack work, I began to write think pieces for foreign newspapers. I was twenty-six, no longer an absolute beginner, and, having studied the dispatches of my elders and betters who had come from New York, London, and Paris, I decided that I could do the job at least as well and probably more reliably. My English was uncertain, but for writing this kind of article I did not need the refinements of style of a Joseph Conrad, let alone a Henry James.

I also began to contribute to the *Palestine Post*, an excellent newspaper at the time. Its stage and readership were small, its attitude partisan, but it was not provincial, and the quality of its editors was high; I have not known a better small newspaper since. The editor was Gershon Agronski, whom I have mentioned before, his deputy was Ted Lurie, and there was also George Lichtheim (who left for Europe in 1946 to cover the Nuremberg trials and stayed in London) as well as Lea Ben Dor. Both Lurie and Ben Dor became editors-in-chief in later years. There was a strong German contingent, including C. Z. Kloetzel, a leading writer in Weimar Germany; "Frango," a gifted but eccentric cultural commentator; and Eugen Meyer, who was literary editor. Above all, there was an Englishman, Roy Elston, alias David Courtney, by far the most famous at the time. He wrote "Column One," which was immensely popular. Courtney was one of the few Englishmen who sympathized with the Jewish cause, and the Mandatory authorities cordially disliked him. I was never among his admirers, as I found too much pathos and sentimentalism and very little substance in his columns. They were a constant variation on the theme that the right cause would prevail, written in elegant English. But the appeal to the emotions was exactly what readers needed at the time; after the state had been established, this kind of journalism went out of fashion. Courtney returned to England but did not quite make it. He was unlucky, because he was neither more nor less talented than some other British journalists who had started their careers in Palestine and who made successful careers in the London Sunday papers or elsewhere.

My beginnings on the *Palestine Post* were modest: From book reviewing I graduated to writing the occasional editorial and eventually alternated with Courtney writing "Column One"— also under a pen name. But for all these various professional breakthroughs, I was still a struggling young newspaperman who had much to learn. I was amused to hear in later years that I did have admirers even then, that they included the chief censor, who (he claimed) had always predicted that I would go far in the world of political journalism.

Toward the end of November the telephone at home was

ringing constantly, especially during the late evenings—what news from Lake Success? The baby, for one reason or another, had not let us sleep for a few successive nights, and on the evening of the twenty-ninth I covered the phone with a duvet, since there was no way to disconnect it at the time. And it was, of course, precisely that night that the decisive vote at the United Nations was taken. Next morning I reported to my paper:

> Jewish Jerusalem forgot last night for a moment its specific status; as a *corpus separandum*, according to the partition plan it was not to belong to the Jewish state. Young and old streamed into the street after a group of youngsters driving in an open car through the inner city had, quite literally, trumpeted the news for those who had not heard it on the radio.
>
> Jerusalem, the inhibited, frozen, sleepy, depressed, suddenly manifested its joy after years of waiting and nights of tension. The news was shouted from rooftop to rooftop, from balcony to balcony, and within a few minutes the whole town knew it. Flags appeared all over and there was singing and dancing in Zion Square and in front of the Jewish Agency building. British police and soldiers were warmly welcomed, even participated in the general joy; on their armored Humbers, they drove singing and shouting boys and girls through the streets.

This report was strictly secondhand, based on the observations of helpful colleagues.

November 30 and December 1 passed quietly.

FROM OUR CORRESPONDENT, DECEMBER 1ST:
I went down to the Old City twice today. The police and army patrols have been strengthened; groups of young Arabs prepare for a general strike. Stones were thrown on the number 7 bus near the Allenby barracks, and on number 2 near Jaffa Gate. Several shots were fired from automatic weapons on Jewish taxis in Romema, but there were no victims. Arab families, living in Mekor Baruch and Romema, left their houses in the afternoon.

On the second of December, soon after I had reached my office I heard that fighting was taking place in Queen Mary Street, a few hundred meters away. When I reached the place, I saw young Arabs trying to enter the center of the Jewish city; they were pushed back by British police and a few dozen unarmed Hagana men. The Arabs did not persist and turned back toward Jaffa Gate. However, an hour later they returned, and burned and pillaged the Commercial Center, located just outside the Old City, which contained dozens of Jewish shops and also some Arab-owned ones. No one was killed in the process, a few people were injured, including a colleague of mine named Lazar, who was stabbed, but forty-four Jewish shops were destroyed and the material damage was considerable. Within a few minutes many families had lost their livelihood. The shop owners organized a demonstration to the Jewish Agency. Why was there no defense, why no counterattack? The official line was, quite correctly, that local Arab attacks were only to be expected and that the commandment of the hour was not to be provoked. After some angry outbursts everyone went home.

The same day, there was an attempt to attack Yemin Moshe, the first Jewish settlement established in the last century outside the Old City walls, and there was also shooting at cars entering the Jewish quarter in the Old City. We did, of course, not know it at the time, but the burning of the Commercial Center was the first battle in the war for Jerusalem that was to last for the next seven months. The early attacks had been quite spontaneous, but gradually a certain pattern evolved, such as sniping from the Old City walls; one of the first victims was an acquaintance, named Stern, an Anglo-Jewish journalist. There were attacks on the small Jewish settlements south and north of Jerusalem and, above all, on the incoming traffic from Tel Aviv. Still, the Arab leadership was calling for calm during this first week, and the Jewish leaders wanted to prevent clashes in any case, be it only because they were not prepared for a showdown.

The second week of December brought a major setback to the

Jews; a convoy from the Etzion bloc was ambushed at Km. 14 on the Hebron Road, and ten Jews were killed. The next day the Irgun rolled a barrel of explosives onto the Arabs cowed in front of Damascus Gate; loss of life was heavy, with fifteen to twenty victims. After that, December passed without any major incidents but small-scale attacks became a constant pattern. There was no day without a number of incidents—the settlements and some of the outlying suburbs were virtually cut off, work in the university ceased, and there was no longer free access to Hadassah, the biggest hospital. Traffic to Tel Aviv became dangerous and had to be organized in convoys with military escort.

In our little world, Mr. Faraj, our landlord, who only a few months earlier had assured me that we were all as safe as if we were in Abraham's bosom, suddenly changed his tune: No, a war was bound to come. When I asked him for the reasons, he said, "Well, it must happen, it has been decided. After that, we shall again live in peace, *inshallah*. . . ." I did not want to press him further—had it been decided by Allah or by the Arab Higher Committee? I took the hint, and a few days later, following several attacks inside the security area, we moved out. It was not easy to find two porters and a van. I had to pay twice the usual sum to my friends among the Kurdish moving experts, and they repeatedly insisted that were it for anyone other than Naomi and me (and a feeling of patriotic duty) they would not have dreamed of entering the lion's den. As it happened, the children from the neighboring houses threw only stones, not bombs. Naomi, with the six-week-old baby in her arms, played a more heroic role than I did. She went with the movers to collect our few belongings. Later she found a small room with acquaintances in the center of town where we could stay until we found a new home.

Our new hosts had not much space in the first place, but in this state of emergency an admirable spirit of solidarity manifested itself, with people making room for those who had been displaced. Eventually, there were twenty-five thousand of us, one in four of the population. At the newly established City Emergency Council, Naomi fought for a new apartment. We were lucky and became the owners of an apartment in Kadima House, which was, of course, well known to me. There were two drawbacks. We had to commit ourselves to accept two other parties, refugees like us from the security zone, so that during the months to come housing conditions were slightly worse than in one of Moscow's less salubrious neighborhoods. Furthermore, the building was quite exposed to attacks from a hill (Shahin) less than a hundred yards away, which was in Arab hands. It was only a question of time until we would come under fire. But this mattered little, and thus, on January 3, 1948, again with the help of our faithful Kurdish movers, we entered our new home.

The months that followed were a period of mounting excitement and even physical well-being such as I seldom experienced either before or since. During the autumn of 1947, I had not felt well at all. I suffered from tachycardia, could not sleep, was subject to a variety of fears. I repeatedly went to see physicians, and though they reassured me, I was afraid that I had not long to live. It was the beginning of an illness that plagued me for years after and severely incapacitated me. Yet as I began to face real danger, the fears temporarily gave way to a feeling of exhilaration.

We had little to eat, but I felt no hunger. There was very little water, not to mention more substantial drinks, but I never was acutely thirsty. During those seven months, I did not mind the indiscriminate shelling. Once Salman Aran upbraided me; he had been sent to Jerusalem as a political commissar of sorts; in later years he became minister of education. We were walking in Ben Yehuda Street when the daily bombardment started. Unlike him, I had no wish to enter the nearest house: "Why do you play the hero?" "It is much more interesting outside," I replied. He shrugged his shoulders, an older and wiser man. Why should I have felt happy and optimistic in a situation in which there was not much reason for contentment? I have read about the curious phenomenon of paradoxical psychological and somatic reactions: During the siege of Leningrad, some reacted to sleeping pills by becoming wide awake. Perhaps I belonged to these unaccountable cases. Perhaps there were other personal motives; intense personal relationships were established during the siege and as quickly vanished, there was the feeling of identification with a community of which I had not been aware before. Perhaps it was a feeling of this being our finest hour, of being lucky to be present (as Goethe said at the time of the Battle of Valmy) at the dawn of a new era. Or was it a manifestation of adventurism unbecoming a husband and a father? I thought it unprofitable to engage in excessive self-analysis.

I was aware that our immediate prospects were not good, but I did not realize until many years later how weak Jerusalem had been. Like many others, I was highly critical of Shaltiel, the new military commander who had arrived in February. A German Jew of Sephardic extraction who had been a sergeant in the Foreign Legion, he probably understood more of haute cuisine than of military affairs, but I doubt whether even a genius would have been much more successful. Of all the cities in Palestine, Jerusalem was the poorest and least organized; there were relatively few young people and of these a fairly high percentage were physically or mentally unfit to carry arms. The ultraorthodox refused to do so as a matter of principle, and the Hagana (which was to become the Israeli army on May 15) had never grown deep roots among the old community (the Sephardim), many of whom claimed to do their patriotic duty with one of the terrorist organizations. No one could check whether these claims were really true, because the terrorists refused to cooperate with the Hagana except on occasional special operations. As a military force the terrorists were useless. There were exceptionally brave individuals among them, but as units they were weak in fighting power.* Thus, when the war broke out, the commander of the Jerusalem front had at his disposal a few hundred men, ill-trained part-time soldiers, with no fighting experience—quite a

---

*When, years later, reliable statistics were published, it appeared that 5 percent of the victims of the Jerusalem siege had been members of the terrorist groups.

few of them under eighteen. The arms situation was even more pathetic; in Jerusalem proper there were 338 rifles, 16 light machine guns, 4 heavy machine guns, 166 submachine guns, 5 two-inch and 2 three-inch mortars, enough to equip one company. Even in May, when the British left, there were fewer than a thousand rifles, 24 light and 4 heavy machine guns—and one "heavy" gun, a two-pounder. In brief, Jerusalem was wholly unprepared. To a certain extent this was inevitable, for as long as the British were present, a major arms buildup was impossible in Jerusalem. But preparations could have been made elsewhere, and it is a riddle, even with the benefit of hindsight, why there was not remotely enough ammunition, or why a food reserve had not been built up in time.

Thus, my optimism was based, in part, on ignorance of the true situation. In a dispatch to a New York weekly, which appeared on November 29, I wrote:

> In spite of conflicting reports it should be realized that there is no danger of war in the Middle East for a very simple reason: there are no armies in the Middle East; there might be clashes, riots, disturbances but no war.

The appraisal was correct as far as it went. Seen against the background of World War II (which had ended two years earlier), the Arab armies would not have been capable of defeating the Swiss canton of Appenzell. But the Swiss army had tanks, heavy artillery, a major arms industry, many divisions of well-trained people, even an air force. The Jews in Palestine had nothing of the sort, and, to occupy a city such as Jerusalem, no dive bombers nor rockets were needed.

My optimism was based on my assessment of the human factor. On March 28, 1948, when Jerusalem had been cut off and things looked grim, I wrote for my New York weekly that the doomsday scenarios for Jewish Palestine, widely accepted in the Foreign Office and the State Department, were wrong—and why.

A new generation of Jews has grown up in Palestine different
from the Jews known to the Near East specialists in Washington
and London. They have been educated in freedom, and the result
will be surprising to those who see the symbol of Jewish resistance
in the fight of the Warsaw ghetto, the heroic martyrdom of a few
untrained people.

I knew this generation; some were my age, some a few years
younger or older, a few had become my friends. I knew them with
their virtues and weaknesses. They were anything but supermen;
their military experience was limited. They had never operated
in larger units, and in the early phase of the war they made
elementary mistakes that cost them dearly. But I also knew that
they were deeply motivated, that they were excellent improvisers,
that they had an esprit de corps, and that they were fighting with
their backs to the wall. In the circumstances I had few doubts
with regard to the outcome of the struggle. But Jerusalem (unlike the kibbutzim) had produced few such youngsters, and
with all the respect due to the locally mobilized Moria regiment, and the sixteen- and seventeen-year-old youngsters who
repulsed the Arab Legion tanks in late May, it was an un-
derstrength and underequipped brigade of Palmach named
Harel that saved the city, first by opening the road for convoys
and later by offensive action in the south and north of Jerusalem.

ELEVEN

The Siege

If *the general preparations* for a siege were wholly inadequate, my own were equally ineffectual. I persuaded my editors to install in my home a short-wave transmitter. They liked the idea, and the next week two experts, members of a kibbutz, appeared; they had served in the engineer corps of the U.S. Army during the war and brought an impressive set (war surplus) and an enormous aerial, which was put up on the roof. But when I tried the transmitter a few weeks later, the mountains effectively barred transmission. But for a relay station somewhere near the Kastel, there was no hope of getting through; unfortunately, the Kastel was in Arab hands. The aerial remained on the roof for a long time and served various useful purposes—the children played with it, washing was hung on it to dry—until one day it disappeared.

Soon after November 29, the telephone lines leading outside Jerusalem were cut, and they remained out of order until well after the cease-fire. As long as traffic to Tel Aviv continued, however sporadically, it was still possible to send out reports with one of the armored trucks. This mail arrived with a delay but it usually did arrive. It became more and more infrequent by February, and then it stopped altogether, even before newspapers had ceased to arrive in Jerusalem. The army had a transmitter and every day a "collective cable" of some 300 to 400 words prepared by all the assembled correspondents, foreign and local, was sent out, but this was hardly a substitute. Some thought of using carrier pigeons; they had been used, after all, at the time of the siege of Paris in 1870–71 and on earlier occasions. Others tried even more outlandish means of communication, and someone even proposed walking through the mountains by night but was turned back by the troops.

It was a most frustrating situation, to be unable to communicate with the outside world. One would have expected a flood of books in later years as a result, but there were, in fact, very few, and with one or two exceptions, they were of no interest. Stoically, I continued to write my reports and articles for Tel Aviv and abroad, and to hand copies to all kinds of people who, one way or another, were about to leave the beleaguered city. I had no idea whether any of these ever reached their destination and were published. When the siege was lifted, there were more urgent preoccupations than ordering back issues of newspapers and periodicals. Only in 1991, in preparation for this book, did I institute a search, and much to my surprise, I discovered that most of my accounts had indeed appeared, albeit with considerable delay. Thus, the following quotations came into my hands forty-three years after they had been written.

Rereading my reports of 1948, I have mixed feelings. I feel some pride at having on the whole correctly assessed the political situation and also having sometimes captured the mood of time and place. But I also realized that it was next to impossible to report anything of relevance and interest about the military situation; the famous fog of war was virtually impenetrable.

I had always thought Tolstoy's description of the Battle of Borodino (in which, after all, he had not participated) somewhat exaggerated. But I soon realized that, if anything, the chaos was even more pronounced. Most of the time, no one, including the generals, knew what was going on. What a veteran correspondent had once told me—to believe only what I saw with my own eyes, and then to accept only half of it—was perfectly true. One never saw very far. I remember two operations in which, as a war correspondent, I was invited to participate. After dark I had to be at the assembly point. At midnight the column began to move. We walked slowly up and down a hill, trying to make as little noise as possible. Then the order was passed on to lie down and wait. After an hour we walked some more. At dawn we had reached our destination. Not a shot had been fired, but the history books report that on that night Malha, an important enemy position, had been seized. Suppose, for a moment, that there had been a battle. I still would have been unable to report anything at all, for my field of vision was limited to the dim contours of the man in front and the one behind; they were armed and I was not. A war correspondent should attach himself to a colonel or general, in which case he will at least have a broader purview. But about the face of battle he will still know very little. Trotsky, in the preface to one of his books, remarks that the ideal observation post for a beleaguered city is on the battlement of the city wall, from which point both the attackers and the defending forces can be observed. It is, alas, an impractical proposition.

I also realize in retrospect that much of what I reported on military actions was factually quite wrong. One example should suffice. On March 29 a long report of mine appeared that began with the following words: "The greatest battle since the beginning of the disturbances ended today at ten past five in the afternoon when the convoy from Kfar Etzion returned to Jerusalem after an armistice had been reached following the mediation of the British army." The reader further learned that the battle had lasted thirty hours, that 12 Jews and 136 Arabs had been killed. True, I reported that the Jewish fighters had to leave their weapons behind, but this was the nearest I came to indicating that this heroic battle had been an unqualified disaster. My account was based on a conversation with the survivors of the convoy minutes after they had returned, but they knew only what they had seen with their own eyes, which simply was not enough.

What really had taken place was briefly the following: It had been decided by the political leadership not to give up even one single settlement. This was a basic mistake, because there were not enough soldiers and weapons, and it overextended the lines of supply. When the Etzion region was cut off early on, supplying it became a constant nightmare. A big convoy was prepared and went on its way during the night of March 27. It reached Etzion but was attacked on its way back, near the village of Nebi Daniel. Everything went wrong from the very outset: It was not clear who was in command—instead of unloading the freight as quickly as possible and returning immediately, there were substantial delays, which gave the Arabs enough time to block the road before the convoy returned. When it came to a halt, there was chaos, and communication among the defenders ceased. The result of the battle of Nebi Daniel was as follows: 15 Jews and 25 Arabs killed (not 136 as I had reported); the Jews also lost 10 machine guns, 140 rifles and submachine guns, 10 armored cars, 4 buses, and 25 trucks equipped with armor plates. And this was, in the words of the official historian who published his work long after the event, most of the armored transport available in Jerusalem at the time. There would be no more convoys to outlying settlements. The accounts of other correspondents were in the same vein; we did not know any better.

The number of enemy casualties has always been exaggerated throughout recorded history—even during the Battle of Britain, when it should have been relatively easy to count the number of enemy aircraft shot down. Even more shocking in retrospect was the inclination to see plots, conspiracies, and treason in an extreme situation such as a siege. Rereading my dispatches, I find constant references to British intrigues. In fact, there were not remotely as many as we thought. True, the British administration and the military commanders did not go out of their way to be helpful and to save Jewish lives, which is not surprising after the terrorist attacks over the previous years. Their attitude varied from place to place. In Haifa it was rather pro-Jewish; in Jerusalem, pro-Arab.

Furthermore, there was much suspicion during the siege, similar to the fifth-column panic in Europe in 1940, which was made responsible for the successes of so many Nazi attacks. In fact, the fifth column did not exist. Nor was there any need to detain the Issei and Nisei in the United States after the Japanese attack on Pearl Harbor and to arrest the Jewish émigrés in Britain in 1940. Jerusalem in 1948 was not free of spy mania, and several innocent people lost their lives as the result of mass hysteria; the case of Meir Tubianski, a former major in the British army and a leading electrical engineer, was the most famous, but there were others.

Hagana intelligence among the Arabs was not too good in those days. Someone informed Hagana that the Arab military command was located in the Semiramis Hotel in Katamon, whereupon the hotel was blown up on January 5, with the loss of forty lives. It was, in fact, just one of Jerusalem's better Anglo-Arab hotels; as a result of this attack, the middle-class Arabs moved out of Katamon and the gangs from Hebron moved in. Thus, another front was quite unnecessarily opened in southern Jerusalem. Admittedly, I had a personal interest, because we lived a few hundred yards from the place, and in the months that followed, we were to suffer as a result of this mistake. Still another fatal error was the case of the Arab driver of the American consulate, who had personally been vetted as an agent and arms supplier by leading Hagana intelligence officers and yet this information was never acted upon. He was the person who, on March 11, placed a bomb in the courtyard of the Jewish Agency (12 were killed, 44 injured).

Nothing went right in Jerusalem during the early months of 1948. The town was gradually strangulated as the result of the battle of the roads, which by late March the Arabs seemed to have won. Inside the town the general mood deteriorated as a result of the constant sniping and the disasters that overtook the city. Among the major disasters were the bombing of the *Palestine Post* on February 22, of the Jewish Agency on March 11, and the Hadassah convoy tragedy on April 15.

The one that affected me directly was the least deadly, the one in the *Palestine Post* building. I had gone home at about ten in the evening. Not long after I had reached home, a friend phoned me, telling me that he was glad to hear my voice, because there had been a major explosion in Hasolel Street and he feared that I had been among the victims. I called the *Palestine Post* and all other offices in that building, but there was no answer. Soon after, I got another call from a colleague according to which the building as well as some others had been destroyed. He offered me his office for the duration. I decided that in the circumstances there was little I could do. I informed my paper (which was just about to go to press) and went to sleep. It must have been one of the last calls to get through.

Early next morning I went to inspect the ruins and found the first reports somewhat exaggerated.

FROM OUR OWN CORRESPONDENT:

. . . the printing presses in the cellar as well as the *Palestine Post* editorial offices are totally destroyed, but most of the damage was caused by fire rather than the blast of the explosion. The foundations of the building are intact. I went up the stairs; a cloud of heavy smoke had settled there, three of the offices on the first floor are burned out, but on architect Kaufmann's door a handwritten note says: Business as usual. Our office is virtually undamaged, only the glass of the windows has disappeared (so have all the windows in the neighborhood). The door and some of the furniture is broken and the telephone cannot be found. As I write these lines electricity is restored, and the *Palestine Post*

employees are resuming their work. They managed to bring out
last night a small edition, with a David Courtney column about
truth being stronger than dynamite. Congratulations.

The death toll was four, sixteen others were injured. For once
Hagana intelligence had been well informed; there had been a
warning three weeks earlier. Even the names of the alleged
perpetrators became known: a British police sergeant from the
Meah She'arim station, two Arab brothers, and two unknown
individuals from Hebron, possibly foreigners.

I reported, as was my duty, the other major disasters that
occurred that winter, but since I had not been an eyewitness, I
had no special contribution to make. On each of these occasions
more than one person I had known was killed, and a few I had
known well.

Our small world in the Kadima House was also affected by
the worsening situation. It was, as I have mentioned, the most
forward Jewish position bar one, a small building called Bet
Hanania. Sniping from the hill opposite began on January 21
and recurred at fairly regular intervals until the Arab irregulars
were driven out of Katamon four months later. The terrain was
ideal for snipers—big rocks, stone walls, and trees offered excellent hiding places. Fire was never very heavy; I suspect there was
only one sniper or two, and he was not a good shot; no one in
the house was ever hurt, even though the distance was not great.
The shooting usually occurred in the daytime when I was at
work, but on a few occasions I was called upon to do my duty
on the roof. A rifle was handed to me, but since I had no binocu-
lars and could not spot the sniper I fired only a few shots on each
occasion, aware of the ammunition shortage.

It was still a nuisance, for it meant that when I returned from
work in the daytime I had to choose my approach in such a way
that I was least likely to be seen from the opposite hill, and the
last hundred meters I had to crawl. A poetess named Ginsburg
was one of the persons with whom we had to share our apartment
at the time; in one of her published works she compared my

approach to a crocodile's. It was well meant, but I found the comparison inappropriate.

Naomi and the other mothers of small children stayed at home; schools and kindergartens in our neighborhood had closed down. A few hundred armed men were present at most hours of the day and night. Their commander was Naqdi, who had been my assistant at the newspaper. He had just published his first literary work, which was a translation of *Pinocchio*. The women had to go out in the open to get their ration of water and kerosene, which was transported in a horse-drawn carriage. (Water was rationed early on, and gradually also electricity.) Some women were killed while waiting in line for the water, but since one could not do without it, the distribution continued; one tried to shorten the procedure as much as possible. There was no fruit or vegetables, and our pediatrician advised us to collect a certain wild grass called *hubeisa* that grew between the rocks and the cyclamen behind the house. Children who disliked spinach would dislike hubeisa even more. But since it allegedly contained vitamins not otherwise available, the mothers persisted in the face of violent resistance.

March 13 was a bad day, sniping continued from morning to evening on the southern front and there were also explosions nearby. On March 31 bread rationing was introduced—200 grams (seven ounces) per person per day. But soon the ration was reduced, and on many days there was no bread at all. Rationing should have been made obligatory much earlier on. Most of the shops as well as other businesses had closed down. In the shops that were still open there was little to buy except tea, some sweet wine, dried fruit, and, for some unfathomable reason, cough drops called Penetro, of which there was an inexhaustible supply. During March less than two thousand tons of food reached the city, far less than the essential minimum needed; two of the biggest convoys had to turn back to avoid destruction. To get a convoy through to Jerusalem became a major military operation; Arab irregulars had seized the high ground on both sides of the road from Tel Aviv, and they closed it at will. To get the convoys to Jerusalem, the hills on both sides had first to be seized; for this, considerable military forces were needed. This was the purpose of "Operation Nakhshon" in April, in the course of which some one thousand tons were carried to Jerusalem by about two hundred trucks. Since it had become pointless to transmit news stories to Tel Aviv, I began to write a "Jerusalem Diary" in countless installments—some, unbeknownst to me, reached the editorial offices after ten days, some after two weeks, and some did not arrive at all.

Much of the time I felt like the chronicler in Thomas Mann's *Mario and the Magician*, describing how one hotel after another closes down at the end of season in an Italian resort. On April 15, I reported that the Public Information Office (PIO) was about to close down. The director was compelled to write the last official communiqués in his own hand. The PIO restaurant and bar had been the last meeting place in town for Jews, Arabs, British, and others. But PIO was under fire from the Old City walls and it became too dangerous to approach it, except in an armored car. Foreign correspondents still continued to arrive, which was, of course, a bad omen. I also noted that Jewish restaurants such as Egged, City, Etzion and Expresso were still open. More people went there than ever before; for the first time in history there were lines in front of these restaurants. It was cheaper than eating at home, and the restaurants got preferential treatment as far as allocations were concerned. No one asked what kind of meat we were eating—horse or camel, or perhaps one of the cows of Kibbutz Ramat Rahel.

On April 22, I wrote in my "Jerusalem Diary" (published on May 6, 1948):

> The chief censor disappeared the day before yesterday, the postal services do not function anymore, Barclay's Bank in the Arab sector closed this morning, all Arab shops outside the Old City walls are shut. Government departments do not operate any longer, there are only some 20–30 senior British officials left and they are waiting impatiently for their evacuation.

Dr. Reynier, the Red Cross representative, talked to us in the old PIO. In the middle there was a bomb alarm but no one took it very seriously. He reported that several camps had been established for women, children, and elderly people, who would be under the protection of the Red Cross if Jerusalem should turn into a battlefield. There was room at present for 15,000 people. These camps would be common to Arabs and Jews, but barbed wire would divide the two communities. He denounced both the Deir Yassin massacre and the murder of the doctors and nurses in the convoy to Mount Scopus.

And I ended:

I cannot continue my diary tonight, there is no electricity. No one is surprised or angry. No one is asking why. This is Jerusalem, the capital, at the end of April 1948, total chaos prevails, *tohuvabohu* (Genesis 1:2).

Everyone at the time understood the reference to *tohuvabohu*, for, in a speech three months earlier, the high commissioner had predicted that, once the British had left, there would be total chaos.

During April our neighborhood was heavily shelled, heavily at least by the standards of those days. The grenades came from far away, and only a few buildings in our immediate vicinity were hit. But the telephone wires were damaged and, since there was no one to repair them, I could no longer work from home. We decided to move to a small hotel in town owned by the father of an acquaintance. Located in Jaffa Street, in the very center of town, it would not have rated a single star in any guidebook. To get a room, however primitive and inconvenient, was next to impossible in those days, and we considered ourselves very lucky that we got a room with three beds—and little else. It was unseasonably cold that April, and the rooms, needless to say, were not heated. Rations for the Passover week (April 23) were two pounds of potatoes, two eggs, half a pound of meat and/or fish, half a pound of matzoth—an enormous amount. Dr. Joseph for once was quite reckless. A Canadian lawyer who had come to Palestine shortly after World War I, he served as the chief civilian commissar. Almost always in bad humor (I think he suffered from stomach ulcers), he was tough, quite incorruptible, and never hesitated to carry out unpopular measures. Had he been able to infuse the population with a little enthusiasm, he would have been a very great leader.

The owner of the hotel had warned us that if one of the big convoys arrived—expected any day—we would have to share our room with a driver or two. This came to pass on the night of April 20. I remember that I was half asleep when two tired men stumbled into our room. One slept on the floor, the other in a bed. The baby was not disturbed, nor were we. "How many trucks got through?" "Who knows? More than two hundred . . ." They were too tired for conversation, and so were we.

Next day I heard that the convoy had brought almost two thousand tons of supplies, but that there had been heavy losses and that some of the best Palmach commanders had been killed. It was the last convoy to succeed in breaking through until the first armistice. The fighting had been done by the Harel brigade of Palmach, which had been dispatched to Jerusalem to help the local forces consolidate their positions, as the Mandate was about to end.

There was an impromptu press conference; I reported: "Have you seized Bab-el-Wad?" This was the critical part of the Tel Aviv–Jerusalem road, with hills on both sides, which was firmly in Arab hands. "Sorry, this is a military secret." "And what is your name and rank, is this a military secret, too?" "It isn't a military secret, but it is totally unimportant. Moreover, the Palmach has no ranks." A colleague told me that the young man (aged twenty-six to be precise) was named Yitzhak Rabin and that he was one of the two commanders of Harel. He had an outstanding military and political career, in the course of which he attained the highest office in both—and made not a few mistakes. As far as I was concerned, he (and his superior officer,

Yigal Allon, the commander of Palmach) deserved a great deal of credit, a conclusion based on the fact that I had watched them in action in the spring of 1948.

I may have mentioned before that I never inclined toward hero worship. But as far as the Palmach was concerned, I certainly felt that, as Churchill said in a famous speech about the Royal Air Force in 1940, seldom if ever had so much been owed by so many to so few. Palmach had been founded early in World War II. It never consisted of more than seven thousand boys and girls. Only a handful were full-time soldiers; what they knew about the craft of warfare they had taught themselves. Yigal Allon was an avid reader of Liddell Hart—but Liddell Hart's theories on the strategy of indirect approach were based on the presence of tanks and air power, neither of which existed in Palestine at the time. There was a Palmach subculture, very far from that of the professional soldier in other countries, closer to the ethos of the youth movement and the romanticism of the campfire. They had their own songs, which for a decade or two dominated Israeli popular culture, and have now finally been classified as "nostalgia" in the record and tape shops—"Finjan,"* "Zipi,"† and all the others. The tradition of anonymity— of no insignia and no distinctions—was too good to last, and Ben-Gurion was of course right when, later in 1948, he dissolved what he regarded as a private army. But it is also true that the Palmach established a tradition of courage, mutual help, and even humanism in war, which largely shaped the character of the early Israeli army. Some of the main figures faded away— Yitzhak Sadeh, circus artist, doctor of philosophy, and participant in the Russian civil war; Benni Marshak, a political commissar with a stentorian voice, a volcanic temperament, and a commanding presence. Among the youngsters fighting in the Palmach brigade in Jerusalem were three future chiefs of staff

* Arab word for a cup (of coffee).
† Zipora, a formidable Palmach girl.

(Rabin, David Elazar ["Dadu"], and Rafael Eitan), as well as three (or more) of the future leading commanders of the Israeli army (Amos Horev, Uzi Narkis, and Zvi Samir).

Their operations began with a most painful setback. Instead of attacking Nebi Samwil, one of the heights dominating the approaches to Jerusalem in the northeast, by night, they did so by day, failing to achieve their objective and suffering unacceptable losses (38 killed, 40 injured). This was on April 23, but then they went on to storm Sheikh Jerah on the twenty-fifth, and Katamon and the Saint Simon monastery on April 29 and 30. Sheikh Jerah, a suburb of Arab-owned villas named after the religious dignitary whose tomb is located there, was far away, on the other side of town, but I had a proprietary interest in Katamon, which was located just over the hill from Kadima House, a distance of less than three hundred meters. I could watch some of the battle. The Arabs fought bravely, every house had to be stormed, sometimes it changed hands twice within an hour. Again Palmach suffered heavy losses, given the small number of these crack units (17 killed, 78 injured); for hours the outcome was uncertain. As Dadu, at the time commander of a platoon, told me many years later, the end came quite suddenly—both sides were equally tired, weakened, running out of ammunition. In this situation the battle for one house decided the battle for all Katamon, and with their escape from Katamon, the whole Arab position in southern Jerusalem collapsed. Suddenly they had all disappeared.

What happened after the conquest of Katamon was saddening. I wrote on May 12 (published May 21):

A supervisor for Arab property has been appointed in Jerusalem, as in other places. Regrettably, this appointment has come too late. Looters made certain that the new supervisor would not have too much work to do. Despite the ban, collective visits are organized to this day—and no one prevents the theft of Arab property. Similar occurrences happened in other parts of town, and they show once again that a special unit of military police ought to be established to confront this new problem.

They were stealing furniture, kitchen equipment, anything of value, even the occasional *Encyclopaedia Britannica*. The pillaging was carried out as usual not by those who had done the fighting but by the scavengers, mainly civilians. There were ugly scenes and demoralizing ones. There probably has been no war without pillaging, but such knowledge did not offer much comfort.

With the conquest of Katamon, our building was no longer under snipers' fire, and Naomi and Sylvia could move back there from the furnished room we had rented in the center of town after we left the hotel. I stayed on for a few more weeks, mainly because Kadima House could still not be reached by phone. Naomi, who had never trained as a telephone repair woman, made a brave effort to mend the cables. She even succeeded up to a point; dozens of parties were connected as a result of her efforts. But in other instances she connected the wrong lines; for a number of weeks life was full of surprises in our quarter whenever the telephone rang.

The room I was staying in was on the fourth floor of what was by Jerusalem standards a high-rise building on King George Street. From the window one could see much of the east and south of the town. To the right, almost at one's feet, was the fortresslike Ratisbonne monastery, which had been founded in the nineteenth century by a converted Jew, Alphonse Ratisbonne. The monks, of whom there were only a few, had agreed to give hospitality to the cows from Ramat Rahel for the duration of the siege. Also, to the right, there was the Terra Santa, a Franciscan college and church; along King George Street a wall had been built to protect the pedestrians from snipers on the Old City wall; the distance, after all, was small. There was little to do in the evening, since there was no electricity and the supply of candles was running out. I always listened to the evening news bulletin on the still-illegal Hagana radio station (Kol Hamagen).

But there were no spare batteries and one could listen only for a few minutes at a time. Thus, we heard on April 22 that Haifa was in Jewish hands and, a few days later, also Tiberias. There had been little, if any, fighting, and the sudden exodus of Arabs came as a surprise.

In later years Israeli and Palestinian Arab historians would engage in long and bitter quarrels as to whether the refugees had been expelled or not. There is no doubt that in June, when the Israeli army was on the offensive, the Arab civilians were called to leave. But before May 15 the Jews were in no position to force anyone to leave, least of all in Tiberias or in Safed, where the Arabs were in a majority and the Jewish community ill-organized, or in Haifa, where the mayor, Shabtai Levy, went out of his way to persuade them to stay.

To some extent I could observe the process in Jerusalem and reported to my paper on April 22. I had talked to foreign consuls who were still commuting regularly between the Old City and the New. They told me that the well-to-do Arabs had no doubt that the Jews would be beaten once the regular Arab army entered the battle, but they had no particular desire to be eyewitnesses. Some went to Jericho and Hebron, others to Egypt and Transjordan. Small private planes were hired—the going rate for a flight to Cairo was £50 (around $120), a considerable sum at the time; fourteen people went in a plane that should have carried six. The Arab Higher Committee appealed to them to stay, but in vain. Once the richer families had left, many poor Arabs went to the neighboring villages. But unlike in Haifa or Tiberias, tens of thousands remained in Jerusalem—or returned after the fighting was over.

And so I looked out of my window, sometimes alone, sometimes in company. Some nights were quiet—from May 8 to 12, there was an unofficial truce in force. On other evenings, and with the arrival of the artillery of the (Transjordan) Arab Legion, there was a great deal of shelling. On May 14 we heard the transmission from the Tel Aviv Museum, when Ben-Gurion announced the establishment of the Jewish state, to be named

Israel. It seemed somewhat unreal in Jerusalem, preoccupied with its survival, and no one paid much attention. In Jerusalem there was a feeling of being discriminated against; everywhere else in Israel things were going well, so why had Jerusalem to carry a so much larger share of the burden? Visibly, all business activity had ceased; there was no entertainment, the streets were dark and empty, while (many imagined) in Tel Aviv and Haifa people were sitting in coffeehouses, dancing, or going for a swim.

A very cold spring had suddenly given way to the heat of the summer. On May 6 a strong *hamsin* was blowing—the dry, enervating easterly wind. And it was, of course, precisely during that week that the Iraqis at Ras al Ain finally cut the Jerusalem water supply, and the daily ration was cut to a few liters, out of which only a liter or two was fit for drinking. However, in the previous months a considerable quantity of water, more than 100,000 cubic meters, had been stored, which, if need be, would have lasted all through the summer. The fuel situation was far more critical. I do not remember a black market during the siege, with one exception, fuel. When the Allenby barracks in the south of town were stormed, the great prize was a few barrels of fuel discovered there.

In daytime I followed my usual routine. Various supervisory committees, official and unofficial, continued to arrive. I have mentioned Dr. Reynier of the Red Cross, but all he could offer was the protection of the flag of the Red Cross, and this was not effective; poor devil, on a visit to the Old City he was stripped of his clothes and beaten. In March, Dr. Pablo Azcarate arrived, a senior UN official heading the advance party that was to supervise the carrying out of the November 29 resolution. Our meeting took place in a cellar next to the YMCA, all the office space the Mandatory government could spare at the time. He was a fine old gentleman who had been a member of the Spanish parliament during World War I, and later a professional diplomat. I talked to him about the Spanish Civil War, and to Colonel Rosher Lund, his military aide, about Norwegian resistance to the German occupation. There was nothing else to discuss, because the

Hebrew University, Mount Scopus, 1938,
home to five hundred students.
(COURTESY ZIONIST ARCHIVES, JERUSALEM)

Concert in the kibbutz, ca. 1938.
(COURTESY ZIONIST ARCHIVES,
JERUSALEM)

Esdraelon Valley (The Emeq), ca. 1942. (Courtesy Zionist Archives, Jerusalem)

The kibbutz watchman in the valley, as shown on a postcard, ca. 1940. (Courtesy Wiener Library, London)

Kibbutz watchmen in the valley—the
authentic version, myself on the left,
Sha'ar Hagolan, 1939.
(COURTESY SHA'AR HAGOLAN)

Naomi, Ben Shemen, 1937.

Working in the kibbutz, 1938.

Issawiya, on the slopes of Mount Scopus, the Arab village that was our home from 1944 to 1945.

Illegal immigrant ship, *Empire Heywood*, September 1946.
(COURTESY ZIONIST ARCHIVES, JERUSALEM)

The last days of peace, Jaffa Street, Jerusalem, November 1947.
(COURTESY ZIONIST ARCHIVES, JERUSALEM)

Main Street in the German colony, Jerusalem, summer 1947. *Emek Rephaim*
(COURTESY ZIONIST ARCHIVES, JERUSALEM)

Kadima House, Jerusalem, 1948, at that time in the middle of nowhere.

Antiterrorist
warfare,
Jerusalem, 1947.
(COURTESY ZIONIST
ARCHIVES, JERUSALEM)

Bombing of the *Palestine Post*,
February 1, 1948. My office
was damaged.
(COURTESY ZIONIST ARCHIVES,
JERUSALEM)

Our home in the center
of Jerusalem, June–July
1948.

Discovering the world of learning, Oxford, ca. 1955.

I arrive in Moscow, ca. 1957.

Sylvia, Shlomit, and their Caucasian uncle Friedrich.

United Nations was quite powerless. With all his goodwill, Dr. Azcarate and his team could do nothing to stop the fighting. In later weeks a committee consisting of the consuls of various foreign countries played a certain role, mainly as intermediaries between Jews and Arabs. Still later, Count Folke Bernadotte arrived as UN mediator.

I reported the last press conference in the old PIO; its head was about to return to his London public relations company, his deputy was about to become editor-in-chief of a newspaper in Nigeria, yet another senior official was to move to Eritrea. It was leave-taking without tears. These Englishmen were decent enough people but in an impossible position, suspected by Arabs and Jews alike, trying to put the best gloss on the activities of a government that had virtually abdicated many months earlier and had made no effort to hand over administration and services to its successors, even though nominally it was still in charge.

May 14 I spent in the Jewish Agency press office in Ben Ye-huda Street. My report was exceedingly short:

FRIDAY MORNING:
The last hours before the end of the Mandate. The High Commissioner has left town. The disorder is great, the people are waiting for the Jewish State to be declared. The eyes of the world are on Jerusalem. And we are hanging around and there is no way to communicate with the outside world.

Later in the day:

No one expected that the occupation of the strategic buildings in town would proceed so quickly and smoothly. Security areas 1 and 2 were taken over without resistance, King David and YMCA are occupied by the United Nations and the Red Cross. The Russian compound was taken over this morning, as well as the Meah She'arim police station, the Italian Hospital, and other buildings. Arab counterattacks began in the afternoon. Our losses so far—one injured. . . .

The number of victims was in fact greater, mainly in the battle for Talpiot in the south, but we did not know it at the time. This was Operation Pitchfork, which had been carefully prepared but there was not enough manpower and even fewer weapons. Not all objectives could be reached and, once the Arab Legion entered the battle three days later, the fate of the Jewish Quarter in the Old City was sealed.

An Irgun unit had occupied the police training center on the road to Mount Scopus; Hagana units had to be sent to extract them in a more or less orderly fashion. Lehi had occupied Barclay's Bank, but they too quickly withdrew following the approach of the Arab Legion.

Some of the heaviest fighting went on in Ramat Rahel, the kibbutz in the south where now Jerusalem's most pleasant swimming pool is located. It changed hands several times, and the kibbutz was destroyed. The Egyptian volunteers, members of the Muslim Brotherhood, were not a very effective adversary, but the Arab Legion's professional soldiers were a different proposition. The other main flashpoint was the Notre Dame monastery and hospital, in the very center of town, where hand-to-hand fighting went on. With its four hundred rooms, this was one of Jerusalem's most substantial buildings, erected by the French Assumptionists around the turn of the century. The Legion armored cars and artillery were not of much use in this densely built-up area, and the locally recruited soldiers of the Moria regiment acquitted themselves well. During a lull in the fighting I went to Notre Dame with a small group of foreign correspondents. The approach was not easy; it took us ten minutes to crawl the last hundred meters. I reported:

The commander's name is Yitzhak. He pointed out that the building dominated the Old City as well as Musrara and other nearby quarters. There are hundreds of rooms in Notre Dame. During the last war it had been headquarters of the Royal Air Force. The Jewish forces reached the building by way of the municipality garden and Dorothy, an old Arab hotel. Fighting continued for many hours and there has been much damage.

I went to the cellar, where I found an interesting collection of artifacts from various historical periods—neolithic knives, bowls, old swords, and Roman statues. The monk who had been in charge of this collection had had to leave the room without prior notice, and on his desk there was an unfinished letter. . . . There is plenty of water. The soldiers proudly said, "We can wash every evening." We envied them. On the way back the Arabs opened fire on us. After every jump, one had to take cover. Only a few minutes from the city center and yet a different world. . . .

On May 28, Friday evening, I was standing on the roof of a building in Yemin Moshe near the Montefiore windmill. The Jewish unit in the Old City had surrendered a few hours earlier. One could not see the Jewish Quarter, but smoke clouds were rising from where the quarter had been. My comments on that occasion ("The last days of the Jewish Quarter," June 4) were somewhat hackneyed:

There had been a heroic fight that had lasted for five months, until the last bullet, the last drop of water, and the last piece of bread.

In broad outline this happened to be true—the ammunition left was sufficient for about two more hours of fighting. I wrote about 150 "boys"—in actual fact, at the time of the surrender there were 69, for 84 others were lying wounded in the makeshift hospital. (Not all of them were boys—during the last days, the girls had shown as much, or more, fighting spirit.) I also noted that Jews had lived in the Old City since time immemorial, for the last 750 years without interruption, and that one day soon they would no doubt return. I hinted that there had been tension between the military command and some of the civilian leaders (largely self-appointed); Weingarten and a few other notables

had been against the Hagana presence. Their assumption that
they would be left alone if they did not try to defend themselves
was, alas, quite mistaken. But today I am certain that the decision
not to evacuate the inhabitants of the quarter, which would have
been easy with the help of the British, was still the wrong one.
Given the very limited resources of the Jerusalem command,
given the fact that from a military point of view the Jewish quarter
was of no importance, the decision to make a stand there was
mistaken, and I find my patriotic pathos misguided in retrospect.
The principle of not giving up a single position without a fight—
and, *a fortiori*, not in the Old City—was indefensible. It is the
kind of principle that has caused countless disasters in military
history. The Palmach commanders knew it. Shaltiel's advisers
knew it, after several attempts to come to the aid of the quarter
had failed. What, then, was the purpose of the exercise? Was it
perhaps because the evacuation would have been a blow to mo-
rale? The eventual surrender was a much greater blow. It was
one of the occasions when emotion got the better of rational
assessment.

My article was dedicated "to the memory of Eliyahu, who
worked in our office and was one of the defenders of the Old
City from the first day to the last." Eliyahu was our messenger,
sixteen or seventeen years of age, who had gone down to the Old
City with a youth platoon in January 1948. There was no reason
to believe that he was still alive. I never saw or heard of him
again. Only forty years later, at a Washington dinner party, I was
introduced to a stranger who thanked me for the article I had
written in his memory. Eliyahu had been taken prisoner by the
Legion, had been relatively well treated, and now worked for
the World Bank, a water expert of world renown.

As I read the war diary for the last days of May, I find that the
bombing of the city went on almost continuously. Four soldiers
and fourteen civilians were killed on the twenty-seventh; the
figures for the next day were six and twenty respectively, and
five and eleven on the twenty-ninth. This refers only to the civilian victims of the bombardment, not to those killed in the fight-

ing. These were not enormous figures in comparison with, say, Leningrad, but Jerusalem was of course a far smaller city, much less prepared for a siege and victims. A quarter of the soldiers defending Jerusalem were killed or injured during that month. There were rumors about white flags appearing among the ultra-orthodox in Meah She'arim; they were not unfounded, as it emerged later on.

I recall one incident as I walked in Jaffa Street toward Zion Square. As a young boy in uniform overtook me, he was whistling one of the favorite tunes of that time: "Give me five minutes more, only five minutes more. . . ." As we reached the square he was perhaps twenty meters in front of me. There was a loud explosion, he fell, and when I reached him he was quite obviously dead, hit by a splinter. Within a minute or two an ambulance screeched to a halt, and I continued on my way.

It would still be wrong to think of those days as one long nightmare. I did not feel like this, nor did others.

FROM OUR OWN CORRESPONDENT, MAY 27:
Now that the cannonade has somewhat abated and most of the Arab Legion forces have been transferred to the Latrun front, life in town has returned almost to normal—at least in some respects. Two- and three-inch grenades continue to fall, but there are again people in the street, despite the heavy *hamsin*. Coffeehouses and restaurants are open, and here and there ice cream is sold. The children emerge from the cellars and the toddlers are playing again outside. But it is also understood that the battle is not over and people prepare for it in the suburbs, the streets, the houses. . . .

How did they prepare for it? On June 1 ammunition was down to 30,000 bullets, 260 two-inch and 12 three-inch grenades, which was a fraction of what it had been at the outbreak of the war, and would have sufficed for only two or three days of fighting.

But it was precisely during these days that I heard, in deepest secrecy, that a way had been found, after all, to get supplies from the coast, and it was not by air drop either. The old road was closed since the battle for Latrun had been lost. But as a by-product of this battle, two little Arab villages, Bet Suson and Bet Jiz, had been seized, and this made it possible to establish contact between the Jewish forces in the plains and those in the Judaean hills. One jeep had, in fact, made the journey. The engineers made a quick survey and found that, but for a stretch of a mile and a half, a new road of sorts could quickly be built. In the night of June 1, some thirteen jeeps went through; two nights later, seventeen. A bulldozer went to work, and on the night of the eighth, four hundred porters carried food and ammunition over the distance that was not yet passable, and from then on, small but significant quantities of weapons, ammunition, and food were transported. From the fourteenth, regular trucks could make their way regularly—at least by night. It was still a dangerous trip, with the Legion less than a kilometer away, but the siege had been broken. Needless to say, it was unthinkable to report about the Burma Road, as it came to be called—an allusion to the famous highway built by the Chinese in Southeast Asia in 1938–39 during the Sino-Japanese War. There had been talks about a truce in the fighting all May, and on May 29 the Security Council passed a resolution to this effect, and after some hesitation the Arab states accepted it. At 10:00 A.M. on the eleventh of June it came into force and was to end on the eighth of July.

On that day I wrote in my "Jerusalem Diary" (to appear only ten days later) that even after the hour that had been agreed upon, shelling continued. Of a group of six boys who had left their homes to play in the street, four were killed.

But at 10:25, peace and quiet descended on Jerusalem. The atmosphere is Sabbath-like. There is no public transport, no taxis, no private cars, no entertainment except announcements concerning some political party meetings. Most people are clothed in khaki— for weeks clothing could not be washed, let alone ironed. Hun-

dreds of women carrying baskets went to the fields near Sheikh
Bader and Bet Hakerem to collect all kinds of grass. The daily
bread ration has been increased to 160 grams. The price of cigarettes is now four times what it was before. Food convoys from
Tel Aviv are expected any hour.

Five days later the bread ration was increased to 200 grams and
schools were reopened, but the food convoys had not yet arrived.
According to the complicated stipulations of the cease-fire
agreement, both sides and the mediators had to agree that there
would be no substantial changes in the supply position of the
two sides. But the first visitors from the coastal plain came; they
brought chocolate and the occasional newspaper. The movie
theaters reopened on the sixteenth. I also reported the robberies
that not only continued in the occupied Arab quarters but spread
to Jewish neighborhoods. The terrorist organizations that had
been dissolved in the rest of the country continued to lead their
separate existences in Jerusalem. They were dissolved only after
the murder (by the Stern gang) of Count Folke Bernadotte.

I went to the front line and witnessed unexpected scenes of fraternization. Arab Legionnaires came up to our positions and offered
"Players" for American "Camels." There were political conversations, from which it emerged that the Legionnaires were not very
enthusiastic about the war but were doing their duty as good
soldiers. Some Jewish soldiers were invited to a meal in Bethlehem, well in the Arab rear, went there and returned, enthusiastic
about the Legionnaires' hospitality.

On the whole the atmosphere was astonishingly friendly. True,
even during the four weeks of cease-fire, almost every day a
soldier was killed by snipers, but not a single civilian. These
breaks of the truce were not one-sided.

Early on during the armistice I went to Tel Aviv. This was a
major adventure since a special permit had to be obtained to get
a seat in a military jeep. We left Jerusalem the usual way, but

then made a detour to the left to reach the Burma Road. We proceeded much of the time at a speed of five miles per hour, sometimes slower, and on a few occasions we had to walk. Altogether the trip took some five hours. As we entered Tel Aviv almost everything seemed unfamiliar, beginning with the new license plates on the cars. In Jerusalem one had not been aware of the fact that a new state had come into being; in Tel Aviv the soldiers wore a uniform I had not seen before, there were traffic jams, shops and offices were open, and there seemed to be no shortages whatsoever. In the lounge of the seaside hotels—Kaethe Dan, Armon, Scopus—newly baked ministers mingled with UN officials, a leading French Communist, a right-wing Italian senator, Jewish air force men, Swedish and U.S. colonels, and newspapermen from two dozen countries, grumbling about Israel's inefficient public relations system.

It took me some time to take it all in. I had come from a city in which time had stood still and had now resurfaced in an almost normal place. Jerusalem had become a frontline city and was likely to remain one. Many years would be needed to recover. On January 1, 1948, some hundred thousand Jews had lived there; by the end of that year fewer than seventy thousand remained. Many residents did not see their future in a divided city and settled elsewhere in the Jewish state.

I went to the newspaper office and gave a short account of what I had not been able to report during the siege. The others listened politely but without excessive interest; there was so much going on all over the country, every day brought major news events and surprises. Unlike in the old days, Tel Aviv was now also the political center. One of the editors put me up in his small apartment—he and his wife slept in one bed, I in the other; it was like in the early days in the kibbutz. Next morning I went for an early swim at the nearby beach, bought a few provisions, including a canister of kerosene, which Naomi had particularly wanted. The canister was heavy and difficult to transport, but seldom was a delivery greeted with greater joy.

The cease-fire period passed, on the whole, uneventfully. The fighting was to be resumed on July 8, and since no one knew how long the siege would last, I tried, in a number of articles written on the eve of the resumption of fighting for U.S. publications, to summarize my views.

> As I write these lines on the evening of July 7th, a few hours only are left until fighting will be resumed.
>
> The army of Israel, however, has considerably grown in strength during the two months' existence of the Jewish State, and will certainly be able to repel all attacks. It seems therefore very likely that, after a few weeks of very heavy fighting, a standstill will be reached which will serve as a basis for further discussions. After a few more Arab defeats, which are bound to happen during the next weeks, these discussions stand a much better chance of success—with or without Swedish counts and United Nations observers.

This was, broadly speaking, an accurate prediction of events during the ten days of fighting until, at 7:00 P.M. on the eighteenth, the war came to an end. But I also wrote in the same dispatch that "arms will not decide the Palestine question," and a little later that year I warned of "dizziness of success." I wrote of the "intolerable burden [of the defense budget] for the new state" and I warned that the "no peace and no war" approach of the Arabs would reinforce those inside Israel who opposed the resettlement of those Arab refugees who wanted to return. In brief, all the major issues of the following decade could be discerned even before the fighting was over.

I concluded a long article, "Birth of a Nation," as follows:

> It would be a major disaster if these right-wing groups [the Irgun and the Sternists] should come into power. It would be tantamount to permanent conflict and an irredenta in Palestine and the whole Middle East. The Jewish State can exist in the long run only on a basis of at least "normal" cooperative relations with its Arab neighbors; the Arabs, however, will never recognize a

Jewish State ruled by people whose chief aim is territorial aggrandizement.

Rereading these lines more than forty years later, I would not significantly change them. I should have added perhaps that there was no certainty that compromises would have worked. For not until much later was there any readiness among at least some Arabs to recognize the Jewish state and to negotiate with it. By then they had to deal with Begin and Shamir. Facing emergent radical Arab nationalism, that unfortunate mixture of fundamentalist religion, resentment, frustration, impotence, and dreams of great power and glory, perhaps no compromise would have worked. But it is still a fact that some concessions could have been offered after 1948 with little or no risk to the survival of the state—and that the attempt was not made.

During the second period of fighting, nothing much changed in Jerusalem. The Arab Legion, which did most of the fighting, was on the defensive, as some of its units had been withdrawn to strengthen their position in Latrun, which commanded the old Tel Aviv–Jerusalem highway. Israeli attempts to storm Latrun again failed, with heavy losses. The Israeli forces in Jerusalem were not strong enough for an assault on the Old City. The only major change in the situation was in the southwest where the Israeli forces occupied Ein Karem, the village southwest of Jerusalem, thus broadening the corridor to the rest of the Jewish state.

The second armistice was never absolute; sniping continued virtually every day, and most nights machine-gun and mortar fire could be heard. There was serious fighting on Mount Zion and around Government House—also known as Jebel Mukabir and the Hill of Evil Counsel. In the first instance the initiative came from the Arabs, in the second case from the Israeli side. Fifty-nine soldiers and civilians were killed during the month of August, and there were thirty more victims in September and forty-five in October. Only in November and December was there a substantial decline in truce violations. Jerusalem was now a divided city, and it remained divided for the next nineteen years.

I continued to work for about a year for my old newspaper, but without much enthusiasm. My old complaints returned. I found it exceedingly boring to attend routine press conferences and to report local events from Jerusalem. There was much less political coverage, for the government offices were then in Tel Aviv. I disagreed more and more with the political line taken by my newspaper, which during that period veered toward a pro-Soviet stance. I had the feeling that, like five years earlier, I had reached a dead end. Daily journalism provided instant but not lasting gratification. Above all, I had the feeling that I had still a great deal to learn.

Thus, in the summer of 1949 I gave up my old job without clearly knowing what I would do. I could perhaps have tried to become a doer rather than an observer or commentator. But I had not served my apprenticeship in one of the political parties; there would have been much competition. I was too young for a senior position and felt too old for a junior assignment. Above all, I felt temperamentally unfit to work in a bureaucratic framework. I became a freelance writer at a time when writing was so badly paid that I was probably the only freelance in the country. Most hours of the day during the next four years I would spend at home reading and writing.

TWELVE

Looking Backward

The *War of Independence* was the only war I witnessed in Israel. In 1956 I was living in London, and my first reaction when I heard about the outbreak of war was one of disbelief: The decision to attack Egypt appeared to me senseless and nothing I have learned since has induced me to change my view. It was different in 1967: Nasser had sworn to annihilate Israel. The issue at stake was not the occupied territories, for they were occupied by Jordan, not by Israel; for Israel it was a fight for survival. It was one of the shortest wars in the annals of military history, there were very few victims, and it led to a brilliant victory. Soon after I went to Israel and, having interviewed many of the dramatis personae, wrote a book (*The Road to War*) that dealt not so much with the military operations of the Six-Day War, but mainly with the prehistory of the war, its aftermath, and the whole international context.

It was a great victory and I invoked the words of Nelson after the Battle of the Nile, that victory was not a name strong enough for such a scene. But I also felt misgivings as I tried to envisage various future scenarios and I quoted the Marquis d'Argenson, who had once observed that there was nothing so dreadful as a great victory except, of course, a great defeat. I wrote about the fatality that would lead sooner or later to a fourth round. While the great victory of 1967 led to the near defeat in 1973, only the Yom Kippur War made peace between Israel and Egypt possible—these are the paradoxes of history that no one can foresee.

One of the results of the 1967 war was the reunification of Jerusalem. Visits to the Old City became again possible for the first time in twenty years. The division of the city had been unnatural and its reunification was, of course, most welcome. But I could not see in it as some others did the finger of divine providence that had allegedly brought about this miracle. My sympathies were with the young paratroop officer who described a visit to a kibbutz to the parents of a comrade who had been killed.

A few of the kibbutz members were there, and the mother was crying. The father was biting his lips to hold back his tears. One of the older members tried to comfort them. "Look, after all, we've liberated Jerusalem," he said, "he didn't die for nothing!" The mother burst into sobs. "The whole of the Wailing Wall isn't worth Misha's little finger as far as I am concerned."

And the young officer added:

"If you tell me that we fought for our existence, then I'd say it was worth Misha Hyman's little finger. But if you tell me it was the Wall we fought for, then it wasn't worth his little finger. . . ."

More than twenty years passed; I went back to Israel fairly regularly every year or every other year. I went again on the eve of the Persian Gulf War. Every evening I jotted down some short notes on what had happened during the day.

❧

January 14, 1991

Flight LY 316, London–Lod, was almost full, mostly young Israelis who have been called back to active duty. There is a bit of patriotism in the air ("and gentlemen in England now a-bed shall think themselves accursed they were not here") but not obtrusively so. Everyone thinks war is inescapable; everyone knows that it will be different from previous wars; no one wants it. I had planned this trip well before the ultimatum (January 15) had been set; a change would have been inconvenient.

Arriving in Lod, I found a long line of those hoping to find a seat on a departing plane: foreign citizens who have been advised by their governments to leave, young orthodox and ultraorthodox families whose faith in the Almighty seems to be less than absolute, U.S. basketball players, and Swedish movie actors (and why should they stay?). There are also some well-to-do Israelis—the kind who normally would go at this time of the year for a long weekend at Biarritz or Monte Carlo, or at least to an Istanbul casino. An elderly lady has taken position opposite the queue, carrying a placard: "Traitors." People avoid looking in her direction. Shlomit brought me a copy of the current bestseller, which covers all the information needed about chemical warfare, how to wear a gas mask, when to inject atropine, how to seal hermetically one room in each apartment.

January 15

A fine, sunny day, about 20° C. [68° F.] in the sun. Traffic in Tel Aviv is quieter than usual, in Jerusalem almost normal. The shops are full of people and merchandise, and special regulations against profiteering have been issued. All kindergartens are closed. Citizens are advised to listen to the radio, which is on the air day and night. The foreign airlines are closing down one by one. My favorite Jerusalem hotel is almost empty. As in 1948 there is a feeling that the tourist season is over. But Jerusalem is not a resort, and for the local citizens it is still business as usual, except for the long lines to obtain the gas masks (plus atropine and the powder to be applied in case of contamination by chemical poison). Since the queues are very long, I decide not to join them. The experts say that it is doubtful whether chemical substances can be used against the civilian population, except when dropped by a plane or by means of short-range shells. The deadline will be at 7:00 next morning (midnight in Washington, D.C.). I phone friends; so does about everyone else. The authorities express fears that the existing telephone network will not be able to cope with the sudden overload.

January 16

I slept well beyond the deadline. Schools are closed, otherwise it still is business as usual. I revisit the main sites of the fighting in 1948. Only a few people are seen in the streets of the Old City; a self-imposed curfew is in force. The old Commercial Center opposite Jaffa Gate, where the Jewish shops were set on fire and all the trouble started on December 2, 1947, has at long last been razed to the ground, but new development has not started. Notre Dame, the Russian compound, and Jaffa Road have hardly changed at all. Ben Yehuda Street, which lay in ruins on February 23, 1948, following a terrorist attack by British deserters (49 killed, 140 injured), is now Jerusalem's one-and-only pedestrian zone; the artists, fewer now than usual, remind one of Moscow's Arbat except that in Jerusalem the musical performers prevail. With all the apparent normality there is a feeling that war is only a few hours away. As usual in such circumstances, people have become more polite, more willing to help, even more patient. An elderly Russian Jew asks me where to find the ministry of social welfare. I can't help him and approach for advice a group of sinister-looking characters. They could not have been nicer and virtually carried him there on their shoulders. Shopkeepers are willing almost to give away their merchandise. A police officer tells me that there has been an enormous decline in crimes committed during the past twenty-four hours.

January 17

Israeli radio, quoting CNN reports in the early hours of the morning, announces that all Iraqi launchers, missiles, planes, airfields, and the Republican Guard have been destroyed. It sounds greatly exaggerated, and the more sober commentators counsel caution. There is now very little traffic in the streets, and all nonessential institutions have been closed—ideal conditions for photographing. The radio asks people to stay indoors, unless they perform vital services, but these are only recommendations. There is no absolute ban.

Next station, Kadima House. Once this was my home, before that the building where UNSCOP, the UN committee that recommended the partition of Palestine, was housed in 1947. Until a few years ago the birds on the trees surrounding it still performed a deafening concerto between five and six in the afternoon. Now they have disappeared; no one knows where they have gone. Many old-timers, my then neighbors who defended the building in 1948, have died; others sit in the sunshine on the steps in front of their apartment and play with their grandchildren. I phone a friend living in the north who tells me that the evening before swarms of migratory birds—storks, cormorants, all kinds of waterfowl—had arrived in Lake Hule and the Tiberias area. Welcome guests, but the fish ponds of the kibbutzim had to be quickly covered.

Later in the afternoon I passed another line for gas masks that was quite short and joined it. The army people in charge of distribution were astonishingly polite. Did I really understand how to put it on? Was I aware that no injection should be made unless at least two of the unmistakable symptoms of poisoning appeared? They had instruction manuals and video films in Amharic, Russian, Persian, English, and other languages. Did I want any of this material? I told them that gas masks had been distributed in Haifa in 1940 after Italy had entered the war, but I am not sure they believed me; for them, history begins in 1980.

January 18

Last night the first missile alert. One of our rooms had been sealed off by means of Scotch tape and plastic sheets; all that remained was to don the gas mask, to stick masking tape around the doorframe, and to put a floor rag soaked in chlorinated water on its threshold. After that, one settled down listening to the radio and watching television. The anchormen make a valiant effort to sound calm and confident; London during the Blitz is the great model. The instructions also mention the desirability of having a few bottles of mineral water and fruit juice in the room; there are special gas masks with a contraption for drinking, just as there are special masks for bearded men and small children.

During the next few nights, this drill became more or less routine, but the mask still did not become a friendly companion. One had to remove glasses and contact lenses. The straps press on the head, one sweats profusely, and it is difficult to breathe if one happens to be afflicted with a cold or other breathing troubles. The gas mask has become a subject of countless jokes and cartoons—people making love in gas masks and suddenly detecting that they have picked the wrong partner. I find them singularly unfunny.

The one slightly comic story concerning a gas mask I heard from a friend and erstwhile assistant. He had been living with a girl for a long time, first in Berlin, later in Tel Aviv. They could not quite make up their mind whether to get married. Then it appeared that she could not obtain a gas mask because she had the wrong kind of visitor's visa. So they went to Nicosia, got married, and she received her gas mask.

I first heard about gas warfare from my father and men of his generation who had witnessed it in World War I. He spoke about it with great horror. I read about it in Roger Martin du Gard's

323

novel-cycle *Les Thibauds*, where the slow death of Antoine, a doctor and a victim of a gas attack, is described in intolerably gruesome clinical detail. I had not thought that I would ever wear a gas mask in my lifetime. Gas had not been used, after all, in World War II, at least not as a means of warfare.

Present-day gas masks, ugly as they are, present a tremendous advance over the clumsy contraptions developed in World War I. At that time soldiers had to carry with them a canister containing charcoal that filtered the poison gas. A nose clip prevented breathing through the nostrils. Today there are no nose clips and no canisters, and the filters are light and can easily be screwed on. All citizens, young and old, have been asked to carry with them the mask, packed in a brown cardboard box. It is the omnipresent symbol of the war of 1991.

Wearing a gas mask, I realized after a day or two, has a curious effect on one's judgment; it wonderfully concentrates one's mind, but it is not conducive to tolerance and moderation. I watch various statesmen through the gas mask, German and American peace demonstrators ("No blood for oil"), as well as crowds from various Arab, Muslim, and third world countries welcoming gas warfare with enthusiasm. Western well-wishers of Saddam Hussein would certainly benefit if in a sealed room they were exposed to the kicking and screaming of little children afraid of the mask, fighting any attempt to make them wear one. Or if they would watch someone dear to them half suffocated because he (or she) does not get air.

Under a gas mask the debates on whether President Bush committed sacrilege when comparing Saddam with Hitler seem a little silly. I always preferred the Mussolini paradigm, but it is also true that with all his blood-curdling oratory Mussolini was not really that bloodthirsty. During two decades of his rule fewer than twenty of his political enemies were given a death sentence—or were assassinated. He was never remotely in Saddam Hussein's league. Mussolini and even Hitler belonged to a tradition in which major crimes had to be hidden. Saddam Hussein is part of a culture in which human life counts for little. If Mussolini used poison gas in Ethiopia, this was done in strict secrecy, whereas for Saddam it seems natural to threaten that he would use it.

January 19

There were three missile alerts during last night; I slept through the second. Indifference grows with repetition. The newspapers have not arrived; most kiosks are closed. According to a radio announcement, they will be distributed in the post office, but no one in the post office seems to know.

In the end I find an open kiosk in Palmach Street. There are only a few customers, and the shop owner gladly cooperates, holding up the newspaper in such a way that I can photograph the front page with its enormous headline.

One hears various horror stories. A newly arrived Ethiopian family did not hear (or understand) the "all clear" and thus stayed up with their gas masks on all night. A family of Russian Jews, just arrived, did not have gas masks or a place to live. So they went into their small Lada (a Fiat produced in Russia), closed the windows, and waited for the morning. Accommodations have now been found for them near Haifa. What of the three- or four- or five-year-olds like Tamar? For the "children of the Scuds" the gas masks of 1991 will be one of their central experiences. Last night, asked to go to bed at eight, she said that since the sirens had not yet been sounded, it was obviously too early. The logic was not convincing, but sirens and gas masks have certainly become a central part of children's fear and imaginations.

As in wartime London, the waiting in sealed rooms and air raid shelters produces a folklore on the adult and juvenile level alike. So far, the songs that have emerged are not on the London level of 1940. The radio incessantly plays a hit song of 1952, "Sugar Bush, I Love You So," presumably an expression of gratitude to the president of the United States. A Baghdadi Jew repeatedly interviewed on radio claims to have been a classmate of Saddam, whom he describes as lazy and not too bright but for his interest in Arab language and literature. The authenticity of the story is doubted by other Iraqi Jews.

My next stop is the Jerusalem Hilton, which together with the Tel Aviv Hilton is now the official press center. The army spokesmen have a big office, so has the Foreign Ministry. And there are countless direct phone and fax lines. Brigadier General Nahman Shai is the first professional spokesman the army ever had, a former journalist and graduate in communications science. True, it still takes too long until the first official announcements are made after a Scud has exploded; in one instance, while phoning Washington, I heard that one of the networks had been on the scene with its cameras well before the local spokesman could give us any information. The reluctance not to be too specific about the site of the explosion is understandable.

Close to a thousand journalists have arrived in recent days. Hotel owners and taxi drivers are overjoyed. But the journalists are frustrated. They take walks in the center of the city and interview each other. The local radio and television people are doing an excellent job; never before has there been so much information available within seconds. They digest it quickly, and intelligently. How different it was during the siege of 1948, when a handful of newspapermen, local and foreign—without telephones, telegraph, wireless, totally cut off from the outside world for three months—tried to do their work.

In 1948 the shops were empty, and the food and water rations were exceedingly small by any standard. Yet there was a euphoria in the air; I for one never felt hunger or thirst. The weapons used by attackers and defenders alike were ridiculously ineffective by 1991 standards—old rifles, light machine guns, a few two-inch mortars. The Arab Legion had a few cannons. Yet the number of victims was higher than in any subsequent war. On January 18, 1948, a whole squad sent on a rescue mission to Kfar Etzion disappeared without a trace. In the small Jerusalem of 1948 virtually everyone had a relation or a friend among "the thirty-five," as they came to be called. It took a long time to establish where the ambush had taken place. Today, by means of a single helicopter, help could have been provided within a few minutes.

Our "press center" was a single room on lower Ben Yehuda Street. At noon every day Gershon Hirsh gave a short press conference, a purely academic exercise, for there was no way to make use of the information. Born in Germany, Gershon went to school in Haifa and attended Oxford, where he was president of the Students' Union. A highly intelligent man and one of the most lively I have known, he became one of the leading Israeli diplomats of his generation, and still later, president of Haifa University. I was to meet him on the nineteenth of January to exchange reminiscences about old days. He phoned—his daughter had arrived with her baby, could we meet the following morning in my apartment? When he did not turn up, I phoned. He had died of a heart attack during the night.

January 20

Another sentimental drive (and walk) through a largely deserted city. Mount Scopus: The university has grown thirtyfold since my days as a dropout. To someone not familiar with the layout it is utterly bewildering. One must not stop in front of the bookshop, and the access to various buildings is barred for security reasons. Dozens of obviously very necessary road signs; in the olden days everything was concentrated in two or three buildings, and everyone knew what was where and who was who. We stop the car on a road from which we have a good look at Issawiya, the Arab village just behind the old Hadassah Hospital where we lived for almost two years. There was no sign of life, human or animal, only bright houses in the sunshine, including quite prominently the one in which we lived. What became of our landlords and neighbors? For a moment we hesitated—should we pay a visit? But past experience in other countries has taught us that such visits in the search of a vanished past are always embarrassing. One does not find what one looks for, the new tenants (who may have lived there for decades) will be suspicious, and the welcome will be less than cordial.

Beyond Mount Scopus, the Mount of Olives, where Jesus predicted the destruction of Jerusalem. But there are no ruins. On the contrary, there are many new buildings that I never saw before, such as the Mormon University and, on the opposite side, the new Hyatt Hotel. With the exodus from Tel Aviv following a few nights of missiles, all of the rooms in the hotel are occupied for the first time. The mayor of Tel Aviv has been angry about the "deserters," but, in fairness, who can blame them? Many thousands leave the city by rail and road every evening, to return the next morning, driving into giant traffic jams.

Thousands of people from Tel Aviv are said to be in town. For many of them, students of history apart, Jerusalem is almost a foreign country, a hundred years away. Some of them know Paris and London better than their capital city.

Back to Zion Square. The cinema after which the square was called has been pulled down; once it was (together with the Edison, which still stands) the center of cultural life. The concerts of the Philharmonic Orchestra as well as mass meetings took place here, as there was no bigger hall. The bookshop where I worked, a stone's throw away, has disappeared, so has the *Palestine* (Jerusalem) *Post*; it moved to an industrial estate to the west of the city close to the television studios.

We have lunch at Shalom's apartment in King George Street. Normally, no parking space can be found in this busiest of all sections of town; today we leave the car on the sidewalk—the danger of traffic warden or police interfering is minimal. We became friends in Breslau in the 1930s, our mothers had been acquainted, we were in the same youth movement, and he was my chief competitor over the hundred meters and in the long jump. Then for many years our paths did not cross; he served in the British army, became a gunnery officer, was one of the founders of the Israeli artillery corps and eventually returned to his old love, athletics, ending his professional life as head of the department of physical education in the ministry of education. His wife, the daughter of a well-known painter, was Israel's chief swimming coach for many years. They are vigorous, busy from morning to night, almost enjoying a second youth.

There is a war on, yet outside the sun is shining, the street is very quiet, and we are talking about the days when we were young and foolish and when the whole world was young.

January 21

Last night the sirens surprised us when we were parking the car in the street. We did not hurry, nor did anyone else; nothing much happened during the earlier air raids, and nothing will happen this time. The slogan immortalized by a great American journalist in 1940, "London can take it," applies to Israel in 1991. There is much less bombing, but it is also true that the Israeli public was quite unprepared for the kind of enemy it faces now. In 1948 the Arab Legion acted according to a code of honor and even chivalry, which would have seemed strange and ridiculous to the likes of Saddam Hussein.

The mood changes from day to day, from hour to hour. The Patriot batteries are welcomed with enthusiasm (and exaggerated expectations). When they fail to provide absolute safety, there is dejection. But on the whole life is becoming more normal, even though schools and kindergarten are not yet reopened. Rain has come and helped to alleviate a serious water shortage; the water level of Lake Tiberias has risen by three inches in two days.

The errors committed during the first days of the war are now put right. It was a mistake to bring the economy to a virtual standstill; most people are better protected at their place of work than at home, because many houses built in the fifties and sixties are rather flimsy. It probably was a mistake to advise the public to use the sealed rooms rather than the air raid shelters during a raid. The air raid shelters would have given greater protection against falling debris, and the number of wounded might have been smaller. But it is easy to understand why the authorities were overcautious—chemical and biological warfare cannot be ruled out. At one stage thousands of Tel Avivians stormed the air raid shelter of the Central Bus Station, probably one of the largest in the world, and had to be removed forcibly. But there have been few scenes of undiscipline since. New immigrants— of whom there are 1,000–1,500 daily—are behaving remarkably calmly.

January 22

More missile alerts. Some of the sirens were not loud enough and had to be reinforced. The sound of passing ambulances has also been confusing at times; they have been asked to use their sirens sparingly. During the alert we watch a debate with Western opponents of the war, some theologians, some professors of moral philosophy. The discussion centers around the concept of the just war, which has been debated for more than a thousand years. The argument most freely adduced on television is that a war ceases to be just if the unjust enemy is very strong and can be defeated only at a high price, such as an ecological disaster. And since Saddam is so strong . . . I turn to a game of Scrabble. Then I read for the nth time the official handbook "Emergency Situations." There is a chapter entitled: "How to Confront Fear—What Can You Do to Reduce It?" The answer is to talk, to help others. It is quite natural to sweat and to tremble. Don't take drugs; you have to be alert. If someone gets hysterical, don't smack him (or her); it is the wrong cure.

January 23

LY 315 leaves exactly on time. The captain announces that, according to the emergency regulation, there should not be too many planes on the tarmac at any given time. Not all passengers have settled down in their seats as the plane rises from the runway, which is quite irregular. With a slightly uneasy conscience, I have taken my gas mask through the controls. But there is no acute shortage, and I would like to keep it.

London–Washington, February 10

I need not have smuggled out the mask. Israeli gas masks priced $34.50 are advertised in the *New York Times*. In the meantime there have been considerable improvements in the outward form of the masks. Special contraptions have been developed for those who wear glasses or contact lenses, and it is now even possible to have a drink with the gas mask on. The ugly brown boxes in which the masks were carried about in the beginning have been replaced by colorful containers. There are masks for sufferers from asthma and for guide dogs for the blind.

I returned from Israel with a bad cold, had to stay home for more than a week, telephoning, listening to the uninterrupted news coverage and the comments, and reading. One morning I had a call that our former little apartment, a few steps from the seashore near the Acadia, had been missed by a Scud, but not by much, and that there was some damage. We had lived there during the 1970s for weeks, sometimes a few months, each summer. I had spent several hours each day on the beach, swimming when the waves were not too high, walking from the Invalides Beach to the Sharon Beach and back, beachcombing, looking for shells and various flotsam and jetsam carried to the beach overnight. Sometimes we went a mile farther north to Sidna Ali, where there had been a glass factory in the early Middle Ages. To this day tiny pieces of glass can be found in the sand and among the pebbles. Over the years we collected many jars of glass. Some we had kept; others were given away. I had become acquainted with the beach community, the mounted policeman patroling the beach, the lifeguards, the owners of the little kiosks and the Zebulon fish restaurant, the few inveterate swimmers and walkers who would appear in any weather. Sometimes they were joined by guests from abroad from the nearby hotel— American tourists, a football team from black Africa, wealthy Maronites from Beirut—a strange and interesting mixture. Over the years the Mediterranean has become progressively more dirty, and the beach was covered with black tar, especially after a storm. It was no longer great fun to swim, and after a walk a few minutes were needed to get the tar off one's feet. There were more and more surfers, especially on weekends, and fewer swimmers; there was no space to park a car in the radius of a mile. Little private planes were skywriting, advertising all kinds of goods and services. These were some of the happiest and most relaxed hours in my life. One met the most extraordinary people on the beach and near it: retired businessmen, politicians, and terrorists; philosophers, illiterates, and paparazzi. One day I had a long conversation with an old Russian lady, the widow of Adolf Abramovitch Joffe, one of the prominent early Bolshevik diplomats, a close friend of Trotsky's who had committed suicide in 1927 anticipating the tragedy of the Communist opposition to which he belonged. All her family had died in Soviet prisons and camps, but she had been permitted to emigrate to Israel to spend there the last years of her life. She knew no Hebrew but there were many Russian speakers in the nearby absorption center. What would a younger generation of immigrants make of someone coming from another world, a member of the old intelligentsia?

To date thirty-five missiles were launched from western Iraq. The last two, a few hours ago, fell somewhere in the desert. There were very few victims but many houses were damaged. Shlomit told me that her daughter, aged four, had nightmares: "Mummy, take my gas mask off!"—but she was not wearing a mask at the time.

It is very sad. But hundreds of thousands of children survived the blitz in London and Leningrad, and the small development towns in the north of Israel who were for years under Katyusha fire from the other side of the border. Time and again I was asked: How does it compare with 1948? I find it impossible to answer. We were so much younger. The community was much smaller and more cohesive. We all had much less to lose, at least as far as material goods were concerned. Every war is a misfortune, even this strange war; every one is different.

October 1991

For a number of years I have been writing an annual review for the *Encyclopaedia Britannica* on the most important developments in the field of international relations during the previous twelve months. Today I met my assistants at the Washington Center for Strategic and International Studies to prepare a list; events in the Soviet Union took pride of place. We then noted Yugoslavia, South Africa, the assassination of Rajiv Gandhi, and so on. "I think we forgot something," one of the assistants said. "What do you mean?" "Well, the Gulf War . . ." How could I have forgotten? Of course, it seems much longer ago than a mere nine months.

THIRTEEN

Postwar Blues

I *have moved far ahead in my narrative* and ought to pick up the thread in 1949. As our cotenants gradually moved out of the apartment, the feeling of an emergency situation faded. I took little Sylvia for walks in the neighborhood; in winter the rocks were partly overgrown by plants, with cyclamen and other flowers to be admired but not to be picked. Today the whole neighborhood is built up, but then it was quite empty and one knew everyone in a radius of half a mile.

These were years of austerity. No one died of starvation but there was little to buy in the shops, with rationing still in force. Even for the renewal of the normal water supply we had to wait a long time. Jerusalem recovered very slowly. A few new hotels were built, but this hardly made much difference as far as the development of the city was concerned. There was as yet little tourism; elementary facilities were still missing. My doctor told me to go swimming as often as possible, but the only swimming pools were in the luxury hotels, and I could not afford them. I was by then fairly well known, mostly perhaps as the result of my Friday evening talks over the radio on world politics. But even so, I had to work harder than ever before, writing a column or an article or editorial every day for the Hebrew- and English-language press. Sometimes I wrote two. Yet the income from all this writing hardly sufficed to make ends meet. Journalistic work was very badly paid in those days; we still lacked basic furniture and kitchen utensils, let alone pictures to put on the walls. I did not have the works of reference essential for my work. To remedy the situation I wrote for foreign newspapers. One longish article made it possible to buy a refrigerator or an encyclopedia; for the royalties from another several food parcels dispatched from Cyprus could be bought. Naomi and I began to suffer from the summer heat more than before. Perhaps we had noticed it less in the years before. There was, of course, no air-conditioning. I hated public transport and virtually never used it. But to own a car was a distant dream, and one had to think twice before calling a taxi; our friendly neighborhood driver was Dr. Samter, who had been a lawyer in Berlin but had found it too difficult in his fifties to qualify for the second time.

In my work I had three major fields of interest—Western Europe, the Soviet empire, and the Arab world—and in my writing I regularly commented on these topics. I had access to newspapers from the neighboring countries, which were brought in by a special messenger by way of the Mandelbaum Gate, the only major crossing point in Jerusalem. I received periodicals from Europe and the Soviet Union. Considering that I had never been to these parts and that my writing was entirely based on reading and listening to the radio, I have no reason to be ashamed of my literary output during those years. But a whole dimension of knowledge was missing, and on occasion my prognostications were widely off target. I suggested that the Western powers should support the democratic forces in the Arab world, failing to realize that such forces virtually did not exist; I thought at one time that there was a fairly high probability that Iraq would go Communist. But I also wrote an article for a British journal, arguing that Israel could work out a settlement with Egypt—twenty-five years before the event. This was a time of constant change in the Middle East. The old order crumbled. King Abdullah was killed in the Old City of Jerusalem; King Farouk had to leave his country; the Hashemites were overthrown in Iraq. Military coups took place every few months in Damascus; every commander of a tank brigade had a fair chance and many made use of it. There was constant excitement, but often it was a mere tempest in a teacup and intellectually of no great interest.

Very slowly life in Jerusalem did become more normal, but I still doubt whether any comparable society suffered so much from rationing and various deprivations in a time of peace, and Jerusalem suffered more than the rest of Israel. Jerusalem became the divided city par excellence. True, Berlin was also divided, and for a time Trieste, too, but one ought to recall that until the Berlin Wall was erected, its residents could move almost freely from west to east and vice versa, whereas in Jerusalem the curtain was nearly impenetrable. There was no telephoning between the two parts of the city, and only one crossing point, the Mandelbaum Gate. This was not really a gate, but the ruins of a house that had been the scene of much fighting. In the course of a day, a few consuls and officials would pass, as well as a few "truce observers," a rare VIP, and some special cases that included a very sick Arab who was to see a Jewish specialist in the new city, having obtained a permit from the UN Truce Commission. But there were not more than a dozen such cases each month. From time to time an Arab family would gather at the gate to take counsel. There were many cases when part of a family had found itself in Israel at the end of the war, whereas other members were in Jordan. In such a meeting they would try to decide whether to be reunited in one country or the other, and there were sometimes stormy scenes. The Mandelbaum Gate also served as a customs clearing station. Since industrial products (say, radios or cameras) were cheaper in the Old City, some smuggling took place, but there was not much of it.

The border between the two parts of the city could hardly be missed. In addition to the barbed wire, there were trenches, heaps of earth and stones, and unexploded grenades and mines. Even so, a few people managed to cross the border inadvertently: children who had run away from home, religious fanatics, or new immigrants looking for a home. They were duly detained and, after a few days, returned.

The United Nations observers (American, French, Belgian, headed by a Danish general) dealt with such prosaic but important issues as canalization in the no-man's-land (so as to prevent the spread of malaria). Furthermore, they had to manage two internationalized areas—namely, Mount Scopus (the Hebrew University and Hadassah Hospital) and the region around the former Government House. Having lost its site on Mount Scopus, the university was housed in a number of buildings all over town, with the center in the Terra Santa.

Jewish Jerusalem was not a lively city. It had the only university at the time and some ten cinemas. Three newspapers were published there, but it was neither the cultural nor the political center of the country. True, Jerusalem was declared the capital, and gradually parliament and most ministries were transferred there. This produced a wave of protest on the part of foreign powers who did not recognize the new capital. The foreign ministry was the last but one to move to Jerusalem in the spring of 1953. The foreign embassies remained in Tel Aviv, except the Dutch, which happened to be located in Jerusalem from the beginning. But most of the ministers and the great majority of members of parliament did not move to Jerusalem, a city that had few attractions to offer. By May 1951 some six hundred thousand new immigrants had arrived in the country, which was more than the entire Jewish community had numbered in early 1948. About half of them came from Europe, the other half from various Middle Eastern and North African countries. But very few of them settled in Jerusalem—the economic situation there was bad; there were no jobs and no entertainment. The ultraorthodox, much fewer at the time but as militant as today, tried their utmost to stop all traffic and whatever little entertainment there was on the Sabbath and, generally speaking, to make life miserable for all those who did not share their rigid practice of religious observation.

From time to time someone in New York, Paris, or Rome would suggest the internationalization of the holy sites. But only one, relatively minor, holy site (the Coenaculum on Mount Zion) was in Jewish hands. Some pilgrims from Europe and America would arrive, but far fewer than in later years, and they all stayed in the Old City. There was no night life in Jerusalem, very much in contrast to Tel Aviv, and there was not much life in daytime either. There was nowhere to go on weekends, except perhaps to Ein Karem. The city had lost not only its hinterland but also its international character, and it had not gained a new character or role. It was again the capital, but mainly on paper. Nevertheless, we never considered moving to Tel Aviv or Haifa. At that time the possession of an apartment (virtually no one had a house) was far more important than having a place of work, and no one would lightly give up his residence. Kadima House was considered a very desirable location. One of our neighbors (and a friend) was a superior gardener (he had been marathon champion of Austria and Palestine before), and the trees and shrubs we planted around the building under his direction were not only aesthetically pleasing but also provided much-needed shade during the difficult summer months.

Shlomit was born in June 1950; fortunately, we had by that time gained possession of the whole apartment. Fortunately, too, there were in our building several children of Sylvia's and Shlomit's ages. While proximity had not necessarily generated close friendship, there still was much of the community spirit that had prevailed during the siege, when we had had to defend our home. There was, in other words, a good deal of mutual help.

One mother would buy provisions for herself and the neighbors; another would take care of her children in her absence. Such division of labor was self-evident. It also existed among the men, and it made life a little easier.

Once the shooting had stopped, it became a very quiet neighborhood. From my window I had a fine panorama, with the Monastery of the Cross at my feet, a fortresslike building with a square bell tower and a brown dome. To the right were the last houses of Rehavia, Metudela Street, and, on the more distant horizon, hills as yet empty, on which in later years the Knesset and the prime minister's office would be built. My own office consisted at the time of a Remington typewriter, which was at least thirty years old, and a small Hebrew typewriter of somewhat more recent date. My typing speed was quite fast, the result of some years of journalistic training, and while I could not compete with secretaries of the old school, it surprised the younger ones among them.

There was an incongruity between the bucolic Jerusalem surroundings and the topics on which I was concentrating during those years: Stalin's last years and the outbreak of the cold war, the Soviet takeover of Eastern Europe, and the economic recovery of Western Europe. I wrote about Sartre and Camus's falling out, about neorealism in the Italian cinema, about Zhdanovism in Soviet cultural life—for the local press as well as for the old *Partisan Review*, for the *Nineteenth Century and After*, and for countless other journals.

As I reread the articles and columns written during those days, I find among the topics covered the origins of the Muslim brotherhood, the philosophy of Etienne Gilson, the fiftieth anniversary of Jules Verne's death, the prospects for proportional representation in Israel, recent trends in town planning and nuclear technology. I was reading very widely, and while this created an aura of omniscience, it was of necessity superficial, based mainly on ad hoc reading rather than any study in depth, perhaps with the exception of some topics that were really close to my heart.

I wrote a little book on oil in world politics; at that time it could be done within a framework of some 130 small pages, after reading a dozen books (this was about all the serious literature in existence) and studying cursorily three or four professional journals.

I wrote a more weighty study of the history of communism in Palestine, which is occasionally quoted to this day, and gave me the inspiration for a wider study on nationalism and communism in the Middle East—my first book in English. Communism had never been a very powerful force in Palestinian politics, but it was still a fascinating phenomenon. The Communists had been against Zionism, and the Palestine experiment, from the very beginning. That being the case, why did they bother to establish a party in the first place? I did face a major problem: The Communists had been opposed not only to Zionism but also to the use of the Hebrew language. Probably all their publications up to World War II were in Yiddish, and to a lesser extent in Arabic. On the basis of my knowledge of German, Hebrew, and Russian, I found Yiddish not too difficult to read, but there was an even greater obstacle. The party had been illegal, so its publications were not accessible in libraries. By a great stroke of fortune I got hold of a unique private collection, including not only most illegal journals, pamphlets, and posters, but even internal newsletters. The owner, who apparently needed the money, had decided to sell it to the government, probably for the archives of one of the secret services. Once it was transferred there, it would disappear for many years, if not forever. I had a week in those pre-Xerox days to make the most of this rare material, and during that week I copied documents day and night, working against the clock.

As far as my political interests were concerned, the Soviet Union and world communism were near the top. If I became more and more critical, and had few illusions about greater liberalization after the war, this was not because I had been fed massive doses of anti-Soviet literature. The general mood during the war in Palestine, as elsewhere, was pro-Soviet, mainly in view of the heroic resistance of the Red Army. Whatever anti-Communism there was came mainly from the Nazi camp, and this, of course, had the contrary effect: Any movement or country so strongly disliked by the Nazis could not be all bad. My critical views had been formed during the war, and *a fortiori* during the early postwar years, by Stalin's socialist and democratic opponents, the Mensheviks and social revolutionaries in exile, and, paradoxically, by the Soviet media. What bothered me was the fact that the Soviet media were so obviously mendacious and that there was a Byzantine cult of the leader, which, if possible, exceeded that of Hitler in Germany. I had the opportunity to talk with people who had recently been in the Soviet Union—there were not a few who had left the country during the years 1945 and 1946, when, of necessity, the borders were somewhat more porous than before or after. The image emerged of a system in some respects not unlike Nazi Germany—a stringent, arbitrary dictatorship ruled by one man by means of propaganda and terror. The fact that there was quite obviously mass support for Stalinism impressed me less than it did others. I had, after all, seen the frenetic jubilation whenever Hitler had appeared, and I also knew that in some German circles at least there was a deep and genuine belief in the just cause of Nazism. I was aware of the important differences between Nazi Germany and Stalin's Russia, but the parallels—concentration camps, secret police, an all-pervasive propaganda, the omniscient leader—were still deeply troubling.

Neither the cold war nor the new wave of show trials came as a surprise to me. It was clear to me early on that the regime was deeply, inherently flawed, that most probably it could not be reformed from within, and that it was a state-of-siege regime that needed enemies to justify its existence and policies. And if there were no such enemies, they had to be invented. I did not engage in discussions with party members; their minds were set. But there were others who did not deny the negative features of Stalinism yet tended to belittle them and, in any case, found a great many extenuating circumstances. They firmly believed that these aberrations were only temporary; after all, Russia was a backward country. To get it out of the barbarous morass, barbaric means had to be used. But since Stalinism had outlived its usefulness, it was only a question of time until Soviet society would transfer itself into the freest society on earth. The most eloquent and influential protagonist of these views was the writer Isaac Deutscher, author of a well-received but deeply flawed Stalin biography. Soon after Stalin's death, he published yet another book, predicting a return to "pristine Leninism," that is to say, democracy and freedom. I derided such wishful thinking. Deutscher answered, and a polemic ensued. I sometimes wonder how Deutscher would have reacted, had he lived, to the final breakdown of Soviet communism, realizing that history had disproved his views. He was a hard man when it came to acknowledging error, and he was not alone in his obstinacy.

But I was also not deeply impressed by Hannah Arendt's magnum opus, which appeared in 1949. It was an original attempt to explain the essence of totalitarianism, in the course of which she equated Nazism and Communism, and brought in all kinds of irrelevant issues, such as the Dreyfus affair and the imperialism of Cecil Rhodes. She struck me as a highly intelligent and educated woman who had somehow adopted the wrong field—namely, politics—in which common sense and judgment are more important than a philosophical training. True, she later modified her views, arguing by 1956 that totalitarianism was finished. She became famous as a result of her writings on the Holocaust, showing again brilliance, perversity, and lack of deeper understanding.

My critical attitude toward Stalinism never turned into anti-Russianism. So great was the desire to see a better future for the Russian people, that for a little while, immediately after Stalin's death, I published some comments and predictions that were clearly too optimistic. I revised my views within a few weeks, partly as a result of discussions with my friend George Lichtheim.

The late 1940s were a period of nightmarish events: the new

show trials in Prague, Budapest, Sofia, and elsewhere, in which the Communist old guard was accused of crimes they clearly had not committed—and confessed to even more absurd ones. At the same time, by means of the "salami technique"—cutting away, slice after slice, of the existing democratic order—regimes were established in Eastern Europe that were replicas of the Soviet model. Having lived through this period, I found it impossible in later years to accept the views of a "revisionist school" in the West, according to which the outbreak of the cold war was largely, or in equal measure, the fault of the West. Of course, certain mistakes were made by the West, but even if it had been absolutely faultless, there still would have been relentless Soviet hostility, for such was the character of a regime that could not have existed without an enemy. Many years later, in a meeting (June 1990) with Soviet historians and policymakers in a dacha just outside Moscow that had once housed Dimitrov and Kalinin, I said as much, and heard no serious arguments in refutation.

The postwar witch hunt found its apogee in the regimentation of Soviet cultural life ("Zhdanovism") and the propaganda campaign against the (mostly Jewish) doctors who had allegedly plotted to poison Stalin and his henchmen. Only Stalin's sudden death prevented further outrages. In an essay for *Partisan Review* I argued that the new cultural policy spelled the end of Soviet literature and probably most other arts. There still would be, needless to say, Soviet writers, composers, and painters, but not Soviet literature, music, and painting in the accepted meaning of the term. This statement might have seemed too harsh, but events in the following years unfortunately bore out this prediction. In some fields, such as the cinema, production literally ceased. In others it continued, but the result was pitiful.

Sometimes the purges would strike nearer home. There was the Oren case in 1952, on which I commented from the beginning to the end. Mordehai Oren, a member of my old kibbutz movement, was an unofficial foreign minister of Mapam. I had known him quite well. Before the war he had cultivated relations with all kinds of left-wing socialist circles in Western Europe.

On one of these trips to Czechoslovakia, in January 1952, he was arrested; someone was needed in Prague in the context of the preparation of a show trial as one of the "missing links" between the local traitors, Titoism, world imperialism, various espionage services, and world Jewry. He duly admitted his guilt and even if no one believed it (he apparently held out for six months), his own party was deeply embarrassed and put most of the blame on "reactionary forces" in the West, while trying to get him released, with appeals for "Communist justice." Such appeals, needless to say, fell on deaf ears.

Oren, who, in the words of the leading Czech newspaper, was "an international criminal who looked like an Apache," admitted all accusations. Accused with him was an Israeli businessman named Orenstein, of whom no one had ever heard before, who claimed that he had been present when the new "Protocols of the Elders of Zion" had been signed in Washington. Orenstein got a life sentence but was released from prison in 1954, whereas poor Oren was about the last to be freed—in May 1956. He was given a wonderful homecoming party in his kibbutz, Misra. On his return, he reaffirmed his unshaken devotion to the cause of peace and progress, as symbolized by the Soviet Union and the governments of Eastern Europe, even though "Gestapo methods" had been used to extract his confession.

The Oren case did not come as a surprise, but it still puzzled me. Not so much because he had confessed—everyone knew by that time that most people could be broken under sufficient pressure—but the credulity of his friends (my erstwhile comrades) and many intellectuals in the West continued to dumbfound me. In the face of all the evidence, in the face of so much information on the gulag and the whole terror system, how could one believe in the progressive mission of Stalinism? I had some sympathy in later years for the scorn heaped by Solzhenitsyn on Western intellectuals who had been willing accomplices, refusing to accept unwelcome evidence. But it was also true that many in the West had never shown any sympathy for Stalinism, a fact either unknown to Solzhenitsyn or suppressed by him.

Political and cultural resistance to Stalinism was the central issue in international affairs in the years 1947–1953. It was not a popular cause; those engaged in it were likely to be painted with the cold war brush. This did not particularly bother me; I regarded anti-Stalinism as essential as antifascism in the 1930s; belief in freedom and democracy involved by definition taking a stand in this great issue of the period. Failing this test was as bad as failing to take a stand against Hitler.

I always believed that a system based on injustice and lies would not last forever, and I was never afraid of the advent of "1984." But I have to admit I did not anticipate that the breakdown would be so rapid and so complete. I had never thought I would live to see articles and books of mine in Russian translation and to be welcomed as an honored guest in Moscow.

I was influenced in my thinking by several people, of whom mention will be made later on, but I should single out a French thinker, much less well known at the time than in later years, with whom I became acquainted after I had moved to Europe. Raymond Aron was then very much in isolation, regarded as something akin to an American agent by many members of the French intelligentsia. Aron was "rehabilitated" only during the last years of his life, when French intellectuals realized that they should have followed him rather than Sartre.

I have again strayed from my narrative. If the immediate postwar period had been one of great fascination, the years after 1948 came as an anticlimax. In Israel these were years of mass immigration, of *tsena* (austerity), of the emergence of a new society and a new state. But I did not feel that I had to make a contribution, however modest, in this context. I felt restless and frustrated: The topics that interested me above all, political and cultural alike, were taking place in countries I had never visited. I was writing most of the time about people I had never met. To become a true Middle Eastern expert, I would have needed a far more substantial grounding in languages, history, and cultures. But my curiosity as far as these countries were concerned was not great enough to generate sufficient enthusiasm for me to make this effort. The United States and the Soviet Union, and Western and Eastern Europe, seemed infinitely more interesting, and thus, in 1953 and 1954, I began to spend part of the year in France, West Germany, and Britain. In 1955 we went to London for what was meant at first to be a sabbatical; eventually it became a permanent stay, but in the United States rather than England. There was no sudden or radical break. I have spent several months each year teaching in Tel Aviv. Had I been a scientist or a physician or an archaeologist, my life might have followed a different course. But, for better or worse, I had opted for another profession, and this led me away from the Kadima House, from friends and acquaintances, and from the seventeen years that I had spent in that new world.

PART THREE

Grand Tour of Europe and Muscovy

FOURTEEN

Grand Tour of Europe

A*s the war in Israel ended in 1949*, I felt I had to make up for lost time. The years in Palestine and Israel had not, of course, been lost years; they had been dramatic and in many ways rewarding, even with all the deprivations involved. I had been privileged to watch from a close angle history in the making. It had been a good school, but as time went by I became more and more restless. In 1951 I celebrated my thirtieth birthday, but it was not a joyous occasion; my education was quite unfinished, I had seen virtually nothing of the world. I had no plan how to remedy this; George Lichtheim introduced me to some of his friends in London and Paris, and this led eventually to offers of work, temporary, uncertain, and not princely paid, but a jumping-off place in a number of directions. But first the young man from the provinces had to broaden his horizons, not only figuratively speaking.

Traveling in Western Europe in the early postwar period was infinitely more complicated than it is today, and to visit Eastern Europe was virtually impossible except for a few select people such as diplomats and some journalists and businessmen— mostly *personae gratae* of the regime. For every country a visa was needed; it always took a number of days to obtain one and sometimes, for whatever reason, was not given at all. I remember applying, on one occasion, for a Swiss visa. When asked for the purpose, I truthfully said that I had been invited to attend a conference. The French-speaking consul told me that he would have to turn down my application because I needed a labor permit, which was seldom, if ever, granted. Upon further inquiry, it appeared that the consul was under the impression that I was to give *une conférence*, that is to say, a lecture. Upon assuring him that I had no such ambitious plans, I was given the visa, albeit with some reluctance.

This incident was quite typical. Few people were traveling at the time, and those who did were suspect. Perhaps they were saboteurs or international spies or, more likely, displaced persons, refugees trying to enter countries that did not want them. The climate in the embassies and consulates reminded one of similar scenes in the 1930s; it was a very unpleasant atmosphere. Within a year there was no empty space in my passport, a second passport was affixed to the first, and eventually I traveled with three or four stapled together.

This was the preturbojet age, and there were no direct flights over long distances. The plane from Lydda to Paris landed in Athens (or Ankara), Rome (or Milan), and Geneva (or Zurich). Those who went on to America changed planes in London, had an hour or two in Shannon (Ireland)—which had at the time the most impressive duty-free shop—and froze for another hour or two in Gander, Newfoundland, before entering the United States. The planes were not yet pressurized, and despite all precautions I was half deaf after many a flight. In brief, flying in those long ago days was a major event, an adventure, sometimes pleasant, at others less so. It would take another decade for mass tourism to develop, sweeping away the need for elaborate questionnaires, visas, stamps, queuing up in consulates, and other bureaucratic chicanery.

I had prepared myself for my first postwar visit to Europe like a young Englishman in the eighteenth or nineteenth century for his educational "grand tour." In fact, I was probably better prepared because I was more highly motivated. I was no longer that young and carefree, and the time at my disposal was far more limited and so were our funds. I had been studying countless books on Paris and London, on Italy, Switzerland, and Germany; I thought I knew what to expect, and I had long lists of places I wanted to see and people to meet. I was full of a somewhat naive enthusiasm of which I see no reason now to be ashamed. For many years I had read and admired English and French literature, yet I had never seen any of the places that I should have known. I had never been to a major museum (except once briefly in Berlin). I had never been to a first-rate theatrical performance or listened to the great musicians of the time. After many years in Palestine and Israel, I had all but forgotten what a forest, a major river, or high mountains looked like. I no longer remembered the sights, noises, and smells of a main street in a big city, with its massive buildings, elegant shops, and department stores. I had never been on a subway, visited a house of parliament, or watched television.

This list could be prolonged. In retrospect it is astonishing that I was not totally overwhelmed, in a perpetual state of amazement, but that in many cases I took to this world I had known only from books as if I had always lived there. I continued to be excited, but then excitement was in the air. Paris in the early fifties was the undisputed cultural center of the world, full of new ideas and impulses. I had grown up in the age-old belief that every civilized person had two homes—his own country and Paris. London was still the capital of an empire, albeit reduced in size. Churchill was still alive; some eighty theaters were opening their doors every evening, and under the Labour party the groundwork had been laid for a welfare state. In Germany democratization seemed to work, and economic recovery was startling. I met a new generation of politicians who impressed me, each in his own way, and who, I felt, would go far in years to come—Willy Brandt in West Germany, Hugh Gaitskell and Harold Wilson in Britain, François Mitterand in France. Few people had heard of them at the time; they were just parliament members at the beginning of their careers, except perhaps Mitterand, who was a junior minister but not yet a Socialist. There was the hope, more than the hope, there was the certainty that a new Europe was emerging out of the ashes.

It was not by accident that I went to Paris first, for this was where most of the action was, and I was to meet there some of those whose ideas and writings had been of particular interest to me—André Malraux and Raymond Aron, Franz Borkenau and Richard Lowenthal, George Lichtheim and François Bondy, and many others.

I well remember the excitement of arriving at Orly close to midnight. We were taken in those days to the city *aérogare* just south of the Seine, somewhere near the Champ de Mars. I tried to identify the quarters and streets we were passing, but quite unsuccessfully, because this was the *banlieue*, working-class Paris, of which I knew nothing. The streets in the inner part of the city were still quite full, and I half expected people to dance; I did not know that this had been the custom only on the fourteenth of July and that after the war it had petered out. At last, we arrived at our destination, which was the Hotel D'Isly, rue Jacob, corner of rue Bonaparte.

For some years to come I would visit Paris in connection with my work virtually every month and this *quartier* of Saint-Germain became our second home; later we moved to the Madeleine district. At first everything seemed wonderful, the romantic little streets in the quarter, the restaurants and nightclubs, the little shops open to a late hour in the evening, the many bookstores—how many books I had missed! In rue Jacob there seemed to be an antique shop in every other building, and a restaurant or bistro in every fourth; the Pré-aux-Clercs became our favorite eating place. We went on long walks along the *grands boulevards* and on the quais along the Seine: Quai Voltaire, Quai Malaquais, Quai Anatole France, Quai d'Orsay—what music to my ears, what associations! I continued to write two weekly "Letters from Europe" to my newspaper and as I reread my dispatches I find that I was far more interested at the time in French culture than in French politics. My reports frequently read like an abbreviated version of "This Week in Paris." My readers had to stand with me in a line several blocks long to watch René Clair's new film *Les Grandes Manoeuvres* even though it was no more than a trifle, hardly worthy of my idol. On another occasion my readers had to accompany me to an avant-garde theater named Antoine in the boulevard de Strasbourg to watch the first performance of *Nekrassov*, a new play by Jean-Paul Sartre—an awful, wholly unfunny farce that went on for four hours. I wrote not only about *Nekrassov*, but also mentioned that Offenbach had lived there, that *Cyrano de Bergerac* had first been performed next door, and other useful information. On a third night readers went with me to watch Jean Anouilh's *Ornifle*, yet another disappointing play, with an elderly music hall songwriter as the main hero. The next column informed my readers that Messrs. Jean Cocteau and Albert Buisson had become members of the French Academy. I have no idea who the latter was, but I do recall that Cocteau's speech was broadcast by French radio though it took several hours. It could not have happened in any other country.

I am amazed, in retrospect, that there were no letters of protest; who cared about second-rate French plays and movies? Perhaps my enthusiasm was infectious; perhaps they enjoyed more my reports about French popular culture. For I also reported the first performance of Clouzot's *Le Salaire de la peur* ("The Wages of Fear"), a thriller that is still shown all over the world. I took them to the Porte Maillot where "ski jumping" was performed in May, with fifty meters of real snow. And I wisely added that there was more fun and more existentialism at the Porte Maillot than in *Nekrassov*.

Above all, I liked going to the small neighborhood cinemas that were showing the films of the 1930s, the great era of the French cinema that I had missed. I saw Duvivier's films and Marcel Carné's and René Clair's and many others. True, one saw them with different eyes after the war. About *Le Jour se lève* (with Jean Gabin as the antihero) it was said that it contributed to a large extent to French defeatism, which led to Vichy. This was not my impression fifteen years later; on the other hand, I was struck by the appeasement atmosphere pervading Feyder's *Kermesse héroïque*. This film, a French-German coproduction, depicted the capture of a Flemish city by the Spanish army in the seventeenth century, with the local women spoiling the Spanish soldiers, softening their hearts and making them leave in good spirits.

It was a very hot summer, and I remember frequenting a *piscine* in the Seine more than once; the river was cleaner than now, and I also reported about what Parisians were doing on weekends—leaving the city for a picnic, angling, watching sports.

Gradually, I became more critical. I realized that the manager of the hotel was exceedingly rude, that Parisians in general were not polite people, that there was no elevator in the hotel, that the plumbing was inferior by any standard. Upon closer inspection it appeared that most antique shops in the street sold rubbish or art nouveau, which I could not stand, or, alternatively, *régence* furniture of strange proportions. I realized that one could exist without reading every single issue of *Esprit* and the other high-brow journals. I had never been a devotee of coffeehouses, but in the beginning I had joined friends when they went to the Deux-Magots or the Flore, or for a dinner at the Brasserie Lipp. (The famous Drugstore did not yet exist.) But it did not take long to understand that I would never meet there Sartre or Camus, who had moved elsewhere long ago, and that most of the guests were either foreign visitors or painters who had never painted a picture or composers or writers who had been equally unproductive. I learned that Racine and Richard Wagner, and more recently, Guillaume Apollinaire and Charles Péguy had been my immediate neighbors, but since I had no particular interest in any of them (with the exception of the last mentioned) I was no longer overwhelmed; one quickly got blasé in Paris.

While I was in Paris, the eighteenth French government since the liberation resigned. Such resignations had become routine and did not attract much attention. The editorials in two leading Paris newspapers that day did not even comment on the event but devoted their columns to Marcel Proust on the occasion of the fortieth anniversary of the publication of *Du côté de chez Swann*. The cabinets consisted either of Pleven, René Mayer, Queuille, and Bidault, or of Bidault, René Mayer, Pleven, and Queuille. There was a permanent crisis and there was no crisis. But for the newspapers no one would have known that the situation was so serious and that urgent consultations went on in the Elysée. I met a youngish politician, named Pierre Mendès-France, but everyone told me that he was too intelligent and radical and would never get a chance. (It took the defeat of Dien Bien Phu to make him prime minister for the one and only time.) On the day the eighteenth government resigned, I concluded my dispatch as follows:

> As you sit in one of the sidewalk cafés of the Boulevard Saint-Germain, the very quarter that is the background to most of Proust's novels, talking with what appear to be not untypical specimens of the academic and nonacademic youth of the Latin Quarter, you are bound to ask yourself: If the twenty-year-olds do not worry about politics, who will?

Some people did, of course, worry. The pundits were saying that the permanent internal crisis did weaken French foreign policy, be it in Indochina, North Africa, or in Europe. People who knew France infinitely better than I did told me that the spirit of France had been broken in 1940, and had never completely recovered.

But I was not entirely convinced. As a student of history I knew that there had been a veritable industry producing books entitled *Finis Galliae* after 1870 and there were a great many "objective" reasons to buttress this thesis. France seemed to be finished in almost every respect. But then around 1905, almost from one day to the next, the mood had changed from despair to aggressive optimism even though the "objective" situation had not changed at all. Could it be that France was not finished even now, but that a comparatively small group of professional politicians had exhausted their ideas and energies, whereas the people as a whole had not been all that much affected by the fashions in mood and thought? I met Herbert Lüthy, a Swiss journalist who had turned academic. (Many of the best journalists at the time seemed to be Swiss. There were Fritz René Allemann, Fred Luchsinger, François Bondy, Hans Tütsch, and a dozen others.) Writing in a provincial newspaper during the war and without access to any privileged sources of information, Lüthy had produced the most perspicacious strategic analysis of the course of the war. In the early 1950s Lüthy was writing a remarkable book on France, full of insights. He pointed to the fact that there were two Frances—the one that had somehow found its way into the twentieth century, and the other, a deeply conservative society, fighting modernization tooth and nail. Even to an outsider like myself it was obvious that there was tremendous overemployment in French agriculture and especially the retail trade, all the little one-family shops called B.O.F. (*beurre, oeufs, fromage*). And since there were a great many small peasants and little shopkeepers, their political influence was great and prevented rationalization. Paris continued to decay, people got accustomed to not paying taxes, the Citroën *deux-chevaux* was the most popular car of the period, and the peasants rejected the 50,000 tractors offered by the government plan. After all, their ancestors had not used tractors and what was good enough for them . . .

For whatever reasons, I did not accept the doom-and-gloom scenarios and wrote in one of my dispatches:

True, many sections of French industry and agriculture cannot compete with the Germans and the British because French prices are 15–20% higher. At the same time it appears that even a modest amount of rationalization of new working methods [I pointed to the success of certain industries] would cause a fall in prices by 15% and make France competitive again.

While Lüthy was writing his book, France changed slowly and imperceptibly: There was a mass exodus from the countryside, whole areas in central and western France got depopulated, the small shops disappeared one by one, new industries began to operate. Even if the governments changed every few months, the civil service, which was much better than its reputation, continued to function. In retrospect it would appear that economic progress during the "troubled years" (1948–58) was considerably greater then in the years after. But de Gaulle and the Fifth Republic reaped the political benefit.

I am amazed that I was not struck even earlier by the constant change. Each time I came to Paris something new surprised me, sometimes small things, but they added up to a major trend. The B.O.F.s were replaced by modern shops; new suburbs were built; the business luncheons became shorter and the consumption of spirits smaller; the hair of young people got shorter; deodorants replaced perfume; American fashions made their appearance, not only in the sixteenth *arrondissement*, called L'Américaine— and it culminated in the great cleaning up of Paris's streets and buildings. Not all the changes were for the better. I happened to prefer Charles Trenet, Yves Montand, and even Tino Rossi to the Beatles, just as I preferred *l'assiette au boeuf* to hamburgers and chips.

I HAVE BEEN WRITING about general events in the world around me and very little about my own thoughts and feelings, not, I believe, out of excessive modesty and reticence, but simply because this was for me a period of learning and absorbing fresh impressions rather than reflection and self-analysis. A new world opened to me. I was invited to various international seminars and conferences; I had to confront new ideas; I met many interesting personalities and from most I learned something. After the Breslau municipal library and the kibbutz and the Jerusalem bookshop, this was my third university, and I tried to make the most of it. One does not usually make many close friendships in one's thirties, but I certainly now had many close acquaintances, and some of them had a considerable influence on me. I did not sit at their feet accepting their obiter dicta without criticism, but they certainly opened new vistas to me and compelled me to rethink ideas that I had taken for granted. As I look back, most of these people were not academics (though many of them ended up teaching in universities) but, rather, *hommes de lettres*, true intellectuals.

I have written elsewhere a portrait of George Lichtheim, who became a friend and frequent houseguest, Richard Lowenthal has written about Franz Borkenau, one of the last of the polymaths, erratic, highly opinionated, but with flashes of real genius. About Raymond Aron several books have been written in recent years, François Bondy had his *Festschrift*, and also Leo Labedz and Daniel Bell and Karl Dietrich Bracher. Edward Shils has recently published a long essay on the Congress of Cultural Freedom, and there has been a book by Peter Coleman on the same subject. A list of those who influenced me during these years would be fairly long and presumptuous, for some I did not know that closely. But I shall perhaps one day write about them in greater detail and also about my own work. This led me more and more into the gray zone between political and cultural journalism and intellectual and political history. I became an editor of a journal and a visiting professor even though I did not even have a B.A. This was still possible then. I wonder whether it would still be feasible now.

While doing the research for this book I came across the horoscope published in the *Washington Post* on May 26, 1921, for those born on that day. Goethe, after all, began his autobiography with his horoscope, and there is no reason why I should not mention it. It caused me considerable amusement: "People born on that day would not experience any financial difficulties in later life." I was, alas, one of the exceptions. We lived as before, very modestly, from hand to mouth.* One day the manager of Lloyds Bank, West End branch, Haymarket, London, asked me to come to his office and told me that he would have expected that a man of my age (and a paterfamilias to boot) would by now have a certain nest egg—which clearly was not so in my case. Perhaps he wanted to get rid of me; that specific branch was mainly frequented by major firms and wealthy individuals. But essentially he was correct, even though it did not cause me sleepless nights at the time.

I was more worried about our children. As the result of our peripatetic life-style, Naomi and I were frequently away, and though in most cases the children were well cared for, I knew from my own experience that separation from parents causes problems. When I was four or five my parents had sent me to a children's home an hour's drive from home with disastrous results. After a few days the director called them to collect me.

I grew out of it; but Sylvia and Shlomit were still very small at this time. Naomi behaved bravely; like the biblical Ruth, she said: For whither thou goest, I will go; and where thou lodgest, I will lodge. But I knew that her thoughts were frequently with the children, and she was fearful, like every mother, that something untoward might happen to them during our absence. Nor did the children take it gamely; many years later, Shlomit told me that she was so angry as the result of our betrayal that she sometimes prayed that we would not return. On one occasion they took part in a mass escape from a children's home in southern England. They attended eight or nine different schools between the ages of six and eighteen, and while this might have

---

*For a long time the month of February was the best month of the year for us because it was the shortest.

broadened their horizon and did not cause any lasting intellectual harm, it also meant that they felt uprooted, that every so
often friendships ended that had just begun. I was aware that our
frequent absences would cause a certain insecurity, but having to
choose between my unhappiness and theirs (which they would
outgrow), I decided to incur the risk. I hope they have forgiven
me over the years.

When I returned to Germany for the first time, eight years
had passed since the end of the war. I did not belong to those
who had sworn never to set foot again in the country that had
been the graveyard of my parents and so many others. If I wanted
to be a chronicler of our times, I could ill afford to ignore a
country that even in eclipse was of considerable importance, not
yet as an active player but as a battleground between West and
East. It was because of Germany that the cold war had broken
out, and the German issue was the topmost one on the agenda
of international politics. There were other reasons to which I
shall refer presently.

And so I took the plane to Tempelhof, the airport very near
the center of Berlin, which was, in fact, Berlin's prewar airport.
Right from the beginning I was surprised by the prosperity even
in those early days.

Berlin had been one colossal ruin in 1945, at least as seen
from the air. I had read that it would take fifty—nay, a hundred—years to remove the rubble, let alone to rebuild the houses.
Yet even in 1953 there was hardly any rubble to be seen anymore,
at least in the Western sector. The supplies in the shops were
plentiful, and the people did not look undernourished and were
not shabbily dressed. Friends took us to a villa in Zehlendorf for
our stay, and as I smelled the coffee and the fresh rolls next
morning, as I saw the back garden with its trees and well-kept
shrubs in the sunshine and also the neighboring villas, and as I
listened to the birds chirping outside, it was difficult even to
imagine that not long ago there had been a major war, that the
country (and in particular this city) had been virtually destroyed.
Everything seemed like before the war, only more modern and

opulent. It happened to be a Sunday and we went in the afternoon to the open-air public beach at Wannsee guided by a young
man named Siedler, then only at the beginning of his career,
who later became one of Germany's leading and most creative
publishers. As we were relaxing among many hundreds of others,
enjoying the water, watching the children playing and their parents laughing, it was easy to forget that there was a cold war on
and that Berlin, a little island in the middle of a hostile empire,
was its focal point.

When we went the next day to the Kaufhaus des Westens, the
leading department store, we realized not only that the selection
of goods was far larger than in Paris (even in the food department) but that the prices were substantially cheaper.

These were the first impressions, and they were correct as far
as they went. But it did not take long to realize that Zehlendorf
and Dahlem, where most of the U.S. military and civilian institutions were located, upper-middle-class suburbs that had hardly
been damaged in the war, were not quite typical. As long as we
looked at the shops, the impact was overwhelming, but if we
lifted our eyes, there was a return to reality. Many of the massive
blocks of offices and apartments had disappeared. This was true
even with regard to the Kurfürstendamm, once one of the largest
and most elegant streets of Europe. It had little in common with
the street I had known before the war.* It was a mere shell, a
facade. One whole architectural dimension had disappeared.
The Emperor William Memorial Church, altitude 370 feet, once
the highest building in Berlin, was decapitated, and remained
so. In comparison with later years, there were as yet few private
cars in the streets. I read in the papers that all the economic
indicators were highly satisfactory. West German industrial production and exports were already considerably higher than before the war, and output was steadily rising. More than ten
million refugees from the east had been absorbed without much

---

*At our first visit in 1953 one did see the Kurfürstendamn from the Witten-
bergplatz; but rebuilding in the center was still at an early stage.

difficulty; on the contrary, they gave a decisive impetus to the West German economy. In school it had been preached to us that Germany was a *Volk ohne Raum*, a people with insufficient living space. Now it appeared that there was more than enough space.

In the cultural field the general picture was less rosy. I found little of interest in the bookshops, and German movies, always with a few exceptions, were pathetically bad. I had grown up in the tradition of classical German literature and of Weimar, so perhaps my expectations were too high. In the field of popular culture, entertainment, hit songs, the situation was not too bad. Berlin had a cabaret called Die Insulaner, which impressed me more than the famous theaters in the West and East sections of the city. The newspapers and periodicals were competent but provincial; the only one with a truly international outlook was *Der Monat*, edited by Melvin Lasky, which was, however, not universally popular because it was edited and financed by the Americans.

By and large there was, however, little anti-Americanism except among sectarians of the extreme Right and Left. The CARE parcels were still vividly remembered, as were the bombers that had brought food when the Soviets had imposed a blockade from 1948 to 1949. German cultural life was Americanized, perhaps too much so, not because the Americans imposed it, but because many Germans thought everything American was wonderful.

The situation in the universities, I was told, was far from ideal; a few of the grand old men of German science and humanities were still alive and active, but the successor generation was not up to the same standards. The decline would not have been that striking but for the fact that pre-Nazi Germany had been leading in many cultural and scientific fields: Mathematicians and physicists from all over the world flocked to Berlin and Göttingen. Germany had some of the best physicians and conductors, philosophers, sociologists; its leading writers were read all over the world; and some German movies were the envy of Hollywood. Germany of the 1950s, on the other hand, was not a country from which many cultural impulses emanated, yet the Germans desperately needed some recognition and encouragement. For many, their victory in the soccer world championship in Switzerland was a much-needed injection of hope: "We made it again!" Provincialism was the bane of German culture in the 1950s and for many years after. Probably it was only natural in view of the great trauma of 1945 and also the fact that the new Germany was only two-thirds the size of what the old had been. Perhaps it was unfair to apply the standards of a past age; seen in a wider perspective, the fact that democratic institutions were growing roots in West Germany and that its economy made rapid strides was more important than a new cultural flowering.

East Germany was an unhappy country. The day I arrived in Berlin four thousand refugees from the east made their way to West Berlin. True, the daily average was lower, only fifteen hundred to two thousand, but during the first three months of the year 1953, one hundred thousand had come, and in the second quarter the same number again. I visited a few of the 105 camps housing the refugees (including one for "Jewish citizens") and came back with the clear impression that there was nothing typically German in this mass escape. I wrote in my dispatch the next day:

> The world would face exactly the same phenomenon of a mass flight from an Iron Curtain country, if those concerned had the facile means to escape.

I was taken to Kaiserdamm 93, where the screening took place, for only those who could convince the authorities that they fled because of an immediate threat to their life and safety were given the right of asylum. There was the case of the elderly farmer who began to weep when he told his story: His farm, which the family had owned for several generations, had been taken away from him. There was the story of a mere boy who had been a member of the Volkspolizei, who had put up a picture of a pinup girl over his bed in the barracks. He fled because he was sure to be arrested. Not a single one had a legally watertight case: The journalist who was accused of deviating from Marxism-Leninism would probably not have been shot at dawn; the chief engineer who had not fulfilled his plan would probably not have been exiled to Karaganda. I asked myself what made these people—most of them beneficiaries of the regime, workers and members of the new intelligentsia—give up their homes and possessions and run for their lives? West Germany in 1953 was not yet that attractive a haven; there still was unemployment, and all they could expect was an uncertain future. My answer was that none (of those screened) could say with certainty that they would have been arrested, imprisoned, or executed had they stayed on; probably they would not have been touched. But they all fled because they could no longer stand the continuous all-embracing and enervating fear that had gripped every one behind the Iron Curtain, which can be understood only by those who have had the doubtful privilege of living under a totalitarian regime.

I was aware that the East German regime was facing a crisis, but I did not anticipate how acute it was. Had I known it, I would have postponed my departure by a few days. For during the week after my departure the great revolt of June 17, 1953, took place, the first of the major spasms that was to shake the Soviet bloc after Stalin's death and that culminated in the Hungarian Uprising of 1956.

I made the obligatory tour of East Berlin driving along Stalin Allee—that copy of Moscow architecture—and visited a museum, a bookshop, a store selling records. But I learned very little, except that the old Berlin, the heart of the city I had known before the war, no longer existed, and that what had replaced it was neither attractive nor interesting.

I returned to East Berlin on the first anniversary of the workers' rising. What lessons had been drawn by the leaders? The official slogan was that the "needs of the people" were now the main consideration. This meant on one hand re-Stalinization, on the other demobilization of the masses. Ordinary people were left alone; the nationalization of small enterprises was postponed. The average number of refugees was now only a few hundred a day. I concluded my report as follows:

> Tomatoes are now two pfennig cheaper, potatoes are plentiful, and more houses will soon be built. What more does one need to be happy if one is not an "enemy agent"? But in East Germany, too, people continue to have thoughts of their own, many in an inarticulate way. The demands of human nature may not be satisfied by a decrease in the price of tomatoes.

The history of East Germany in the subsequent decades oscillated between crisis (the Berlin Wall) and consolidation. It had some wonderful achievements in athletics and swimming, partly owing, as we now know, to hormone therapy. During the 1980s the regime seemed more securely in the saddle than in any of the Eastern bloc countries. It was the Communist success story par excellence. But it was rotten to the core. It was my good fortune to watch some of its last days from Unter den Linden and the Alexanderplatz and I shall not deny that the indescribable joy felt by the masses, many of them weeping, was infectious. For a few days it seemed that "bliss was it in that dawn to be alive." I had not doubted that one day that dawn would come, not so suddenly perhaps. But I also felt that soon enough the jubilation would give way to a more sober feeling and perhaps even dejection, for it would take a long time, and great effort and suffering, to dismantle the heritage of forty-five years of Communist rule.

I had no particular difficulty in the first postwar decade to converse calmly with my contemporaries in Germany, let alone with those younger than I. I had known that generation well. They had been eighteen or nineteen when war broke out, too young to belong to the Nazi party. Some were deeply influenced by the official indoctrination, and there had been a few fanatics among them, just as there had been a few opponents. They fought in the army as disciplined soldiers, because everyone did;

esprit de corps was far more decisive in this context than political belief. Most talked to me openly about their experiences before 1945 and I had no reason to disbelieve them.

It was more difficult to confront the older generation; with them there was often room for suspicion. I never believed in the collective guilt of a people. I knew from my own experience that if it had been up to most individual Germans, there would not have been a Gestapo, or military attacks in every direction, or the mass killings of Jews and others. But I also knew with what blind enthusiasm so many had followed the Führer while the going was good. From my work in the Nazi archives after the war, I realized that many who after the war pretended to be free of individual guilt had been accessories to crime, wittingly and unwittingly. I remember a dinner in Tübingen, the town of humanists and Hölderlin. I had given a lecture, which was followed by a walk along the Neckar. Our host was a distinguished professor of international law, a *Geheimrat* of the old school, a most charming man of the world and a brilliant raconteur who behaved most graciously.

A week later, working in the archives, I looked out of curiosity at Geheimrat Rödiger's file and found that he had been instrumental as a foreign ministry official in having all German Jewish passports stamped with a "J." And this, as it happened, was tantamount to a verdict of death, in many cases, for carriers of this sign of Cain did not receive foreign visas. I remember a conference on Soviet affairs when an elderly professor named Bolko von Richthofen welcomed me particularly cordially. But I ignored the outstretched hand, for he was the author of several particularly nauseating and mendacious works on "Judaeo-Bolshevism." He was offended and claimed that he had joined the party only to "prevent worse," a phrase that one heard rather frequently in those days.

I came to know and interview not a few old Nazis in the course of my work on twentieth-century German history, including some senior aides who had been with Hitler almost from the beginning. They usually argued that National Socialism had initially not been a bad idea, but that its execution into practice had been lamentable: There had been too many gangsters in the leadership. I did not enter into long disputes with them; I simply mention the argument as a line of rationalization frequently encountered. But there were also some who did not look for excuses but felt genuine shame and guilt. The problem of the old Nazis was a moral problem, not a serious political one; those I encountered in public life had all become staunch democrats— some, no doubt, out of genuine conviction, others out of opportunism. I knew that they would gradually die out. By the 1980s the last of them had disappeared from view.

I had not yet been eighteen when I left Germany and I had known only three of its major cities, two of them only very superficially. The Germany I came to know after 1945 was in many respects a different country, physically, politically, and culturally. Yet I believe that I understood Germany better than France or Britain, even though I have spent much more time there than in Germany. This is largely a matter of instinct, of feeling in one's bones how people will react in a certain situation. But what is instinct? A little inspiration based on experience. The fact that I was born in that country and spent some of my formative years there apparently counts as much as learning and observation in later life. My instinct told me not to take left- and right-wing extremism in the new Germany too seriously—from Baader-Meinhof to the sporadic neo-Nazi upsurges. It taught me to distrust the political judgment of many sections of the German intelligentsia; as a student of German intellectual history, I knew that German thinkers had always been stronger on the level of abstraction than of reality.

In fields of particular interest to me I found myself frequently out of sympathy with the prevailing mentality. I have great admiration for some of the leading scholars and writers, some of whom became my friends. But among others I often encountered a mind-set that did not appeal to me: dogmatism, extreme views aggressively pronounced, an unwillingness to accept unwelcome evidence and to admit mistakes, a lack of both self-criticism and a sense of humor. From the 1960s to the Persian Gulf War, sections of the German intelligentsia have behaved with a lack of judgment and a shrillness that I found difficult to explain on a rational level.

I never thought of myself as a German expert even though some of my work in later years was in that field. I did not find German postwar politics and culture particularly fascinating; in any case, the lack of passionate interest has been mutual. With a few exceptions, my books have been more widely read in Italy or in Japan than in the country of my origin.

WE HAD BEEN WARNED about London rain, fog, and smog, but when we arrived late one morning in early June we were pleasantly surprised—the sun was shining and there were more trees and parks than in either Paris or Berlin. London airport (Heathrow) did not yet exist, and we were taken by a red double-decker bus, the first I had seen, to the terminal in town, which in those days was in Waterloo Station. The trip seemed endless, for much of the time we were stuck in a giant traffic jam along the Thames embankment. But it did not matter, for it gave us a wonderful chance to have a good first look at the city that was, or had been until recently, the most important in the universe. Gladstone had once advised a group of American tourists that the best way to see London was from the top of a bus, and this was still sterling advice seventy years later even though buses and London had changed considerably.

As in Paris, the first impression was overwhelming—above all, the bigness of the city. Never had we stayed in a hotel with seven hundred rooms; the neighboring one even had a thousand! The corridors were enormous; the dining room seemed as big as a football field. Never had I seen that many people in the streets, especially during the rush hour, yet another new phenomenon of which I had not heard before. Our first appointment next morning was in Primrose Hill, for late morning we were to visit someone in Twickenham, and we had a lunch appointment in the City. We quickly learned that such a schedule was possible perhaps in compact Paris or truncated Berlin but not in London with its enormous distances.

Our time in London was more or less equally divided between sightseeing and meetings with book publishers, editors, academics, writers, and old and new friends. I had done my preliminary homework and knew how to reach Piccadilly from Oxford Circus and how to proceed from there to Trafalgar Square and the House of Parliament. Still, there were many surprises. I had great difficulty understanding many of the natives, who spoke a language that bore a certain similarity to English but that at times I could understand only in part. I had never heard cockney spoken; neither in France nor in Germany nor in any other country were there such linguistic differences along class and educational lines. I did not understand why (as I read everywhere) Guinness was good for me or why the Windmill Theatre never closed, for I had never heard of these institutions. I had never seen buskers and pavement artists. I had never tasted a "spaghetti sandwich," steak and kidney pie, or suet pudding. In brief, I had a lot to learn. As in Paris, I found almost everything interesting during the first days, even the sweet, black tea in the ABC chain stores and the Lyons Corner Houses, even the dark cavernous underground stations, even the gray unending rows of houses in the less-affluent quarters. I even found London as seen from the window of a train out of Paddington or Liverpool Street stations of fascinating ugliness.

But the critical faculties reasserted themselves more quickly than in Paris. I soon realized that while the Imperial Hotel on Russell Square was as grimy as it was enormous, the same was true with regard to much of the London scene. One did not see much war damage—this had mainly occurred in the City, the East End, and Docklands—but as in Paris, there had been little new building. I enjoyed the pageantry—Whitehall and Buckingham Palace, the Georgian and Regency architecture in the West End. I was grateful for the extreme politeness and helpfulness on the part of total strangers whenever we were in need of advice or help. Partly it was, of course, my fault, because I knew so little about the English way of life, about the enormous respect for privacy, about the sometimes grotesque tendency toward understatement, about the right to be eccentric.

Within my first week in England I went unannounced to see an Oxford don in his quarters; this was an elderly man who had spent half his life in covert intelligence services but had to take early retirement because one of his subordinates had crossed the Iron Curtain in the wrong direction. The don was almost apoplectic as a result of this intrusion and within less than a minute I found myself in the street. In Palestine and Israel it had been customary to drop in unannounced, not just on good friends but on perfect strangers, and our don, though having spent many years abroad, had no wish to make concessions to foreign habits. (We later became good friends; he realized that it had been innocence on my part, not deliberate rudeness.)

I realized soon that I was far more critical about Britain and the British than most of the Continental immigrants who had come before the war and who found almost everything wonderful and worthy of emulation. Some of them had taken elocution lessons so that their Continental accents would be less pronounced. They were glad if their children were invited to join the school choir to sing "Onward, Christian soldiers / Marching as to war" and to be invited to one of the Royal Tea Parties was the pinnacle of achievement. I tried to look for an explanation. Perhaps because they had had the good fortune to be among the British in their finest hour it had generated a deep sense of identification. I came to realize in later years that in an emergency the British were more likely to do the right thing than almost any other people but that, unfortunately, it usually took an emergency to bring out the best in them. In no other country have I found so profoundly decent people in all classes of society, but seldom have I encountered so much arrogance, not only in the upper classes but also among the intelligentsia. If among the Conservatives there was the firm conviction that they knew best, not only how to run their own affairs but those of the rest of the world, the Left was equally firmly convinced that they had all the answers for the third world. I found the pervasive class spirit repugnant; this was not one nation but, as Disraeli and others had noted, two, three, or even four. I was not then aware of the growing divide between the south of England and the rest.

Above all, there was a feeling of living in the past, of basking in a glory that belonged to bygone days. Despite my deep ignorance about things British I could not fail to sense decay in the air, but this was at the time far from common knowledge. Churchill had again become prime minister. Britain still had a sizable empire despite the loss of India; British industrial output and per capita income was still higher than the German and French, let alone the Italian. This created the illusion that Britain was still a great power, that it was playing a leading role in the postwar world. For an illusion it was, followed by a bitter awakening as the years went by.

Culturally, Britain in the 1950s seemed a wasteland. The prewar years had been the age of Wells and Shaw, of Bloomsbury and D. H. Lawrence; their successors clearly belonged to a lesser league. In the writings of George Orwell I found a running commentary on the reasons why. As far as satire was concerned, the British were still unsurpassed—I discovered Evelyn Waugh, Malcolm Muggeridge—but it was bitter satire, which left a taste not wholly enjoyable.

True, I saw some encouraging signs such as the growing interest in music (the promenade concerts), especially among the younger generation, or the earnest talks on the BBC Third Programme. What impressed me most during my early weeks in Britain was popular culture, the thrillers, the music halls, a Wembley Cup final or an athletics championship in the White City. But the music halls were on their way out, Gracie Fields had gone to the isle of Capri, George Formby had retired, and Vera Lynn and "Underneath the Arches" were superseded by a younger generation of singers who appealed much less to me.

I had believed, in my innocence, that every educated Englishman was reading the *Times* or the *Manchester Guardian*;

George Lichtheim explained to me that these newspapers were mainly read by Indian and African graduate students, which was no doubt an exaggeration. But I soon realized that the mass media had preoccupations that were new and unfamiliar to me. The first Sunday in London I read in the *Sunday Dispatch* a report by Mr. Geoffrey Wynn that "there was one subject that is on everyone's lips, in everyone's thought, this weekend. For only someone in whom all natural feeling is dead could fail to be stirred and fascinated by the culminating steps . . ." The writer, it said, was the only correspondent who had been received by Her Royal Highness. I did not want to be among those in whom all natural feeling was dead, but I still did not know what he meant. To gain deeper insight I bought the *Dispatch*'s main rival, the *News of the World*, with a circulation of seven or eight million, but it did not shed much light; its main story was entitled: OUR WORLD SCOOP: WE SIGN FUEHRER'S VALET TO TELL EVERYTHING.

Only toward the end of the day did I learn that Mr. Wynn was referring to the question whether Princess Margaret's wedding should take place in Balmoral, Glamorgan Castle, or Saint Giles's Cathedral, Edinburgh. If the popular press was pathetic, radio was on a considerably higher level, and British television was infinitely superior to American, which I came to know a few years later. A great controversy was raging at that time: whether a commercial TV channel should be permitted to operate alongside the BBC. The fears voiced at the time, that a general decline in standards would ensue, were not unjustified, but British television still compares favorably with that of most other countries.

London in the early 1950s was, for better or worse, far more British than today. There was a black colony in parts of Brixton and some Indians in Southgate, but the great influx began only in later years. There were no Arab residents, no Cypriots, and no Japanese, no mosque in Regent's Park, and few Americans. There were no European tourists, only some from Australia, South Africa, Canada, and other English-speaking countries who frequently came for a year or forever.

When we first arrived in the early 1950s, London (and England) was approaching its nadir. The Suez expedition in 1956 showed that though the country had won the war, it was no longer a great power; economically it was overtaken by France and Germany, and eventually Italy caught up with it. Neither Conservatives nor Labour seemed to have an answer to the country's problems. There was a general malaise, a discontent that expressed itself even on the faces of the people one met in the Underground and on buses: Why did other countries seem to manage their affairs more efficiently?

In later years there were sporadic signs of improvement, and in the sixties there were reports about "swinging London"— central heating became quite common, the quality of food improved, and the smog disappeared. Why did we settle in London if our relationship was not that of a passionate love affair? I could write about London at considerable length, for I pride myself on knowing its streets well; for months we systematically explored this giant city and we lived in parts unknown even to many native Londoners, such as south of the river. At one stage I even contemplated preparing a dictionary of London cabdrivers' slang. I knew what it meant when a cabby said: "During the kipper season, a legal asked me to take him to Buck House."* But I doubt if my observations and comments would be of great public interest and originality. London was in many respects a convenient vantage point to watch events in Europe and beyond. It was a good place for our children to go to school; in this respect, alas, there has been palpable deterioration. One had only to drive outside London for an hour to be in a lovely countryside, to walk through a real meadow, to pick fruit in summer, to sail down the Thames. Of English beaches I never thought highly. In my specific field of interest at the time, Soviet studies, London had the greatest accumulation of talent in the world; some were men and women of world renown, others less well

---

*The kipper season is the slack period between Christmas and Easter; a legal is a passenger who pays only the legal minimum and does not give a tip; Buck House is Buckingham Palace.

known, but immensely knowledgeable, such as the late Victor Frank. Half the time I believed with Samuel Johnson that when a man is tired of London, he is tired of life, "for there is in London all that life can afford"; half the time my sympathies were with Dr. Johnson's contemporary, Edward Gibbon, who had written about London in his autobiography: "crowds without company, and dissipation without pleasure." But then I had not mainly come to London for company and only partly in the pursuit of pleasure. Since I had no ambition to be accepted by the local establishment, and since, in any case, we were part of the year away from London, it seemed a logical choice at the time.

FIFTEEN

Discovering Muscovy

For *years I had steeped myself* in Russian history and culture but I had never been in the Soviet Union. Had I been a historian or a student of Russian literature this would not perhaps have mattered. But I was equally interested in the contemporary Soviet scene and I had never assumed that *Pravda* and the political and literary magazines could possibly provide a full picture. I had learned to understand the Aesopian language of Soviet politics, but this, too, was not sufficient, for although life in the Soviet Union was permeated with politics, it was not all politics. If the Western media were not sufficient to convey a real picture of what life in America or Europe were like, this was *a fortiori* true with regard to the Soviet Union. I had a fairly detailed mental image of Russia and the Russians, but how true was it? I was to have a good opportunity to find out, for beginning in the fifties, we went on yearly, prolonged trips to the Soviet Union, and I think I learned about as much as a foreigner could come to know about that country short of actually settling there. I knew this was not the way to gain important insights into Soviet high politics; one knew as much (or as little) about this from the outside. But one could learn a great deal about the quality of life and the mood of the country.

There was yet another reason that made us look forward to these trips; for Naomi it meant a reunion with her family. She had been born in the city of Frankfurt, which she left in 1936. The next year her parents, with two of their five children, departed for Moscow, not for reasons of political affinity—her father was a very learned but deeply unpolitical man—but because like so many others he had lost his job and the only offer for work came from the Soviet Union. His field was internal medicine, but his professorship was in the history and philosophy of medicine; he had been one of the founders of the discipline in this century. How the invitation came about we do not know; it was very rare that anyone from the West was permitted to enter the Soviet Union.

Thus, in 1937 Professor Richard Koch found himself knocking on the door of the Ministry of Health in Moscow. But those who had invited him had meanwhile disappeared in the great purge. When he came back again a month later, those whom he had seen the first time had also vanished. He was bewildered, unable to understand what was going on, and he was running out of money. Fortunately, he accepted the advice given, according to legend by the doorman of the ministry, to get lost as quickly as possible and move far away from the capital. He had become a Soviet citizen when entering the country, and thus he could no longer leave it had he wanted to. There were two offers: to proceed to the Volga German Autonomous Republic or to go to a resort, of which he had never heard, in the northern Caucasus, called Essentuki (the name in the local language meant "live water"). Luckily, he opted for the latter offer; the Volga Germans were deported to central Asia during World War II and many did not survive. According to another version, someone in the ministry recalled that he had once written a book entitled *Goethe and Health Resorts: The Magic of Spas.*

His life in Essentuki was not easy, to put it cautiously. Local colleagues warmly welcomed the distinguished newcomer who did not know a word of Russian (and did not bother to learn much to the end). With the older generation he conversed in a mixture of Latin and French; for conversation with the patients and younger colleagues he had a translator. Within a short time he became a well-liked member of the community. But living conditions were incredibly primitive. It was one thing for Naomi and me to live for years in a tent—or in a room in an Arab village—without electricity, running water, or an indoor toilet. But her parents were no longer young, and they had been accustomed to European comfort. It cannot have been easy for four people to live huddled in an old, decrepit house, in an apartment of a room and a half.* The fact that Gertrud, Naomi's sister, was bedridden much of the time did not help. But they did survive and were not unhappy. When the German troops approached the northern Caucasus, the family wisely decided to join the stream of refugees; wisely, because of the Jews who stayed behind, virtually no one survived, though the occupation of the German forces lasted not even six months.

The evacuation was hard. Naomi's father had a stiff leg, the result of a sepsis he had contracted while doing military service before World War I. He could not move easily, and crossing the mountains of the Caucasus on foot, without provisions, was hard even on younger and healthier people. The Georgians were less than hospitable with regard to the evacuees. When the parents

---

*Because of a legal oversight, Naomi became the owner of this apartment upon her sister Gertrud's death in 1991. Since she had no desire to be a woman of property in the Caucasus, she tried to renounce this inheritance. In view of the bureaucratic difficulties involved, it proved exceedingly complicated but in the end she succeeded.

returned to Essentuki, they found that their apartment had been plundered, including the cherished library. There was no electricity, no heating, hardly any food. The years 1943 and 1944 were the most difficult of all. During the long winter evenings Professor Koch jotted down his recollections of the years before 1914; he had almost total recall, and when he died in 1949 he had written more than two thousand pages, a fascinating cultural and social document that has not been published to this day.

When we first came to the Soviet Union, several years after Stalin's death, Naomi's mother was still alive and also her brother Friedrich and one of her sisters. Correspondence between them had never ceased, not even during the years of terror and the war, except when they had been evacuated to Georgia. This was a very rare, perhaps unique, case, because at that time few people in Russia wanted to attract attention to the fact that they had relations abroad. But Naomi's family, partly out of political naïveté, partly because controls in the Caucasus, which were slightly more liberal than in Moscow, ignored such practices. Naomi's father wrote letters of many pages in a handwriting that was virtually illegible; an indulgent censor may have given up in despair. But letters could never replace physical contact, and twenty-three years were to pass before Naomi saw them again in the hall of Vnukovo Airport, waiting with a bunch of flowers as is customary in Russia. Vnukovo, I should say in passing, was a small airport but perfectly adequate for the few travelers flying in and out of the Soviet Union at the time. The years had taken their toll—Naomi's mother, who had been a well-groomed, elegant lady, now looked like many other old Russian women, except that she never wore a babushka or anything else on her head. Her brother, whom Naomi remembered as a young devil aged fourteen, with open shirt and in short trousers, was now a solid citizen in his best years, a father of two sons, a lecturer in a leading institute, working on a dictionary and on various other linguistic projects.

Almost every time we went to the Soviet Union in subsequent years, we went to see them or they came to meet us in Moscow.

As a result we probably learned more than others about a very interesting part of Russia—not secrets of state, of which they knew less than we did, but elementary facts of life, which few foreigners could possibly know and understand. We came to know a great deal about the mentality of people, about their fears and hopes, about their prejudices and superstitions.

In later years we invited them for long visits, always one or two members of the family at a time. I half expected that there was a price to be paid for these meetings and I assume that Naomi's relations were interviewed after each visit, but no attempt was ever made to approach us. Naomi's mother had reached the age of retirement by that time, her sister was ill, and Friedrich was quite fearless.

He had an uncanny ability to assess correctly situations that were unfamiliar to him and to judge people whom he had never seen before, not just in the Soviet Union but in England and Germany. The only person who wholly baffled him was a Hassid (of the Satmar persuasion), whom we met in Golders Green, wearing his Sabbath best. Friedrich had never seen anything like it and disbelieved my explanation—that this was a Polish nobleman of the late eighteenth century. I have come across this facility (of making instantaneous judgments) far more often among Soviet citizens than among Westerners, perhaps because in their country there was much less room for misjudgment, which, in certain conditions, could be fatal.

When we first came to the Soviet Union, only Moscow and Leningrad were open to foreigners, and only one hotel in all of Leningrad, the Astoria. But the country quickly opened up. The year after, Sochi and Yalta—the Black Sea resorts—were added to the list; the third year it was the turn of Kiev; and on the occasion of our third or fourth annual visit we could proceed to the Caucasus. Controls there, as I have mentioned, were less stringent than elsewhere; thus, we were among the first foreigners to enter certain areas such as the Checheno-Ingush region, from which the inhabitants had been expelled by Stalin's orders.

But in the beginning we were restricted to Moscow, and in

later years, too, every trip began and ended there. The city then had five million inhabitants but only a dozen hotels. We came to know most of them, from the National on Red Square to Ostankino in the far north. I tried to explore Moscow as thoroughly as London, but because I had much less time at my disposal, I did it far more intensively, which no doubt aroused the suspicion of taxi drivers. "Why do you want to go to Krasnaya Presnya?" "Well, it played a role in the revolution of 1905. . . ." "But what is so great about the Proletarskaya district?" "I want to see how people live. . . ." This they accepted with great reluctance—the Kremlin, yes, the old churches, the Donskoi Monastery, and the museums. But why should anyone be interested in how Russians live? I was careful not to take photographs in those years; it would have been interpreted as anti-Soviet propaganda.

On my second day in Moscow I found myself in the very center; walked twice around that giant square and wrote:

Red Square, an unending stream of visitors: guided tours, delegations, and even some individual travelers, buses from Huddersfield and Hamburg, Citroëns and minibuses, Uzbeck cotton growers and Sverdlovsk steelworkers, Russians hurrying to work and foreigners photographing the entrance to the Kremlin.

This has been the center of Russian history. It is, of course, in no way red, the name (*krasny*) is probably derived from beautiful (*krasivy*). In the Middle Ages it was a fairground and marketplace; the Cossack rebel Stenka Razin was executed here, and Peter I established the first Russian theater around the corner. After the great fire of 1812, the square was completely reconstructed; Minin and Pozharsky, who saved Moscow from the Poles, were commemorated with a statue and Lenin and Stalin with a mausoleum.*

* Stalin was reburied in 1961 at the Kremlin Wall, where he rests together with some of his faithful paladins such as Kalinin and Maksim Gorky and a strange medley of foreigners such as John Reed, the German Communist Clara Zetkin, and the Japanese Sen Katayama.

Moscow had always a special place in the hearts of the Russians. Chekhov's three sisters dreamed day and night of "going to Moscow." Can one imagine English poets raving about London as Russian poets rave about Moscow? Lermontov, for instance: "I loved her like a son, like a Russian—with a strong passionate, delicate love" . . . Or Pushkin: "*Moskva, kak mnogo v etom zvuke. . . .*" (Moscow, how much there is in this sound. . . .) Visitors from Voronezh, Murmansk, and Nizhni Tagil still come to Moscow to admire the tall buildings and the new fashions, the big open spaces and the shops. For them Moscow is the pattern of things to come. It sets the fashion, intellectual and otherwise; it is the center of Russia, and Red Square is still the center of the capital.

The Square is bordered by the Cathedral of St. Basil (now a bit decrepit and supported by much scaffolding), GUM (Russia's biggest store), and the Kremlin. Ten years ago there was a standard scene in Soviet fiction: on a rainy, cold November evening the hero, with or without wife or girlfriend, crossed the empty Red Square and looked toward the towers of the Kremlin. Everything was shrouded in darkness but one window gleamed with light—the omnipotent, omniscient Father of the People was still busy, never relaxing in his work for the good of his children. Now, the Kremlin is open to the public during the day. Most of the political decisions are made, I surmise, not here but at the Central Committee of the Party at Staraya Ploshchad (about half a mile away), or in Khrushchev's own office nearby. The Kremlin is now mainly used for receptions and conferences.

By and large, Moscow has less to offer by way of sights than any comparable European capital, certainly less than Leningrad. My first impressions were the usual ones—the neoclassicist monumental architecture of the Stalin period, which to this day dominates the character of much of this city; the fact that Muscovites seemed always in a hurry, between one queue and another after a long working day; the fact that the metro was splendid but that there were so many grim faces. I was struck by the fact that there were far more people in uniform than in any other country; how could I have known, for instance, that a blue badge merely meant that the bearer had graduated from an institution of higher education? At first sight, the city, especially the inner part, gave an impression of a certain prosperity—the roads were broad, the buildings massive, and I saw no one in rags. Only the few foreigners who ever visited a Soviet home came to realize that the housing shortage was desperate; each room housed a family, the quality of the buildings was shoddy. True, Muscovites became more fashion conscious after 1957, the first time that thousands of young foreigners invaded the capital to attend an international youth festival, but they were still very, very poor.

More houses were built, but the number of Moscow residents grew even more rapidly. Even now, there are only estimates with regard to the number of Moscow's permanent inhabitants. There has been an official ban on moving to Moscow for many years but there are many hundreds of thousands of *limitchiki*, illegal residents, those above the limit. Miserable as the supply situation was in the capital, it was still infinitely better in those days than in the rest of the country. (Under *perestroika* this changed; it became worse in the capital.) Yet with all this there was still widespread belief among many people that the Soviet system was the best of all possible political and social systems, and, in any case, the only suitable one for this country. Generated by the propaganda machinery there was a basic optimism, an assumption that life was getting a little better every year.

A few months ago I had a letter from someone who complained that in a recent book I had not sufficiently emphasized that the great majority of Soviet citizens had always hated the regime. More recently I listened to the interview of a well-known Russian lady of letters, aged about forty, who claimed that no one she knew had ever believed in communism. This was not my impression thirty-five years ago. I do not claim that the majority of Soviet citizens fervently loved the party and the regime. But many respected it, or at least lived in awe of it, and thought that for better or worse, the future belonged to it.

On my second trip I noted:

A mere eleven months I have been away and so much seems to have changed. The airport (Sheremetovo) is new and so is the skyline—not new skyscrapers but a forest of television aerials, sometimes up to fifteen on a single building. Men wear better-quality shoes and hats than last year and women more colorful and daring dresses; customers in the shops who last year were willing to buy just about everything have become more selective. There is canned food from Mexico and Southeast Asia, crème de cacao from Czechoslovakia, even a few pineapples. Moscow suddenly seems prosperous. It is pointless to engage in comparisons with the West. All a Soviet citizen knows is that he is slightly better off this year than last, even though not all classes enjoy the new prosperity to the same degree. But people begin to dream of a very small car and a few keep a poodle.

Soviet citizens were still very much influenced by the official indoctrination; they had never been abroad; there were no foreign newspapers (except a few Communist ones); only relatively few listened to foreign radio stations. They genuinely believed that if their country was in some respects behind the West (no one knew as yet about Japan) the reason was that little more than ten years had passed since the end of a war in which they had suffered more than anyone else. Many firmly believed that in the near future they would catch up and overtake the most developed "capitalist" countries as they had overtaken them in the field of space travel.

Some of this optimism persisted for another ten or fifteen years. The great majority of Soviet citizens had no idea that economic progress in most foreign countries was much quicker, or that to stand in long lines every day for essential requirements was not a normal state of affairs.

Only in the 1970s did it gradually dawn on many of them that something was basically flawed with their system, that the ravages of the war could not indefinitely serve as an explanation for their poverty and backwardness. Some intellectuals had their doubts even earlier, but they kept their opinions to themselves. There is reason to believe that many Soviet leaders, living in isolation from the masses, were genuinely uninformed about the true state of affairs in their country; unlike Mrs. Thatcher, they never went to shop in the supermarket or waited in an outpatient queue at a hospital clinic.

Back in the 1950s my first exposure was to a Russia as yet full of self-confidence and naïveté. "Are you a capitalist or a proletarian?" I was frequently asked. This at least was the official stance; some would have talked to me more openly had I been a close friend or a member of the family. When I first went to Russia, I took a firm resolve to eschew political discussions and not to write about political topics. It was a wise decision, and up to the event of *glasnost*, when the situation began to change, I have given this advice to successive generations of Western correspondents about to leave for the Soviet capital. But it was very difficult to stick to this resolve consistently. I wrote long articles about Soviet television, about religion, about Russian taste in literature and the arts, about the young generation, about the progressive embourgeoisement of Soviet society as far as manners, morals, and aesthetic taste was concerned.

Yet in a country so deeply permeated with politics there was no escaping it. Following a longish stay in Sochi on the Black Sea, I wrote about the life of the Soviet *nomenklatura*, the privileged stratum, many years before the term entered the language. I wrote about the subtropical climate, about palms and cacti, cedars, lemon trees. I wrote about the seven hundred doctors and the many thousands of Russian Hans Castorps who came as patients to the sanatoria; they had to be very tough, even the cardiac patients. In some of the big rest houses I counted two hundred steps up from the road and no elevator. I mentioned that alcoholism was a problem; since the local newspaper had a daily column reporting cases of public drunkenness, this was a safe subject. I reported that, while in theory medicine was free, the unofficial fee for a private consultation by a specialist was 150 rubles, about as much as in Harley Street or Park Avenue. I reported that Russians were talking with great enthusiasm about their respective diseases, and I stressed that only very hardy people could possibly go through all the exercising, drinking the water, walking, swimming, being massaged, and so on, imposed on them by their doctors. I listened with attention and some enjoyment to their jazz orchestras playing "Creole Love Call" and "Yes, Sir, That's My Baby." But at the end of the day there was no escaping from politics.

I had developed a certain routine in Moscow. My favorite haunts were the markets, bookshops, railway stations, cemeteries, and some "culture and rest parks." I soon realized that one met far more interesting people there than, say, in the Writers' Union or the university. Cultural life I found disappointing. There was no originality, no individuality; there seemed to be not much to choose between one writer, or one historian, and another even during the thaw, let alone after its end. True, in the plastic arts the state of affairs was a bit better, but these developments belong to the 1960s rather than the 1950s and following Khrushchev's visit to the Manege exhibition hall in Red Square, painters and sculptors, too, again became the object of strict regimentation. Naomi visited a kindergarten, where the children's drawings were shown to her. All of them were exactly alike—the same house under the same sun shining from the same blue sky. They all looked rather as if they were drawn from the same template.

There was no reason to believe that Soviet writers or historians (or philosophers or economists) were intrinsically less gifted than their opposite numbers in the West. I always assumed that below the official line, with its indescribable boredom, there was another culture—poems, novels, and plays that were written and kept at the bottom of one's drawer without any hope of publication in the foreseeable future. But I had no idea whether such surmises were correct. This was a good ten years before the first dissidents appeared, and no one had as yet heard of *samizdat* or *tamizdat* (literature smuggled out and published in the West). The nearest thing to spontaneous action were the recitals of young poets at the bronze Pushkin statue in Gorky Street. This is how I first heard of Yevtushenko, Voznesensky, and the young rebels of the 1950s. Even in 1990, with the editorial offices of *Moscow News* around the corner, this was still one of the rallying points of the opposition. Yevtushenko's mother I had known before; this friendly lady was selling newspapers and periodicals in one of the kiosks in front of the White Russian railway station. When I last went there, the last part of Gorky Street had reverted to its old name, Tverskaya, and a great many other changes had taken place, but Mrs. Yevtushenko, well beyond retirement age, was still there. She said that she had worked all her life, and she found it much too boring to stay at home.

Thus, the official culture quite apart, there had been a second culture all along, at least in Moscow and Leningrad. But for a foreigner it was next to impossible to gain access: I had vaguely heard about the existence of an institution called the Moscow kitchen, where, after dinner and a drink or two, people would open up among themselves in a small circle. But outsiders could not enter this inner sanctum of Russian life; it was too risky. When *glasnost* came many years later, it suddenly appeared that below a deceptive gray surface there had been much individuality, that many Soviet intellectuals were well informed and able to discuss just about every issue under the sun, on an enviably high level of sophistication. Some had moved to the far Right, others had been converted to Social Democracy or liberalism in every form or shape. The only school of thought that, in contrast to the West, had virtually no disciples was Marxism-Leninism. I had never assumed that the alienation of the intelligentsia was so complete.

Twenty-five years later on more than one occasion I was told by a Soviet colleague that if he had made some derogatory reference to my work in a Soviet journal or a book at the height of the cold war, this had, of course, been in line with the general mood of that unfortunate period—and that he hoped that I had taken it in the right spirit. . . .

I made a special effort to meet and to talk to young people. For I assumed that change in the Soviet Union would come with the rise of a new generation. I jotted down my impressions at the time:

A procession approaches from Sverdlov Square—a trumpeter in the small car leading, followed by several buses of singing boys and girls in white blouses and red ties: out-of-town Komsomol—or, more probably, the pioneers, its younger section—on an excursion through Moscow. *"Me Molodaya Gvardiya Rabochikh i Krestian"*—they are singing the old song of the Komsomol about the young avant-garde of workers and peasants, which brings back memories of the twenties: the storming of Perekop and Kronstadt, how the Komsomol fought always and everywhere for the "general line"—collectivizing agriculture, working at Magnitogorsk, building the city named after itself, Komsomolsk-na-Amure. It reminds one of the generation of the children's republic, of Kostya Ryabtsev and the Rabfak (the workers' faculties), of endless discussions about free love, revolutionary literature, and art.

Pavel Korchagin (in Ostrovsky's *How the Steel Was Tempered*) was the great hero of that period. Paralyzed and incurably ill, he continued his political activity up to his last breath. Pavel Korchagin's contemporaries are now grandfathers and grandmothers, if they were lucky enough to survive the war and the purges. In the high command of the party there are now many who, born after the 1917 revolution, joined the party only during World War II. And the youngsters in the white shirts were just a few years old when Stalin died; for them the Stalin era belongs to the distant past.

There is much speculation about the character of this new generation, "the Russia of tomorrow." Today's Soviet student is very different in his mental makeup and outlook from his predecessor twenty, or even ten, years ago. "Too different," their elders complain. The teachers say that these youngsters are not at all accustomed to receiving an order without discussion. Parents complain that their sons and daughters want to enjoy themselves; they get very impatient when faced with the "what was good enough for us . . ." argument. True, they will take over unthinkingly much of the doctrine, which does not mean that they are content with Soviet society as it is now. They are impatient with bureaucratic chicanery, they want a better life and more freedom; they don't think Russia is developing and changing fast enough.

They earnestly believe that less control plus *izobilie* (abundance of goods) equals communism, which is a synonym for the good life. They are more interested in literature and the arts than in ideology, more in their professional training than in politics. "Only the less savory type," it is said, choose politics as a career these days.

Looking back, this assessment of the mood of the younger generation in the Soviet Union more than thirty years ago was not far from the mark. But it was also true that for this generation Soviet ideology was in large part still self-evident; they had no fundamental doubts with regard to the Soviet system at least as long as they were in school, protected from any exposure to the realities of Soviet life.

This changed only later when the young progressively lost all belief in the faith of their parents: true, lip service was still paid to the official slogans, but no one took it very seriously. They knew exactly what to say at school and the Komsomol, but they did not believe a word of it. And so the party gradually lost the younger generation. The song about the Young Guard* was heard less often, and if anyone now mentions "*Molodaya Gvardiya*," this refers to a monthly magazine of the extreme right, quite out of touch with the spirit of the younger generation.

Life as a foreigner in Moscow was not enviable. Many of those who had been staying there for more than a year or two were showing signs of claustrophobia. The summers were not too bad—one could meet people in the streets, the parks, the beaches of the rivers, the holiday resorts. But the long winters were deadly—the same round of cocktail parties, national holidays celebrated by the embassies, and visits to the theater or ballet. Foreigners were kept in three or four little ghettos with Soviet policemen in front so as to deter any Russian visitor. If a foreign correspondent (there were about fifty at the time, including the Communists) spoke Russian too well or succeeded in some other

---

*Written by a Soviet poet of Jewish extraction, Alexander Bezymensky.

way in breaking out of the ghetto, he was bound to be attacked in the Soviet press as a foreign spy. True, from time to time the authorities showed a little liberalism. Thus, on one occasion, they arranged for diplomats and correspondents a guided tour of the Lenin Library, the biggest library in the country. Imagine the Foreign Office arranging a visit to the British Museum, or the Quai d'Orsay a trip to the Louvre! It was this fear of claustrophobia that made me never seriously consider staying in the Soviet Union for more than a few weeks at a time.

And yet, it is amazing in retrospect how much one could learn about many aspects of this closed society simply by keeping one's eyes open, by traveling a great deal, by watching movies and plays, by reading between the lines of the literary magazines. There was no information to be extracted about nuclear arms or the secret operations of the KGB, or about the weekly deliberations of the Politburo and the intrigues in the top leadership. But there was a great deal one gathered about the mood of the country. Thus, the extent of corruption—above all, in Central Asia, but also in other parts of the Union—was never a secret; it had become part of the system. On the other hand, the working class remained a book with seven seals; one knew more about the state of affairs among the peasants, even among remote and exotic nationalities. But even the supreme party leaders knew little about the mood among Soviet workers and their families. One sensed discontent and resentment against the bosses and other classes in society—especially the intelligentsia. But these were mere impressions; one could not be certain.

Moscow in many ways was not an ideal place for watching the Soviet Union; there was the anonymity of the big city reinforced by strictest police control; people were less open and friendly than elsewhere. We used every opportunity to escape from Moscow, and the region we came to know best was the Northern Caucasus, where Naomi's family had settled twenty years earlier. My introduction to the Caucasus was at Pyatigorsk, the town of the five hills. I arrived at night and inevitably began my account with a quotation from Lermontov:

"Yesterday evening I arrived in Pyatigorsk and found lodgings on the outskirts of the town, fairly high at the foot of the Mashuk; if a storm comes the clouds will hide my roof. When I opened the window at five o'clock this morning my room was full of the scent of the flowers in the small garden; cherry blossom gazes into the room and sometimes the wind covers my desk with white petals. The panorama is magnificent: in the west one sees the blue peaks of the five-headed Beshtau, in the north the Mashuk rises like a Persian fur cap; in the east below me there lies the clean new town; one hears the murmuring of the mineral springs and the voices of the cosmopolitan crowd. Further away the mountains form a kind of amphitheater, blue and hazy in the distance; and on the edge of the horizon one sees the silver chain of the snow-covered summits from Kasbeck to Elbruz. It is a pleasure to live in such a place. . . ."

I continued:

Thus Lermontov's Pechorin in *A Hero of Our Time*—the amazing work of a twenty-five-year-old. The journey to Pyatigorsk has become faster but the jet age, fortunately, has not yet reached the Caucasus. It takes fifty-four hours by train from Moscow or seven by plane; arriving in the town at midnight in bright moonlight, the traveler feels something of the old romantic magic of the place.

In the early morning such illusions fly away. The traveler opens the window at five o'clock, wakened not by the murmuring of the mineral springs or the scent of the flowers but by the infernal noise of the kolkhoz market opposite. The crowd outside is cosmopolitan, but the fine gentlemen from Petersburg and Moscow are gone, as are their elegant ladies whom Lermontov saw and fell in love with. It consists of highlanders (*gortsi*) with their large hats, Kabardines, Georgians and Russians, Armenians and Ukrainians. There are no Westerners in this crowd: Until recently they were not allowed in the area at all. Neither the mountains nor the magnificent panorama have changed, but there is a gigantic television mast on the top of the Mashuk and on a single day the indomitable Elbrus, at 5,633 meters (18,481 feet) the highest mountain in Europe by far, was recently climbed by 1,300 Alpinists.

Nowadays Pyatigorsk is a rather dull provincial town with 69,000 inhabitants, seven public libraries, fifteen sanatoria, an Institute of Education and a pharmaceutical college, factories where bricks, reinforced concrete, machinery, butter, liqueurs, and chemicals are produced, four cinemas, four large and several small bookshops, five restaurants, fifteen nursery schools, a newspaper, and a television station. The traveler can get this and other important information from the telephone book that, very much in contrast to Moscow, he finds in his room. There is a special quality about the only hotel in the place; it appears to date from the period of Pushkin and Lermontov, but the sanitary installations were probably in a better state then. A modern hotel in another part of the town is, however, to be opened shortly, and the traveler cannot complain about bad service even in the old *caravanserai*; everyone is courteous, friendly, and obliging. One has to leave Moscow to become acquainted with Russian hospitality.

In the entrance hall of the hotel there is a branch post office with large pictures of Lenin, Stalin, and Kalinin. In the main post office, which is a modern building, there is, however, only a picture of Khrushchev; there are more portraits, busts, and memorials of Stalin in the Caucasus than anywhere else in the Soviet Union. The locals are not prepared to give up the great son of Georgia.

Various queues form in front of the post office counters, including one for telephone coupons (or "*talons*"). In the Soviet Union it is not at all easy to ring up somebody in another town even in the immediate vicinity; first of all one has to go to the post office (which is impossible at night) and buy coupons for a trunk call. Armed with these, one books the call at home or from a public call box; to avoid these complications many Russians prefer to send a telegram.

Pyatigorsk is also a cultural center. Notices on the walls of the houses announce performances by leading theatrical companies from Moscow, Leningrad, and Saratov, who appear in the summer months. Deborah Pantoffel sings arias from *La Traviata* and *Rigoletto*. *The Great Waltz* appears twice—as a film and as a ballet. The movies show Leslie Caron in *Lili* and Gregory Peck in *Roman Holiday*. Comrade Filimonov of the Society for the Propagation of Political and Scientific Knowledge is giving a lecture on "the cunning methods of foreign espionage organizations."

Pushkin lived in Pyatigorsk and Tolstoy was stationed here as a young officer; above all, however, the town is bound up with the life and work of Lermontov, who was killed here, in 1841, in a duel at the age of twenty-seven. In the presence of a lady, he had called a fellow officer a "highlander (*gorets*) with a big dagger." Martynov was in Circassian clothes and did have a big dagger, but he took offense and insisted on a duel. Lermontov, who was the first to shoot, fired into the air, but Martynov took good aim. An obelisk has been erected on the spot where the duel took place and beside it a large stone plaque on which the events that led to the duel are described; around the obelisk there stand four stone figures, a symbol of mourning. Groups of Pioneers and *Oktyabryat*, the youngest members of the Communist youth organization, with their red scarves, are here on a visit from their holiday camp. Their leaders tell them the story of the great Russian poet and his tragic end.

In the morning the place is deserted, apart from a young man who, leaning on the pedestal with one hand, recites poems in a loud voice. They seem to be his own, not Lermontov's. Then there is a Lermontov Gallery, the Grotto of Diana, the "Restoration" House, where the ball took place that is described in *A Hero of Our Time*, and finally the building in which Lermontov quarreled with Martynov. Pechorin, the "hero of our time," was a romantic wastrel—his preoccupations were card-playing, the seduction of young girls and married women, duels, and, above all, how to escape boredom. One might expect that a character like Pechorin would not mean very much to the Pioneers except as a warning. But no one likes renouncing a world-famous work of literature and so the Lermontov cult is more developed now than ever before. A local writer has just published a long and learned treatise to prove that Lermontov did not die immediately after the duel but lived for another day or two, and his thesis has given rise to a great deal of discussion.

The day begins very early in the provinces; people are already on their feet or, more precisely, in the streets, by seven o'clock. The crowds are greatest in the kolkhoz market and the wooden stalls surrounding it. Men and women with shopping bags stream through the gates of the great market hall, which is adorned with portraits of the Party leaders, and inscriptions about the coming victory of Communism. The Soviet authorities are very touchy about the kolkhoz markets, and taking photographs is very much frowned on.

They regard it as a relic of capitalist economy, since the hundreds of peasant women on their little stools, offering their goods for sale, do so on their own initiative and fix their own prices; it is really a bit of a free-market economy inside a completely different economic system. According to the Moscow guidebooks, there are no longer any such markets in the capital, but one can see with one's own eyes that this is not true. The Moscow telephone directory contains the addresses of no fewer than twenty-nine such institutions.

From Pyatigorsk we went to Essentuki, where Naomi's mother and sister lived, and farther on to Kislovodsk, probably the most famous Soviet spa (and, incidentally, Solzhenitsyn's birthplace). My impressions at the time are recorded below.

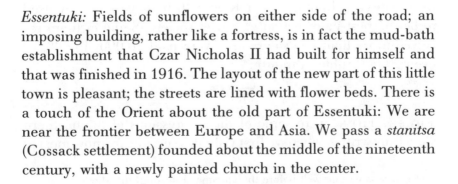

Essentuki: Fields of sunflowers on either side of the road; an imposing building, rather like a fortress, is in fact the mud-bath establishment that Czar Nicholas II had built for himself and that was finished in 1916. The layout of the new part of this little town is pleasant; the streets are lined with flower beds. There is a touch of the Orient about the old part of Essentuki: We are near the frontier between Europe and Asia. We pass a *stanitsa* (Cossack settlement) founded about the middle of the nineteenth century, with a newly painted church in the center.

Kislovodsk: The main road climbs to about 1,000 meters (3,280 feet) and it is not long before we reach Kislovodsk. For the Soviet citizen Kislovodsk means Narzan, the mineral water that is drunk all over the Union. There is a Narzan Street, a Narzan Hotel, a Narzan bookshop, a Narzan gallery, and, needless to say, a Narzan sanatorium, and countless other institutions where the name occurs. It comes from the Kabardian and refers to the carbonic drink of the legendary heroic tribe of the Nartens. Nowadays the mineral water is bathed in by patients suffering from circulatory or other internal complaints, but plenty of Narzan is still drunk. Around the original spring in the spa park, which is now mechanized and surrounded by glass, a few young girls in White Russian blouses stand pouring out the Narzan for visitors. The patients subject themselves to a strict regimen: for there are fifteen different diets and baths and innumerable variations in fifty sanatoria. Not without good cause: Soviet doctors think highly of walking as a cure and there are three standard walks, ranging from nearly a kilometer for the infirm to eleven kilometers (6.8 miles) for those with no organic disorder. On the way there are twenty checkpoints where one can have one's pulse and blood pressure taken and where inquiries are made about one's general state of health.

The best place for sociological studies is the central park, where thousands take the prescribed walk in the afternoon or evening. There are Armenians and Georgians who come with their large families by taxi or in their cars; there are professors from Moscow, Leningrad, or Kiev with their wives. They used to be the best-paid section of Soviet society. Some of them received more than one salary and were paid 10,000, 15,000, or even 20,000 rubles a month.*

⁂

THESE, THEN, were some of the impressions of the northern Caucasus written when we first visited. We came to know most of

---

*This was written well before the currency reform of the 1960s.

the drinking pavilions and the bathhouses; we ventured farther afield on the Military-Gruzinian Highway and to the Dombai Valley, which had not yet become a well-known ski resort at the time. The scenery was spectacular; unfortunately, I could not photograph it because that was frowned upon—there were so many military installations about that included for good measure railway stations, bridges, and so on. Nor could one photograph nonmilitary objects; more often than not, this was considered anti-Soviet propaganda. On a good day I would talk about "Switzerland without the tourists," which was true as far as the scenery was concerned. The amenities, to be sure, were not Swiss; they were not even southern European. Having been exposed to living conditions in some of the less-developed parts of the Middle East, and having come to the Soviet Union without excessive expectations, I was certainly not shocked. Had I been born a Soviet citizen, I would probably have opted for living in that part of this enormous country. But it also occurred to me that if living conditions were so deplorable in one of the most beautiful regions of the Union, how much more miserable life must be in the industrial cities of the Ural, the mining towns of the Donbas and Kuzbas, the villages of the nonblack-earth region.

I became acutely aware of tensions between the nationalities. There was no better place to observe this than in the Caucasus. I was not a naive believer in Soviet propaganda, but I had thought, like most foreigners, that the Soviets had somehow solved their national problems even though not just by persuasion. This was true to the extent that there was no open conflict—Azerbaijanis did not slaughter Armenians and Georgians, or vice versa; the KGB would have made short shrift of them. But I soon realized that there was no such thing as a Soviet nation or a Soviet citizen. All the nationalities kept very much to themselves, and there was a great deal of distrust and even ill will between them. This would come out on occasion when waiting in a long line in front of a shop and sometimes without any provocation. Some of the non-Russians pretended not to understand when I addressed them in Russian. When they realized that I was a foreigner, their linguistic faculties rapidly improved.

The trips to Moscow and the Caucasus came to replace our annual holidays, but one could never truly relax. I remember one occasion when, walking along Essentuki's main street with Sylvia and Shlomit, then in their early teens, a man accosted me, trying to hand me a letter for his brother who, he said, lived abroad. I shouted at him that I was a law-abiding citizen (*poriadochi*) and that he ought to use the local post office. Sylvia and Shlomit were very indignant; how could one treat anyone so rudely? It took me a little time to explain that I did not feel too good about it myself, that the man was probably quite harmless, but that there was always a certain risk involved in this country.

These visits and extended stays contributed a great deal to my political education in a wider sense, but gradually I felt that the returns were diminishing. It must have been soon after Khrushchev's fall that I was sitting in front of the Pirogovsky* Baths in Pyatigorsk when it occurred to me that I had probably learned as much as a foreigner could about this (still largely closed) society, that there was no reason to believe that any major changes would take place for years—perhaps for many years—and that time had come to break the habit of these frequent visits. Naomi went on seeing her family from time to time; every few years one of them came out for a visit to the West. But I did not return to the Soviet Union for twenty-five years. My professional preoccupations shifted. I still followed Soviet affairs from afar in a desultory way but more out of a feeling of duty than with genuine interest. Russia under Brezhnev was a predictable country politically, and intellectually very unexciting. This changed only from 1986 to 1987, when my interest reawakened and we renewed our visits to Moscow and Leningrad. I wrote a

---

*Nikolai Ivanovich Pirogov (1810–81) was one of the leading Russian physicians of his time. Like Lenin's, his body has been preserved as a mummy and is displayed on his estate.

book on *glasnost* and *perestroika*; recently I received by chance a copy of the Russian edition, which had been published (needless to say, without asking permission) in three hundred copies for official use only—that is to say, for members of the Central Committee of the Communist party of the Soviet Union. It might well have been the last Western book published in this way, for a few months later the Central Committee, the party, and the Soviet Union had ceased to exist.

In 1990 I went with Naomi on a sentimental journey to some of the places in the Caucasus that we had known so well at one time. It began inauspiciously: A short time previously I saw a Soviet film entitled *Lermontov*, which was not just intellectually overambitious in a tasteless way but in parts permeated by raving madness. It claimed that the great patriotic poet had been the victim of a satanic Judaeo-Masonic plot. In actual fact, Lermontov was an arrogant and irritable young man, had a sharp tongue, and was given to merciless ridiculing, in word and caricature, of friends, foes, and innocent bystanders alike. He was quarrelsome, and the duel in which he lost his life was not the first he had fought. Lermontov had certainly provoked Major Martynov, the man who shot him. Martynov, now, according to all accounts, was a pompous fool. But as far as his ancestry was concerned he was pure Russian, in contrast to Lermontov, whose family had come from Scotland, where they had helped King Malcolm defeat the historical Macbeth. Lermontov was not a chauvinist; one of his most famous poems, written before he left Moscow for the Caucasus, begins with the words

> *Farewell, unwashed Russia,*
> *Land of masters, land of slaves . . .*

Lermontov, I was told, had become something like a cult film in some circles, which bothered me: Having seen various instances of collective madness in my time, were we now to face yet another one in the Soviet Union?

The expedition to the Caucasus began for once not in a Mos-

cow hotel but in a suburban dacha belonging to the Soviet Foreign Ministry. It was a charming place, belonging to the later
nineteenth rather than the twentieth century; it would have been
ideally suited as a site for filming a Chekhov play. We had to
get up very early in the morning and there was a great deal of
pushing and shoving at Vnukovo. But the flight time was now
much shorter, one hour and fifty-eight minutes, no longer than
from Washington to Tampa–Saint Petersburg, Florida. The
wooden shack in Mineralnye Vody that had once been used as a
waiting hall, information and ticket office, and luggage-delivery
center had been replaced by a good-sized building. If thirty years
earlier a car (as distinct from a truck) had been a rare sight,
there was now a traffic jam; and it would have been even more
congested, we were told, but for the shortage of gasoline. Pyatigorsk had grown; the number of inhabitants had almost doubled.
There were many new sanatoria, catering to miners, army officers, and professionals. There were many more trees, and the
old hotel in the main street had been replaced by a modern
thirteen-story building with a discotheque and probably the
loudest floor show I have watched in my life. The women, old
and young, no longer wore the traditional head scarves; some
had the most elaborate hairdos this side of Vidal Sassoon. A
foreigner was no longer a rare bird; once upon a time they had
waved us good-bye when we left the hotel for the day, and in
the evening a cup of tea was always waiting for us, free of charge.
The sons and daughters of the ladies of the 1950s were more
polished; many spoke some English, German, or even Japanese.
But the old warmth and hospitality had apparently gone out of
fashion.

One of our first visits was to the cemetery on the outskirts of
Essentuki, where Friedrich is buried next to Naomi's parents.
The last time I had seen his sons they had been aged ten, playing
football in a far-too-small backyard next to the Essentuki central
park. Now they were middle-aged men very much preoccupied
with their work and the usual family problems; their children
continued the football tradition. Despite modernization and

fashion consciousness one still had the feeling one was far away from Moscow, and I came back with the conviction that out in the country there had been far less change than in Moscow. Thirty years earlier, upon visiting the big open-air market, I had written that it was only a question of time, perhaps only a few years, until these free markets would disappear, for more and more of the supplies would go to the state shops. Famous last words. The shops in 1990 were quite empty, and the market was the only place to buy fruit, vegetables, meat, and fish—and just about everything else.

We went back to Kislovodsk; we drank Narzan at the source and rested among the bathers at a nearby lakeside. One afternoon we went to Zheleznovodsk, the smallest of the resorts, and had an ice cream in the parlor in Central Square. We shared a table with a Muscovite who drew our attention to several women cutting the grass and the hedges and, generally speaking, embellishing the place. I found nothing extraordinary in their work, but our neighbor, with the sixth sense of a Soviet citizen, did: "I wonder what they are doing; probably some VIP is about to visit. . . ." He seemed a nice enough man, not very sophisticated; to me it was a textbook case of the roundabout way in which citizens in this regime were accustomed to think and how rumors started.

The next day, alas, Gorbachev arrived in Zheleznovodsk and with him Chancellor Helmut Kohl, and a few steps from our ice-cream parlor, in the municipal building, they agreed that the Soviet troops would be withdrawn from East Germany—a milestone in postwar European history. It taught me that after all these years I still had a lot to learn about Russia.

Epilogue

In *my story* I have reached the 1950s, when I was in my thirties. Naomi and I had married early and had two children who were growing up fast. It was time to settle down at long last. I was about to start a new career far away from the sites of my childhood and adolescence, equally remote from the places that had shaped my outlook and character as a young man. It was the beginning of my "third existence"—to paraphrase the title of a well-known but now-forgotten novel of the 1930s. I hope to write one day about the later years; today I feel not yet ready to do so.

I have written on a variety of subjects and tried my hand in various genres; this was quite common in the last century but is frowned upon in ours. But autobiography is a genre *sui generis* and I approached it with trepidation. Almost every other book can be written by other authors; an autobiography only by the self. From my superficial studies of the theory of autobiography (there is such a discipline) I gathered that there are various approaches—spiritual, confessional, apologetic, psychoanalytical—to name but a few. I learned that garden scenes and early sins play a prominent part in many traditional autobiographies. I also gathered that their value as a source of historical insight is very limited because they shed more light on the state of mind of the author when he wrote his recollections than on the events when they actually occurred.

This is probably correct, but my ambitions were much less far-reaching. Nor did I want to engage too much in self-examination and self-revelation, not out of personal reticence (though this also played a role—my father was one of the most reticent people I have known). It seemed to me inappropriate: Had I lived in a quieter time and place and had I still felt the urge to write my recollections there would have been stronger emphasis on the "I" and "me." Against the background of Germany from the 1920s and through the 1930s and World War II and its aftermath in what was then Palestine such concentration on the ego seemed to me out of place.

I tried to forget quickly all I learned about the theory of autobiography—which was not too difficult. But one quotation stuck in my mind. It is from the preface of the autobiography of a German writer named Karl Immermann entitled *Memorabilia* (1840), and it says: "My life does not seem to me of sufficient importance to bring it on the market in all its details. I shall deal only with my encounters with history." This translation is unfortunately much too vague; Immermann used an untranslatable turn of phrase, *"wo die Geschichte ihren Durchzug durch mich hielt,"* which, literally translated, means "where history marched through me."

History, fortunately, never "marched through me," but it

affected my life more profoundly than Immermann and his generation.* Immermann also wrote a three-volume semiautobiographical novel called *The Epigones*; the title is still widely used when referring to the cultural history of the 1840s and 1850s. Perhaps we were also epigones? I considered the idea only to dismiss it. Who were the great masters to whom we could look up to? They were several generations distant; nor did we follow in their footsteps. But the original meaning of the term *epigoni* ("those born after") is different. It refers to the children of the "Seven against Thebes" in Greek mythology. The Seven had unsuccessfully tried to fight the city; their children continued the fight and prevailed. There is a faint resemblance here because in my lifetime I witnessed the crumbling of two of the most tyrannical regimes in history.

But such comparisons are not very helpful either. Some recollections are written because the authors were men or women of great achievement, others because they had the insight and the powers of expression of a great writer. Mine, needless to say, belong to neither category, and I have tried to keep the story as simple and straightforward as possible. I have never been fond of intellectual and social pretentiousness and of originality at any price, and my aversion has not diminished with age. I wrote this account of the first part of my life because I lived through a period of history full of drama and tragedy, an era which is now receding into the distant past. A great deal is now written on this period, but I feel that those who were not witnesses, however thorough their research and innovative their explanations, are missing one whole dimension. That age was in many respects so different from the present that an enormous amount of imagination and empathy is needed for understanding it.

My intention, to repeat once again, was not to present the

---

*Karl Immermann (1796–1840) was a judge and one of the most important novelists of the postclassical period. Today his novels are studied only by those specializing in the history of German literature; they are still of some interest but are usually far too long.

panorama of an age, but something far more modest—a personal account of a wanderer between various worlds, neither comprehensive nor altogether systematic.

When the Abbé Sieyès was asked what he had done during the Terror, he gave the famous answer, *"J'ai vécu."* Since I also lived through a stormy age, this is the only answer I can give; many of my contemporaries did not survive, and in this respect, as in some others, I have been lucky.

INDEX